The History of Live Music in Britain, Volume 3, 1985–2015

To date there has been a significant gap in existing knowledge about the social history of music in Britain from 1950 to the present day. The three volumes of *The History of Live Music in Britain* address this gap, and do so from the unique perspective of the music promoter. The key theme of the books is the changing nature of the live music industry in the UK, focused upon popular music but including all musical genres. Via this focus, the books offer new insights into a number of other areas including the relationship between commercial and public funding of music; changing musical fashions and tastes; the impact of changing technologies; the changing balance of power within the music industries; the role of the state in regulating and promoting various musical activities within an increasingly globalised music economy; and the effects of demographic and other social changes on music culture. Drawing on new archival research, a wide range of academic and non-academic secondary sources, participant observation and a series of interviews with key personnel, the books have the potential to become landmark works within Popular Music Studies and broader cultural history. The third volume covers the period from Live Aid to Live Nation (1985–2015).

Simon Frith is Emeritus Professor of Music at the University of Edinburgh. From 1985 to 2000 he reviewed live music for the *Sunday Times*, *Observer* and *Scotsman* and from 1992 to 2016 chaired the judges of the Mercury Music Prize.

Matt Brennan is Reader in Popular Music at the University of Glasgow. He has served as Chair of the International Association for the Study of Popular Music (UK and Ireland branch) and is the author of two monographs, *When Genres Collide* (2017) *and Kick It: A Social History of the Drum Kit* (2020).

Martin Cloonan is the Director of the Turku Institute for Advanced Studies in Finland and coordinating editor of the journal *Popular Music*. He chaired Freemuse for its first 20 years and, with John Williamson, co-wrote a history of the UK's Musicians' Union, *Players' Work Time* (2016).

Emma Webster completed her PhD, *Promoting Live Music: A Behind-the-Scenes Ethnography*, at the University of Glasgow in 2011. She has held a fellowship at Oxford Brookes University and AHRC-funded post-doctoral positions at the Universities of Edinburgh and East Anglia, working on the UK Live Music Census and Impact of Festivals projects. She co-founded Live Music Exchange and is currently working in research support at the University of Oxford.

Ashgate Popular and Folk Music Series

Series Editors:
Lori Burns, Professor, University of Ottawa, Canada
Justin Williams, Senior Lecturer in Music, University of Bristol, UK

Popular musicology embraces the field of musicological study that engages with popular forms of music, especially music associated with commerce, entertainment and leisure activities. The Ashgate Popular and Folk Music Series aims to present the best research in this field. Authors are concerned with criticism and analysis of the music itself, as well as locating musical practices, values and meanings in cultural context. The focus of the series is on popular music of the twentieth and twenty-first centuries, with a remit to encompass the entirety of the world's popular music.

Critical and analytical tools employed in the study of popular music are continually being developed and refined in the twenty-first century. Perspectives on the transcultural and intercultural uses of popular music have enriched understanding of social context, reception and subject position. Popular genres as distinct as reggae, township, bhangra, and flamenco are features of a shrinking, transnational world. The series recognises and addresses the emergence of mixed genres and new global fusions, and utilises a wide range of theoretical models drawn from anthropology, sociology, psychoanalysis, media studies, semiotics, postcolonial studies, feminism, gender studies and queer studies.

The Tragic Odes of Jerry Garcia and The Grateful Dead
Mystery Dances in the Magic Theater
Brent Wood

Another Song for Europe:
Music, Taste, and Values in the Eurovision Song Contest
Ivan Raykoff

The History of Live Music in Britain, Volume 3, 1985–2015
From Live Aid to Live Nation
Simon Frith, Matt Brennan, Martin Cloonan and Emma Webster

For more information about this series, please visit:
www.routledge.com/music/series/APFM

The History of Live Music in Britain, Volume 3, 1985–2015

From Live Aid to Live Nation

Simon Frith, Matt Brennan,
Martin Cloonan and Emma Webster

LONDON AND NEW YORK

First published 2021
by Routledge
2 Park Square, Milton Park, Abingdon, Oxon OX14 4RN

and by Routledge
52 Vanderbilt Avenue, New York, NY 10017

Routledge is an imprint of the Taylor & Francis Group, an informa business

© 2021 Simon Frith, Matt Brennan, Martin Cloonan and Emma Webster

The right of Simon Frith, Matt Brennan, Martin Cloonan, and Emma Webster to be identified as authors of this work has been asserted by them in accordance with sections 77 and 78 of the Copyright, Designs and Patents Act 1988.

All rights reserved. No part of this book may be reprinted or reproduced or utilised in any form or by any electronic, mechanical, or other means, now known or hereafter invented, including photocopying and recording, or in any information storage or retrieval system, without permission in writing from the publishers.

Trademark notice: Product or corporate names may be trademarks or registered trademarks, and are used only for identification and explanation without intent to infringe.

British Library Cataloguing-in-Publication Data
A catalogue record for this book is available from the British Library

Library of Congress Cataloging-in-Publication Data
A catalog record has been requested for this book

ISBN: 9781409425915 (hbk)
ISBN: 9780367752958 (pbk)
ISBN: 9781315557168 (ebk)

Typeset in Times New Roman
by Newgen Publishing Uk

This volume is dedicated by Matt Brennan to his parents, Terry and Ann, and by Emma Webster to Jan Webster, 'my Best Thing'.

Contents

Preface	xi
Acknowledgements	xiii

1	New times	1
2	We Are the World	10
3	Taking care of business	29
	A snapshot of live music in Bristol in October–November 2007	53
4	Live music and the state	57
5	The political economy of music festivals	83
6	Festival worlds	97
	A snapshot of live music in Glasgow in October–November 2007	120
7	DJ business	123
8	Moving to a different beat: jungle, bhangra, garage and grime	145
9	Making a musical living	169
	A snapshot of live music in Sheffield in October–November 2007	194

x   *Contents*

10 Live music experience in the digital age   197

11 The live music ecology   219

    The Rolling Stones, Twickenham, August 20 and 22, 2006   244

12 Conclusion: the value of live music   247

    Bibliography   258
    Index   269

Preface

This book brings to an end a project that began as a research proposal in 2007. Our history of live music thus has a history of its own: from proposal to grant to publication, from speculation to research to writing, editing and rewriting. Like the organisation of Volumes 1 and 2, the organisation of this volume reflects the questions that we initially asked and the research strategy we followed to answer them.

As we explained in the preface to Volume 1, we wanted to shift attention in popular music studies from the recording industry to the business of live music. We had therefore decided to focus our research on the historical role of the promoter. Our volumes thus chart three eras of promotional activity. As it turned out, our focus on promotion was a useful way to make sense of the complexity of the live music business, the interplay of social forces involved: the market, state regulation, technology, demography, ideology and so forth. As in our other volumes, considering the history of live music from the promoter's perspective gave us a structure for the narrative in this book.

We also explained in Volume 1's preface that a history of live music is a history of place: concerts are necessarily promoted in specific venues and localities. In this history, we draw material systematically from three cities—Bristol, Glasgow and Sheffield—and include in each volume snapshots of the gigs and concerts taking place in each period in these cities. The cities were chosen partly to explore similarities and differences from the north to the south of Britain, but also because each city has fostered a unique music scene and is large enough to feature in national and international touring circuits. The snapshots in Volume 1 explored the three cities in 1962, the year before The Beatles exploded in Britain, while Volume 2 focused on 1976, the year before punk did the same. In this way, the snapshots show the cities on the cusp of something new while also highlighting business as usual in venues across town.

So why did we choose 2007 for this volume? Rather than a game-changing music group or genre, 2007 was instead the year before the financial crash of 2008, the repercussions of which are still being felt across all worlds, musical and otherwise. It was also the year before the formation of the Association of Independent Festivals and the year before revenue from live music overtook that from recorded music for the first time. In the context of a general

xii *Preface*

history, these examples serve to illustrate our arguments about continuity, change and the differences between the local music ecologies in the context of the wider world.

We also include in each volume a capsule account of a Rolling Stones concert. More than any other band, the Stones encapsulate the transformation of live music promotion since the 1950s even as their line-up, their music and even a core section of their audience remain remarkably unchanged. These inserted sections also pay tribute to live music history as a popular form, whether on local websites featuring scanned tickets from every local gig or on fan websites documenting a band's every concert playlist.

There is a third issue that we had to address specifically in this volume: when to end it. The starting and ending dates for any history are usually somewhat random—there is no significant difference between people's lives on December 31 and January 1, whether the dates mark the end of a year, a decade or a century. That said, our starting point was easily resolved. World War II *did* mark a clear break in everyday activities but by 1950 its most disruptive effects were over and a new chapter in the history of live music history was underway. Our end point was not so easily determined. Our funded research had a cutoff point and the bulk of our interviews and our most systematic archive research were completed by 2010. On the other hand, the underlying dynamic of the changes in music in this period, whether the effects of digital technology on the relationship between the live music and the record businesses or the evolution of music festivals and dance culture, were now attracting increasing academic and media attention, providing us with further research material. We therefore decided to suggest 2015 as our formal cutoff point, if only because this gave our book the neatness of a 30-year period.

What we didn't anticipate was the coronavirus and a pandemic that clearly marks an end to the live music worlds described in this volume. There now can be no doubt that in the future histories of music will be organised around the pre- and post-COVID-19 periods just as twentieth-century European histories are organised around pre- and post-war periods. The point here, though, is that the virus did not disrupt live music in the period of this volume and its history can't be written by reference to an event that was so unanticipated. It will be for other scholars to take the history of live music forward, just as we expect that other scholars will write their own histories of live music since 1950, drawing on—but hopefully challenging—our judgements.

Acknowledgements

This is the third volume of three. *The History of Live Music in Britain, Volume 1: 1950–1967. From Dance Hall to the 100 Club* was published by Ashgate in 2013; *The History of Live Music in Britain, Volume 2: 1968–1984. From Hyde Park to the Hacienda* was published by Routledge in 2019. The original research for this project was made possible by the Arts and Humanities Research Council (AHRC) (AH/F) (437/1) and this book, like the original project and the previous volumes, is a collaborative work. Matt Brennan did the majority of the national industry interviews and archive research. Martin Cloonan did the remaining national interviews as well as the archive work on the Musicians' Union, state regulation and political policy, and wrote the Rolling Stones' concert review. Emma Webster did the interviews and archive work in Bristol, Glasgow and Sheffield, and wrote the snapshots of these cities. Simon Frith wrote the book's final version and takes responsibility for all errors and infelicities.

We are grateful to the AHRC for supporting this project and for enabling us to set up *Live Music Exchange*, "the online hub for anyone interested in live music", and to Derek Scott, Stan Hawkins, Lori Burns and Justin Williams, editors of the Ashgate Series, and Heidi Bishop at Taylor and Francis for supporting this publishing project over its long life. Thanks too to Adam Behr, a valued colleague in our continued live music research, to John Williamson and the late Dave Laing for sharing their music industry wisdom, and to Jenny McKay for her editing skills. Our biggest debt of gratitude is to the promoters and agents who were willing to talk to us. In the first of his crime novels, Paul Charles (who with Paul Fenn runs the Asgard agency) describes a journalist who "had discovered that there were two main things that the majority of people in the music biz loved. It wasn't doing drugs and having sex; it was making money and giving interviews" (Charles 1997: 55). This may perhaps explain why our interviewees were so generous with their time but we are very grateful to them anyway.

1 New times

> Above me the sky was blue. The sun seemed at its zenith and it filled the stadium with the brilliant untainted light of an English summer's day ... Before me was the largest audience the world has ever known ... This was 13 July 1985. It was Live Aid.
>
> (Bob Geldof 1986:10)

> So what exactly is Red Wedge? Is it a cynical device via which the Labour Party hopes to get the vital youth vote for a general election now just over two years away? A front for a faction like Militant? A Live Aid for Lefties? An ideologically sound haircut?
>
> (*New Musical Express* January 18, 1986: 19)

> Mass production, the mass consumer, the big city, big-brother state, the sprawling housing estate, and the nation-state are in decline: flexibility, diversity, differentiation, mobility, communication, decentralisation and internationalisation are in the ascendant. In the process our own identities, our sense of self, our own subjectivities are being transformed. We are in transition to a new era.
>
> (Stuart Hall (1988: 24)

Introduction

In some ways the live music world in Britain changed remarkably little in the decades after 1985. An analysis of global box office returns in the first decade of the twenty-first century found that the Rolling Stones were the top grossers ("the wizened rockers made more money than any other touring band this decade, earning almost $1bn over 264 gigs") just as they had been in the 1980s,[1] while *Les Misérables* continued its run in London's West End.[2] In 2015, there were still five London-based symphony orchestras and the BBC still ran its Concert Orchestra and its orchestras in Scotland, Wales and Manchester. There were still regular discussions in the 2010s about the Arts Council's support for the Royal Opera House and Edinburgh City Council's support for the Edinburgh International Festival. The summer holidays were

2 *New times*

still marked out in the media by the Glastonbury and Reading festivals, and by the Proms at the Royal Albert Hall; the promoters and agents who had been important players in the live music business in the 1980s (Harvey Goldsmith, Barrie Marshall and Barry Dickins, for example) were still important players 30 years on.

In other ways, however, the role of live music in the cultural economy changed radically, something brought to public attention by a widely reported Mintel finding in 2008 that "spending on live concerts and festivals has overtaken recorded music for the first time since the birth of rock'n'roll". Mintel estimated that in 2007 Britons had spent £1.9 billion on live music and £1.5bn on CDs and downloads[3]; it concluded that the music industry was undergoing a profound redistribution of power as the internet drove down both the price and sales of records:

> The traditional relationship was one in which the LP or CD was the focus, with concerts primarily there to sell more records. In today's downloadable world, where the price of music has tumbled, and in some cases is even given away free, records, CDs and downloads have been demoted to the status of promotional tools for selling tickets and merchandise. Album sales are in meltdown. Much of the action is moving to the live arena. Live music has become a key route to profitability.
>
> (quote taken from *Evening Standard*, 10 September 2008: 21)

The arrival of digital technology in the form of CDs had initially restored the fortunes of the record industry following the 1970s recession. Introduced into the UK market in 1983, initially for classical releases, CD sales took off in 1985 with the release of Dire Straits' *Brothers in Arms* and overtook vinyl and cassette sales in 1989.[4] Digital technology did not become a sales threat until the end of 1990s, with the development of mp3 files and file-sharing services such as Napster, which operated between 1999 and 2001, the year iTunes and the iPod were launched.

US economist Alan B. Krueger has suggested persuasively that the beginning of the end of what in Volume 2 we called "the rock era" relationship between the recording and the live music industries predated Napster's launch. It was in 1997 that "the price of concert tickets took off and [overall] ticket sales declined", and it was this process that was accelerated by file sharing.

> In the past, when greater concert attendance translated into greater artists' record sales, artists had an incentive to price their tickets below the profit-maximising price for concerts alone. New technology that allows many potential customers to obtain recorded music without purchasing a record has severed the link between the two products. As a result, concerts are being priced more like single-market monopoly products.
>
> (Krueger 2005: 1, 25–26)

CDs and concert tickets were, in other words, no longer treated as price-competitive goods. If artists and their managers had previously been wary about making tickets for a concert much more expensive than the record it was promoting, they now followed a new economic model: maximising returns from live performance; treating a CD as a promotional cost. In his detailed analysis of changes in the "wallet share" of musical expenditure in the UK (the percentage of people's disposable income spent on live and recorded music), Will Page shows that between 2000 and 2010, when the average price of an album fell from £11.99 to £7.99, concert and festival ticket prices more than doubled: a full-price ticket for Scotland's T in the Park festival, for example, rose from £75 to £195 (Page 2011: 4).

The economic effect of treating concerts as "single-market monopoly products" was immediately obvious in the USA. For example, in 1981 the top 1% of artists took 26% of US concert revenue; by 2003 they were taking 56% (Budnick and Baron 2011: 55). An analysis of the top 35 music income-earners in the USA in 2002 found that only four "made more money from recordings than from live concerts", while "for the top 35 artists as a whole, income from touring exceeded income from record sales by a ratio of 7.5 to 1" (Connolly and Krueger 2005: 4). Such figures also illustrate the increasing earnings gap between the superstars and everyone else on the live music circuit and their realisation that, as "heritage" or "legacy" acts, they no longer needed to keep ticket prices below their market value in order to "buy" the loyalty of fans for future releases or appearances. Fan loyalty was established firmly, if not always permanently, by an act's previous record sales. Agent John Giddings remembers the change in the music business power structure in this way:

> They [record labels] were the powerful people, they controlled all the money, they controlled all the tools. They could make groups successful by spending lots of money marketing them. And so we used to listen to what they had to say. But I remember one classic moment when Virgin Records said to me, "You're doing the Iggy Pop tour before the album's released" and I said, "Who cares about a new Iggy Pop album? They're playing to people who want to hear *The Passenger*." And the swing in power between record companies and live music has been incredible.[5]

Krueger's second point about the changes in the live music market must also be stressed here: increasing ticket prices for the big stars meant decreasing ticket sales for everyone else. For the majority of musicians, who had always got most of their income from performance rather than recordings, this was a significant problem. In the 1960s, as veteran promoter Jef Hanlon remembers, even a band as internationally successful as Herman's Hermits spent most of their time on tour because their record deals were "so crap". Fifty years later, Guy Garvey (from another successful Manchester band, Elbow) was equally clear that, "You couldn't really live on the money you'd make from an album

4   *New times*

these days." Now, though, even constant touring was not always viable given both the lack of suitably sized venues and audience competition from superstar tours. As Garvey concludes, "It's lucky there are so many festivals." We will come back to the festivals business and its growing importance for all music worlds in Chapters 5 and 6.[6]

From another economic perspective, the changes in the UK live music sector over the last 30 years can be described as "Americanisation". This has partly been the effect of US live music companies directly buying up British promoters but also describes the changing role of British agents and promoters in the global live music economy. London-based agents have long expected to represent artists for "all territories outside the USA" and this has remained the case, but as the market has been globalised so the UK's role has increasingly been to support American corporate concert-promotion power. The UK's status as the key English-speaking country in Europe has enabled UK agents and promoters to consolidate their value as the organising centre for EU tours and beyond. On the one hand, UK companies have become subsidiaries of US companies; on the other, the UK live sector has been integrated into the US model of arena tours and venue chains (thus achieving new economies of scale). We describe the emergence of this model in detail in Chapter 2 and examine what it meant for British promotional practices in Chapter 3.

In introducing this volume, however, there are two points we need to emphasise about our approach to live music history. First, we do not think it is possible to treat live music as a business in isolation from other kinds of music commerce. Rather, our aim is to situate live music in a dynamic relationship with other music businesses—recording, broadcasting, the cinema, telecommunications and so forth. Second, this is a social rather than an economic history and, while changes in the live music business provide a context for everyday musical activities, those activities have their own causes and effects. It could be argued, for example, that the biggest changes in live music culture in this period reflected the impact of electronic dance music. DJ-ing, a musical practice that was once considered either antithetical or marginal to live music-making (we had to justify its inclusion in Volumes 1 and 2) now holds more sway over the popular music night out than the previously dominant gig conventions of rock and pop. We discuss these issues in Chapter 7 (on the rise and effects of rave and acid house) and Chapter 8 (on the rise and effects of jungle and grime).

Our argument here is that live music practices have not only adapted to the digital music business, but have also helped shape it, and in this volume we explore these processes with reference to rock, classical, jazz and folk musicians (Chapter 9), audiences (Chapter 10) and venues and localities (Chapter 11). We conclude in Chapter 12 with a discussion of the various ways in which "the value of live music" is now understood.

A key factor in value arguments, of course, is ideology. What do people involved in music think live music is *for* and how and why do these ideas

New times 5

change? In Chapter 4 we address these questions with particular reference to policies of the state, but changes in political ideology are central to the story we tell throughout this book. We can best introduce this theme by describing two live music enterprises dating from 1985, our starting point for this volume. The contrasting fortunes of Red Wedge and Live Aid can be seen to symbolise the ideological transition between musical eras with which we are concerned.

Red Wedge

"One of the most striking economic shifts of the eighties," wrote sociologist Bill Osgerby in 1998, "was the massive decline in the numbers of youngsters entering full-time employment" (Osgerby 1998: 156).[7] Between 1985 and 1992, the number of 16- to 17-year-olds in full-time education rose from 37% to 66%; by 1991–92, roughly a third of 19- to 20-year-olds were entering full- or part-time higher education. As Osgerby shows, the rise of youth unemployment in the 1980s was not simply an effect of economic recession; it was more significantly the result of a "deep-seated restructuring of the British economy" and, in particular, of the reduced number of jobs in the manufacturing sector:

> This shift impacted especially on young people since many of the jobs that disappeared were the less skilled manual occupations that had been the bedrock of youth employment during the fifties and sixties [and, we would add, the underpinning of the rise of rock 'n' roll].
>
> (Osgerby 1998: 157–8)

This was the context of the Labour Party's Jobs for Youth campaign, which Billy Bragg toured in 1985 to support. It was the success of that tour that, coupled with the failure of the left to get youth votes in the 1983 General Election, led to the formation of Red Wedge. The need for popular musicians to have an anti-Thatcher platform seemed particularly pressing by then, given the imminent dissolution of the Greater London Council following the 1985 Local Government Act. (The GLC had been a highly visible promoter of musical events—see Frith et al. 2019: 99.)

The first Red Wedge concert was staged at the beginning of 1986, and *New Musical Express* (January 18, 1986: 19) suggested to its readers that "when a decidedly motley troupe of musicians step onto the stage of the Manchester Apollo on January 25, a new chapter in the course of politically active British pop will begin".

Red Wedge's general purpose was to instil "a greater political awareness among young people"; its immediate task was indeed to help the Labour Party win the next general election.[8] This was clearly a continuation of the strand of 1970s cultural activism we described in Volume 2, a time when musicians were involved with a variety of political causes—Rock Against Racism and the Anti-Nazi League, CND and AAM (the Anti-Apartheid Movement), as well as support for the miners' strikes and other trade union struggles. In terms

6   *New times*

of its political objectives (a Labour electoral victory thanks to a large youth turnout), however, Red Wedge failed (even if its concerts were well enough attended).

It was suggested in the music press that Red Wedge's problem was that its politics weren't very jolly. In *Melody Maker*, for example, under the headline "Rebels Without Applause", Carol Clerk wondered after the election whether Red Wedge had "anything left to offer" and interviewed Billy Bragg, now on tour with the Nicaraguan Solidarity Campaign:

> In much the same way that Bragg's own worthiness has been isolated and dwelled upon, so the simply earnest face of Red Wedge is the one that's ended up in the picture frame—nobody ever told me that Red Wedge would be *fun*—and this has served to limit its communicative potential. Lots of people are simply put off.
>
> (September 21, 1987: 10–11)

This offsetting of earnestness and enjoyment was commonplace in music press discussions of cultural politics in the second half of the 1980s. The pleasures of consumption were contrasted to the dreariness of political organisation or social responsibility; writers drew freely from new academic fashions in cultural studies and postmodernism.[9] Such music press articles reflected the more general media agreement that the failure of the Red Wedge and Labour campaigns in the 1987 election was evidence that the Conservative Party's proffered solution to the UK's economic crisis, "consumer empowerment", had resonance with young as well as older voters despite the employment situation. By 1988 a Tory-supporting paper like the *Daily Star* could claim that:

> Britain's youngsters are riding the roller-coaster boom of Mrs Thatcher's economic recovery. They have seen a new kind of revolution—giving power to the consumer—and they want to join the action before it ends.

Market researchers were now eagerly documenting this youth movement. A 1988 Mintel report, *Youth Lifestyle*, concluded that young people had a "new consumption and success ethic", generated by "the sustained economic growth of the enterprise culture", while a large survey of *The New Generation* by the advertising agency McCann-Erickson identified

> a "New Wave" of "post-permissive" youngsters who were committed to a new spirit of possessive individualism and who exhibited "the most highly developed form of the new multi-profile consumption in our society".
>
> (Quotes from Osgersby 1998:159)

Britain was, in short, entering the "new era" described by Stuart Hall in the opening quote to this chapter—a new era of live music introduced most enthusiastically (if unknowingly) by Bob Geldof.

Live Aid

Live Aid is perhaps the most famous concert ever staged. It was still being celebrated in the 2019 Oscar-nominated film *Bohemian Rhapsody* and its statistics are embedded in pop's historical mythology. A transatlantic benefit concert masterminded by Bob Geldof and staged simultaneously at Wembley Stadium (for an audience of 72,000 people) and the John F. Kennedy Stadium in Philadelphia (for an audience of 100,000 people), it was the first and remains one of the largest-scale satellite link-ups and live television broadcasts ever watched, with an estimated global audience of 1.9 billion people across 150 nations. As Wikipedia notes, if press reports were accurate, the Live Aid concerts were seen by about 40% of the world's then population. The exact sum of money raised for Ethiopian famine relief from the individual donations phoned in during the shows is impossible to document with academic accuracy, but seems to have been well over £100 million, to which can be added the income from concert ticket sales, programme and advertising sales, broadcasting and DVD rights, and so forth.[10]

In his own account of how the Live Aid concerts were organised, Bob Geldof focuses first on how he persuaded the big rock names to appear and then on how the ever more difficult logistical staging problems were resolved—primarily by the lead promoters, Harvey Goldsmith in London and Bill Graham in Philadelphia. But in his determination to raise the maximum amount of money (the object of the exercise), his key insight was that the concerts needed to be organised as a televisual rather than a live musical event. As he explained to Goldsmith:

> Look, the object is to make money. If people watch a concert on TV they get bored, it doesn't matter who it is. We want them to give money, so the more multi-million record-selling acts the better, because people will watch their favourites and contribute. Secondly, they won't get bored because bands will only have time to play their hits. And because there are so many of them, each band only gets fifteen or twenty minutes, which will suit them better than doing a whole concert. In fact, I'll specifically ask them to do that. It's like a global juke-box.
>
> (Geldof 1986: 330)

As a concert, Live Aid was above all a global event. One of the professional organisers Geldof recruited early on was Michael C. Mitchell, a specialist "event manager" who had recently been involved in coordinating the worldwide TV coverage of the 1984 Los Angeles Olympic Games. When he was appointed executive producer of the Live Aid broadcast, Mitchell named the company he set up Worldwide Sports and Entertainment (Geldof 1986: 333). In their bills of "multi-million record-selling acts", the Live Aid concerts celebrated the superstars created in the rock era. As an event, however, Live Aid pointed forward to the development of a new way of organising the live

8 *New times*

music promotion business, to the use of international entertainment and event corporations.

Conclusion

On June 11, 1988, Wembley Stadium hosted another global televisual event, the Nelson Mandela 70th Birthday Tribute Concert. This was reported as reaching an audience of 600 million people in 67 countries and, according to Robin Denselow (1990: 276), was thus the "biggest and most spectacular pop-political event of all time, a more political version of Live Aid with the aim of raising consciousness rather than just money".[11] The concert combined the logic and logistics of Live Aid (it was organised for and sold to world-wide television stations as entertainment; its success depended on booking big-name acts) with a particularly British tradition of moral protest. Jerry Dammers, a stalwart supporter of Red Wedge, was also a key figure in the Mandela event's conception and planning.

The Live Aid and Nelson Mandela concerts combined two ways of thinking about the world: the unabashed admission of Western political responsibility for global poverty and injustice, and the equally unabashed enjoyment of Western technological and cultural power. The contradictions here, much discussed at the time (e.g. see Rijven et al. 1985) were implicitly resolved over the next decades by the ideological suggestion that global poverty and injustice were, in fact, *best* addressed through an unfettered global market for both technology and culture. This is the context for the rise to dominance in Britain and much of the rest of the world of three US-based music companies, Live Nation, Ticketmaster and AEG, whose business models were to have a profound effect on the organisation of the British promotional sector and to which we now turn.

Notes

1 Quote from Sean Michaels' *Guardian* report December 18, 2009: see www.guardian. co.uk/music/2009/dec/18/rolling-stones-top-touring-act.
2 *Les Misérables* opened at the Barbican on October 8, 1985 before transferring to the Palace Theatre in December. In 2004 it was moved to the Queen's, where its run continues (in 2019 the theatre was renamed the Sondheim).
3 Mintel broke down ticket sales by genre: £1.05 billion for rock and pop concerts; £500 million for classical concerts; £200 million on jazz; £150 million on opera. It also noted that spending on recorded music had peaked at just under £2 billion in 2001 but had been in steep decline since 2005.
4 In the late 1980s, cassettes were Britain's best-selling recording format—see Rogers (2013).
5 Giddings interviewed by Matt Brennan, May 4, 2010.
6 Hanlon quoted from an interview with Martin Cloonan, May 4, 2010. Garvey quote from https://www.theguardian.com/lifeandstyle/2019/nov/30/this-much-i-know-guy-garvey-i-have-gone-back-to-playing-lego-fanatically.

New times 9

7 In 1976 research suggested that 32% of school leavers got the first job they applied for and 86% were employed within a month of leaving school; by 1992 "only 13 per cent of sixteen- to seventeen-year-olds possessed full-time jobs" (Osgerby 1998: 156).

8 See *Melody Maker*'s four page report on the debate it organised on Red Wedge's politics, featuring Jerry Dammers, Billy Bragg, Paul Weller and Clare Short MP on one side and Chris Dean of the Redskins, Stewart Copeland and Greg Knight MP on the other (January 25, 1986: 23–6).

9 In November 1986, for example, *Melody Maker*'s resident intellectuals Simon Reynolds and Frank Owen wrote a lengthy diatribe against "Social Realist Pop", epitomised by Red Wedge and nostalgia for punk (Reynolds and Owen 1986).

10 In Britain almost everyone involved (including the bands and promoters) worked for nothing, though Wembley Stadium cost $250,000. In the USA all the technical crew had to be paid, and the Philadelphia gig cost $3.5 million. Event costs were covered by sponsorship; all money paid by the public went to Live Aid. For these details see Geldof (1986: 356–7)—he gives the sums in US dollars.

11 A possible rival for this description is Bruce Springsteen's free concert in East Berlin on July 19, 1988, which drew a live audience of 300,000 with millions more East Germans watching it on state TV. This event is often claimed to have accelerated the fall of the Berlin Wall (e.g. see Schulze 2015) and certainly could be said to symbolise the victory of capitalism over communism.

2 We Are the World

You'd better be prepared for doing a lot of touring because that's really the only unique situation that's going to be left.

(David Bowie, 2002)[1]

When I'm pitching to local authorities for the management of their buildings, they'll say to me "that sounds all very well and you're good at being music promoters, but what if musical tastes change?" And I say, all entertainment changes. To be honest, if I was sitting here 200 years ago, you'd be talking to me about public hangings and floggings that people came to, or bear baiting. Now I'm not proposing to put those back into the public portfolio, but ultimately these are spaces that we sell, and we will sell what people want, and that's what happens.

(Paul Latham, president of Live Nation UK, 2009)[2]

Introduction

It may seem odd to devote a chapter in a history of live music in Britain to an account of developments in the USA, but in order to explain how the UK live music industry was reconfigured by the corporatisation of the global live music sector we need to describe in some detail how the three key corporate ways of thinking about the core business of live music were initially developed. In this chapter, we focus on the Live Nation model, the Ticketmaster model and the AEG model.[3]

Live Nation: live music as a marketing opportunity

Live Nation was formed by the political economy of US radio. Robert F. X. Sillerman bought his first radio station in 1978, had acquired seven more by 1985 and in 1992 launched SFX Broadcasting, a company that expanded rapidly once the 1996 Telecommunications Act allowed a single company to own "an unlimited number of radio stations in the same market".[4] Later the same year, by which time SFX owned 86 radio stations in 24 cities, Sillerman bought New York-based concert promoter Delsener/Slater Enterprises, announcing that:

> While this acquisition is immediately attractive on its own, it has the added dimension of benefiting all our radio stations with a direct association with leading concert tours and shows ... [and] great opportunities for promotional tie-ins.

As Budnick and Baron note, the concert business "was the last entertainment and media industry to be consolidated", and in the words of SFX CEO Mike Ferrrel:

> When we bought Ron Delsener, what began was a dialogue with every major concert promoter in the United States. We had an opportunity to see [the concert] business from the inside and from the perspective of an operator. It gave us insight as to the opportunities there.
>
> (Quotes from Budnik and Baron 2011: 159)

What followed was another busy year of takeovers. SFX bought Sunshine Promoters of Indianapolis, Bill Graham Presents in San Francisco, Contemporary Productions in St Louis, Concerts/Southern Promotions of Atlanta, the Network Magazine Group/SJS Entertainment in New York and PACE Entertainment of Virginia.

Robert Sillerman was not the first person to realise that the US live rock business had not changed much since it had been established in the late 1960s and that it needed to evolve. The established way of doing things involved a national network of fiefdoms run by regional promoters whose collective collaboration was necessary for artists to mount national tours. As early as 1978, the Rolling Stones' business manager, Prince Rupert Lowenstein, was bemused by the obviously corrupt elements of the US live rock industry, by the bags of cash that were passed around (he worried that the Stones would be charged with tax fraud if they were suspected of having undeclared income) and by the amount of ticket income the group lost to scalpers and touts. "There's nothing you can do about that. That's the promoter's business," he was told.[5] After discussing his problems with more experienced music business colleagues, Lowenstein concluded that "there was an irreducible core of approximately 10 per cent [of concert earnings] that would never come our way" (Lowenstein 2014: 133).

Come 1989 and Lowenstein was planning the Stones' first US tour for seven years, to promote the *Steel Wheels* album, and was in negotiation with Bill Graham. Graham had been overall producer of previous Stones tours, working with the usual network of local promoters. One morning, Lowenstein got a telephone call from one of these locals, the Canadian promoter Michael Cohl, who said he'd double whatever offer Graham made. The Stones accepted Cohl's proposal and, in Lowenstein's words:

12   *We Are the World*

> Under his guidance the [1989] tour became the most financially successful rock tour up to this point: there was huge pressure on him and his team to deliver, since his advance had acquired the rights to handle not only the concerts, but also all the sponsorship, merchandising, radio, television and film exploitation.
>
> (Lowenstein 2014: 193)

Cohl's promotional ideas emerged from his Canadian experience with Concert Promotions International (CPI), whose problem had been how to organise a national tour in a country with a limited number of large venues. The obvious solution was to use the profits from large venues to cover the losses from small ones, but for this to work a promoter had to have cost control of all the venues involved and to be booking acts with big enough pulling power to sell them all out. The inspiration here was Elvis Presley's 1970 comeback tour. Promoter Concerts West paid Presley's manager Colonel Parker a million dollars for the right to book a national tour and then negotiated directly with local venues about the costs of security, merchandising and so forth; the usual middlemen were bypassed. Presley's drawing power was big enough that venue owners were willing to upset the promoters on whom they were usually dependent and the tour's success showed that regional promoters' control of local venues could be challenged (Budnik and Baron 2011: 201).

The second strand of Cohl's approach to tour promotion is shown by CPI's purchase of the Brokum merchandising company in the early 1980s. (Brokum was essentially a manufacturer of t-shirts).[6] This gave Cohl access to bands' inner business circles and a share of the income from tours put together by other promoters. At the same time, in investment terms, CPI was a joint venture with Labatts Brewery, which sponsored the Stones' *Steel Wheels* tour.

In summary, Cohl's unprecedented financial bid for the rights to promote the Rolling Stones depended, first, on his ability to maintain complete control of each night's costs and returns and, second, on his success at expanding and developing new revenue streams. For the Stones tour, he developed travel packages, TV deals and VIP seating; he put in place a bigger range of ticket prices than had been the norm on Stones tours and negotiated lucrative merchandise and licensing deals alongside Labatts' sponsorship. The tour generated around US$260 million, a record for the time. Indeed, in this model a big act could earn *more* than 100% of ticket revenue (given the centralised merchandise deals, for example), so it is not surprising that CPI went on to promote not just future Stones tours but also such major earners as U2's 1992 *Zoo* tour. Throughout the 1990s, Cohl was the promoter of choice for most big British acts embarking on US trips—including Pink Floyd and David Bowie.

Cohl's promotional strategy makes further sense of Alan B. Krueger's finding discussed in Chapter 1: in the second half of the 1990s, as the price of concert tickets took off, overall ticket sales declined. These developments reflect the emergence of a superstar concert economy on the one hand, and the decline of local promoters on the other. But they also explain the business opportunities that Sillerman spotted in live music and the business changes he made. He understood, to begin with, that concert promotion involved a very large cash flow but very small profit margins. This meant that the only way to increase box-office profits was by increasing the *scale* of concert tours. He perceived, second, that the boundaries to such expansion were artificial. They were an effect of the bargaining power of local promoters and venue owners—hence the SFX strategy of taking their companies over.[7] By 2000, SFX controlled 14 amphitheaters in nine of the top ten US markets alongside 69 concert venues in 28 of the top 50 markets.

On February 29, 2000 Robert Sillerman sold SFX to Clear Channel. By now SFX was a company with a remarkable annual income but even more remarkable debts (the result of all its takeovers). The sales talk was still in terms of the untapped returns from a radio/concert promotion synergy (Clear Channel was also a commercial radio company), and it was true that this meant that a chunk of concert promotional costs could be kept in house, as it were. But there was also a broader and more significant argument: a successful live concert business could maximise sponsorship and advertising possibilities (just as a successful commercial radio business did). From this perspective, Budnik and Baron (2011) argue, SFX was selling not a concert business as such but an *audience-gathering business*, a way of delivering the right consumers to the right marketing campaigns ((2011: 107).[8] One inspiration here was Disney World. In Sillerman's words:

> Disney's relationships with corporate sponsors are a good model for what we want to do in the concert-promotion business. It's extremely difficult to make money just selling tickets. We want to make money both by selling tickets and by putting a live audience in front of Madison Avenue.
> (quoted in Budnick and Baron 2011: 176)

Clear Channel Communications shared this vision. This company had begun in 1972 when investment banker Lowry Mays found himself owning a radio station as a result of a bad loan. By 2000, Clear Channel owned or controlled more than 1000 radio stations, 550,000 outdoor billboards and 19 television stations. For Mays, Clear Channel was neither a radio business nor a music business: "it was in the business of selling our customers products" (quoted in Budnick and Baron 2011: 224). The appeal of SFX was that it would expand the number and availability of "our customers".

In 2001, Clear Channel became Clear Channel Entertainment (CCE) and in 2005 CCE was spun off from Clear Channel as a new, separate company, Live Nation Entertainment, with Michael Rapino as CEO. He had previously been CCE's chair of European Music, but had started his professional career in promotion as a sales rep at Labatt, rising to be senior marketing executive with responsibility for music sponsorship, before leaving in 1998 when Labatt divested its concert assets. Rapino then formed Core Audience

14   *We Are the World*

Entertainments, which became Canada's second largest promoter until it was sold to SFX in 2000.

Rapino was now the dominant player in the global live music industry; Live Nation took a significant percentage of the sector's annual earnings. At the same time, Live Nation itself still had big debts, which didn't seem to reduce much year by year (the company was yet to make a profit) and hadn't solved the basic problem of any live music business—even one focused on audience-gathering. What happens to the financial model if the audience doesn't gather? The company was in need of new revenue streams and sought them in other parts of the music industry.

In October 2007, *Music Week* reported that Live Nation had paid Madonna more than $100 million for "her services". Michael Rapino announced that the company would now control "everything Madonna will do music related over the next 10 years anywhere in the world, including touring, private events, corporate sponsorship, studio albums, DVDs, film, TV" (*Music Week*, October 27, 2007: 2). Madonna was the first signing announced to a new Live Nation company, Artist Nation, which would be run by Michael Cohl (whose own company, CPI, had been taken over by Live Nation in 2006).

Before he hooked up with Live Nation, Cohl had been involved in discussions with the Rolling Stones regarding a similar offer, which Rupert Lowenstein had advised the group to accept, calculating that the sum on the table was rather more than the group could expect to earn in the coming years.

> If touring would be the primary source of income, and if Rolling Stones tours were going to become less frequent and more difficult, if not peter out entirely, then there was considerable uncertainty ahead, and my aim had always been to minimize uncertainty.
>
> (Lowenstein 2014: 224)

For once, Mick Jagger and Keith Richards rejected Lowenstein's advice (they feared losing control of the group),[9] but they had been happy to work with Cohl on another business venture which informed his (and Live Nation's) thinking about such artist deals.

In 1998, David Bowie and his business managers (who also worked with Lowenstein) launched Ultrastar:

> a management/technology partnership that specializes in the area of Internet services, bringing major entertainment, sports and fashion clients to the world in a community-based forum delivered over the Web.
>
> (Quoted in Budnick and Baron 2011: 215)

The company's first clients after Bowie were sports teams; the company's sales pitch was the sophisticated use of the web to develop "fan connection and artist interaction". SFX was sufficiently interested in the income potential of owning web rights to a touring artist and the possibilities of content development in driving e-commerce that in 2000 it bought into Ultrastar, acquiring 10% of the company. Cohl and the Stones used the company for the 2002–03 *Forty Licks* tour, and Cohl was sufficiently impressed by the results to buy a majority stake in the company. By now it was clear to everyone in the concert business that, as "an artist services platform", Ultrastar had created an effective way of "capturing fan data while simultaneously driving website traffic"; the online sales of "exclusive" fan merchandise had a rather better profit margin than at-venue sales. What Ultrastar couldn't crack, though, was how to provide efficiently what fans most wanted: exclusive tickets. Enter Ticketmaster.[10]

We will return to ticketing shortly. The final point to make in this section is that the application of the Live Nation model to the artist deals made by Artist Nation, vastly overpaying musicians for their exclusive services, was a bit of a disaster. The company's shares fell sharply after Madonna's signing (by 83% in little over a year) and if anything, the fall was accelerated by subsequent deals with Jay-Z, Nickelback, Shakira and, in March 2008, U2. U2's deal didn't include their recordings but, like Madonna's, did include Live Nation shares (1.6 million in U2's case) with a price guarantee. In December 2008, *The Guardian* reported that U2 had sold its shares at an extra cost to the company (given how much the actual share price had fallen) of $25 million (*Guardian* December 19, 2008: 40).

It became clear that Artist Nation was not the solution to Live Nation's problems. Michael Cohl left the company and Michael Rapino looked for salvation elsewhere. In May 2010, after a year-long investigation of the deal by competition regulators in both the USA and the UK, the merger of Live Nation and Ticketmaster was approved (for the UK findings, see Competition Commission 2010).

Ticketmaster: live music as a ticket-management business

The history of live music as a business can be written as a history of ticketing. The commerce of a concert is that people who want to enjoy it have to pay money to attend. This may just involve turning up on the night and handing cash over at the door (as at pub gigs or club nights), but once a concert audience is seated or if there are likely to be more people demanding entry than can be accommodated then tickets are essential. They can be used to attach person to seat, to guarantee customers' entry and to help promoters get the maximum crowd. From their origins in the eighteenth century, concert halls, like theatres, were built with box offices.

To begin with, music venues were expected to handle their own ticket sales. To get a ticket meant visiting the box office—in previous volumes, we described the all-night queues for tickets that were a routine part of the pop and rock fan experience in the 1960s and 1970s. But both venues and the promoters using those venues quickly realised that they needed additional methods of ticket distribution to enable would-be audience members

16   *We Are the World*

to get tickets without needing to visit the hall in person in advance. One strand in the history of ticketing can be traced through developments in communications systems, from the postal service and mail order through the telephone network and the credit card to the various online services in use today. The earliest way of distributing tickets, however, was through ticket agencies.

In 1786, under the headline "The New System of Ticket Agents", the *London Morning Chronicle* ran an article about Theatre Ticket Messengers, a company that used messenger boys to go to theatres to hold seats or collect seat tokens for favoured clients. In 1830, this company was acquired by musical instrument dealers Robert Keith and William Prowse, who renamed it Keith Prowse and advertised that they could now "book and hold the best theatre seats for their clients who could thus have the best experience with the least trouble". From the very beginning, according to its website, Keith Prowse was "at the forefront of innovation": it was the first ticketing company to have a telephone installed, its number appearing in the earliest UK telephone directory in 1880.

A hundred years later (after going through many changes of fortune and ownership), Keith Prowse was still a significant ticket agency, its street-side and hotel lobby sales booths a familiar London sight. It was, as a Mintel report in 1986 noted, "the leading name" among the 146 theatre ticket agencies in the UK, owning 21 of the 46 ticket outlets in the capital (Mintel 1986: 115, 134); as we write, the company continues to advertise its services online in terms hardly changed since the 1830s:

> Keith Prowse offers tickets for all London Musicals, from the oldest to the newest show. Choose a ticket which best suits your budget; we offer tickets from top price all the way down to the best value ticket. Guarantee your seat at your show of choice at a price which suits you.[11]

This model of ticketing—tickets available at the box office, from brokers or via the post or a telephone call—remained dominant in the live entertainment economy for much of the twentieth century. In 1992, for example, Manchester agent and promoter Danny Betesh (Kennedy Street) bought a local ticket agency, Piccadilly Box Office, when its owner retired. This was, in fact, "a kiosk in a street in the centre of Manchester" with telephones and had only just started taking credit card bookings. Betesh's first move was to open a call centre and change the company name to Piccadilly Ticketline.[12]

From a promoter's point of view, this way of marketing tickets had two significant problems. First, by controlling the primary sale of tickets, box offices and ticket agents also, by default, controlled what would later be called secondary ticketing. They were the source (hard to police) of most of the tickets made available to touts and scalpers. (This was one reason why Piccadilly Box Office owner Barry Ansel offered his business to Betesh before putting it on the market—he and Kennedy Street had built up mutual trust.) Second,

We Are the World 17

management of the inventory (the industry term for the ticket stock) got more complicated (and inefficient) as venues and ticket sales expanded. The coordination of the supply to and returns from the various agency outlets got more time consuming and the need for effective marketing—to ensure maximum sales—more urgent.

In Volume 2, we described how these problems were exacerbated in the rock era by the mismatch between the demand for concert tickets and a supply limited by the size of the available venues. In the USA, as is well documented by Budnick and Baron (2011), such ticketing problems led to the emergence of a variety of entrepreneurs who believed they could be solved by computers. As early as 1965, the *New York Times* drama critic Howard Taubman was calling for "a computerized ticket system" so that "the process of acquiring tickets would become infinitely easier and pleasanter" (quoted in Budnick and Baron 2011: 5) and the first attempt at this, Ticket Reservations System, was launched in 1967.

To have any chance of success, TRS and its numerous successors (most notably Ticketron) needed three things: clients (initially theatres and sports teams); a computer system capable of dealing with surging demand (when tickets first went on sale); and outlets (computer equipment was usually installed in department stores and had to be easy for shop assistants to use amidst their other activities). The profits from such ticketing services would, on paper, come from a combination of a service charge (paid by the ticket buyer), an "inside" charge (paid by the client) and an equipment rental fee (paid by the outlets).

In developing an effective business model, however, these companies faced various snags. They were given only part of the inventory and were therefore in competition with both the box office and other kinds of broker, who didn't necessarily apply a service charge; their systems were most likely to fail when ticket demand was at its highest; and ticket buyers often doubted that the outlets really had the best seats. These problems were exacerbated by the rise of rock as the most lucrative sector of the live music business. Rock fans were the biggest buyers of tickets, but were particularly sensitive to being "ripped off".

This was the context in which Ticketmaster, under the direction of lawyer Fred Rosen from 1982 to 1998, became the dominant player in the market. Ticketmaster, in Rosen's words, distinguished itself from its competitors by being "a ticket service that makes use of computers, rather than a computer company that sells tickets" (quoted in Budnick and Baron 2011: 70). What this meant in practice was a new business model. If Ticketron, for example, was paid by a venue to sell and distribute (some of) its tickets, Ticketmaster paid the venue for exclusive rights to handle *all* its ticketing services. Rosen regarded ticketing as a profit-making activity rather than as a customer service and developed his company's strategy accordingly.

Rosen treated the right to sell tickets for a particular event as an *exclusive* concession, like the right to sell merchandise or beer. In return Rosen

18   *We Are the World*

offered venues and promoters a share of the service fee his company added to ticket prices. Part of Rosen's calculation here was that in market terms concert tickets were significantly under-priced. For the big shows at least, demand was far greater than supply and insofar as Ticketmaster was taking a risk here, this was not with the price-elasticity of the live music market but with the robustness of the company's computer systems. Ticketmaster's success had as much to do with the skills of its computer engineers as with Rosen's ruthlessness. Gene Cobuzzi, who worked for a time as Ticketmaster's chief operating officer, summarised the company's policy this way:

> Fred came into [a venue] and said, 'Right now you have a cost centre, it's called your box office. You pay for the equipment and you have to pay for the labour to sell the tickets. I'm giving to give you the equipment for free. I'm going to equip your entire box office with terminals. I'm going to teach your people how to sell tickets over those terminals, and I'm going to support those people. What I'm going to ask you to do is close down the first day of sale on concerts and let me sell those tickets through my outlets. So now you don't even have to pay the labour on the first day of sale. But if that's not enough, I'm going to give you a piece of every ticket I sell. So I've just turned your cost centre into a profit centre.'
>
> (Quoted in Budnick and Baron 2011: 75)

Add Ticketmaster's concert-marketing clout and willingness to offer venues an advance against returns or a sign-on fee, and it is not surprising that Ticketmaster rapidly built up its business. By 1994 *Pollstar*, the US concert industry's trade paper, was reporting that Ticketmaster had exclusive contracts with 63.2% of America's halls and arenas. As R.E.M.'s attorney, Bertis Downs, told a congressional hearing that year,

> at this point in 1994, for at least the last few years, there really isn't any choice. If you want to do a major tour, a major arena level tour in major markets, you have no choice. [Ticketmaster] comes along with the building. It comes with the building the same way concessionaires do.
>
> (Quoted in Budnick and Baron 2011: 132, 136)

There are two further points to make about this stage in the rise of Ticketmaster. First, the company's ticketing dominance and aggressive use of service charges ensured that it was loathed by ticket buyers; however, this was part of the deal it made with the venues and promoters who used its services: Ticketmaster took the flak for the service fee add-ons from which its clients were equally benefiting. Second, the pressure driving concert ticket prices up was the demand made by performers and their managers and agents for increased guarantees and higher percentages of the gate.

The next chapter in the Ticketmaster story involved different technologies, different owners and, eventually, a different business model. The company launched its website (as an events database) in 1995 and made it transactional (a place to buy tickets) in 1996. The internet, in the words of Alan Citron, the chief operating officer of Ticketmaster Multimedia, "allows you to offer everyone access to everything" (quoted in Budnick and Baron 2011: 234). By the end of 2001, 41% of the company's ticket sales were online. But the most significant aspect of the e-ticket was to change Ticketmaster's client base: its clients had been venues and promoters, now they were the people who used their website. Ticketmaster had become a "customer-facing" company; its concern was to ensure its website was so user friendly that its customers would return not only to buy tickets but to explore Ticketmaster's other offers. The company's aim, in the jargon of the time, was to provide "a better transactional experience". In addition:

> For the first time – *the first time* – Ticketmaster began leveraging its mammoth data base to proactively contact customers about upcoming events they might be interested in attending, based on their previous purchases. Armed with its new-fangled Ticket Alert email system, Ticketmaster could now offer a clear solution … to the industry's age-old problem: the biggest reason people don't go to a concert or event is that they simply don't know about it.
>
> (Budnick and Baron 2011: 242, authors' italics)[13]

The change in Ticketmaster's sales pitch is well captured in a 2011 report by Chuck Salter on a ten-date US tour featuring new Ticketmaster CEO Nathan Hubbard, whose brief was to develop Ticketmaster "as a fan-centric e-commerce company rather than merely a transaction engine for live-event venues and sports teams". As a merchandiser, the company was, Hubbard claimed, up there with Amazon and eBay: "We've rolled out more products in the last six months than we've rolled out in the last six years". The Ticketmaster site now included an interactive venue map that "puts fans in control of choosing from all available seats" while "a forthcoming Facebook app will pinpoint where your friends are seated". As Salter notes, "Hubbard wants to expand the definition of a ticket beyond access to a two-hour event, offering exclusive content to tap the anticipation beforehand and the memories afterwards" (Salter 2011).

Ironically, in becoming more consumer friendly, Ticketmaster found itself involved in competition with fan ticketing sites. The catalyst here was the success of Music Today, "a hub of online fan club ticketing and merchandise" formed in 1998 by Dave Matthews Band manager Coran Capshaw. By 2000, this company was providing services for 45 acts. Fan club ticketing was of interest to Ticketmaster for two reasons: it provided a significant revenue stream for bands (as mail-based fan clubs had done in Britain since the 1960s)[14] and it offered fans premier seats at the price of an event's cheapest tickets by reducing or removing service fees. (This was a good reason for joining the club in the first place.)

20 *We Are the World*

The Ticketmaster problem was how to restrict the number of fan tickets on offer, and the dispute here was primarily with the musicians, who if they did not exactly "own" the tickets did have a degree of control (depending on their drawing power) over concert policy. The Ticketmaster solution followed its usual approach to competition. In the words of John Pleasants, company CEO from 2000–05: "You say, 'The only way I wouldn't care if [artists] sold twenty per cent of the inventory through this fan club is if *we* ran the fan club" (quoted in Budnick and Baron 2011: 271). This was also the moment Ticketmaster decided it needed to buy a stake in the USA's biggest artist management company, Front Line.

What everyone involved had realised by now was that premier seats had a monetary value that was not restricted to their cover price. As well as being offered to fan club members, they were a key ingredient of VIP packages, which offered to those who could afford them not just the best seats but also such add-ons as exclusive merchandise. Bands began to employ specialist VIP packagers, who requisitioned tickets from the inventory, making them unavailable to either regular fans or the general public. This was one of the ways Michael Cohl tried to develop a new revenue stream to meet his extravagant guarantees on the Rolling Stones' *Steel Wheels* tour; it was "the first large-scale VIP ticketing operation". Cohl had earlier pioneered a scheme in Canada by which a tranche of premium tickets was assigned to a transportation company, which packaged the seats with a bus ride to the show and an on-bus party (Budnick and Baron 2011: 302). This model is still in use in Britain (with an added overnight stay in a hotel) to take people from the provinces to see a London show or a star such as Cliff Richard in concert.

VIP packages enabled artists to sell seats at ticket touts' prices while apparently doing their fans a favour, but if this was partly a way of taking on the scalpers, the continuing development of e-commerce saw the emergence of online ticket exchange sites, which created a whole new scale of secondary ticketing. The pioneer here was LiquidSeats, established in 2001 to manage the ticket resale market for sports teams before evolving in 2003 into the consumer-focused StubHub, which by 2005 was recording ticket sales of around $40 million annually (the company took 15% of ticket value from sellers and 10% from buyers). In January 2007, StubHub was taken over by eBay but by then co-founder Eric Baker had already moved to Europe to start a new secondary ticketing site, Viagogo, which in November 2019 announced its own plans to buy StubHub, in a $4 billion deal.[15]

We will return to secondary ticketing in Chapter 4. In the final part of this chapter, we examine the third US corporation that came to dominate the live music business in the UK: AEG.

AEG: live music as a property business

The Millennium Dome in London's Greenwich (or Millennium Tent, as *Private Eye* named it) was, as Tim Burrows (2009: 224–5) writes, "a widely derided structure—the British [Labour] government's monumental white elephant". When it closed, on December 31, 2000, no one knew what to do with it—something that became increasingly embarrassing for ministers as the building cost the taxpayer around £240,000 a month just to keep empty. Originally planned (by a Conservative government) as the hub of Britain's Millennial celebrations, it was conceived as a huge exhibition centre, designed by architect Richard Rodgers (with reference back to the Dome of Discovery at the 1951 Festival of Britain) and built on derelict land known for its toxicity and unexploded bombs.[16] The Dome was planned not just to be an inspiring place to visit but also as a contribution to the regeneration of an abandoned, unvisited and under-populated area of East London.

In 2005, a Dome deal was finally struck with an American property company, AEG, which was already involved in the redevelopment of the Greenwich peninsula. In a naming deal with the Spanish company Telefonica, the building was now to be called the O2 and its centrepiece was the 23,000-capacity O2 Arena.[17] The venue opened on June 24, 2007 with a performance by Bon Jovi but had already, some months before, run a full-page advertisement in *Music Week* (2 June 2007: 32) announcing a million ticket sales. By the end of the year, AEG's Europe CEO, David Campbell, was telling the paper that, "rather than having to woo artists, the venue's problem is now how to accommodate all the acts that want to play there" (*Music Week*, December 17, 2007: 1). *Pollstar's* 2008 "Worldwide Music Arena Industry Chart" confirmed that the O2 Arena was now the most popular venue in the world: its sales of 1,806,447 tickets were "a country mile ahead of the second best-selling building", Madison Square Gardens (*Music Week,* January 24, 2009: 6).

For most British commentators, there were two stories here: the transformation of Britain's most pointless leisure building into its most successful one, and the revelation of how comfortable a purpose-built rock-oriented arena could be. In Tim Burrows' (2009: 227) words, "critics gushed about the padded seats and abundant loos" and the UK's leading promoters were equally enthusiastic. Simon Moran of SJM Concerts said, "It is a great venue, much needed in London. It's very well done, with very good facilities, nicely done up, looks good. I'm very pleased with it." Harvey Goldsmith stated, "I think it has had an amazing impact on the whole business. It has allowed acts to go into a great new space and actually sell more tickets than they thought they would sell" (quotes from *Music Week*, June 8, 2008: 13). In a *Music Week* editorial, Martin Talbot spelled out the lesson of the O2 Arena's success for other venues: "It's not just about the music—although that is very important—it is about the broader experience, the bars, the concessions, the comfortable seats, the price of the merchandise" (*Music Week*, June 30, 2007: 12).

For us, though, the interesting story is how the O2 came to be established in the first place. How was it that the British venue business was transformed by an American corporation? AEG, the Anschutz Entertainment Group, was owned by Philip Anschutz, "who made his fortune in oil and gas, real estate,

22   *We Are the World*

railroads, telecommunications, and sports and entertainment". The O2 development in London was modelled on his earlier Staples development in Los Angeles.

> Fifteen years ago, the area was an urban wasteland: thirty acres of flophouses, bars, strip clubs, and empty lots, forlornly situated near the 10 and 110 freeways. Now [Tim] Leiweke [AEG CEO from 1996–2013] can point to Staples Centre, a twenty-thousand-seat arena, and to L.A. Live, a bustling entertainment district, which are almost entirely owned by AEG. Beneath flashing billboards advertising L.A. sponsors like Coca-Cola and Toyota, there are dozens of restaurants, a J.W. Marriott/Ritz-Carlton Hotel, the Nokia Theatre, the Grammy Museum, and a multiplex Regal Cinema. Across the plaza from Leiweke's office window is the entrance to Staples Centre, home to the Lakers [basketball team](partly owned by Philip Anschutz) and the Kings [ice hockey team] (majority owned by AEG).
>
> (Bruck 2012: 47)

Leiweke, whose pre-AEG career was as a sports executive, notes in this *New Yorker* article that, "We've built more arenas and stadiums than anyone in the world, ever—including the Romans!" and he explains that AEG's goal was to create "entertainment palaces where citizens can gather". As Connie Bruck writes,

> Anschutz and Leiweke had a specific model in mind. "When we started thinking this up, we went to Universal Studios and Disneyland," Leiweke said. "The theme parks have a very brilliant concept. If twenty million people go through Disneyland, why can't we build hotels, restaurants, and retail that service twenty million people? That's all we did here."
>
> (Bruck 2012: 47)

Anschutz exported this "American model" globally, and was so successful that by 2012 the company owned or operated nearly a hundred venues around the world, including O2 arenas in London, Berlin and Dublin. The plan was "not only to control facilities worldwide, but also to have a stake in their content". The company's concert division, AEG Live, was thus formed in 1999 and within a decade was second in size only to Live Nation as a concert promoter. "The strategy was to own a piece of everything, cross-promote, and reap the benefits, in a synergistic conglomerate for the new century" (Bruck 2012: 48, 52). AEG's most startling musical deal was struck in 2000 with Celine Dion, her manager and Caesars Palace. A new theatre was built (to be operated by AEG) specifically for Dion, who signed a $150 million deal for a five-year residency: the show opened in 2003 and sold out for 723 consecutive shows (Bruck 2012: 52).

AEG's strategy for the O2 was therefore familiar to anyone who had followed the company's activities in the USA: first, develop an arena as part of a state supported urban development project; second, buy into "content provision" (AEG acquired a 49% stake in Marshall Arts, Barry Marshall's promotions and talent agency: "The move potentially provides AEG with a pool of talent to book for shows at the O2"); third, promote residencies (early O2 Arena events included a 17-night Spice Girls run, and 21 nights of Prince—"Sold out. Every seat. Every night. Tickets: 351,527. Gross: £10,971,157").[18]

AEG was not just in the rock and pop concert business. In the words of its own slogan, London's O2 offered "a world of entertainment under one roof". The O2 Arena was used for promoting sporting events such as the World Gymnastics Championships, the ATP Masters tennis finals, and various wrestling and boxing bouts. The O2 complex included IndigO2, a smaller music space for comedy, rock, jazz, pop and classical music (the Royal Philharmonic Concert Orchestra made regular appearances), which was purpose-built for television and live recording; the O2 Bubble, an exhibition space that initially held a Tutankhamun display (a million tickets for this were sold between November 2007 and June 2008) before hosting the *British Music Experience* exhibition from 2009–2014; and Matter, a dance space operated by Fabric, one of London's leading clubs.[19]

Of course, the site also included 20 bars and restaurants, and a multiplex, Cineworld; on a busy day, 65,000 people might visit. David Campbell, AEG Europe's CEO, explained the thinking: "For many, the restaurants and bars of Entertainment Avenue are a big attraction." While "hard-core music-lovers" might just arrive for the concert, many people wanted to make an evening of it, filling the venue from four or five o'clock in the afternoon. "That is kind of what is happening in the live music market now—we have given people a much better experience and that is why they are coming earlier, that is why they are staying later" (quoted in *Music Week,* June 17, 2008: 20).

And the people flocking to the O2 were not just punters. Matt Botten, head of hospitality, said:

> We have got 96 suites here, the VIP Club Lounge, Backstage Bar, the Chairman's Club—we have anything up to 3,500 guests in the hospitality areas every evening. No two nights are ever the same. During the week, it is very much suite-holders using their tickets for corporate hospitality. Then at the weekend, it is far more likely to be friends and family of the suite-owners coming along.
>
> Our suite-holders get tickets for every single event, so we do try to see them make the best use of it, and we encourage them to do that as well. At the Led Zeppelin show, every single suite was about entertaining and suite-holders making the most of their facility.
>
> (Quoted in *Music Week,* June 17, 2008)

24   *We Are the World*

For many rock fans, the O2 experience seemed to replicate a trip to the Bluewater shopping centre (opened in 1999) rather than to offer any kind of musical adventure,[20] while for critics the sound often seemed ... well, too perfect. This, for example, is Anthony Holden, reviewing a concert for *The Guardian* in November 2008:

> Had there been a programme, I could perhaps tell you how long the Berezovsky Trio have been together. But this was an evening as informal as classical music gets. Comfortable seats with holders for drinks in plastic glasses; no nagging interval bells; people wandering around at will, as at a jazz concert—this is musical life down at the Dome.
>
> Yes, classical music has recently arrived at the O2, or in this case IndigO2, the smaller of the halls that have turned Richard Rogers' stately pleasure dome from millennial morgue into pulsating fun palace. A tenth the size of its 18,000-seater big brother, the Indigo is capable of seating some 1700 in its sleek, Las Vegas-style lounge, where artists of the stature of Bryn Terfel, Sarah Connolly and pianist Garrick Ohlsson are on this autumn's bill of fare.
>
> Will they, like Berezovsky, eschew the electronic "enhancement" on offer in a theatre which normally hosts the likes of Billy Ocean, Shakin' Stevens and the Bootleg Beatles? The RPO didn't last month, when I attended a concert of Sibelius, Tchaikovsky and Rachmaninov's third piano concerto, with soloist Peter Donohoe. Indigo's dry, clean acoustic is fine for chamber groups and soloists, but orchestras fare less well in a venue built for jazz and pop, whose every surface is designed to absorb heavily amplified sound. So microphones are hung high above the stage to relay "fill-in" sound to the seats on the side, and at the back of the balcony, thus simulating a more reverberant acoustic.
>
> Having now sat all over the auditorium, I can testify that the effect is akin to being a guest at a recording session.[21]

The final point to make here is that even in the British context, the O2 was not entirely novel. This model of arena economics—a British city council investing in a space for sports events, conventions and concerts; US companies being brought in to manage it—was in place well before the Millennium Dome was built. The Sheffield Arena, for example, opened in 1991 (it was built to host the World Student Games), while the Manchester Arena was developed by the local authority (with Whitehall and EU financial support) in support of Manchester's 1996 and 2000 bids to stage the Olympic Games. Since 2000, it has been operated by SMG, a US specialist in managing publicly owned facilities, which took over from another US based company, Ogden Entertainments—SMG had previously been running the Sheffield Arena.[22] In a *Music Week* special feature in 2010, the Manchester Arena's general manager, John Knight, was keen to contrast its local grittiness to the O2's metropolitan gloss.

It's not about money and it's not about marble floors or moving stairwells—it's about atmosphere. We are not a capital-city venue and we are never going to have that cachet. We are a solid, no frills, give-people-a-good-night-out, working venue, and that is what I think people feel comfortable with here.

(*Music Week*, July 19, 2010: 13–15)[23]

This is a nice soundbite—plucky northern venue takes on corporate US behemoth—but it is misleading. Over the years, the Manchester Arena has not only had various corporate names (as naming rights have been sold and resold) but its site has also been owned by various real estate companies, mostly US based and including AEG before it switched its attention to Greenwich. As a music venue, its continued success (like that of the O2) depends on a regular calendar of big names rather than local music acts.

In Chapter 4 we will further consider the argument that for British cities in the twenty-first century, an arena has come to be as significant for city prestige as a town hall was in the nineteenth century. The point here is that whatever their political origins to survive such venues have had to become part of the global corporate arena business. For example, the Cardiff International Arena, which opened in 1993, is now owned as well as operated by Live Nation UK.

Conclusion

In its end-of-year round-up for 2007, *Music Week* suggested that if the year "is remembered for anything in the live sector, it will be how the traditional relationships between artists, manager, venues and record companies turned on their heads". It was the year in which record companies started pushing for 360-degree contracts with their artists (covering all their activities and sales, merchandise as well as recordings, performing as well as publishing) and "live companies expanded beyond their traditional revenue streams"—AEG taking on representation of Prince, Live Nation signing Madonna. It was the year in which "the secondary ticketing market emerged as a major new revenue stream"; Wembley Stadium was re-launched and AEG's O2 became the world's most popular arena; the year when Live Nation and the Dublin based Gaiety Investments became majority owners of the Academy Music Group, in the process (to meet competition requirements) selling the Hammersmith Apollo and Kentish Town Forum to the Mama Group, which itself acquired six venues from Melvin Benn's Mean Fiddler, "which in turn rebranded as Festival Republic" (*Music Week*, December 22, 2007: 12).

We will discuss the complexity of the relationships between the small number of promoters who now controlled most live music in Britain in the next chapter. As we have outlined in previous volumes, oligopoly is not a new feature of the entertainment business—think of the chain of Mecca Ballrooms or the showbiz empire of the Grades. What was new by the turn of the century

26 *We Are the World*

was, first, that the dominant players in British live music were now American corporations and, second, that their interest was not the market value of the music experience itself, but in the supplementary income it could generate. Robert Sillerman, Fred Rosen and Philip Anschutz did not start out as music lovers; rather, they were visionaries in their grasp of the untapped income-generating possibilities of live music. This was, it could be said, the major effect (and perhaps one of the causes) of the post-digital shift of musical power from record companies to live music entrepreneurs.

In Britain, this regime change was also demonstrated by the increasing interest taken by investment companies and hedge fund managers in promoters, venues and festivals. This, for example, is how RJD Partners, "an equity investor specialising in buy-outs and buy-ins" explains its involvement in live music:[24]

RJD originally backed the £33.5 million management buyout of Academy Music Group (AMG), the UK's leading owner and operator of live music and club venues, including South London's award winning concert venue, O2 Academy Brixton and O2 Shepherd's Bush Empire, in August 2004. The company owned further Academy venues in Birmingham, Bristol, Glasgow, Liverpool and Islington (London) and Bar Academy sites in London and Birmingham.

We were introduced to the deal by a boutique intermediary. We won the mandate based on our leisure sector track record, which gave us a clear insight into the sector dynamics, the strong relationship developed with the management team and an innovative deal structure which met the objectives of several different stakeholders.

We were attracted to AMG because of its leading position in the live music venue sector, its strong relationships with the principal promoters of live music events and the track record and strong reputation of the management team led by chief executive John Northcote. In addition the business operated in a sector with high barriers to entry.

We took a majority stake in the business, investing alongside AMG's management team and three of the UK's leading concert promoters, Metropolis Music, SJM Concerts and MCD Productions. These three promoters were responsible for promoting many international acts on the touring circuit, as well as collectively owning and promoting some of the biggest outdoor music events, including the annual V Festival, thus making them excellent strategic partners.

The buyout provided AMG with financial strength to pursue its strategy of rolling out the award-winning "Academy" brand across the UK, building on its existing successful venues.

During RJD's ownership, new venues were opened in Oxford and Newcastle and growth was driven through improved asset utilisation within existing venues and developing in-house promotions.

AMG's success created interest from trade buyers and in March 2007, RJD sold its investment in AMG to a consortium led by LiveNation, the largest producer of live concerts in the world. The transaction valued Academy at £57 million, giving a return to RJD of 2.6x its original investment. The sale represented the first exit from our first fund, raised in 2003.[25]

In Chapter 1 we described how, in 1985, the most publicised rock concert, Live Aid, was organised as a means to a charitable end. Twenty years later, the most successful rock concerts had primarily become means to ends more appropriate to a new era: retail expenditure, returns on speculative investment and data mining. We now turn to the effects of these changes on the everyday activities of the British live music business.

Notes

1   Quoted from an interview with Jon Pareles in the *New York Times*, June 9, 2002: 30.
2   Quoted from an interview with Matt Brennan, June 2, 2009.
3   The discussion below draws extensively from Budnick and Baron (2011), by far the best-informed history of the US concert industry in this period.
4   This act was a key moment in the political impact of neo-liberalism on the USA; among other things, it enabled Rupert Murdoch's News Corp to establish Fox News.
5   Lowenstein writes that Bill Graham operated "one of the worst examples of scalping", not just by having a special (unofficial) turnstile for his "friends" but also by encouraging acts he promoted to keep ticket prices low "for their fans", omitting to mention that this increased his profits on the scalper tickets he sold at market value (Lowenstein 2014: 133–5).
6   By far the biggest music merchandising company in North America at this time was Bill Graham's Winterland Productions.
7   It should be stressed here that, while SFX formally bought promotion companies, effectively the company bought people, promoters valued for their contacts, experience and knowledge of their markets. Such promoters took on key roles in upper echelons of both SFX and then Live Nation.
8   Clear Channel was cognisant of the commercial success of EMCI, a company that matched entertainer and sponsor (Budnick and Baron 2011: 177).
9   This decision was the beginning of the end of Lowenstein's relationship with the Stones. He stepped down from his business management role in 2008 (see Lowenstein 2014: 227–9).
10 For full discussion of the issues here, see Budnick and Baron (2011: 216–21).
11 Keith Prowse's main business today is, however, sports hospitality. Details of the company's history taken from www.keithprowse.co.uk and https://en.wikipedia.org/wiki/Keith_Prowse.
12 Information taken from an interview by Matt Brennan, November 23, 2010.
13 LiveAnalytics, "an independent team charged with innovating around the company's data", was launched by Ticketmaster USA in 2010 (See Salter 2011) and rolled out internationally in 2013 to sell customised data to artists, venues and

28 *We Are the World*

promoters, and to potential sponsors and brand partners (see *Music Week*'s June 2013 story: www.musicweek.com/news/read/ticketmaster-rolls-out-analytics.

14 Budnick and Baron (2011) note that in 2005 U2's fan club, run through its website, had around 100,000 members paying $40 each; the Rolling Stones had even more fan club members while charging a $95 membership fee.

15 At the time of writing this acquisition was being investigated by the UK's Competition and Markets Authority.

16 See www.theguardian.com/culture/2015/mar/17/how-we-made-the-millennium-dome-richard-rogers.

17 Telefonica, owner of the mobile phone network O2, signed a 15-year contract for naming rights, at a cost of £6 million/year plus 2000 seats a show to offer to their customers. Other 'commercial partners' were ADT, BMW, Credit Suisse, InBev, NatWest, NEC, Nestle, Pepsi and Visa. "As with O2, their dividend comes in association with the music: prominent branding, privileged tickets and all manner of corporate hospitality" (Burrows: 227; *Music Week*, June 18, 2008: 15–16).

18 See *Music Week,* October 29, 2006: 4; October 13, 2007: 7.

19 Fabric ran this space from 2008–10; it then became the Proud2 nightclub. There were always issues about late-night transport for O2 clubbers. In 2006, AEG purchased Thames Clippers, the river bus service, to ensure that its boats would run through the small hours on club nights; in 2010, Matter's closure was blamed on financial difficulties caused by delays in developing the Jubilee Line.

20 Head of event marketing, Dawn Jones, explained, "We have 300 screens around the venue that we use to market our events" (*Music Week,* June 17, 2008: 18).

21 See www.theguardian.com/music/2008/nov/16/boris-godunov-berezovsky-review.

22 SMG, a subsidiary of American Capital Strategies, signed a new 25-year lease deal for the Manchester Arena in 2010.

23 The best evidence that the Manchester Arena was in certain respects an authentic *local* venue was the remarkable success of comedian Peter Kay's 35-night run in 2010. Kay worked at the arena as a steward before his stand-up career took off.

24 The company was incorporated as a private investment company in 2001, going through various name changes before becoming RJD in November 2005.

25 See www.rjdpartners.com/portfolio/academy-music-group.

3 Taking care of business

It's not a job; it's a way of life. And none of us play instruments. None of us pretend we're in showbiz 'cause we're not really, it's just, it's like a subculture. And Danny Betesh has more money that the Aga Khan, you know, he doesn't have to work, but he still does. And he'll still turn up at Van Morrison dates to get bawled and shouted at ... it's just something in the blood.

(Paul Latham, Live Nation UK)[1]

Where are the buccaneers, the pirates, the chancers? They are now all working for Live Nation and sending their monthly plans to accountants in New York and it just stifles everything.

(Jef Hanlon, Jef Hanlon Promotions)[2]

I suppose the worst ever gig should be the one you lost the most money on if you're a promoter, but I don't see it like that—I can lose money on a gig and still think it's fantastic.

(Mark Mackie, Regular Music)[3]

Introduction

The most obvious feature of the live music business in the UK in the decades after 1985 was the consolidation of the ownership of promotion companies and music venues by the US entertainment corporations we discussed in Chapter 2. By 2011, five major companies controlled most of the British live music economy: Live Nation Entertainment, AEG Live, Gaiety/MCD, SJM and Metropolis Music. In terms of cross-company share ownership, this apparent oligopoly is better described as a duopoly, with Live Nation and its subsidiaries on one side and AEG Live and its subsidiaries on the other (Brennan 2011: 71).

The business model adopted by these promoters was essentially collaborative. They routinely worked together to promote big tours; they shared ownership of the UK's most used concert venues. The complexity of the financial relationships here can be illustrated by a case study of Glasgow, home to Scotland's biggest concert promotion company, DF Concerts. DF promoted

30 *Taking care of business*

everything from small venues to stadium gigs and ran the country's premier rock event, T in the Park. But the assumption (in most local media reports, for example) that DF was a Scottish company was misleading. In 2011, DF was 78% owned by LN-Gaiety Holdings, a joint venture of Live Nation and the Irish concert promotion company MCD (owned via the Jersey-based Gaiety Investments and controlled by Denis Desmond and Caroline Downey), 19.5% by Simon Moran's SJM Concerts, based in Manchester, and 2.5% by Geoff Ellis.[4] Along with Metropolis, Live Nation, Gaiety and SJM also had controlling shares in the Academy Music Group, which in Glasgow owned the 1300-capacity O2 ABC and its sister venue, the 300-capacity O2 ABC2, as well as the 2500-capacity O2 Academy. Through their shares in DF, LN-Gaiety and SJM also co-owned King Tut's, Glasgow's most famous small venue (350 capacity).

This pattern of venue ownership could have been found by then in Britain's other major cities (Live Nation owned 42 UK venues) and was replicated in the ownership and operation of the music festival business, to which we will return in Chapter 5. In this chapter, we focus on the effect of this interlocking corporate ownership on the everyday activity of live music business.

Promoter careers

For the British promoters (all men) who were established in the mid-1980s (the starting point of this volume), the impact of Live Nation and AEG became apparent at the turn of the century. As veteran Manchester promoter Danny Betesh put it, if there were around twelve major national promoters in the UK at the end of the 1990s, over the next decade Live Nation and AEG each "condensed a few".[5] The effects of this can be seen in the detail of a sample of promoters' careers.

Paul Latham's life in the entertainment business began at Granada (in bingo halls and night clubs)[6]; he joined Apollo Leisure as an assistant venue manager and by 1985 was running the Manchester Apollo:

> As venue managers we were treated like local promoters. It was part of our job to go out and get stories, to get placements, to have the journalists work in those areas, to be part of it. That was where I made my reputation. I used to work really hard.[7]

The Apollo Circuit had been established in 1973 by Paul Gregg, an ex-employee of ABC (Associated British Cinemas) who started buying decaying urban venues for himself, restoring them as flexible entertainment spaces for music, theatre and films; over the next 25 years, Gregg expanded his interests into ticketing, promotion and agency. In 1999, Apollo Leisure was sold to SFX and Paul Latham thus became a SFX employee. He rose within the company as it was sold to Clear Channel and became Chair of Live Nation UK in 2002.[8]

Taking care of business   31

Barry Clayman, who had started out in 1969 at MAM (discussed in Volume 2), launched Barry Clayman Concerts (BCC) as a joint venture with Apollo Leisure in 1986. After the Apollo sale to SFX, Clayman also found himself on the Live Nation payroll, as did his number two in BCC, Phil Bowdery, who had begun his live music career as a tour manager. Initially Clayman and Bowdery worked as "entrepreneurial promoters" within Live Nation, but in 2005 Bowdery took on the corporate job of managing Live Nation's European tours.[9]

Barry Dickins, who also began at MAM, became co-owner of International Talent Booking (ITB) in 1978; it was sold to Live Nation in 2001. While Dickins was now technically a Live Nation employee, the money he brought into the company came from the artists signed to ITB, and in providing agency services to ITB acts, Dickins' policy was still "to do the best deal for the client", which might mean using a promoter from outside the Live Nation family.[10]

In 1987, John Giddings, another ex-MAM agent who had started out as the social secretary at Exeter University, sold half of his own agency and promotion company, Solo (established in 1986), to the North American International Talent Group (ITG), which was, in turn, half owned by Michael Cohl, thus forming a global agency, Solo ITG. Five years later, he regained majority ownership of Solo but Cohl's company retained shares. When Cohl sold out to Clear Channel, it therefore got a percentage of Solo, which it acquired outright in 1999. Again, Giddings initially ran Solo *within* Clear Channel before (in 2004) re-forming it as an independent company and becoming a Live Nation "consultant": "I implement their global touring ... The Live Nation office in Oxford Circus is what I would call the regular army, we're like the SAS. We're separate but close." In this role, Giddings was working not as an independent agent (as with Solo) but as a representative of Live Nation's global promotions business.[11]

Rob Hallett started out in 1980 as an agent and manager in Derek Block's office and worked with Duran Duran's Andy Taylor at the refurbished Trident Studio before joining Marshall Arts, where he was based from 1990–2000. In 2000, Marshall Arts was absorbed into AEG and Hallett became president for international touring (his job was acquiring touring rights), a post he occupied from 2004 to 2014, when he left AEG to start a new independent live music company, Robomagic. Robomagic was merged with Live Nation in 2018.

In 1984, Stuart Galbraith joined the promotion company Midland Concert Promotions (MCP) straight from Leeds University, where he had been entertainments officer.[12] MCP was sold to SFX in 1999 and by 2005 Galbraith was managing director (music) of Live Nation. He was sacked from this job in 2007, "accused of conspiring with global rivals", and in 2008 founded Kilimanjaro Live, following an approach from AEG Live.[13] The aim was to create a pipeline of artists to play in AEG-owned and operated venues. In 2012, Galbraith acquired AEG's share of Kilimanjaro; in 2014, he sold a controlling stake to DEAG, the Berlin-based entertainment group.[14]

32 *Taking care of business*

Bob Angus began his live music career in the late 1970s as entertainment officer at Surrey University and set up his own promotions company, Metropolis, in 1985. "It was a struggle in the early days," he remembers. "It was a struggle to get business. It was a struggle to do anything. Once I'd got acts to a certain level, I'd get them nicked off me" (quoted in Forde 2016: 44). Metropolis initially developed by specialising in small London gigs for emerging artists (for example, at the University of London Union), but Angus developed a broader national reach when he started working with northern promoter Phil McIntyre (who later became a specialist in live comedy), and broke through to the big time by promoting Robbie Williams' solo tours just as the artist took off as a superstar.

Although Angus saw Metropolis as "proudly independent", he understood early on that his promotional risks needed to be offset by more secure live music earnings. In 1995, he and Simon Moran launched the V Festival as an alternative weekend to the established Reading and Glastonbury events (Manchester-based Moran, who started out promoting gigs as a student at Sheffield University in the mid-1980s, had launched SJM Concerts in 1992.)[15] The V Festival was set up to operate across two sites, one in the north of England (where Moran promoted) and one in the south (where Angus was based) and at around the same time, again in partnership with Moran and Desmond, Angus bought 35% of what was to become the Academy Group, which at that point operated only the Brixton Academy and Shepherds Bush Empire. Even as an independent, then, Angus became involved with Live Nation, which in 2008 took over management of the Academy Group and in 2013 bought a significant stake in the V Festival.[16]

Vince Power, who started out in the furniture business, opened the Mean Fiddler venue in Harlesden in London in 1982 and was always aware of the financial importance of venue ownership:

> When I started the business, I loved music of course, but I always had one eye on the till and one eye on the talent. So the till was like selling beer. Generally when you do a venue, if you're lucky, you make a very small amount on the door, once you've paid for advertising, promoting, and the fee of the bands, PA, lights, dressing room, everything. You make the money on the beer … that's where the profit is. This is what enabled me to pay money. Before promoters never had their own venue. I was the first promoter to have my own venue. They all have now, people like Denis [Desmond] and all, they copied the same format of the Mean Fiddler. But they used to just hire places like the Hammersmith Apollo, and they'd have to make all the money on the door.[17]

A decade later, in 1994, John Northcote, whose company Break for the Border had been running the Borderline, a venue in Charing Cross, since the early 1990s, bought the Shepherd's Bush Empire and reshaped it as a live music venue; in 1997, he bought the Brixton Academy.[18] Northcote's aim (which echoed Paul Gregg's plan for Apollo Leisure in the 1970s) was to develop a national venue network and in 2000 he established the Academy Music Group with investment, as we have seen, from SJM Concerts and Metropolis Music, soon to be followed by Live Nation/Gaiety as additional shareholders. If Vince Power was a venue owner who became a promoter, Northcote was a venue owner whose success depended on doing deals with promoters; this eventually meant the Academy Group too being absorbed into Live Nation.[19]

Vince Power also acquired other venues, most significantly the 2100-capacity Forum in Kentish Town,[20] but his key purchase was the Reading festival in 1989. As Simon Parkes, then running the Brixton Academy, recalls:

> Controlling Reading gave Vince enormous leverage on the industry. He could offer agents a much-coveted slot at Reading, on the condition that their bands do their warm-up shows at the Forum rather than their natural choice, the Academy. Now, for the first time in years, I had some credible competition to keep things interesting.
>
> (Parkes 2014: 326)

By the end of the 1990s, Power was the leading player in the UK festival market but in 2005 the Mean Fiddler Group was sold to Clear Channel; Power now focused on developing the Benicassim festival in Spain. Other new ventures were less successful; Vince Power Music Group went bust in 2010; Vince Power Music Festivals went under in 2012.

Two points can be made immediately from this brief survey. First, although many of the promoters who emerged in the 1980s began (like their 1960s and 1970s predecessors) as entertainment officers at universities, their careers flourished as student unions (though not students) became less and less important for the live music business. Second, they started out, as Eamonn Forde remarks,

> at a time of immense potential for smaller players who were smart enough and swift enough to seize on things. "We were living in a world of small operators in those days," says [Rob] Hallett. "People like me, Bob [Angus] and Simon Moran were all trying to get ahead then. It was a time of opportunity. We were all independent."
>
> (Forde 2016: 44)

The problem these promoters faced, as small operators taking risks on new acts, was that once they had built their artists up to a certain level of success, the bigger players would swoop in and poach them. This is the context for the developments we describe in the next section.

Loyalty and calculation

There were many reasons why British promoters became cogs in US corporate entertainment machines—the same reasons, of course, that had been behind the original success of Live Nation, AEG and Ticketmaster in taking over the

34 *Taking care of business*

promotion business in the USA, as we discussed in Chapter 2. To begin with, by the nature of their business, promoters lack fixed or physical assets, hence the need to own or invest in venues and festivals. Vince Power also understood incorporation as a way of giving a promoter a marketable asset: company shares. The Mean Fiddler Group became a Public Limited Company (PLC) in 1999, claiming to be the first publicly quoted live music company on the UK Stock Exchange. Power recalls:

> Well, I was never very good at board meetings but, having said that, it was a great discipline with the Mean Fiddler and it did get us to realize a value for the company. That is one plus about having a PLC, it gives you a value, which is whatever people are prepared to pay you to buy the shares. On the other hand, I'm not very good at being told what to do.
> (*Music Week*, June 10, 2006: 15)

As we have seen, small promoters have also long realised the advantages of teaming up with big promoters—it was only when DF had become part of Live Nation, for example, that Geoff Ellis had the clout to bring Bruce Springsteen to Glasgow. Matt James and Mark Kemp, who launched SPC in Essex in 2005, similarly welcomed their acquisition by Marshall Arts/AEG in 2009. It enabled them to reach "the next level" of the promotion business. As Kemp explained, if SPC were "to take artists from the very, very beginning of their careers to international success", then the problems arose at the most "competitive stage of development ... fighting against other national promoters".[21] For James and Kemp the deal meant that

> SPC will remain its own entity and the company will focus strictly on promoting. We will still work with all the agents, but the difference to us is that we can plug into the infrastructure of Marshall Arts and AEG for finance if we need to, as well as marketing support and accountancy if we need backup.
> (Mark Kemp quoted in *Music Week*, December 12, 2009)

The problem for new promoters, as Conal Dodds (of Metropolis) notes, is persuading agents to go on dealing with them as their act gets bigger,

> unless the agents are really fair and a lot of them *aren't*, because they want an easy life and they'd rather have one or two promoters promoting a whole tour, because it's one or two phone calls or emails for them, as opposed to fifteen (Dodds' emphasis).[22]

It has always made sense for promoters to be part of larger consortia, and this was why even the biggest British promoters—relatively small in global terms—needed to make deals with AEG and Live Nation.

Barrie Marshall, for example, explains that he sold 49% of Marshall Arts (which he founded in 1976) to AEG "so that we had money to put up for international tours". As an independent company Marshall Arts simply hadn't got the sort of financial resources necessary by the 2000s for such tours. Live Nation had upped the stakes: "they bought around the world ... so if you weren't a part of them in the UK, you didn't get the shows, as a promoter. You couldn't compete with them." AEG's financial support was needed if Marshall Arts were to come up with the advance money needed to book a show or tour.[23]

Bob Angus explains his sale of a stake in the V Festival to Live Nation similarly:

> When you have global players buying acts globally, we felt that it was better that we align ourselves with one of the global operators to make sure that, hopefully, we can maintain the ability to get better acts. You could imagine the scenario where we might *not* be able to get an act.
>
> (Forde 2016: 49)

For Live Nation and AEG, a key contractual element in such deals was that the promoters and agents taken over would stay in charge of their companies for a period (usually around five years), so their acts wouldn't notice any changes.[24] For Paul Latham, "the consolidation [of the live business] changed [things] for the business and the people doing the business, but I don't think it changed a huge amount for the people on the ground". This was certainly the case, for example, at King Tut's in Glasgow in 2010–11, when Emma Webster carried out her field research there. Few of its regulars seemed to know that it had been part of the Live Nation empire since 2008—and why would they? Its branding, personnel and booking policies hadn't noticeably changed. And for at least one small Scottish promoter, there were some advantages in dealing with a global corporation:

> I'd rather work with Live Nation than with some of the small-time gangsters that work in Glasgow ... I mean, Live Nation, if you fall out, what's the worst they can do? I don't pay them or they don't pay me. That's *it*, isn't it?[25]

There were, though, people who doubted the long-term feasibility of corporate promotion. Tony Smith, whose career started in the early 1960s, suggests:

> The thing with tours is, things happen on tours very quickly, quite often and you've got to react. And you've gotta have a point person to go to, who calls the shots and knows what they're doing. Once it becomes a corporate thing, who do you call? The accounts department, legal?[26]

36   *Taking care of business*

Simon Parkes of the Brixton Academy said:

> I had always known that I wasn't built for the world of the Public Limited Company: for board meetings, decisions by committee, and corporate hierarchies ... the accountants, lawyers and financiers called the shots now ... I wasn't used to decisions made at monthly board meetings. It drove me insane. I was used to thinking on my feet, to finding the angle and going for it before the next guy got in there; to being cut-throat in business, but generous with the spoils; to the music business as it once was: piratical, volatile and fun ... These accountants and lawyers lacked the slightest feel for how the industry actually worked.
>
> (Parkes 2014: 391–2, 393)

For Barrie Marshall, by contrast, what AEG and Live Nation offered was a way to *go on* doing what he'd always done but with more financial clout and less financial risk:

> To me, still to this day, a great promoter is a promoter who puts together the concert and the marketing and turns the radio on in the morning, or gets on the internet or drives down the streets and sees the billboard ... and sees the front of the theatre, or sees the event. And knows it's happening. You can't do that 3000 miles away in an air-conditioned office: you don't know what's going on. Similarly you need to be at shows to see what the audience is like; a tour manager is great, but it's no good for them to be telling you what it's like. As a promoter you stand there and see: did the people stay for an encore ... how many left? Was it because the band was late, so they needed transport? Or was it they'd just seen enough? Those things, you've got to be there to understand. It's an old-fashioned view, but it's the view that I have.

The challenge to this old-fashioned view was not so much the new corporate model itself as what had shaped it: the earning power of the biggest acts. In Paul Latham's words, "the one thing we don't control is the artists".

> I've got some lovely venues, but nobody comes to sit in the venue and say, "Isn't this nice?" They come in to see what's on stage. And unless you've got the right person playing at the right fee, it doesn't work.

"Getting the right person at the right fee" is the essence of a promoter's business, but it has never been a straightforwardly financial transaction. Rather, one could say, it involves juggling conflicting forces of loyalty and calculation. Promoters' relationships with in-demand artists involve both acceptable financial terms *and* their trust. As Latham puts it, "ultimately it is still down to 'alright, you can pay the most money, but can I trust you to deliver?'"

Taking care of business   37

Many of the promoters we interviewed referred their success to the key relationships they had built up over their careers with particular acts: Barrie Marshall with Tina Turner; Jef Hanlon with Duran Duran; Danny Betesh with Take That. Betesh had a share of Take That's Ultimate Tour in 2006, one of the most financially successful promotions in British live music history, "because I worked with the boys all through the nineties and there was a loyalty factor there". Bob Angus talks of "the fierce loyalty" he established with his artists: "about 90% of the acts we work with today we have worked with since day one" (Forde 2016: 44).

For corporate promoters like Live Nation, then, it wasn't enough to buy out rival promoters and their clients; the company also had to ensure that they were involved at the start of the careers of new acts. As Paul Latham explains, Live Nation needed a portfolio of venues:

> It's like hardware and software. The hardware are the venues, the software are the gigs that you have playing there. So yes, it is very much part of our methodology over here that we touch on every strand of the promoter's game.

In 2009 the company employed 13 promoters in its London office, three or four of whom "did nothing else but go to pubs" because "that's where acts are". It was important to be there at the start because "if you were the ones that gave them their first chance, they won't forget you when it comes to the big money". Such calculations also had an effect on ticket pricing policy. Promoters might underprice an act at an early stage in its career to ensure sellouts and an audience buzz from getting such good value for money; this kind of investment would reap its rewards for the promoter when the act moved into the major league of live attractions.

As the big money got ever bigger, though, the ties of loyalty were stretched. The rise of global live music businesses with apparently unlimited funds combined with the decline of tour support from record companies led artists to expect much better concert deals, an expectation driven by what Conal Dodds describes as the "funding vacuum" that appeared as the cost of shows increased. Bands were playing larger venues with more elaborate stage technology; they needed more funds in advance to prepare concerts as the *spectacles* that audiences now expected; and they had to rely on their promoters rather than their record companies to look after them—to guarantee their returns. In Paul Latham's words, "artists now have to come to us for their bread and butter, whereas in the past it was record companies … We're the last arbiters of how many drugs they use and how many Ferraris they buy!"

As a long-established promoter, Barrie Marshall felt that acts' expectations

> got to a point where the share between the promoter and the artist became unbalanced … I thought it was okay at 85/15, but if a promoter was honest, and lost money, it was very hard to make it back on time.

38   *Taking care of business*

When it got to 90/10 then it was up to the promoter to try and find a way to make a profit, because the risk was not proportionate to the return.

For Paul Latham, too:

The artists are taking too much out of the [live music] pot … The risk in promotions is now too great. If you get it wrong it's because an agent's jacked up the fees too high, created a bidding war that was artificial, and then got it guaranteed, and everything's guaranteed now. If you get one of those wrong, it can wipe out your entire promotion's profit on one tour. And that has happened. You know, we've been that fool, who was the last one in the ring in a bidding war, through the ego of the individual making the bidding, or maybe some strategic reason why we thought that artist was important to us, and it went wrong because the market had gone cold, the ticket price was too high to justify the fee that they were getting, thereby disenfranchising the audience that they had, and of course it's a double whammy, when somebody decides that someone's got too greedy. Unless they're real diehards, people that you need to go to these gigs to make up the numbers say, "Sorry, that's too much, who the fuck do they think they are?" and don't go.

From this perspective, it takes just one promoter to offer a ridiculous sum to get an established act "to kill the golden goose for everyone else". Some fool, to use Latham's term, offers too much money, all acts take this to be the going rate, and the odds shorten that a failed event or tour will means bankruptcy. Harvey Goldsmith's Allied Entertainments collapsed in 1999, for example, following its losses (reported as £1 million) on the Eclipse Festival. Neil Tennant of the Pet Shop Boys remembers that this happened mid-tour: "We were playing half-empty stadiums and losing a fortune."[27]

In his illuminating discussion of live music promotion as a risk business, Martin Cloonan (2012: 155–62) points out that corporate promotional strategies were not designed to *eliminate* risk (an impossibility—it is an essential feature of live music) but to *manage* it. Promotion got more corporate partly because of the way the shift of power from record companies to major acts changed the risks involved in promoting them. Concert profit margins became too small to sustain independent promoters or box office failures—or, indeed, a fully competitive live music market. We will return to this.

Arenas and ticketing

Another change in the UK live music sector in this period that enabled the development of the corporate model was the opening of a network of much larger venues (i.e. arenas that, as we noted in Chapter 2, were for the most part funded and owned by local authorities but managed by American entertainment companies). As Gordon Masson wrote in *Music Week* in 2010:

The fact that arena tours have become part and parcel of the live entertainment sector owes much to the work of the National Arenas Association, which this year celebrates its 20th anniversary. Indeed, the rapid development of the arenas sector and its absorption into popular culture belies those early days two decades ago when arena-sized venues were few and far between and even the biggest global acts were confined to performing in theatres and town halls if they wanted to embark on a UK tour.

(*Music Week,* July 17, 2010: 27)

As we have already noted, GMEX in Manchester opened in 1986 and the Sheffield Arena in 1991. These were followed by the Belfast Arena in 1992 and the Cardiff Arena in 1993; by 2010, the NAA had 20 members around the country. Paul Latham points out that acts could now do UK tours using their US tour equipment, while to get overall ticket sales of 80,000 it was no longer necessary to play 40–50 UK dates over a couple of months; artists could sell as many tickets doing eight dates over a week and a half. It was, in short, for the first time possible for acts to make serious money from a UK tour.[28] This changed the culture of touring. "The accountants came in," as Latham puts it, and bands and their entourage became, in Clayman's words, "a money making machine rather than actually enjoying the 'being on the road' scenario".

Digital technology also had an impact. Tour planning could now be much more centralised, for example. Local promoters' local knowledge became less significant. Barry Clayman said:

I mean today, if we [were planning to book] a theatre and [had] never played it before, we would have an e-mail within five minutes with a spec of the whole place, stage size, width, height, it would be there.

Of course, as we also discussed in Chapter 2, digital technology had a major effect on ticketing services. Vince Power claims to have been the first major promoter

to embrace Ticketmaster over here. They [other promoters] said, "Ticketmaster is going to ruin the whole business …" [but] I had a lot of venues, a few festivals, and as far as I was concerned my ticketing system was a nightmare. So Ticketmaster came in … And it worked. It was such a pleasure to get them to deal with our tickets. In the old days, in the 90s, we used to have a room full of people just answering the phone, ticket for this, ticket for Reading, for Fleadh, 40 operators.[29] And all of a sudden, gone.

In Chapter 2 we noted Danny Betesh's 1992 purchase of local Manchester ticket agent Piccadilly Box Office. By 2009, Ticketline (as it had been renamed)

40 *Taking care of business*

was processing 100,000 ticket transactions an hour and selling 1.75 million tickets a year. As an independent ticketing company, Ticketline courted independent festivals to be its key clients but it followed Ticketmaster in its digital initiatives: "bundling merchandise with tickets", launching a mobile phone ticket service, offering bespoke on-site box office facilities and "developing security measures such as holograms and barcode scanning entry systems" (*Music Week*, December 26, 2009).

What promoters now expected from a ticketing service was, first, its ability to deal with a big demand for tickets in a short time (around 65% of ticket sales for a tour or concert happen in the first day and a half) and, second, its ability to supply audience data. TicketWeb, for example, which claimed to be the first company to sell tickets online in the UK, told prospective clients that, "You log on, you can build your own events, you can pull off customer data, put more events on sale, it gives you total control over your box office."[30] In 2000, the company was bought by Ticketmaster. TicketWeb's Tim Chambers (ex-venue manager at the Brixton Academy and now Ticketmaster UK's Vice-President Sales and Music Services) explained the logic of the deal to *Music Week*: "We could cross-market and that just opened up a whole new world for our clients because they were getting the exposure on Ticketmaster" [and access to its vast customer base] (*Music Week,* Marc 28, 2009: 17).

For promoters, the main issue here, as the TicketWeb sales pitch suggests, was "control over your box office". For Paul Latham, Live Nation's subsequent merger with Ticketmaster (which we discussed in Chapter 2) was a matter of promotional common sense:

> Our business strategy is to have a relationship of more than just two hours, both with the artist and the customer. We want to talk to them when a ticket goes on sale, and we want to share in that experience afterwards. We want them to trust our brand to deliver quality entertainment in a manner that you want, to bring people to talk to them, marketers that will enhance the experience.

For Jane Donald, then head of sales and marketing at Glasgow's Royal Concert Hall, it was equally obvious that the Hall should control its ticket sales and thus box office data, which had become the new gold:

> If a commercial promoter comes in and doesn't want to use the box office, then they should be charged for it … We provide a very good ticketing service so you either use it or pay to opt out of it.

In terms of data protection laws at this time (2010), Donald said, "We have all the customers' data." The box office has the power "because they're the only people who can get permission for customer relationship marketing". The Concert Hall (a publicly funded venue) had "data partners", other publicly funded bodies, such as Royal Scottish National Orchestra, that might be "trying to fulfill audience development opportunities", but if commercial promoters wanted to use the Concert Hall's box office data in their own marketing, "we do that on their behalf; they don't actually get the names and addresses and email addresses, and we charge them for that service".[31]

For a small promoter such as Mark Kemp, it was ticket sellers' audience reach that was the problem:

> My main frustration with selling tickets is that once we've sold a ticket to somebody, that should be the opening point from when you are able to start freely talking to a customer, based in conjunction with the artist. So if you put ticket sales [in the hands of] a ticket vendor, the chances are that they will keep the ticket stock, keep the inventory and then you'd lose your chance to build a dialogue, or build a brand with that customer, because, ultimately, the information now lies with See Tickets or with Ticketmaster.[32]

Then, of course, there was the problem of the secondary ticketing business and promoters' control of their ticket *prices*. We will return to this in Chapter 4.

Agents, affiliates and associations

Historically, promoters have always seen competition as well as risk as an essential feature of their business, with agents as essential live music figures. Mark Kemp, for example, suggests that when an agent is looking for promoters for a "hot" act,

> more often than not there's a massive fight. Because if an act's hot then, you know, every promoter wants to work with them ... back to the gambling thing, it's just like, you know, you think you're in and you're going to bet the house on it coming through.

As a new promoter in the 1980s, Vince Power took it for granted that success meant winning bidding wars, by fair means or foul:

> Well I found it hard to get in. From my point of view, it was a very small club of promoters, agents and managers that seemed to control the business in the 1980s. And it was obviously very hard to get into that elite group of agents and promoters, because they obviously had their favourite agents and promoters, the bands had their favourite agents. The only way I could do it was by being a bit more aggressive and offering more money, and if the agent didn't listen I spoke to the manager, and if the manager didn't listen I spoke to the act, causing a little bit of discomfort for everybody.
>
> When Oasis did their first festivals in Reading and Leeds, everybody was bidding and bidding and getting nowhere, and in the end I just

42 *Taking care of business*

decided to go £500,000 more than anybody else, which was unheard of in those days. I think I paid them £2 million for two shows, way back in 1990-something. Promoters said I was crazy, but I knew the strength of Oasis, so all I did was actually just stick another £20 on the tickets.

Simon Parkes remembers outwitting Power in a similar bidding situation:

One of my favourite steals from Mean Fiddler occurred when I got taken to see an unknown group called Jamiroquai at the Orange, a 200-capacity toilet-venue in north Kensington [and realised immediately that] these guys were going to be stars ... I made some surreptitious enquiries about album release dates and touring schedules, only to discover that Vince was about to announce a flagship London concert to promote Jamiroquai's upcoming record at the Clapham Grand ... Just as the gig was finishing, I found Jamiroquai's agent, pulled him into the men's toilet, and asked him straight out how much Vince was offering as fee. "Eight thousand pounds," came the reply. "Bring them to the Academy three months later and I'll double that," I shot back ... We announced our Academy show the day after Vince went public with his Clapham gig and completely killed him on sales.

(Parkes 2014: 327–9)

But by the turn of the century, such stories seemed nostalgic, looking back to an "authentic" way of doing live music business that was becoming archaic. In describing his combative relationship with Vince Power in the 1990s, Simon Parkes remarked that:

There were two things in particular I admired about him. The first was that anyone could tell a mile off that he had got into this game out of a genuine love of live music. He had the authentic spirit written all over him. The other was that he absolutely hated agents, especially the established big-power agents that ran the industry. These were both character traits that I could very much relate to.

(Parkes 2014: 326)

From Parkes' perspective, the agent/promoter set-up was straightforward: a promoter takes the risk, an agent gets paid whether a promoter wins or loses, promoters always feel hard done by. But the power relationship here began to change as early as the 1970s, when Barry Dickins realised in his dealings (as an agent) with American artist managers that to tour the UK, top-tier US acts didn't need to use an agency; they could deal directly with a promoter. In John Giddings' words, "they didn't want to pay agency commissions" so, from a UK agent's perspective, "it was better to promote them in the UK, and retain the agency representation out of the UK". Giddings also realised that the same strategy made sense for popular UK acts:

Taking care of business   43

It got to a stage where they were so successful your mother could have promoted them, it was just collecting the money and putting them in the right place at the right time.

This downgrading of the agent's role was reinforced by Michael Cohl's world tour model, discussed in Chapter 2. Giddings again:

He put a check down and said, "Okay, I'll promote all your concerts worldwide, and I'll pay you x amount of money, and I want to earn money from the ticket income, merchandising, TV, everything."

As Giddings notes, "There's always *someone* you have to phone up to book a gig," but it is no longer necessarily an agent. It may be the manager, the tour manager, the artist or even another promoter. In short, "Agents, at least on major acts, are no longer an important factor. And so the relationship has changed between the manager and the promoter and that's a big change over the years."

If absorbing or eliminating agents (and their fees) was one effect of the new kinds of deal promoters were making with artists and their managers, another—as we suggested at the beginning of this chapter—was that promoters increasingly treated each other as affiliates rather than competitors. Simon Moran, for example, describes his relationship with Bob Angus in this way: "We were competitors to begin with so it probably took a few years to gain trust in everything which we definitely do have now"—now that Metropolis and SJM routinely join forces to promote national and international tours (Forde 2016: 52).

In one sense, this had always happened. Historically, agents booked UK tours by dealing with the "best" (most reliable) promoters in each region. As Paul Latham remembers, that meant Phil McIntyre and Danny Betesh in the North West, MCP in the Midlands, Harvey Goldsmith in London, DF and Regular in Scotland and so forth. This was the promotional cabal that newcomers like Simon Moran, Vince Power and Bob Angus found it difficult to break into.

But in the 1990s, as promotional costs rose and profit margins shrank, the strategy changed. It was no longer agents who divided up promotional returns, it was promoters making sure they had a little cut of everyone else's business. In John Giddings' words, "it means everybody's doing everybody favours, to help everyone". In his experience, the most "connected" person in the UK live music business was the Irish based Denis Desmond:

He's a sleeping partner with me in the Isle of Wight festival, he helped me form it because he loaned me money in a handshake. [Desmond had also been Stuart Clumpas's sleeping partner in the creation of the Scottish festival T in the Park.] People like that are worth being in business with. He's in business with Simon Moran, he's in business with Metropolis, he's

44 *Taking care of business*

in business with Live Nation. He believes in having fingers in a lot of pies, he likes control![33]

The point here, as Paul Latham puts it, is that "nobody's there to wipe each other out". The corporate strategy is to *share* risks: "it's an affiliative business". This is Michael Cohl's cross-collateralisation model (described in Chapter 2) applied by promoters collectively. According to Latham:

> It goes back to the model of who controls what competition is. So every promoter knows each other and may have co-promoted at some stage, may have shared risk. And the problem is, the bigger the risks are now, the more you want to sort of share that and not go out on a limb. So two of our biggest losses this year, we were promoting with Simon Moran, so we shared the risk. In terms of Live Nation's *raison d'être*, while I have buildings to fill, we as Live Nation will never fill more than 25% of our time with our own promotions, and this will probably get less ... there is too much risk in bidding for everything. You can't give the artist the service they need in terms of marketing, support, you know. I'd rather do less and do it better. We'd anyway need more staff, etc. A better model is not to out-bid competitors but to add our services to theirs.

Here, Latham is in part challenging the notion that Live Nation is becoming a monopoly—if the profit margin on an event is only 4% at best, "Why would you try to take more of the business?" But this is a little disingenuous. The strategy *is* actually to have a cut, one way or another, of as much of the live music income stream as possible, to have fingers in *every* pie, to "monetise" *every* aspect of the live music "experience". As Conal Dodds explains, "from a promoter's point of view, it makes more sense that we put shows into venues that we've, you know, got a shareholding in", and this is a matter of control as well as income. Dodds gives the example of John Dunn,

> who's at Live Nation, who also books Latitude [Festival]—even though it's not a Live Nation event, it's a Festival Republic event, he books it on Festival Republic's behalf. He will use that as a carrot to work with an artist ... "I'll give you a slot at Latitude but I've got to be your main national promoter in London", so that's kind of the way it works.[34]

It was this kind of collaboration (and not just the fact of corporate ownership) that led to the live music business being, it seemed, largely organised around deals made by "suits" rather than by Jef Hanlon's "buccaneers, pirates and chancers". Risk-taking, as Cloonan (2012) puts it, had become risk management and one aspect of this collaborative approach was the creation of a promoters' trade association.

Trade associations, conventions and B2B magazines

The oldest trade association in the live music business, the Association of British Orchestras (ABO), was founded in 1948 as the Orchestral Employers' Association. It was set up primarily to negotiate with the Musicians' Union, and its membership consisted "almost entirely at that time of those orchestras receiving annual funding from the newly established Arts Council of England". It was renamed the Association of British Orchestras in 1973 (becoming a limited company in 1982) and its most significant role continues to be to represent orchestras' interests in the continuing negotiations of the MU's Orchestral Agreements. Full membership of ABO is open to "professional orchestras and ensembles which have existed for not less than two years in the UK, and have undertaken no fewer than 24 public performances". In 1989, the ABO had 35 members; by the end of the period of this volume, membership had risen to around 175.[35]

The Concert Promoters Association (CPA) was formed in 1986. If ABO originated in orchestra managers' need to negotiate with the MU as a bloc, the CPA was created so that promoters could negotiate collectively with the Performing Right Society. As Jef Hanlon recalls:

As the 70s became the 80s there was a constant group of between 20 and 30 people who were earning a serious living promoting concerts in the UK. Most of them were out of the rock generation with some exceptions such as [Derek] Block and some still attached to the old showbiz industry. *That* generation, *my* generation—not the old style cigar-smoking "I'm an impresario" type. The jeans and t-shirt rock promoters (his emphases).

In the mid-1980s, PRS wanted to raise the licensing fee rate for live shows, from 2% of a show's net income (total ticket sales less VAT) to something closer to continental European rates (which were nearer to 10%). Promoters already communicated routinely with each other; they agreed now that they needed a formal collective voice at the Copyright Tribunal hearings planned for 1987. In Hanlon's words, "So 20 or 30 people put money into a pot and contributed to funding a secretary, chair and operating board—it's all very loose and informal."

The CPA was successful in its immediate aim: the Tribunal ruled that PRS could raise its rate to just 3%, but, as Stuart Littlewood remarks, the hearing (and its media coverage) revealed a widespread misunderstanding of the live music market. Ticket prices may have been rising rapidly, but promoters' percentage of box-office revenue was steadily falling; it was actually the artists who were taking the lion's share of the bigger cake.[36] It was apparent that promoters needed a permanent representative body,

to promote the interests of its members, and to represent them at a national level both to the public, and to other organisations, such as UK

46   *Taking care of business*

Music, the Office of Fair Trading, the Home Office, and the Department of Culture, Media & Sport.[37]

By 2006, the CPA had around 40 members (at the time of writing there are 57). Most of these were in the rock/pop field but members included Raymond Gubbay Ltd (classical)[38] and Serious Ltd (jazz) as well as what one might call high cultural entertainment centres (the Barbican and the South Bank) and civic entertainment venues (the Bridgewater Hall in Manchester and the Civic Hall in Wolverhampton). Over the next few years, these would be joined by Sage Gateshead, Bristol's Colston Hall, Birmingham's Symphony Hall, the Liverpool Philharmonic Hall and the Usher Hall in Edinburgh.[39] Folk/roots music also had members: the Green Man Festival and Glasgow's Celtic Connections.

Promoters had clearly become part of the establishment—in more ways than one. One of the most enterprising new promoters in the early years of the twenty-first century was Liz Hobbs, once the world water skiing champion, who now persuaded an increasing number of racecourses to finish a racing day with a concert (Newmarket, Newbury, Epsom, Cheltenham and Doncaster quickly became her clients). Hobbs signed a contract with the Jockey Club and established both a new concert circuit and a new concert audience. Artists were guaranteed 10,000 ticket sales; racecourses carried the risks of poor box-office figures; and Jockey Club Live duly became a member of the CPA (*Music Week*, June 20, 2009: 21–3).

Professional organisations such as ABO, CPA and the NAA both encouraged and reflected the way the live music business was becoming more collaborative and less competitive. In the words of Guy Dunstan, manager of the (Birmingham) NEC Group's Arena Division and a member of NAA:

> The networking that goes on between NAA members has helped us move away from the old situation where arenas were simply competing with each other to a much healthier environment where we can all work together for the common good.
>
> (Quoted in *Music Week*, July 17, 2010: 29)

This was also the thinking behind the launching of the International Live Music Conference (ILMC) in 1989, which is best summarised on its own website:

> When it began in 1989, this was the first ever dedicated gathering of leading figures involved in the world's concert industry, many of whom had only ever spoken on the phone. It swiftly grew to become the most respected meeting place for live music professionals in the world.
>
> Bringing professionals together to air their common goals, aims and issues, while providing unique networking opportunities, ILMC

has developed into a year-round organisation that also publishes *IQ* magazine ...

While the ILMC adapts and changes in response to innovations and events affecting the industry, two major factors have always remained constant: first, the ILMC is designed, organised and supported by active members of the concert industry not an outside organisation; and secondly, attendance is by invitation only. Only acknowledged professionals may attend ...[40]

One of ILMC's achievements was to put Britain at the centre of discussions of the global live music business, even though its biggest companies were American. In 1999, another live music business magazine, *Audience*, appeared; it advertised itself as "the leading B2B publication dedicated to the international contemporary live music industry". For British-based promoters and venue owners, Audience Media UK published *Live UK* (and its regular *Festival* supplement). In its professional self-consciousness, live music had become a business like any other.

Live music skills

In 2009 Creative and Cultural Skills published a report on "the economic impact of the creative industries" that included a breakdown of employment statistics in the music industry. The live music sector now accounted for five times more jobs than the recording sector. In terms of social variables, "promotion work" was revealed to be particularly male-dominated—around 70% of its workers were men (*Music Week*, June 6, 2009).

Creative and Cultural Skills (CCS) was one of the licensed sectors of the Sector Skills Council, which had been set up under the auspices of the Labour government in 2005. In 2007 it had published the results of its first skills survey of the live music and theatre labour markets. The headline finding had been the scale of the skills *shortage*: "the live music sector is facing a massive crisis in skilled staff" (*Music Week*, May 5, 2007). This survey found total employment in live music and theatre of 40,000 (half in music, half in theatre); it calculated that 20,000 employees would leave or retire in the next ten years while the continued expansion of live events would mean that an *extra* 10,000 workers would be needed (events attracting 5000 or more ticket buyers had doubled in the previous decade). All told, the sector had to recruit at least 30,000 new people by 2017. If not, festivals and major tours would be cancelled or else run by foreigners!

This report was obviously useful ammunition for CCS's established aim of creating a National Skills Academy for the live entertainment sector. *Music Week* had already reported the CCS proposal to build a Live Academy. It would cost £10 million and the live music industry would contribute £3 million. Up to 2000 students per year would be able to complete a "live entertainment

48 *Taking care of business*

apprenticeship" (*Music Week*, September 30, 2006). By 2010, the project had the support of Prime Minister Gordon Brown:

> The National Skills Academy will help to support young people in the creative industries, and is of international importance for a live performance sector that generates over £6 billion per year for the UK economy.
> (Quoted in *Music Week*, March 17, 2010)[41]

As it finally emerged, the sector's National Skills Academy (whose launch chair and chief flag-waver was Live Nation's Paul Latham) was a nationwide operation, involving 500 employers and 40 Further Education Colleges offering training courses and a programme of apprenticeships and paid internships (supported by funding from Arts Lottery administered through the Arts Council). The Live Academy itself (now called The Backstage Centre and built beside the Royal Opera House Production workshop in Purfleet, Essex) opened in 2013, giving visiting students access to the most up-to-date back stage technology.

The development of the National Skills Academy reflected both promoters' newly acquired political significance for the British economy and the formal occupational status of live music workers. Road crews, stage hands and security teams in the early rock days would have been bemused by the requirement to have *qualifications* for their jobs, but this was a natural outcome of the professionalisation of live music promotion discussed in Volume 2. In the words of Stereophonics' stage manager Derek McVay:

> People aren't just roadies anymore; there's no such thing as a roadie, you can't do the job now if you're just a roadie. A lot of people are very highly qualified mathematicians or physicists, or really highly qualified electrical engineers, who transgress into this business now because they like the lifestyle, they get paid very well and we need them! [laughs] ... If you think you can just hump a box to get a job, forget it. That's not the qualities we're looking for anymore ... The responsibility they have, the amount of money that one single technician can be responsible for can be in the millions in each department.[42]

But the creation of the National Skills Academy did also seem paradoxical: the British state was intensifying its engagement with the live music business at the moment it had become dominated by global corporations. We will return to live music policy in Chapter 4.

Conclusion

We end this chapter by returning to an issue that we raised at the beginning of Volume 1: the typology of promoters.[43] We suggested that there are two ways of classifying promoters: either in terms of their business models (independent, artist affiliated, venue based) or in ideological terms (in pursuit of commercial profit, to fulfil state policy, as a matter of enthusiasm). The evolution of the corporate practices described in this chapter challenges our typology of business models. Companies like Live Nation and AEG could be said to be independent and artist affiliated and venue based in terms of both the variety of their sources of income and the different contractual deals they make for different events. Ideologically, the lines have been blurred over the last couple of decades too. When it is state policy to make a profit, then there is little distinction between state and commercial promoters. This is most obvious in the case of arenas, built (and maintained) with state funds and then handed over to commercial management companies.

What is most interesting to us, though, is the relationship between commercial and enthusiast promotional values. In previous volumes, we have shown how enthusiasts inevitably become commercial operators—if only as a way of making an enthusiastic living! But in our promoter interviews for this volume, what we heard recurrently was corporate promoters explaining that they were really still enthusiasts, and that musical enthusiasm was still necessary for successful promotion. We cite Mark Mackie at the head of this chapter, but he was by no means the only interviewee to distinguish a "good" gig from a profitable one. A successful gig for these promoters was *not* measured by the retail expenditure it generated, its returns on speculative investment or the value of the audience data mined. Our interviewees, in effect, sought to mark off what they did *as promoters* from the marketing, ticketing and property activities of the companies they ultimately worked for.

We can illustrate this by reference to a number of recurring themes. *Risk as a personal matter*: "The promoter takes the risk ... You've got to sell the tickets, you've got to produce the show, you've got to deal with all the people that it takes to do that on all levels." *Hands-on engagement with the audience*: "A promoter has to be *very* hands-on: distribute flyers at gigs, know every market in every region we work in; know the shows our audiences will go to; work out the demographics from 16-year-old indie kids at their first gigs to 40 to 50-year-old musos." *The ceaseless urge to find new bands*: "It's what we do. You can't get away from that. I am in this because I love it. I love music and I love going to live shows. That's the way it is." *The need to be a fan*: "A promoter has to understand the artists, get inside the artists' vision of where they're going."

As descriptions of the business logic of corporate promotion such statements are misleading: it is organised around reducing risk, exploiting audiences, upping the earnings of established stars and treating fandom with a healthy degree of cynicism. But as expressions of promoters' sense of themselves—even as successful players in corporate empires—they are revealing and indicate a continuing belief in promotion as a craft, with its own mysteries, mentors and magic. It is perhaps not surprising, then, that a significant number of the promoters we talked to (Barry Clayman, Danny Betesh, Stuart Littlewood, Barry Dickins and Vince Power among them) had

50   *Taking care of business*

sons and daughters also now working in the live music industry. Perhaps this was what Paul Latham meant when he said that promotion is in the blood!

Notes

1 Interviewed by Matt Brennan, June 3, 2009.
2 Interviewed by Martin Cloonan, May 4, 2010.
3 Interviewed by Emma Webster, July 1, 2008.
4 Geoff Ellis had taken over as CEO of DF from its founder Stuart Clumpas in 2001; the company was taken over by LN-Gaiety and SJM in 2008.
5 Unless otherwise noted, all Danny Betesh quotes taken from an interview with Matt Brennan, November 23, 2010.
6 Granada, founded in 1930, was one of Britain's major owner/operators of theatres and cinemas and, from 1954, television stations and services.
7 Unless otherwise noted, all quotes from Paul Latham taken from an interview with Matt Brennan, June 3, 2009.
8 Paul Latham retired from the live music business in 2018.
9 For Philip Bowdery's career, see the *Music Week* tribute feature, October 31, 2009: 29–48.
10 Unless otherwise noted, all Barry Dickins quotes taken from an interview with Matt Brennan, June 5, 2009.
11 As a promoter, Giddings had also by then re-launched the Isle of Wight Festival. Unless otherwise cited, all John Giddings quotes taken from an interview with Matt Brennan, May 4, 2010.
12 MCP was established in 1978 by Tim Parsons and Maurice Jones.
13 Quote taken from an interview with Galbraith on the Virtual Festivals website: www.virtualfestivals.com/latest/interviews/6632/-/-Stuart-Galbraith-Sonipsheres-comeback-king.
14 Kilimanjaro details taken from the company website: www.kilimanjarolive.co.uk/history.
15 Denis Desmond and DF's Stuart Clumpas also invested in V Fest.
16 Details of Bob Angus' career taken from Forde (2016). Live Nation took over Metropolis in 2017.
17 The Mean Fiddler had previously been a boxing gym; Power remodeled it as a 'honky tonk bar', initially specialising in country and Irish music. Unless otherwise noted, all Vince Power quotes from an interview with Matt Brennan, June 5, 2009.
18 Break for the Border paid Simon Parkes £2.5 million for the Academy; he had acquired the venue in 1982 for just £1 (Parkes 2014: 386).
19 Northcote died in 2011. For an obituary, see www.completemusicupdate.com/article/amg-chief-dies.
20 The previous leaseholder had run the space as the Town and Country Club. The Forum was sold to the Mama Group in 2007 and acquired by Live Nation in 2015. It is now the O2 Forum.
21 Unless otherwise cited, all Mark Kemp quotes taken from an interview with Martin Cloonan, February 17, 2011.
22 Unless otherwise cited, all Conal Dodds quotes taken from an interview with Emma Webster, March 29, 2010.

Taking care of business 51

23 Unless otherwise cited, all Barrie Marshall quotes taken from an interview with Martin Cloonan, February 17, 2011.

24 Most large promotion companies and agencies work much like advertising agencies or law firms: employees get a basic salary plus a percentage of their earnings as individual promoters or agents. The most successful may be offered partnerships.

25 This promoter requested anonymity!

26 Tony Smith, interviewed by Matt Brennan, November 15, 2010.

27 See www.theguardian.com/music/2018/oct/21/neil-tennant-pet-shop-boys-collection-lyrics.

28 The money-making possibilities here were first indicated by Michael Jackson's 1988 UK visit: seven nights at Wembley Stadium, an eighth at the Milton Keynes Bowl and an Aintree performance in Liverpool with, according to Barry Clayman, an audience of 120,000–135,000. (This may be promoter's hype! The official capacity was 100,000.)

29 Fleadh was an annual Irish music festival, staged in London from 1989.

30 TicketWeb in the UK originated (in 1999) as a box office operation for the McKenzie/Academy Group. It was a joint venture with the US TicketWeb company and soon attracted SJM and Metropolis as clients. A third global ticketing company, the German-based Eventim, entered the UK ticket market in 2010. Ironically, its first major contract was with Live Nation, as it turned out shortly before the Live Nation/Ticketmaster merger (*Music Week*, October 1, 2008).

31 Jane Donald quoted from an interview with Emma Webster, February 17, 2010.

32 See Tickets began in the 1990s as a company selling concert tickets out of Way Ahead Records in Nottingham. It became See Tickets in 2004 after being bought by various investors, led by Andrew Lloyd Webber's Really Useful Group. In 2011 it became a wholly owned subsidiary of the global entertainment group Vivendi.

33 In August 2018, Dennis Desmond and Caroline Downey sold 50% of MCD to the Live Nation Group. At the time of writing, Desmond is Live Nation UK's CEO.

34 The relationship of Festival Republic (which owned Latitude) and Live Nation is even more complicated than this suggests. As a company specialising in the promotion of festivals, Festival Republic was originally a component of the Mean Fiddler Music Group (its MD, Melvin Benn, ran political and campaigning events before being employed by Vince Power to develop his festivals operation; Benn was the operator of the Glastonbury Festival from 2002–12). In 2005, the group was taken over by Hamsard, owned 50.1% by LN and 49.9% by MCD; in 2007, the bulk of the Mean Fiddler business was sold to the MAMA group. The festival part of the business was retained and renamed Festival Republic. See Webster (2011) for a diagram of UK festival ownership at the end of the 2000s.

35 Details here taken from www.abo.org.uk/about-us/history.aspx.

36 Littlewood was the second chair of the CPA (following Harvey Goldsmith). Information here is taken from an interview with Matt Brennan, November 22, 2010.

37 In 1997, the CPA drew up a Code of Conduct for all its members; it has also liaised with the Office of Fair Trading in drawing up Concert Ticket Terms and Conditions. Information and quote taken from the CPA's official site: www.concertpromotersassociation.co.uk.

38 Raymond Gubbay himself left Raymond Gubbay Ltd in 2016, by when it was partly owned by Sony Music (Sony took full control in 2018). He told *The*

52   *Taking care of business*

Stage, "I didn't like the new owners. I didn't like Sony. I thought for a music company they were remarkably ignorant about music and were only interested in the bottom line. For me, this is a business about passion and having an interest in it and putting your life and soul into it." See www.thestage.co.uk/news/2018/raymond-gubbay-couldnt-work-sony.

39 As already noted, arenas had their own organisation, the National Arena Association, formed in 1991.

40 Taken from www.ilmc.com/index.php/about/about-us.

41 This figure seems to be purely rhetorical. PRS statistical analysis for that year suggests that the sum was actually around £3 billion (see Page and Carey 2010).

42 Quoted from an interview with Emma Webster, March 2, 2010.

43 Our arguments here draw on Webster (2011), the definitive account of promoters' understanding of their business in this period, and Brennan and Webster (2010).

A snapshot of live music in Bristol in October–November 2007

The year 2007 was the 200th anniversary of the Abolition of the Slave Trade Act and October 2007 was the 20th anniversary of Black History Month. Forming part of Bristol's celebrations was the two-week long celebration of African culture at the second Afrika Eye Festival, featuring music, food and dancing at venues across the city, including the Arnolfini and Cube Cinema (Wright 2007a). Bristol has an uneasy historical relationship with the slave trade and at the time of writing the main council-run venue in the city, Colston Hall, was in the process of changing its name following protests—including a boycott by Bristol's own Massive Attack—due to its eponymous connection with merchant, philanthropist and slave trader Edward Colston (Morris 2017). In the autumn of 2007, the Hall featured a range of musical styles from classical to jazz and "world music" to rock and pop, including Kate Rusby (Thursday October 4, £18.50/£16.50—postponed due to illness), The Proclaimers (Monday October 15, £22.50) and Ladysmith Black Mambazo (Monday October 29) ("History" 2017). The amateur group New Bristol Sinfonia celebrated their tenth anniversary by performing Mahler's *Resurrection Symphony* at the Hall (Saturday October 6), while an amateur choir, the Bristol Choral Society, performed Elgar and Vaughan Williams with the (professional) Bournemouth Symphony Orchestra (Saturday November 24). Tackling traditional English folk songs and featuring artists including Billy Bragg, Martin and Eliza Carthy, poet Benjamin Zephaniah and bhangra drummer Johnny Kalsi, the Imagined Village folk supergroup also performed at the Hall (Friday November 16, £18.50/£16.50) (Sloan 2007a). Between July 2007 and 2009, the venue underwent extensive construction work while its striking golden foyer was built.

In late November, "jazz legend" Keith Tippett returned to Colston Hall to perform *From Granite to Wind* (Tuesday November 27, £7/£5) ("Jazz legend …" 2007). At the smaller end of the scale, jazz fans were provided for by the Old Duke pub—a stalwart of the local jazz scene, which (then as now) was still putting on regular gigs, as was the Tantric Jazz Café. The Albert Inn jazz pub in Bedminster reopened in late October 2007 following a major £100,000 refurbishment after closing over two years earlier amid speculation that it

54   Snapshot: Bristol October–November 2007

would be turned into flats. However, the new owners said music would play a key part in its future ("Jazz back on the menu" 2007).

St George's Bristol—which had reopened with a new look and a new name in 1999—was by 2007 providing a year-round programme of jazz, classical, folk, world music and small-scale opera. In the period of our interest, one of the world's leading pianists, Artur Pizarro, produced a "magnificent performance" in a programme that included Beethoven, Schumann and Liszt (Reid 2007), while Eduardo Niebla performed flamenco jazz guitar. Over at the Bristol Hippodrome, the Welsh National Opera staged the Bristol premiere of James MacMillan's *The Sacrifice* (Wednesday November 7), conducted by the composer (Hale 2007), while theatre-goers in Bristol were the first British audience outside London to see the Abba jukebox musical *Mamma Mia!* when it opened at the end of November for a nine-week run ("Thank you for the music" 2007).

Other than Colston Hall, the most significant (standing) venue in the city for major touring rock and pop artists was the Carling (now O2) Academy, part of Academy Music Group. The 1800-capacity venue originally opened in November 2001 and hosted both bands and club nights ("O2 Academy Bristol" 2019). Artists performing in 2007 included Happy Mondays (Wednesday October 3, £25), Manu Chao (Sunday October 7, sold out), Super Furry Animals (Monday October 29, £17.50) and Lethal Bizzle (Thursday November 22). The "Bristol sound" of Portishead and Roni Size brought the city to international prominence in the mid-1990s with drum'n'bass and its stoner cousin, trip hop. By 2007, the legacy could still be seen in club nights and occasional live events. For example, drum'n'bass producer TC played at the Carling Academy on Saturday October 13 (£16.50), mixing his "hyperactive, insistently changing rhythms" with the "unmistakable Bristolian burr" of vocalist MC Jakes (Wright 2007b).

Enthusing beforehand in the *Evening Post* that he loves Bristol because of the "famous music culture" going back to the days of the Wild Bunch and Daddy G (Wright 2007c), DJ Norman Jay MBE played at the Western Soul night at the 300-capacity Native club on Saturday October 6 (£5 before 11.00pm, £6 after). Native closed two years later, citing rising costs and noise complaints caused by city centre development, no doubt exacerbated by 2007's smoking ban in England.[1] Further highlighting the precariousness of the local scene, the Lakota club in the rapidly gentrifying Stokes Croft area—a club that then hosted underground club nights from dubstep to trance—was under threat from a developer who wanted to knock it down to develop the adjacent building into flats ("Popular club…" 2007). The Lakota survived but a similar headline in 2018—"Legendary Bristol nightclub Lakota could be turned into accommodation and offices"—illustrates some venues' persistent difficulties in the face of ongoing city centre development (Murray 2018).

The floating Thekla had run as an underground nightclub into the early 2000s but, reflecting a general shift away from nightclubs and towards live music venues, was bought and relaunched as a live music venue in October

2006 by Nottingham's DHP group. In a "bit of a coup", Thekla put on Babyshambles on Saturday October 13, led by notorious Libertines frontman Pete Doherty, in a secret gig ahead of their arena tour in November (Sloan 2007b); other gigs included British Sea Power (Tuesday October 30) and the Young Knives (Monday November 12). The Fleece and The Louisiana were two other significant smaller independent Bristol venues at the time, with The Cribs playing at The Fleece (Thursday October 4) as part of *Lamacq in the City*, BBC Radio 1 DJ Steve Lamacq's occasional trip outside London to check out the latest music in the UK's regional cities ("6 Music heads west" 2007). Other (mostly pub) venues in the city provided space for regular open mic and folk sessions, including the Moon & Sixpence, The Oxford, Joe Public's and adult education centre the Bristol Folk House. At the other end of the scale, in December 2007 *BBC News* reported that Bristol's arena plan had been abandoned due to "spiralling costs" ("Bristol's arena plan is abandoned" 2007).

Note

1   As ex-Native owner Ben Dubuisson (2009) explained, "[A small club is] a very, very difficult model … to make work now. You're better off opening the doors for free and letting people in all night."

Bibliography

"6 Music heads west" (2007) *Bristol Evening Post*, October 4: 36.

"Bristol's arena plan is abandoned" (2007) *BBC News*, December 13, http://news.bbc.co.uk/1/hi/england/bristol/7141884.stm. Accessed April 2, 2019.

Dubuisson, Ben (2009) Personal interview with Emma Webster, October 12.

Hale, Natalie (2007) "Tribal warfare", *Bristol Evening Post*, November 1: 64.

"History". 2017. Colston Hall website, http://stage.colstonhall.org/history. Accessed 22 January 2019.

"Jazz back on the menu" (2007) *Bristol Evening Post*, October 26.

"Jazz legend to bring his unique vision home" (2007) *Bristol Evening Post*, November 8: 28.

Morris, Steven (2017) "Bristol's Colston Hall to drop name of slave trader after protests", *The Guardian*, April 26, www.theguardian.com/uk-news/2017/apr/26/bristol-colston-hall-to-drop-name-of-slave-trader-after-protests. Accessed April 2, 2019.

Murray, Robyn (2018) "Legendary Bristol nightclub Lakota could be turned into accommodation and offices", *BristolLive*, October 9, www.bristolpost.co.uk/whats-on/music-nightlife/legendary-bristol-nightclub-lakota-could-2089280. Accessed March 28, 2019.

"O2 Academy Bristol" (2019) Academy Music Group website, https://academymusicgroup.com/companyo2academybristol. Accessed January 22, 2019.

"Popular club could be turned into flats" (2007) *Bristol Evening Post*, November 9: 17.

Reid, Helen (2007) "A masterful trip through romanticism", *Bristol Evening Post*, October 15.

56   *Snapshot: Bristol October–November 2007*

Sloan, Helen (2007a) "Community spirit", *Bristol Evening Post*, November 8: 42.

Sloan, Helen (2007b) "Pete is weakest link in live show", *Bristol Evening Post*, October 15.

"Thank you for the music" (2007) *Bristol Evening Post*, November 30: 8.

Wright, Steve (2007a) "Celebrating the past", *Bristol Evening Post*, October 11: 64.

Wright, Steve (2007b) "The singing DJ", *Bristol Evening Post*, October 11: 66.

Wright, Steve (2007c) "Storming Norman", *Bristol Evening Post*, October 4: 62.

4   Live music and the state

In my experience of four years' standing, I can assure your Lordships that many projects are put on by the arts sector for the enjoyment, entertainment, education, and enlightenment of those who work in the sector. Not too often do you hear the question asked, "Will the man or women in the street benefit from this?"

> (Baroness Detta O'Cathain, Managing Director
> of the Barbican, 1994)[1]

For several years the Magistrates' Association has been concerned that the 1964 Licensing Act fails to address the needs and requirements of today's society.

> (Anne Norton to Hamish Birchall, 1999)[2]

Public disorder issues have always arisen whenever large groups of people gather together, particularly at night, to enjoy popular pastimes.

> (Jack Straw, Home Secretary, 2000)[3]

Introduction

In November 2003, MTV Europe's annual Music Awards show was staged in Leith. This star-studded, globally televised event had been established by the head of MTV's European business, Brent Hansen, a New Zealander who earlier in his career had been in charge of the New Zealand broadcast of Live Aid. "The central objectives" of these events, as Gavin Reid explains, were "delivering a youthful audience to advertisers and marketing [the MTV] brand" (Reid 2007: 483), but Hansen had also had the smart idea of persuading hosting European cities to cover some of his costs. Edinburgh, it seems, didn't need much persuasion to contribute to MTV's £4.5 million budget for a show: "Scottish officials developed a £750k package to part fund a structure capable of protecting MTV's brand from Scotland's November weather and the outside broadcast costs of a simultaneous concert in Edinburgh's Princes Street Gardens." The necessary funds came from the

58 *Live music and the state*

Scottish Executive (£125,000), Scottish Enterprise (£500,000) and Edinburgh Council (£125,000)—although, as Reid (2007: 484–6) points out:

> This was not a concert with thousands of public tickets, but a private event for MTV's music industry clients and sponsors (American Express, Vodafone Live, Replay Blue Jeans, Foot Locker). Locals could obtain one of 2000 public tickets by competing with European callers on a single hotline. These sold out in 14 minutes with few locals successful.

Why did both national and local state agencies in Scotland agree to subsidise what was essentially an extensive advertisement for an American entertainment corporation? One argument was that the event would have significant economic benefits for the local community (these were initially estimated at £4 million; a later impact study suggested £9 million),[4] but the policy-makers were equally convinced of the MTV event's "symbolic benefits". It would help to establish Edinburgh as a vibrant and ambitious modern European city, a tourist destination and "a global brand with a rich waterfront in Leith". The MTV Show would be a unique opportunity for "place promotion" and provide "priceless celebrity endorsements" from the featured superstars. For Henry McLeish, former Labour First Minister, "there [was] no way of quantifying the effect of the rest of the world looking at Scotland in such a new light" (Reid (2007: 486–8).

What is clear from such statements is that state support for MTV had little to do with the promotion of Scottish music or the support of Scottish musicians, but rather was taken on as a way to give Edinburgh a new kind of commercial status. In Reid's (2007: 491) words, "in trying to create the most prominent Northern European city by 2015 Scottish officials played by the neo-liberal rules of culture-led regeneration". These rules underlie much of what we will discuss in this chapter. In the period of this book, Britain was governed variously by the Conservatives until 1997, (New) Labour until 2010 and a Conservative/Liberal Democratic coalition until 2015, but there were clear continuities in cultural politics, not least in the way such politics affected live music. On the one hand, throughout this period there was a sustained policy of deregulation and privatisation; on the other, the transformation of arts policy into creative industries policy was as much a New Labour as a Conservative project.

As an example of deregulation, we will take an issue that had long been dear to the Musicians' Union: "needletime". Needletime agreements were built into the terms of radio stations' licences to play records. The licensing agency, Phonographic Performance Ltd (PPL), founded by EMI and Decca in 1934, required broadcasters to *restrict* their use of recordings (needletime), thus ensuring that they continued to programme (and pay for) live performances.[5] In 1980, the commercial radio stations' trade body, the Association of Independent Radio Contractors (AIRC) took a complaint about PPL's terms and rates to a meeting of the Performing Right Tribunal.

Live music and the state   59

The AIRC lost the immediate case but legal arguments about PPL licensing conditions continued and in 1988 the Monopolies and Mergers Commission (MMC) undertook an enquiry into the effects of such collective licensing deals on music market competition.

After detailed examination, the Commission concluded, in Martin Cloonan's (2016: 364) words, that "needletime was an anti-competitive practice that should be abolished" and also recommended that PPL "should no longer require discotheques to employ musicians as a condition of licensing" (see Cloonan et al. 2016: 203–7; MMC 1988: 1). These rulings, as Cloonan (2016: 364) goes on to remark, "signalled the end of an epoch", putting an end to licensing arrangements that been designed (under the guidance of the Musicians' Union) "to provide employment opportunities for live musicians" *even as* they were being replaced by broadcast or dance-floor recordings.[6]

A more direct example of the Thatcher government's determination to open the state sector to commercial competition, the Education Reform Act of 1988 was not obviously a matter of cultural policy but its provision for the creation of City Technology Colleges (CTCs) did lead to the BRIT School for Performing Arts and Technology, which opened in Croydon in 1992.[7] The BRIT School was sponsored by the BPI's charitable arm, the British Record Industry Trust (money made from the annual BRITS Awards show is fed into the school's budget) and became famous for such successful graduates as Katie Melua, Amy Winehouse and Adele. It can also be seen as a precursor to the Skills Academy discussed at the end of the last chapter. The point here is that when the New Labour Government took power in 1997, it did not get rid of CTCs but rather encouraged them to become academies, another version of business-sponsored schools funded by central rather than local government.

This is unsurprising when one considers the New Labour government's approach to cultural policy. In 1998, Chris Smith, Britain's first ever Minister of Culture,[8] published *Creative Britain*, a collection of the speeches he had made in his first year of office, when his big decision had been to establish a Creative Industries Taskforce to "map" the UK's cultural sector (Smith 1998). Not the least significant aspect of New Labour cultural policy was its obsession with empirical data—necessary to impress the Treasury.

Smith's concept of "creative industries" was shaped (as was his political career) by municipal socialism, by the cultural strategies developed by the GLC and other Labour-controlled UK cities in the 1980s.[9] The urgent task for such municipal authorities was to find new jobs following the collapse of the industrial sector. Something was needed to replace manufacturing, and creative industries (such as music) could be encouraged by the provision of cheap spaces (such as empty mills and warehouses) and appropriate skills training. In developing such policies at the national level, Smith sought institutional collaboration with the industries themselves—the Music Industries Forum was established in 1998.[10]

Investment in creative industries was not just a strategy for regeneration; it could also boost the local economy through tourism and inward investment

60 *Live music and the state*

(this was, as we have seen, one argument for Edinburgh's support of the MTV Awards). "Culture" was defined here as something that made a city a good place in which to live and work—hence the importance of the selections of Glasgow (1990) and Liverpool (2008) as European Capitals of Culture. Images of these cities' industrial decay and urban dinginess were replaced with an emphasis on the vitality of cultural heritage and local creative imagination. For both cities, live music was particularly significant to such rebranding.[11] In 2008, when Glasgow was successful in its bid to become a UNESCO City of Music, it announced that "the award gives the city an edge as an international cultural destination for tourists and strengthens Glasgow's image".[12]

In the previous volumes of this history, we discussed the role of the state in terms of two kinds of activity, regulation and promotion, and at two institutional levels, central and local government. We will do the same here— although, as we have been describing, the ideological context of state activity was by now rather different. On the one hand, there was no longer a policy belief in an *artistic sphere of production* that needed protection from market forces or profiteers; on the other, there was a new policy belief that the value of *artistic experience* could be measured economically. The assumptions here (shared by the various governments) had clear effects on how cultural policy was conceived and pursued.

We will come back to this. First, though, we will discuss legislation that reflected long-held political concerns: the control of public gatherings, the regulation of public behaviour and the licensing of public houses.

Regulating raves

We will be examining the history of rave culture and the rave business in Chapter 7. Here we want to focus on the aspects of rave that most concerned politicians: the *unregulated* gatherings of dancers and their use of a new *drug*, MDA, or ecstasy. MDA had, in fact, first been synthesised in Germany in 1910, although it didn't reach the West Coast of the USA (as "the love drug") until 1968. MDMA (first synthesised in 1914) "appeared as a legal alternative [to the now banned MDA] around 1972". Recreational use of this drug, soon known as ecstasy, "reached proportions significant enough to cause the drug to be banned in America in 1985" (Shapiro 1990: 241–2). In the UK, ecstasy had been outlawed earlier, in the Misuse of Drugs Act of 1971, but its widespread use developed with the 1980s rise of raves, "dance music parties arranged in secret", initially in abandoned inner city warehouses and then, as they got bigger, "in country barns and fields" (Shapiro 1990: 241–2).[13]

Such gatherings were mostly unlicensed and usually involved trespass; from the start, then, they were of interest to the police. As Bill Osgerby (1998: 177) explains:

> As warehouse parties became larger in scale they attracted greater police attention. Having established the location of a party the police would mount a raid on the illicit gathering—though if the event was already

Live music and the state   61

in full swing, rather than closing it down, officers would usually simply turn away newcomers to avoid engendering a confrontation with the assembled crowd.[14]

It became clear to the most enterprising rave organisers, such as Sunrise's Tony Colston-Hayter, that the bigger the rave, the less likely the police were to stop it, so rave promoters prepared their events as if preparing for war. Sound and lighting systems were set up surreptitiously in the chosen venue; phone lines were put in place to "release spoken directions to a specific meeting point" (on the M25, for example); party-goers would find the phone number by buying a ticket.

> Once a crowd of sufficient size (usually several hundred) had gathered, Colston-Hayter and his colleagues would then use mobile phones to record and release details of the party venue—reasoning that the police would be unable to halt such an enormous convoy of party-goers.
>
> (Osgerby 1998: 177–8)

By 1988, the tabloid press was beginning to draw once more on its rich stock of shock horror youth headlines: it was easy enough to rewrite 1960s LSD stories as 1980s acid house stories, and "the evil acid house cult" became a matter for political attention.[15] In 1990, a Private Members' Bill was introduced to Parliament by Tory MP Graham Bright. His "Acid House Bill" came into law as the Entertainments (Increased Penalties) Act. Its basic purpose was to strengthen existing laws on unlicensed public entertainments by increasing the penalties for breaking them (Osgerby 1998: 182). Many players in the rave scene believed then (and believe still) that Bright's Bill was driven less by the media-led moral panic than by the drinks lobby. This is the view of rave promoter and DJ Terry Farley (quoted in Brewster and Broughton 2010: 381), for example:

> The Bright Bill was funded by the breweries to get people into their pubs. The breweries suddenly started doing alcopops and cleared the tables and chairs out and put music on ... and now they're the ones paying for it with a nation of binge-drinking teenagers, when you could have had a nation of E-takers but not causing any problems. Now they're stuck with every casualty in every major city, with glassings, stabbings and policemen being sorted. No one got sorted at Sunrise and it's the same kids. Without doubt there was a definite boardroom decision taken. They said, "We've got to get them out of these fields and back into our pubs, how we gonna do this?"[16]

It is certainly true that brewers were concerned about the effects of ecstasy and club culture on their profits. The Henley Centre's 1993 report on Britain's Leisure Futures revealed that between 1987 and 1992, "pub attendance in the UK fell by 11%" and it "predicted a further fall of 20% by 1997". The report

62 *Live music and the state*

also suggested that "UK ravers were spending £1.8 billion a year on entrance fees, cigarettes and illegal drugs. Money they weren't spending on alcohol" (Phillips 2009: 313). In this context, parliamentary moves against acid house were complementary to the major brewers' decision to rebrand (and redesign) pubs as trendy dance clubs (see Hadfield 2006: Ch. 3). In 1996, for example, another Tory MP, Barry Legg, introduced the Bill that came into force in 1997 as the Public Entertainments Licences (Drug Misuse) Act. It gave local authorities further powers "to revoke licences from clubs where drugs are known to be dealt" (Phillips 2009: 314).

Bright's Bill itself coincided with what Osgerby describes as "a spate of police raids on unlicensed parties, with numerous arrests and confiscations of sound equipment". Blackburn-based rave promoter Sparrow, who had set up 76 illegal parties over the previous 18 months, and dedicated party-goer Dave Beer, who went on to promote the successful Back to Basics club night in Leeds, remembered Sparrow's last illegal party, at Nelson (near Burnley) on February 24, 1990:

> It got so hot in the warehouse you had to open the side shutter. As this big shutter opened you could see these rows and rows of police officers, all with their riot gear on, all ready.
>
> (Sparrow, quoted in Phillips 2009: 75–6)

> It was ugly, they were coming down the hill like Romans, with the shields and just laying into girls and everything. They charged in and squashed everything. Everybody was climbing on top of each other and they lost all their shoes and clothes. It was just the most dangerous thing I've ever seen
>
> (Beer, quoted in Phillips 2009: 76)

Later the same year, in July, police "violently arrested" 836 partygoers at a rave at a disused warehouse on the M62 near Leeds. Only 17 were actually charged, though "the DJ, Rob Tissera, because he had encouraged the dancers to barricade the doors and carry on partying, was sent to jail for three months" (Brewster and Broughton 2000: 391).[17]

Such aggressive policing also had an impact on the free festival and New Age traveller movements we described in Volume 2. They too "experienced a siege mentality" that, for a moment, "tightened the bonds" between the rave and traveller communities.

> Traveller-influenced sound systems such as Spiral Tribe, Circus Normal and Bedlam toured a circuit of raves and free festivals ... the cross-over [of these scenes] culminating in May 1992 at Castlemorton Common in Hereford. Here, up to 40,000 travellers and ravers joined forces, camping out for over a week and enjoying the biggest free festival in six years.
>
> (Osgerby 1998: 190)

Live music and the state 63

This event was peaceful; the crowd broke up once the landowners posted an eviction notice. But media and politicians nevertheless echoed each other in their criticism of the police for not preventing the gathering in the first place, and when Parliament passed a new Criminal Justice and Public Order Act in 1994, it included "a series of new criminal offences that were expressly designed to deal with the problems thrown up by the acid house party and New Age movements of the late eighties" (Osgerby 1998: 190). Section 63 of the Act therefore applied

> to a gathering on land in the open air of 20 or more persons (whether or not trespassers) at which amplified music is played during the night (with or without intermissions) and is such as, by reason of its loudness and duration and the time at which it is played, is likely to cause serious distress to the inhabitants of the locality.[18]

In the long term, these clauses of a Bill that was designed to "curb the rising criminal element" generally were less significant for youth culture than its other measures, not so much those aimed at squatters, travellers and hunt saboteurs as the increasing police powers to stop and search and to detain people on "reasonable suspicion" of being involved in political subversion (Hutnyk 1996: 156–8).

Unlike free festivals, most raves were essentially commercial enterprises. Tony Colston-Hayter, who launched the Freedom to Party Campaign in 1989, was a right-wing rather than a left-wing libertarian.[19] And he, like the other big rave promoters, by now had the resources, the experience and the determination to stage licensed events and become part of the legitimate club and festival scene. The rave promoter Universe, for example, teamed up with Mean Fiddler to stage the entirely legal Tribal Gathering '95, which drew 25,000 dancers for a weekend on a 60-acre site in Oxfordshire, while the decline of rural raves meant the rise of much larger licensed urban clubs, such as Ministry of Sound in South East London and Cream in Liverpool, and in the number and popularity of outdoor festivals with dance stages. We will come back to these clubs and festivals, their licensing strategies and commercial development in Chapter 7.

Cigarettes and alcohol

The Criminal Justice Act was unusual in referring directly to a particular kind of music: "sounds wholly or predominantly characterised by the emission of a succession of repetitive beats". What promoters usually had to worry about was legislation that was not in itself about music but could, nevertheless, have significant effects on their business models.

In June 2006, for example, *Music Week* reported on venue operators' anxieties about the potential effects of a UK-wide smoking ban and examined the experience of Scottish venues (where the ban had come in a year earlier).

64   *Live music and the state*

Fiona Rosie from King Tut's in Glasgow noted that, "People seem to arrive just before stage time now, rather than coming early for a drink. Also, during the interval, people are outside smoking rather than standing at the bar" (*Music Week,* June 20, 2007).

Although venues now had to organise pass-outs and outdoor places where smokers could gather, the smoking ban was also seen as a good thing and Fiona Rosie reassured *Music Week*'s readers that

> The positives vastly outweigh the negatives. Our bar takings might be down and our security and cleaning bills have gone up, but, on the plus side, our food trade has increased. Overall it's a nicer environment and the general health of our staff has improved.

Promoters were more worried by the prospects of a ban on alcohol advertising from events attended by young people, as recommended by both the Advisory Council on the Misuse of Drugs (in 2006) and the National Alcohol Harm Reduction Strategy (in 2007). A spokesperson for Carlsberg, which was in the process of investing £5 million into the re-launch of Tuborg, explained the problem from the perspective of the alcohol industry:

> A significant part of that investment is tied up in buying music rights. Through our deal with Live Nation, Tuborg has the pouring rights to five key festivals—Download, Global Gathering, Escape, and the two Wireless festivals—as well as in 45 Live Nation venues across the UK.
> (Quoted in *Music Week*, June 16, 2007: 7)

Geoff Ellis, promoter of T in the Park (for which Tennent's had always had the "pouring rights") put the promoter's point of view:

> Tennent's Lager has acted like an arts council in Scotland for musical events. Without them world famous events such as T in the Park and T on the Fringe would have struggled to get off the ground in their early years because there certainly wasn't the option of government or arts council funding.
> (Quoted in *Music Week*, June 16, 2007: 7)

Unsurprisingly, in the end the government of the day followed corporate rather than medical advice.

The rise and fall of public entertainment licensing

For musicians, particularly folk and jazz musicians, the most pressing problem in this period was the decline of playing opportunities in pubs. In previous volumes of this history, we traced the development of Public Entertainment Licences (PELs), introduced by the 1964 Licensing Act with further provision made for local authorities to set their own licence fees in the 1982 Local Government (Miscellaneous Provisions) Act.[20]

It was undoubtedly the increasing financial demands made by local authorities that led to publicans' disinclination to apply for PELs—not just the rising licence fees, but also the expenditure additionally required to meet local inspectors' unpredictable demands on health and safety. Live music campaigner Hamish Birchill summarised the changes:

> The sharp decline of small gigs in pubs coincided with the reform of entertainment licensing in 1982, when local authorities were given powers to set their own fees. These quickly rose by several hundred percent, and by 2000 the Home Office estimated fewer than 10% of pubs had entertainment licences, although all of them could still have one or two live performers, the "two in a bar" rule.
>
> (E-mail to the authors, 22 January 2012)[21]

The peculiarities of the PEL system are probably best symbolised by this "two in a bar" rule. Under Section 182 (1) of the 1964 Licensing Act, a PEL was not required if the entertainment was provided by no more than two players (and if no one was dancing).[22] In practice, this was not straightforward. Did the rule mean two players at any one time or the same two players throughout the evening? Did a pre-recorded accompaniment count as a player (or, indeed, as several players)? If the audience joined in the chorus as is normal at a folk gig did that instantly break the "two in a bar" rule? How was the line to be drawn between public and private entertainment when, for example, musicians were employed to provide musical entertainment in a hospital ward?[23]

The problem here was that such questions didn't have straightforward answers and different local authorities treated them in different ways (as did different licensing officers within the same authority). It was the consequent irrationality of licensing decisions that fuelled public interest in Birchall's anti-PEL campaign. How could it make sense, for example, that in 2000 the annual cost of a PEL for Bridgewater Hall in Manchester (capacity about 2400) was £1040 and for the Boatman pub in Bermondsey (capacity about 150) was £1000 (*Classical Music*, September 23, 2000)?

The Labour government addressed the "two in a bar" problem in its "modernising" 2003 Licensing Act (which came into force in 2005) by getting rid of the exemption altogether[24] but ignored Birchall's underlying question: why was *live* music treated as a potential source of noise and disorder when other forms of pub entertainment (the showing of live football matches on big-screen television, for example) were not? Section 182(1) of the 1964 Act had also explicitly exempted the "reproduction of recorded sound" from its definition of regulated entertainment, and this exemption remained: recorded sound was not treated as a potential noise problem. At the same time, it was not clear why the health and safety of live music audiences should be treated

66 *Live music and the state*

any differently from the health and safety of people gathering in the pub for any other reason.

The new act "modernized" the PEL system by getting rid of historical anomalies and subjecting *all* live music performances to the same licensing rules, but its starting point was familiar: live music was treated as if in itself, *if unregulated*, it was a threat to public order. This was, as Birchill later put it,

> the legislation that marks the highwater point of regulation of live music through licensing. It was under this Act that even providing musical instruments became a potential criminal act unless licensed. This ranged from pub pianos to instruments provided by schools for concerts.[25]

Certainly from an academic perspective, the 2003 Act was a singularly ill-drafted piece of legislation (see Cloonan 2007: Ch. 3). An immediate, well-publicised effect was apparently to make carol singing illegal. Hasty attempts were made to clarify what was meant by music "that was incidental to activity not in itself regulated entertainment" (congregational singing, for example) and therefore not subject to licensing law. It was equally quickly apparent that different licensing authorities defined "incidental" music differently.

Given that this was a New Labour government, industry involvement and the gathering of statistics necessary for "evidence-based" policy had quickly been put into place. A Live Music Forum of representatives of "seventeen key industry bodies" (*Music Week,* March 24, 2007: 4) was set up under the chairmanship of Fergal Sharkey in 2004. Its first task was to survey the state of live music; its second, once the Act was law, was to measure its effects. Initially, there was optimism that the new law would increase playing opportunities, but as the number of people going to gigs decreased and it became increasingly difficult for small venues to survive, the argument got louder that there needed to be an PEL exemption for concerts below a certain *audience* size (200 was the agreed figure). This was suggested by both the Live Music Forum's 2007 Survey and, in 2009, by the Culture, Media and Sports Committee of the House of Commons.[26] At this point the Live Music Forum was quietly dissolved and the Department of Culture Media and Sport increasingly became involved in wrangles about the statistical validity of its own still sunny figures.

It took a Private Member's Bill and a change of government to address the problems of the 2003 Act. Lord Clement Jones' Live Music Act was given Royal Assent in 2012.[27] Hamish Birchall said:

> It has taken more than 30 years of lobbying and campaigning by musicians, backed by a coalition of the music industry, arts organisations and performers' unions, to arrive at this historic moment for the regulation of live music in England and Wales.
>
> (Email to the authors, 3 July, 2012)[28]

Live music and the state 67

The performance of all unamplified live music between 8.00am and 11.00pm in all venues was now exempt from licensing, as was amplified music for audiences of less than 200. In venues licensed for the sale of alcohol (such as pubs), the existing conditions for live music were not enforceable between the same hours, although noise complaints could lead to enforceable conditions being applied (we discuss noise complaints further in the next section). Morris dancing could now be accompanied by amplified music!

That is not the end of the story, of course. Not all musicians or promoters think the 2012 Act solved the problem of finding affordable spaces in which to play and it is, in practice, difficult to measure the impact of the Act on live music in a local area. The question here, as Tim Knowles (2017: 2–3) points out in his ethnography of the folk scene in Sheffield, is whether making it easier for pubs to supply live music has a positive or negative effect on the local music ecology. We will return to this question in Chapter 11.

Hamish Birchall attributes the long life of "the presumption" against live musical performances unless first licensed (a presumption with a 250-year history) to "the puritanical streak in English culture", which was equally apparent in the local authority responses to rock'n'roll in the 1950s and punk in the 1970s that we discussed in our previous volumes. But there was also a sense of people *getting away with things*, captured in a Music Tank panel discussion between Lord Clement-Jones and Detective Chief Inspector Andrew Stud of the Metropolitan Police, who explained why he opposed the licence exemption for venues with a capacity of under 200:

> If we set a number like that, all venues would claim they have a 199 capacity. And if we exempted jazz, everyone would call themselves jazz musicians.[29]

If, from a historical perspective, the Live Music Act could be seen as a belated victory for the 1960s cultural move towards a "permissive society", this victory was not uncontested.

Local regulations

One of the recurring themes of this history is that, by its nature, live music happens in a particular place—it is always a *local* event. In both promotional and regulatory terms, national laws and initiatives are always subject to local variations. The 2003 Live Music Act was thus as open to different local interpretations by councils, magistrates and the police as any previous licensing regime. The most notorious example of this in our period was the use by London councils of the Metropolitan Police's event risk assessment form, commonly known as Form 696. As *Music Week* reported in November 2011:

> London boroughs are now asking promoters to complete a four-page event assessment form, which UK Music chief executive Feargal Sharkey says is akin to vetting for threats to national security.[30]

68 *Live music and the state*

Form 696 requires promoters to provide comprehensive details about themselves, the event they wish to mount and details about the artists who will be appearing and then inform both the local borough licensing unit and police clubs and vice unit 14 days before the event is to take place.

(Music Week, November 22, 2008: 6)

Over the next couple of years, *Music Week* ran constant reports on the problems caused by these demands, with stories about individual promoters, events and venues falling foul of the form; the paper also described the variations in how the form was used (if at all) in different boroughs' determination of different venues' licensing conditions.[31] *Music Week* gave space to the police position —"Form 696 is just part of our overall strategy to combat violence in the night-time economy"—but cast doubt on the claims that it had led to a significant drop in the number of shootings and assaults (*Music Week,* May 30, 2009: 10.). In September 2009, the Met admitted that, "by looking back over the past four years, we found that the events that caused most problems were those after 10pm which featured recorded music rather than live performances". It also now agreed to drop "the music style or genre stipulation" and remove the need for artists' phone numbers and "all reference to ethnicity of the audience" (*Music Week,* September 19, 2009; 10; October 24, 2010), but in its new reduced format the form continued to be used until 2017.[32]

Otherwise local promoters' licensing disputes were, as ever, about drugs and noise. In 2015, the Association of Licensed Multiple Retailers (ALMR) claimed that more than half of the UK's nightclubs had closed since 2005.[33] This was in part an effect of changing leisure habits but also a consequence of local licensing decisions. In Glasgow, for example, the Arches, an arts and community centre (opened in 1991), which used the revenues from its highly successful club nights to fund its promotion of live music, fell increasingly foul of unsurprising public and police concern about its use as a site for drug dealing, particularly following drug deaths in the club:

Police put the onus on the Arches to comply with incredibly strict searches and security measures or face being shut down. The club said they complied with everything asked of them, but the police still persuaded the council to limit the club to a midnight licence. This effectively made it impossible to run the club and the huge community arts centre that ran during the day.

Guardian, August 14, 2015: 5)[34]

Even without the problems of working with the police to deal with night-time violence and drug abuse, local authorities still had to adjudicate between some people's right to sleep and other people's right to party. In the first decades of the twenty-first century, this recurring problem was increasingly dominated

Live music and the state 69

by a new narrative: long-established live music venues being threatened by new residential property developments. The most high-profile example here was the Ministry of Sound, the club founded in a disused bus station in the Elephant and Castle in 1991. As the BBC reported on February 26, 2010:

> The Ministry of Sound nightclub is fighting a battle to stop a new residential development being built nearby which, it says, could spell the end for the club after nearly two decades.
> The problem is this. If flats are built nearby, residents could complain about the noise from the club. The council would be obliged to investigate and might issue a noise abatement notice. Such a notice could put the club in jeopardy.[35]

As the BBC reporter explained, there was a pattern in such disputes:

> Pubs, clubs, venues and galleries colonise a former industrial area in the middle of a city that has been plagued by dereliction. As they make the place buzzier, so people become interested in living there. But when the residential developments arrive, they bring the possibility of complaints.
>
> (BBC, February 26, 2010)

A more locally publicised media story concerned the troubles facing Birmingham's "creative quarter", Digbeth. As *Music Week* reported in 2009:

> The Spotted Dog [in Digbeth] was served with a noise abatement order in 2007. After 22 years of live music, the pub, which hosted music in its outdoor area, came under scrutiny after a block of 178 flats was erected next door and three residents complained about the sound levels. After a long, bitter and ultimately unsuccessful campaign, The Spotted Dog has been served with its noise abatement order.
>
> (*Music Week*, August 8, 2009: 10)[36]

Over the next decade, such local protests coalesced into a national campaign (spearheaded by the Music Venue Trust) to include an "agent of change" clause in planning regulations. In January 2018, the Ministry of Housing, Communities & Local Government announced that in future "developers building new homes near music venues should be responsible for addressing noise issues". We return to these issues in Chapter 11. Here we turn to the state's role in *promoting* live music.

Arts councils and clients

In his history of the London Sinfonietta, David Wright remarks that in the 1990s the ensemble had to come to terms with

70 *Live music and the state*

> the contingent realities of the turn-of-the-century funding situation in which the "Thatcherite" drive towards public–private enterprise subsidy [was] replaced by the "Blairite" virtues of inclusiveness and relevance … One consequence has been the increasing difficulty of representing the case for the public subsidy of music that is branded elitist and of minority interest.
>
> (Wright 2005: 119–20)[37]

For the UK's arts councils, the shift in establishment cultural sensibility was most clearly marked by the launch of the National Lottery in 1994.[38] The arts were one of the Lottery's five good causes, getting 5.6% of the money raised, which was then awarded to applicants by the arts councils, on the understanding that Lottery funding was for new initiatives, not running costs or existing projects.[39] In its first year, the Lottery raised £271.6 million for the arts—the annual budget of Arts Council England (ACE) was £190 million—and in July 1995 ACE announced its largest Lottery grant so far: £78.5 million given to a jubilantly self-satisfied Royal Opera House to cover the costs of its redevelopment. While Arts Council funding decisions weren't usually of much interest to the tabloid press (unless they involved sex or someone naked), the *Sun* by then had a lottery correspondent, Larry Lottery, who reported Royal Opera's largesse with the headline "FURY AS MORE LOTTERY CASH GOES DOWN THE DRAIN. IT'S THE GREEDY BEGGAR'S OPERA!" For Genista McIntosh, who in 1997 was briefly the Royal Opera House's (ROH) Chief Executive:

> The allocation of £78 million to the ROH in 1995 (and their reaction to it) was probably the most single damaging event in the recent history of the arts in the UK. It gave licence to the latent hostility to art and artists that has been evident in this country for a long time.
>
> (Quoted in Lebrecht 2001: 410)

The New Labour Party certainly took note. One of its more popular manifesto promises in the 1997 general election was to cut Lottery arts funding by half, so as to give the other half to a new good cause: projects in health and education (see Witts 1998: 503).

There were, nevertheless, significant differences between Conservative and Labour Party thinking about the arts. For Thatcherite Tories, all state activity was suspect, and even the high arts needed to be subject to market discipline and open to private enterprise. By 1987, as Wright (2005: 123) notes, the Arts Council's Annual Report "referred to art works as 'products' and audiences as 'consumers', with calls for value for money (understood in terms of measures of consumer take-up)".

For Labour, state arts activities were worth supporting if they helped realise the Party's political and economic ends: improving people's lives and driving economic growth. The key term here, as we've seen, was "creative

Live music and the state   71

industries". In Scotland, the institutional culmination of such thinking was the 2010 merger of the Scottish Arts Council and Scottish Screen (created in 1997 to help develop the Scottish film and TV industry) to form Creative Scotland.[40] Nod Knowles, head of music at SAC from 1998–2005, notes that arts/enterprise collaborative projects were already well established:

> We did an initiative with Scottish Enterprise with music record labels ... We gave [labels] the investment support that they needed, since the record label *is* the platform, well, one of the platforms, especially in rock music ... It's like investing in a theatre company which is the platform for new drama or a festival which is the platform for new jazz compositions or in traditional workshops or whatever.
>
> (Quote taken from an interview by John Williamson, September 10 2002)[41]

For arts councils and their clients, whatever the differences between Conservative and Labour ideologies, their policies had the same effects: to blur the line between commercial and non-commercial creative practice (and therefore between high and low culture)[42] and to expand the demands of bureaucratic accountability, which meant in practical terms ever more complex form-filling (there were now social and economic as well as artistic "targets" to be met)[43] and opaque management-speak.[44] The pressures here for ACE clients were intensified in England by its regional policy. In 1991, the 12 Regional Arts Associations—once, in Richard Witts' (1998: 382, 497) words, "full of well-meaning amateurs, running things themselves" and still with a degree of local idiosyncrasy, were replaced by 10 Regional Arts Boards, which were steadily brought under more bureaucratic control.

In 2005, Clive Gillinson left the London Symphony Orchestra to run New York's Carnegie Hall. He had earlier told Richard Morrison:

> Compared with when I started in orchestral management, twenty years ago, the whole music business has become so much harder. There's so much less recording work around. International touring is much harder to organise and negotiate. Revenues from the box office haven't kept pace with costs ... We find everybody is being tougher and tougher on budgets. Everybody argues over every penny. Now you often get promoters saying: "Can you change the repertoire, because we want to pay for fewer players?"
>
> (Quoted in Morrison 2004: 235)

In Volume 1, we suggested that the Arts Council "brought stability and a new kind of professionalism to orchestral life and established a structure for live classical music in Britain that is still recognizable" (Frith et al. 2013: 49). This remains true, but by the turn of the century there was a sense that it was the orchestras rather than the arts councils that were shaping the survival tactics

72 Live music and the state

for classical music in the twenty-first century. In response to the decline of the classical record industry, for example, the LSO launched its own record label, LSO Live, marketing CD recordings of the orchestra's concerts for £4.99 and reaching sales of 750,000 in its first three years.[45] The Royal Liverpool Philharmonic Orchestra had pioneered the way here, establishing its own label in 1998 (see Morrison 2004: 206–7).

The key to orchestral survival now was commercial sponsorship. Even by the end of the 1980s, the LSO had an annual sponsorship income of £700,000 on top of its City of London funding as the Barbican's resident orchestra, while between 1994–95 and 2001–02, "the funds above core grant" the London Sinfonietta raised for itself "increased by almost 600%" (Morrison 2004: 211; Wright 2005: 124).[46] The exigencies of corporate sponsorship were now built into arts companies' decision-making. When in 1984 John Drummond led an Arts Council enquiry into dance theatre provision in London, the pressing problem was already to find a venue with a front of house "geared to the demands of the new world of sponsorship and corporate entertaining" (Drummond 2000: 304). And, as Lebrecht (2001: 482) writes, when the Royal Opera House reopened at the end of 1999 after its Lottery-funded redevelopment:

> The Crush Bar had been demolished and the space turned over to corporate entertainment ... The Hall itself looked like a cross between an airport concourse and a shopping arcade. It was soon to be hired out for bar mitzvahs and weddings.[47]

Looking at the succession of new (or newly restored) concert halls built in this period makes it clear that what was at stake now was not just their acoustics, more audience friendly auditoria and dedicated rehearsal spaces, but also the creation of buildings fit for commercial exploitation. Iain Crawford (1997: 229) writes that:

> The star of the 48th [Edinburgh] Festival in 1994 was obvious before it began. It was—it had to be—the new glassy gleaming, plush and gilt Edinburgh Festival Theatre, the longest and most eagerly awaited cultural icon in the city's chequered artistic history, which had been a gleam in some ambitious planner's eye ever since the Edinburgh International Festival of Music and Drama first took off as a major world event in 1947.

Despite its name, the Festival Theatre was a council-owned commercial space for entertainment and events of all kinds, and the same could be said of the more obviously orchestra-focused buildings such as the Lighthouse, Poole for the Bournemouth Symphony (opened in 1978), the Glasgow International Concert Hall for the Royal Scottish National Orchestra (1990), St David's Hall Cardiff for the BBC National Orchestra of Wales (1982), the Symphony Hall for the City of Birmingham Symphony (1991), the Bridgewater Hall in Manchester for the Hallé and BBC Philharmonic (1996) and the Sage Gateshead for Northern Sinfonia (2004).[48] The restoration of Glasgow's City Halls (home of the BBC Scottish Symphony Orchestra) and Liverpool Philharmonic Hall (for the Liverpool Philharmonic Orchestra) followed the same logic.

The role of ACE and the SAC in these developments was, if necessary, to award hefty financial contributions to building costs from its Lottery fund; otherwise the major investors were local councils and development agencies, often drawing on European Union support, and the challenge for concert hall administrators was to balance commercial, artistic and local authority demands.[49] Their financial stability was continuously threatened by cuts in arts council and local authority income (whether for political or economic reasons); their strategic task was to resist the need for commercial income dominating programming decisions. An added problem was that buildings that were state-of-the-art in the 1990s were not necessarily adapted to shifts in commercial use; further funds were constantly needed for building renewal. The pressures here are captured in a 2018 press release from Nick Reed, CEO of Birmingham's Symphony Hall, announcing a £12 million foyer development project, "opening the building onto a regenerated Centenary Square and reinforcing Symphony Hall's place in Birmingham city life".

> This project will finally give Symphony Hall the foyers and public spaces to match its world-class auditorium. Boasting a much improved audience experience and a dedicated entrance, this permeable space will be energised with new artistic adventures, creating a sustainable future for Symphony Hall, and developing an audience that looks like the city it serves: young, diverse and creative.[50]

In contrast to these commercialised public arts buildings, London's Kings Place, which opened in 2008, was an entirely private concert hall venture, built more on a nineteenth- than a twentieth-century economic model. Its upper floors were let commercially—primarily to the *Guardian*; its music spaces were in the basement: a small concert hall (415 seats) and a smaller rehearsal and performance space. It was the first brand new music venue in London since the Barbican and, unlike the Barbican, was designed specifically for chamber music, providing, for example, a new home for the London Chamber Music Society's Sunday concerts, which had been running since 1887 (since 1929 in the Conway Hall).[51] Kings Place put in place a resident ensemble, the Aurora Orchestra,[52] and provided office space for the administration of two others, the Orchestra of the Age of Enlightenment and London Sinfonietta.

These music spaces were run by a charity, the Kings Place Music Foundation (which leased them on a peppercorn rent); it was built into the project that the Kings Place music programme would be funded entirely by box office revenue and the income generated through event and conference

74 *Live music and the state*

hire. As it developed. Kings Place also offered a range of educational programmes and activities.

These days, the classical music world takes the importance of educational work for its mission and survival so much for granted that it is startling to recall that in his 1965 Report on the London Orchestras, Lord Goodman noted in passing that "we think it wrong that [the orchestras] should spend their own resources and the public funds allotted to them in attempts to educate potential concert-goers. This is not their primary function" (quoted in Noltingk 2017: 52). By the end of the century, arts councils were expecting all music organisations applying for support to lay out their educational plans. In this, the arts councils were following rather than initiating trends. The London Sinfonietta, for example, had established an educational programme in 1983,

> taking its lead from the education departments found in theatre and dance organisations, but not yet a feature of orchestras. Gillian Moore was appointed education officer, and during her ten years the Sinfonietta's concept of participatory educational work (with the emphasis on practical involvement in creating and performing music) quickly spread across schools, higher and adult education, and community outreach projects. Educational work not only provided a means of engaging and communicating with wide cross-sections of adults and children outside the concert hall, but also gradually built an important income stream for the organisation. This was an example that other orchestras followed.
>
> (Wright 2005: 116)[53]

The LSO set up its new educational programme in 1990. It was, in Richard Morrison's words, "soon to assume a significance in the orchestra's life that few players might have anticipated". In 1992, Richard McNicol was appointed "official LSO Musical Animateur" to run what was now called LSO Discovery, which "quickly grew to be the biggest [educational project] run by any British orchestra", developing, among other things, "packs of back-up material for hard-pressed classroom teachers who were not necessarily music specialists". When LSO St Lukes opened in 2003, it was "not primarily a concert venue or a rehearsal hall, though at times it *is* both of these things. It is primarily an orchestral education centre—the first in the world" (Morrison 2004: 217, 237, 240).

The Scottish Chamber Orchestra appointed Kathryn McDowell as the orchestra's development manager in 1985.[54] McDowell's remit was to develop "education in its broadest sense of in- and out-reach". Ian Ritchie, the orchestra's then MD, remembers that at the time of McDowell's appointment, the SAC's music director "firmly stated that their funding could not be used for this kind of work", and to fund her most famous project, the Strathclyde Concertos, McDowell therefore persuaded Strathclyde Regional Council to contribute £10,000 annually for seven years (see Noltingk 2017: 167–8).

Live music and the state 75

The educational work of orchestras was driven by their need to build audiences but it also involved a commitment to music education as a valuable and creative activity in itself. For most classical musicians, teaching had always been a necessary source of income and a significant context for the development of such work was the decline of music education in schools following the introduction of the National Curriculum in 1988. "At the same time," as Richard Morrison (2004: 231–2) puts it, "the trend towards 'local management of schools' turned out to have unforeseen and disastrous consequences for music". As an expensive "minority" subject, music was squeezed out of the curriculum in many schools, and local authorities were increasingly unwilling to fund such local music services as youth orchestras and peripatetic music teachers.

This was not just an issue for the classical music world. In late 2010, an article in *The Word* got wide media coverage for suggesting that a clear majority of UK chart acts were now either privately educated or from prestigious stage schools. The point being made here was that formal music education was becoming more important for popular musical careers *at the same time* as it was becoming less accessible.[55] One consequence had been the emergence of a music-school business, beginning with Drumtech in London in 1983. It started by offering tuition in drums, but soon added other rock instruments, changing its name to Tech Music School. In 2010 it was taken over by BIMM, founded as the Brighton Institute of Modern Music in 2001 "to provide students with degree and diploma music qualifications while connecting them directly to the UK music industry". 2010 was the year BIMM was bought by the private equity firm Sovereign Capital and it now grew rapidly: in addition to its existing Brighton home, Bristol campus (opened in 2008) and new London base, BIMM Dublin opened in 2011, BIMM Manchester in 2013, BIMM Berlin in 2015 and BIMM Birmingham in 2017. In 2019, the BIMM Institute was granted "taught degree awarding powers" and its website could proclaim:

> From our beginnings as Drumtech to the opening of BIMM Hamburg in 2018, our musical journey has been one of continual growth, culminating in our position today as one of the largest providers of modern music education in Europe.[56]

This was also the period when careers in jazz and folk music increasingly meant following degree courses. In Scotland, the Royal Scottish Academy of Music and Drama established its BA (Scottish Music) in 1996, "the first of its kind in Britain"; in England, the first folk music degree was launched by the University of Newcastle in 2001. By then, jazz education in Britain had already begun to develop along these formal educational lines and by 2010 Tony Whyton found that jazz was on the curriculum of at least 50 HE institutions in Britain (Whyton 2015). In the 2010s, it seemed that the majority of successful new British jazz musicians (those nominated for the

76   *Live music and the state*

Mercury Prize, for example) were graduates of the conservatory courses at Guildhall, the Royal Academy of Music, the Royal College of Music and the Royal Northern College of Music or had studied at City Music Schools such as those in Leeds and Birmingham. We will return to the effects of these developments on musicians' careers in Chapter 9.

Conclusion: the state and free market ideology

Throughout the period of this volume, the political problem that most exercised promoters was the *lack* of the state regulation of secondary ticketing and the consequences for both their own business models and their customers' live music experiences. For the Concert Promoters Association, formed in 1986, "ensuring that concertgoers have the opportunity of seeing their favourite artists at reasonable ticket prices has always been a primary concern". An early lobbying campaign was thus for "legislation to protect consumers from ticket touts", which led the Department of Trade and Industry's Price Indications (Resale of Tickets) Regulations 1994, introduced in February 1995 to ensure that secondary ticket buyers were clearly informed of the price of the ticket and its seat number before purchase.[57] For the CPA, "while these regulations did not go as far as concert promoters would have liked, it was felt that they were a step in the right direction".[58]

The CPA's lobbying continued, but so did an unsatisfactory political response: while the DTI was concerned to protect consumers from ticket fraud, it regarded secondary tickets in themselves as occupying a legitimate place in the live music market. In February 2009, the CPA announced the launch of its own secondary ticketing service, Officialboxoffice.com. CPA chairman Rob Ballantine told *Music Week*:

> We had a three-year campaign to try to get touting outlawed, getting all the way to a Government Select Committee, who rejected our proposals. We are obviously disappointed about that, but we have accepted it and we know that touting is inevitably here to stay.
> (*Music Week*, February 28, 2009: 10).[59]

By then, the CPA and its members had given evidence to an Office of Fair Trading (OFT) enquiry into *Ticket Agents in the UK* (which reported in 2005), to at least four "touting summits" organised by the Department of Culture, Media and Sport in 2006 and to a House of Commons Select Committee's hearing on ticket touting in 2007; the responses were much the same. The OFT concluded that "secondary agents can provide a useful function and benefit to consumers" (Office of Fair Trading 2005: 73).[60] The DCMS made it clear that the government supported the view that "the secondary sale of tickets brings benefits for consumers" who "welcome the existence of a well-functioning, legal secondary market for tickets". Such a market provided access to tickets beyond the initial period offered by primary sellers and was a means of selling

Live music and the state   77

unwanted tickets "so as not to be out of pocket if the primary seller refuses a refund" (Department of Culture, Media and Sport 2009: 8).[61]

The net effect of these debates was to suggest a distinction between legitimate and illegitimate ticket touts. In *Music Week*, for example, stories about ticket fraud—"Serious crime squad called in after non-delivery of V and Reading tickets" (*Music Week*, August 20, 2008)—ran alongside quotes from the newly established Association of Secondary Ticket Agents (ASTA) and increasingly gushing reports about the success of companies like Seatwave and Viagogo (who were not actually ASTA members). For example, under the headline "Coming in from the Cold" (*Music Week*, October 25, 2008: 15), it was suggested that, "For so long the pariahs of the live sector, secondary ticketing businesses such as Viagogo are now winning over customers and clients alike and seem set for mainstream success." In 2009, it reported that Viagogo had been appointed "the official secondary ticketing, and ticket exchange partner" for Festival Republic (*Music Week*, April 11, 2009: 11) and that Seatwave was attributing its record rise in profits to the recession (*Music Week*, September 19, 2009: 11). By then, Tixdaq had published the results of the first systematic survey of secondary ticket data. One million tickets had been sold in this market in 2008; the average price paid for a ticket was twice its face value; 85% of sales were, unsurprisingly, for best-selling tours, festivals and acts in the primary ticket market (*Music Week*, February 7, 2009: 14). Equally unsurprisingly, by then Ticketmaster had also bought a secondary ticketing agency, Get Me In (*Music Week*, February 9, 2009: 5).[62]

That was not the end of the story: lobbying, consultations and reviews continued through the next decade.[63] This was inevitable. Ticket touting (whatever name it goes by) is as essential to the business of concert promotion as ticket selling, and symbolises the underlying contradictions of treating a transient experience as a commodity. On the one hand, secondary ticketing services are loathed by both musicians and their audiences as greedy and exploitative. When in 2018 Ticketmaster closed its secondary ticketing sites in Europe, Get Me In and Seatwave, the decision was thus taken at least in part because of the perceived reputational damage: "We know that fans are tired of seeing others snap up tickets just to resell for a profit on secondary websites, so we have taken action," said Andrew Parsons, head of Ticketmaster UK.[64] On the other hand, people continue to use them. A year later, Viagogo was confident enough of its business model to announce a $14 billion deal to buy StubHub from from eBay. Viagogo CEO Eric Baker explained why: "Bringing these two companies together creates a win–win for fans – more choice and better pricing."[65]

This is the context in which "legitimate" promoters (as represented by the CPA) turned to the state to solve a problem that was a consequence of the logic of a free market. Much of this chapter has been about the effects of neo-liberal ideology on the state's live music policies. It is a nice irony that when it came to ticket touting, promoters demanded market interference, and not surprising that the state's response was simply to compel secondary ticket

78   *Live music and the state*

sellers to provide more ticket information so as to enable buyers to make more informed choices in the secondary market! We turn now to one of the sectors with recurring secondary ticketing issues: the music festivals business.

Notes

1   Quoted in Morrison (2004: 219).
2   Quote taken from a letter from Anne Norton, Chair of the Magistrates Association's Licensing Committee, to live music campaigner Hamish Birchall.
3   Quote taken from the Labour Government's Licensing White Paper, published on April 10, 2000.
4   As Reid shows, this figure rests on rather dubious data. The word on the street at the time was that the only local beneficiaries were taxi drivers and the portable toilet business (Reid 2007: 489).
5   Dance halls and discotheques faced similar licensing restrictions.
6   On December 1, 1996, the UK legally acknowledged "performer rights", as part of the process of harmonising British and EU laws. *All* performers on a commercial recording made since 1946 (whether featured artist or session musician) were now due money if the recording was broadcast or played in public. These rights were initially administered by a new organisation, the Performing Artists Media Rights Association (PAMRA), which merged with PPL in 2006. For an early discussion of the implications of this right for performers' income, see Taylor and Towse (1998).
7   CTCs were to be independent of local education authorities and were expected to get at least 20% of their funding from the business sector; the rest came from the Department of Education. In this case, the business sector was the British Phonograph Industry (BPI) and its investment in a CTC was at least in part motivated by the need to develop a good relationship with government in its lobbying for copyright reform.
8   Smith now headed the Department of Culture, Media and Sport; it had previously been the Department for National Heritage.
9   Policy here was strongly influenced by Comedia, a consultancy specialising in research into the economy of cities, founded by Charles Landry in 1978 (Frith 1999). Iain Crawford also notes the influence on Scottish political thinking of the Policy Studies Institute's 1988 report on the benefit of the arts to Glasgow's economy. Edinburgh's Labour council, for example, thereafter developed an unexpectedly positive attitude to the Edinburgh Festival (Crawford 1997: 206). The development of Red Wedge, which we discussed in Chapter 1, was another component of Labour's municipal socialist thinking.
10   This involved regular meetings of industry figures, chaired by Smith, at which ministers could be lobbied to address music business problems (such as copyright) and music company bosses lobbied to support Labour's flagship policies such as the New Deal for Musicians, a training programme for young would-be music workers launched in 1999. For an incisive account of NDfM's history see Cloonan (2002).
11   For Liverpool Council's use of music in its rebranding policy see Cohen (2007).
12   Quote taken from the Edinburgh UNESCO City of Literature webpage: www. cityofliterature.com/glasgow-named-unesco-city-of-music. For an enlightening

Live music and the state 79

account of the policy thinking here see Martin Cloonan's analysis of the political economy of the SSE Hydro in Glasgow, which eventually opened in 2013 (Behr et al. 2016: 18–23).

13 We discuss the origins of warehouse parties in Volume 2.

14 Osgerby's account of rave is drawn from Saunders (1995).

15 The evil acid house headline is cited in Osgerby (1998: 181). As Harry Shapiro points out, the dance floor use of ecstasy had more in common with the Mod and Northern Soul use of amphetamines than with hippie use of LSD—MDMA was an amphetamine-based drug (Osgerby 1998: 242).

16 Paul Oakenfold claims that Bright's links with Ian Greer Associates, whose clients included Whitbread, "were disclosed in 1994 during the 'cash for questions' scandal" (quoted in Brewster and Broughton 2010: 144). For the early history of alcopops, see https://allmyownresearch.wordpress.com/2015/09/09/the-story-of-uk-alcopops-and-ready-to-drink-rtd-beverages-1984-to-2003.

17 The DJ at the Nelson rave was still at work when "a fireman began attacking the decks with a sledgehammer" (Phillips 2009: 76).

18 See www.legislation.gov.uk/ukpga/1994/33/part/V/crossheading/powers-in-relation-to-raves.

19 Sunrise's highly effective PR man, Paul Staines, was a member of the Libertarian Alliance and went on to run the influential right-wing blog site Guido Fawkes (see Garratt 1998: 164–6).

20 These Acts applied to England and Wales; in Northern Ireland, a pub needed "a Liquor Licence and an Entertainment Licence if it provided entertainment to the public". In Scotland, the Civic Government (Scotland) Act of 1982 required that a PEL would be required for all places of public entertainment *except* when the premises already had a licence to sell alcohol. For discussion of the origins of PELs, see Frith et al. (2013: 34–5).

21 Hamish Birchall is a jazz drummer who started his anti-PEL campaign for the Musicians' Union before pursuing it independently.

22 In November 2002, Soho branches of the Pitcher and Piano pub chain were fined £5000 for allowing "rhythmic moving" to occur to their piped music. For an entertaining follow-up article, see "Twist and Out!" by Grace Dent. She describes how Soho publicans desperately tried to stop people "changing shapes to fill the space of the floor available", as amplified dance music was blasted through their bars (*Guardian Guide* December 7–13, 2002: 8–10).

23 We take the examples here from a series of articles Hamish Birchall wrote for *Classical Music* magazine in 2000–1. See, for example, *Classical Music,* March 31, 2001: 12.

24 Again, this Act only applied to England and Wales.

25 Quote taken from email to the authors, January 22, 2012. For a useful guide to government and parliamentary thinking about the "two in a bar" exemption, the 2003 Act and subsequent amendments and debates, see Philip Ward's 2011 House of Commons Library notes on Music in Small Venues, http://webarchive.nationalarchives.gov.uk/+/http:/www.culture.gov.uk/images/research/Increases_in_live_music_between_2005_and_2009updated.pdf.

26 See https://publications.parliament.uk/pa/cm200809/cmselect/cmcumeds/492/492.pdf.

27 Tim Clement-Jones was a Liberal-Democrat peer and tireless parliamentary champion of live music.

80 *Live music and the state*

28 Scotland retained, and indeed, was in the process of strengthening, its entertainment licensing laws (see Lorraine Simpson's 2012 report for the Scottish Artists' Union on the Criminal Justice and Licensing (Scotland) Act 2010 at www.sau.org. uk). Northern Ireland retained without any changes its own entertainment licence system.

29 Quoted in Helienne Lindvell's *Guardian* report on the event. See www.guardian. co.uk/music/musicblog/2009/oct/15/small-venues-struggle-live-music.

30 Form 696 had been in existence since 2005, although its use did not get much media attention until 2008.

31 *Music Week* reported that by June 2009 more than 100 venues were "currently required to comply with Form 696 as part of their licensing conditions", but noted that this was a conservative estimate and that the figures (and their availability) varied greatly between boroughs (*Music Week,* June 6, 2009: 10).

32 The BBC Radio1 News report of its demise (on November 10, 2017) noted that versions of the form had also been used by 16 other local authorities.

33 See Sam Wolfson's report for the *Guardian*: "Is the British Nightclub in Danger of Extinction?" (August 14, 2015: 4–6). The ALMR is the trade body or, in its own words, "the voice and champion of over 90% of managed pubs & clubs, branded restaurants & cafes" in the UK (www.almr.org.uk/about).

34 The Arches soon closed altogether, despite a widely publicised campaign for the restoration of its nightclub license.

35 See http://news.bbc.co.uk/1/hi/magazine/8535219.stm. Ministry of Sound eventually did a deal with the developer on soundproofing costs and the development was completed without the club being jeopardised.

36 For a good account of similar issues in Liverpool see Cohen (2007).

37 Wright notes that in Ken Livingstone's draft cultural strategy, *London—Cultural Capital: Realising the Potential of a World-Class City*, circulated by the Mayor of London's office in 2003, there was no "mention of traditional concert events as an aspect of the city's cultural life".

38 The Arts Council of Northern Ireland, which administers lottery funds for the region, was set up in 1962 to take on the work of the Committee for the Encouragement of Music and the Arts (CEMA), established in 1942. It became a statutory body in 1995.

39 The money was divided between the arts councils on a population basis. ACE got 83.3%, the Scottish Arts Council 8.9%, the Arts Council of Wales 5.0% and the Arts Council of Northern Ireland 2.8% (Witts 1998: 509).

40 Three music companies, the Royal Scottish National Orchestra, Scottish Opera and the Scottish Chamber Orchestra, which had taken the bulk of the SAC's music budget, became "national organisations", funded directly by the Scottish Government.

41 For excellent accounts of SAC music policy in this period, see Cloonan (2007) and Tom Bancroft's "History of Scottish Music Funding" interviews with three SAC Heads of Music: Matthew Rooke (1991–97), Nod Knowles (1998–2005) and Ian Smith (2005–16). See https://bellacaledonia.org.uk/2018/04/25/the-history-of-scottish-music.

42 The Tune Up live touring programme launched by the SAC in 2003 included "music of all styles from traditional Scottish to cutting edge jazz and salsa, from contemporary classical to the latest indie rock music" (quote from SAC News Release, November 17, 2003).

Live music and the state 81

43 In 1997, Tony Blair adopted "diversity" as a key principle of New Labour's cultural policy (Wolf 2017: 295).

44 The same thing was happening at the BBC, for the same reasons. John Drummond remembers asking John Birt, his new director-general, what he thought of the BBC's orchestras. Birt replied that they were "a variable resource centre whose viability depends on the business plan of the Controller of Radio 3" (Drummond 2000: 425).

45 LSO Live was launched in 2000. For an excellent account of its origins and development, see Aguilar (2017).

46 In 1993, Kenneth Baird, the Arts Council's Music Director, calculated that in the season 1991–92 Council grants accounted for just under 20% of its client orchestras' funding. See Wolf (2017: 293).

47 Lebrecht (2001: 490) also notes that

> The Met [in New York] and the Bastille [in Paris] kept tickets affordable by building new houses with 4,000 seats. Covent Garden kept them exclusive by rebuilding with just 2141. This cardinal misjudgment alone will prevent the ROH from ever again becoming a popular venue.

48 The Waterfront Hall in Belfast (1997) is used regularly by the Ulster Orchestra, although the Ulster Hall, which opened in 1862, is still regarded as its home.

49 The only building for which ACE had direct responsibility was the South Bank (which included the Royal Festival Hall, Queen Elizabeth Hall and Purcell Room), which it took over following the abolition of the GLC in 1986.

50 Quoted from www.thsh.co.uk/news/building-to-the-beat-of-a-new-foyer.

51 Information from Peter Fribbins, Artistic Director of the London Chamber Music Society, interviewed by Matt Brennan in November 2008.

52 The Aurora Orchestra also had Associate Orchestra status at the South Bank.

53 Wright (2005: 119) notes that in the mid-1980s, when it was difficult to get businesses interested in its concerts of new music, "the majority of its sponsorship was attracted by the more widely appealing work of the Sinfonietta's education arm in projects for schools and community outreach work, including prisons, which sponsors felt gave them credit by association".

54 Richard McNicol had already been involved in education work for the SCO.

55 See the report by Tom Bateman for the BBC's *Today* programme on January 28, 2011: "Has Pop Gone Posh?", http://news.bbc.co.uk/today/hi/today/newsid_9373000/9373158.stm.

56 BIMM now stood for British and Irish Modern Music—see www.bimm.ac.uk/about-bimm.

57 See www.legislation.gov.uk/uksi/1994/3248/regulation/8/made.

58 Quotes taken from an in-house biography of the CPA provided to the authors by its secretary, Carole Smith, in 2010.

59 We couldn't find evidence that this site did much business.

60 For detailed critical analysis of the OFT Report see Cloonan 2007: Chapter 4.

61 For full further discussion of the issues here see Behr and Cloonan 2018.

62 Ticketmaster later also took over Seatwave.

63 For a good summary of developments in the 2010s, see Adam Behr's 2018 report for Live Music Exchange: http://livemusicexchange.org/blog/the-tide-turning-on-ticket-touts-adam-behr.

82 *Live music and the state*

64 Quoted in a BBC news report, August 13, 2018 (www.bbc.co.uk/news/entertainment-arts-45133094). This action only seemed to apply to Ticketmaster's policy in Europe.
65 Quoted in *The Guardian*, November 25, 2019. See www.theguardian.com/money/2019/nov/25/ebay-agrees-sale-stubhub-swiss-ticket-reseller-viagogo-4bn-deal.

5 The political economy of music festivals

> We are the fifth biggest town in Scotland when T in the Park is on, with all the issues that come with running a major town.
>
> (Geoff Ellis)[1]

> For Celtic Connections we're really all pretty much folk fans now! And, you know, it would probably be much more important, in *my* opinion, for people to have a good sense of people and a good sense of music than a marketing degree, and I want to share that kind of love, pass it on. Sounds a bit cheesy but you know what I mean.
>
> (Jane Donald, Head of Sales and Marketing, Glasgow Royal Concert Hall)[2]

Introduction

Music festivals have long played a significant role in British live music culture. In previous volumes we have described their importance in the post-war period, tracing, for example, the development of the Edinburgh International Festival (launched in 1947), the Reading Festival (originating as the National Jazz Festival in 1961) and the Glastonbury Festival (which began as the Pilton Pop, Blues and Folk Festival in 1970). These annual events still take place, of course, but in the period of this volume they became just the best known of a rapidly increasing number of competing music and arts festivals that, taken together, came to occupy a central place in both the live music economy and the tourism business, as well in the pursuit of various political ends.

In Europe, arts festivals have been thought of politically since at least the start of the 1960s. As early as 1957, the European Music Festival Association (EMFA), founded in 1952, responded to criticism of its members' elitism by interviewing "eighty celebrities from the music industry" in order to "show the positive role of festivals in European culture" (Autissier 2009b: 126). Between 1960 and 1980, "[European] festivals came to serve more diverse purposes" than simply staging classical music concerts and celebrating European high culture. They were already seen as useful for the promotion of

84 *The political economy of music festivals*

tourism and were encouraged now to promote the development of "minority cultures" as well, while from the 1980s "festival-related activities also became integrated into local authorities' urban strategies" (Autissier 2009a: 34, 41). The Edinburgh International Festival was an early member of the EMFA; the British Arts Festival Association (BAFA) was launched in 1969 (at the behest of the Arts Council).[3] The British Association of Festival Organisers, representing community festivals, was created in 1987.

The changes in commercial music festivals at the turn of the twentieth century were well summarised in a 2013 article by Geoff Ellis, who had promoted Scotland's T in the Park since 1994:

> People thought we were mad and that a big music festival in Scotland would never work, but here we are approaching our 20th consecutive edition. Festivals have changed dramatically in this time—when the first T in the Park took place in 1994 the only other UK [outdoor] festivals were Glastonbury, Reading and WOMAD—now there are literally hundreds all over the country and they have gone from just being a place where you watch bands outdoors, to an entire four day experience or a long weekend away.[4]
>
> In year one we had about 2000 campers and 17,000 people in total at T in the Park, whereas this year we will have 70,000 campers and 85,000 festival goers on the site each day—this alone obviously calls for major changes to the festival, from facilities to campsite entertainment, that were not required in the early years ... From fencing to building 11 stages, bars, a campsite big enough to hold 70,000 people, police presence and security, medical provisions, power, lighting, transport, waste management (we've won the best toilets at the UK Festival Awards three times), land rental as well as preparing the site year round for all weather conditions, to getting licenses etc.—it's not a cheap gig.[5]

Ellis goes on to describe some of the essential components of the festival economy to which we will return in the next section: the need for commercial sponsorship, for example. In 2006, *The Guardian* (August 28, 2006) ran a story on "How the Summer Rock Festivals Became One Big Branded Beer Tent" but the Cambridge Folk Festival was already officially known as the Abbot Ale Cambridge Folk Festival in 1985.[6]

Another significant economic factor here was the increasing importance of the European festival network for big acts' promotional tours. Anderton gives the example of Björk's 2007 *Volta* schedule. The tour's European leg began at the Glastonbury Festival in June, continued at Rock Werchter in Belgium and the Roskilde Festival in Denmark, and called in at numerous smaller festivals before ending the summer at the Connect Festival in Scotland (Anderton 2018: 41–2). A decade later, the Arctic Monkeys' tour promoting their 2018 album, *Tranquillity Base Hotel and Casino*, was made up of 20 arena shows in six countries and 17 festival appearances in 15 countries. For

The political economy of music festivals 85

major rock stars at least, the global festival circuit now provided the most effective sales platform.[7] As Anderton (2018) suggests, this promotional use of rock festivals has been facilitated by international operators like Live Nation, which both owns festivals worldwide and controls the touring schedules of potential headliners, but the same calculations are significant for world music, jazz and folk tour promoters: the increasing number of European festivals in these genres "helps to guarantee scale efficiencies" and "decent" fees for travelling artists (Autissier 2009a: 40).[8]

In Chapter 2, we suggested that for Live Nation musical events are primarily important as marketing opportunities and this is certainly the case for its music festivals. From this perspective what matters about a music festival is not the music but the *festival experience* to which it is an accompaniment. T in the Park, for example, routinely sold out *before* its line-ups were announced and Geoff Ellis describes the festival's history as the "continued enhancement of customer service quality"—the provision of gourmet food outlets, for example, or "shower and pamper areas" or, as Denise Winterman reported for the BBC in 2010, tipis with double beds. However, as Winterman goes on to suggest, what was happening here was not only improved customer service. Festivals were now designed to nurture the consumer identities reflected by musical tastes.

As the number of festivals increased (and a new kind of festival entrepreneur emerged to promote so-called "boutique" festivals), deciding *which* festival to attend became a more important decision than just deciding "to go to a festival" (the starting point for rock fans in the 1970s).[9] In Winterman's words,

> With so much choice and such a range of "experiences" on offer, where to go says more about you than ever before. It's why people continue to wear the wristbands for weeks afterwards. It's about making a statement.

Winterman quoted *Independent* journalist Alice Azania-Jarvis:

> The reputation of a festival is more important to some people than the acts who are playing. If watching your favourite band means standing in a field of people who look like mobile phone salesmen, then some people will decide not to go. It's not what you're watching, more who you are watching them with.

And Winterman found academic support for this argument, quoting Professor George McKay:

> I often make the point that people don't go to festivals for the music, which is a secondary attraction. They go for the mass experience, the event itself. Some festivals are simply "cool" and others not ... If you go to Glastonbury or WOMAD you are probably interested in ethical

86   *The political economy of music festivals*

issues around the environment or multiculturalism or a global consciousness. You may even have an allotment. If it's Latitude you're a bit older and possibly taking the kids but don't want to be too uncomfortable—perhaps thinking you'd like to hire one of those tipis.[10]

By now the *Guardian* was providing annual consumer guides for would-be festival-goers under a range of labels. Festivals were recommended not just for, say, country music, Irish music or soul and funk but also as "best for health", "if you really don't like crowds", "for foodies", "for steam train enthusiasts", "for surprises", "for listening and learning", "for campfire sing-alongs", "for Brazilian vibes" and even "for summer sledging" (*Guardian*, April 24, 2009: 3; May 21, 2010: 3).[11]

By 2010, music festivals were clearly commodities in themselves, a sector of the much broader market for "events". One sign of this development was the evolution of Virtual Festivals.com. Originally set up in 1999 as a live music business website, in 2004 it launched Festival Awards, an annual gathering for the festival sector. There were soon 21 prize categories, including not only best hospitality, best toilets and best brand activation, but also best non-music festival. Virtual Festivals provided guests with its annual Festival Census and encouraged them to subscribe to *Festival Insights*. Its 2010 data, for example, suggested that the average festival attender was aged 31 and earned £18,000 per year; 26% of festival-goers had children and 20% took drugs as part of their festival experience.[12] When Virtual Festivals went into administration in 2014, the Festival Awards show was taken on by Mondiale Publishing, a business-to-business media company based in Strawberry Studios in Manchester. Mondiale specialises in the Food Service sector, with publications including *Sleeper* and its supplement *Supper* for the hotel trade. Its concern in these titles is to show how "F&B [food and beverage] concepts and brands are developed and how products, produce and personalities interact to deliver a coherent guest experience".[13]

"A coherent guest experience" would have seemed an odd way of talking about the Glastonbury Festival in the 1970s, but by the time of Glastonbury's 40th anniversary event in 2010, this had become the language of the festivals business. Such marketing talk was, though, in some ways misleading. The financial health of most music festivals continued to be dependent on state investment and support of various sorts. Hence the importance for festival promoters of economic impact studies—purely commercial ventures would have measured their success simply by reference to profit margins. Arts Council funded music organisations had long had to justify their grants and demonstrate their social and cultural value, but in the 1990s "impact" came to mean measurable economic results, especially as local development agencies also got involved in arts investment (as an aspect of the cultural industries policies we discussed in the last chapter), and such impact studies were now routinely commissioned by all festival promoters.[14] In their comprehensive survey of the festival impact literature, Emma Webster and George McKay (2016: 23–6) summarise the economic findings from 25 music festivals of all sorts and sizes,

The political economy of music festivals 87

from Glastonbury and Glyndebourne to the Shetland Accordion and Fiddle Festival.

Yet, as these authors note, neither the precise figures for extra jobs and added value nor their accuracy are what really matter here.[15] The general purpose of these studies was, above all, to prove that a festival was *a good thing*—good, that is, in a particular way: for the local economy, for tourism, for employment, for geographical branding. No festival has ever published a study that showed its lack of (or declining) economic impact or damaging social effects.[16]

One way of thinking about music festivals in this period is to see this as the moment when they reached the final stage of their journey from the disruption to the celebration of leisure consumption, and this has certainly been a significant theme in scholarly work on rock festivals. Chris Anderton (2008 and 2011), for example, organises his festival studies around the tension between "carnival" and "commerce", while Vanessa Valéro (2002) describes rock festivals as moving between "*passion et désenchantement*".

Disenchantment is a topic for this and the next chapter. But this is because of the continuing belief that festivals are—or should be—places where one can be enchanted. In 1957, the European Music Festivals Association proposed this as its festival definition:

> A festival is most of all a *festive event*, a comprehensive programme featuring art performances transcending the quality of regular programmes to reach a *unique* quality level in a specific place. As a result festivals boast remarkable beauty that can only be attained *for a limited period of time*.
> (Quoted in Autissier 2009b: 126—authors' italics)

Compare Michael Eavis's description of the Glastonbury Festival in 1995:

> It's going to sound corny, but, well, it's a kind of utopia really, something outside of the normal world we live in.
> (Quoted in Webster and Mckay 2016: 11)

Beauty and brand management, utopia and the consumer experience: such contrasting perceptions of music festivals run through this chapter, in which we examine festival economics, and Chapter 6, in which we examine festival cultures in different music worlds.

Festival economics

On June 7, 2010, under the headline "Festival Survey Reveals Cause for Celebration", *Music Week* reported:

> The live sector is providing the Government with a timely reminder of its economic and cultural impact with new figures suggesting the festival market is contributing more than £1bn a year to the British economy.

88   *The political economy of music festivals*

A report from the Association of Independent Festivals, released this week, demonstrates festivals are the number-one entertainment choice for Britons this summer, with its 24 member festivals injecting more than £130m into the UK economy and a further £12m into local businesses near the sites.

Live [sector] experts say the UK now hosts around 400 festivals each year—many of which are much bigger than the AIF's events. This leads them to estimate the true extent of the value of the outdoor market to the Exchequer's coffers has now topped the £1bn mark.[17]

Six months earlier, under the headline "Funding Woes Force Festivals to Pull the Plug", *Scotsman* journalist Brian Ferguson had reported:

EXPERTS have warned Scotland is unlikely to see any new festivals launched for the foreseeable future, as it emerged that a string of top events have been axed. Connect, Outsider, Big in Falkirk, Live at Loch Lomond and EH1 are among festivals shelved in the wake of poor ticket sales and funding problems.

The festival businessmen quoted blamed this situation on various factors: the economic downturn, infrastructure problems caused by bad weather and the squeeze on public spending.[18]

The point of juxtaposing these stories is not to show that "experts" can be found to say anything, however contradictory, but to illustrate why even the most successful players in the festival business are always aware of the risks of their ventures. In August 2010, Melvin Benn, Britain's most successful festival promoter, explained to *The Guardian:*

It's not like a regular business. It's gambling in its crudest form. Before the tickets go on sale, you promise to deliver a festival that contains a certain amount of things for the customer. Then you have to deliver, whether or not the customer decides to buy a ticket. Your income is made up of 85%–90% ticket income and 10%–15% ancillaries such as food and beverage, traders, merchandising and sponsorship. When people start buying [tickets] late, the smaller festivals tend not to have the cash flow to sustain themselves. Everyone still has to be paid even if they're not certain tickets will sell.

(*The Guardian*, August 27, 2010: 9)[19]

Outdoor festivals, in particular, carry numerous risks. Benn notes that he

took a 40% stake in Glastonbury when it was threatened with closure after being gatecrashed by more than 100,000 people in 2000. An aerial photograph has revealed that there were twice the number of festival-goers than had bought tickets.

The political economy of music festivals   89

Emma Webster and Adam Behr's systematic review of festival cancellations reveals the range of factors that can be involved. Weather, particularly heavy rain, is a common one—as Gareth Cooper of Festival No 6 said, "You plan for a year and it could all be washed away. That's not a sensible business. It's a reckless business."[20] Other issues have included the flight disruption caused by the Icelandic ash cloud; overcrowding and safety concerns (the 1989 Monsters of Rock Festival was cancelled following the death of two fans in a crowd surge the preceding year)[21]; fuel costs; a lack of sponsorship; changes in acts' touring schedules and/or their increasing fees (as a consequence of changing currency exchange rates, for example); foot and mouth disease; the London Olympics; local authorities withdrawing licences; a bomb scare; drug overdoses; and, most commonly, poor ticket sales due to an overcrowded festival calendar.[22]

Festivals can even be announced and cancelled before a single ticket has gone on sale. On September 19, 2008, for example, the *Reading Evening Post* "exclusively revealed" that a new festival was being planned for 2009 on the Rivermead site:

> The brainchild of Reading Borough Council, Reading Festival organiser Melvin Benn and Womad's ex-artistic director Thomas Brooman, the festival will feature various genres of music from across the world and will be aimed at families and teenagers with entertainment which will appeal to all generations.[23]

A couple of weeks later, under the headline "After 26 Years in the Business I Know that Promotion has Always Been Risky", Thomas Brooman gave *Music Week* more details. Heavenly Planet, "a new innovative, diverse and outward-looking festival", would be launched as an annual event for 15,000 people on July 10, 2009. It would use the Rivermead site left vacant following WOMAD's move (after 25 years) from Reading to Charlton Park in Malmesbury (*Music Week,* October 4, 2008: 12).

Brooman, like Benn, had already had a successful career as a festival promoter: he was the artistic director of WOMAD (the World of Music and Dance) from its first staging at Shepton Mallet in 1982 until it left Reading in 2006.[24] Both Benn (as promoter of the Reading Festival) and Brooman were well experienced in working with Reading Borough Council.[25] Nonetheless, in March the following year, Live Nation (owner of Benn's Festival Republic) announced that the Heavenly Planet idea had been dropped, "due to the effect of the current economic climate"—that is, the 2008 financial crash.

While festivals do compete with each other for limited customer resources, the festival sector as a whole also competes with other kinds of leisure business. Most festival promoters agree, for example, that Glastonbury is valuable not just in terms of its own takings but also in the way it generates favourable publicity for the general activity of "festival going". In the words of Steven

90 *The political economy of music festivals*

Corfield of Serious Stages, "when Glastonbury is on, it's on the news the whole time, the BBC is pumping it out, and everyone thinks ... festivals!"[26]

By 2010, the festival business was certainly understood to have the potential for substantial returns on investment. According to the *Financial Times*, pre-tax profits at Festival Republic almost quadrupled between 2005 and 2010, while PRS for Music calculated in 2009 that the spend on live music in the UK had risen 9.4% in the previous 12 months to £1.45 billion, of which the festival market accounted for 19% (and for the sharpest increase in spending, rising by £50 million to £275.5 million). By 2011, festivals were apparently the largest sector of the live music market, generating £397 million.[27] But festival investment never ceased to be risky, and as a consequence the underlying strategy for the growth focused more on collaboration than competition, as we noted in Chapter 3.

The result, to use Brennan and Webster's (2010: 26) words in the 2010 Festival Awards Report, is that:

> The UK festival market remains fairly convoluted in terms of ownership. Many festivals are owned and operated by joint ventures between two or more different promoters, making exact market share calculations diffi-cult ... [Further] the festival sector seems to be imitating the indie/major dynamic of the recording industry: just as major labels have traditionally acquired the most successful independent labels, so too larger promoters move in to acquire successful independent festival brands.

The economic model here involves promoters both sharing risk and collect-ively putting together the resources needed to cover what can be huge advance costs. There is no such thing as a typical event in financial terms, of course, but Eamonn Forde (2015: 13) provides a useful example of an unnamed fes-tival promoter's basic balance sheet:

> *Costs*: artists 36%, site infrastructure 23%, personnel 9%, venue licensing and legal fees 9%, security 8%, technical production 6%, marketing 5%, policing 2%, other 2%.
> *Revenue*: tickets 70%, bar 15%, sponsorship 6%, food 3%, merchandise 2%, car parking 1%, other 3%.

These percentages would, in fact, be familiar to the promoters of all large music venues and events, but the scale and settings of festivals pose particular cost problems. Take the case of the licensing fees charged by the PRS for Music. In a polemical piece for *Music Week*, Alison Wenham, chair of the Association of Independent Festivals, pointed out that there was "a lack of distinction between concerts and festivals in PRS for Music's tariff system". Even though AIF research showed that "up to 60% of a festival's audience is not motivated by who is playing", the PRS was still taking 3% of the ticket price, especially galling for festival promoters as the higher price of their

The political economy of music festivals 91

tickets reflected the extra money they had to spend on *non-music* facilities and entertainment (*Music Week*, July 11, 2009).[28]

Even for festivals, though, booking artists was a requisite skill—balancing who was accessible or affordable with who was "right" for the event, but now with additional decisions: who would/should play which stage? At what time? For how long? On which day? Who should appear where and in what size font on the festival poster? At some festivals, the booking and programming of a particular stage might be the responsibility of a sub-promoter; different stages were, in effect, competing for audience attention. Other promoters, such as John Giddings at the Isle of Wight, put all live acts on the same stage so that every ticket holder could see them.[29] The way a festival line-up is constructed doesn't just reflect the different fees the acts demand but is also used to influence the audiences' perception of a festival's ethos. Promoters have to decide, for example, whether to feature ageing "heritage acts" (relatively cheap compared with contemporary stars, but with a known following) or new acts (even cheaper but with unknown audience appeal). Should a festival have a reputation for reliability, adventure or some combination of both? This is a question for jazz as well as rock promoters, for folk as well as arts festivals, and indeed for the booked artists themselves, who have to consider the effect on their careers of their appearance at one festival rather than another.[30]

In purely financial terms, though, the biggest problem for outdoor festival promoters is site management. As Isle of Wight Festival promoter John Giddings explains, "a greenfield site isn't immediately fit for a festival just because you've made it fine for campers and live entertainment". He spent £250,000 building roads to the site's car park and noted that:

> When it rains, you have to pay a lot of extra money for straw to go on the mud. When the sun shines you have to pay a lot of money to give away water for free.
>
> (Quoted in Forde 2015: 12–3)[31]

Giddings had to employ around 5000 people to ensure he could "lay on all the necessary amenities"; the cost of security and policing was around £1million. In 2002, T in the Park employed 500 staff from Rock Steady (its contracted security provider) and 200 direct employees: stage managers, production managers, health and safety officers—"we give a lot of work to people who are freelancers in the industry", while also using specialist PA companies, lighting companies, staging companies and so forth.[32]

If a significant amount of festival promoters' advance investment is to ensure that a festival will work as a musical event, an equally significant financial investment is necessary to meet the licensing requirements of various local authorities. Such requirements can be impossible to meet. In 2015, for example, T in the Park moved from Balado (widely regarded as the best festival site in Britain) to Strathallan Castle Estate after a four-year dispute with

92   *The political economy of music festivals*

the local Health and Safety Executive over the hypothetical risks posed by a BP oil pipeline that ran under the festival area.[33]

Throughout its time in Balado, T in the Park had been strongly (if, in the end, vainly) supported by Perth and Kinross Council (which among other things paid for the festival's impact studies). Outdoor festival promoters from Glastonbury onwards were well aware of the threat posed by a lack of local support.[34] According to Vince Power:

> The biggest obstacle you face is usually the neighbours, especially in Britain where licensing is so political. There's a lot of scaremongering about people coming into your village to take drugs and rape your daughters.

Kate and Oliver Webster-Jones, promoters of the Deer Shed festival in North Yorkshire, echo Power's argument:

> Our problems started when an elderly couple who own a static caravan site next door complained. To run a festival, you have to engage in local politics. Deer Shed's future depended on three councillors in Harrogate, all of whom were over 60.
>
> (Quotes from *Sunday Times*, May 16, 2010)[35]

Promoters seek local community support not only with the economic impact studies we have discussed but also through direct engagement. T in the Park gave charitable donations to local organisations such as the Rotary Club and Round Table, who provided volunteer stewards. A nearby church centre and rugby club were used to provide travellers with breakfast and showers; the local pipe band was employed to pipe ticket holders on to the site; the festival itself ran a community helpline and distributed regular newsletters. On its Malmesbury site, WOMAD uses 5000 volunteers, while at Glastonbury in 2007 Oxfam "recruited, trained and managed" 1400 stewards, who worked three eight-hour shifts over the weekend in return for a free ticket. In 2005, the festival gave Oxfam a donation of £200,000 (Stone 2008: 218). Many small events, such as the Tiree Music Festival in the Inner Hebrides (launched in 2010), are entirely dependent on the willingness of local residents to volunteer for the various onsite tasks.

In 1997, T in the Park faced a major financial disaster when one of its ticketing agencies, Tocter, went into receivership, depriving the festival of a significant chunk of its ticket sales revenue (around £500,000). The festival was saved from immediate cancellation by an interest-free loan from the Scottish brewery, Tennents, who explained that it was "good PR for us, we're seen to be helping the event when this ticket agent collapsed".[36]

This is a good example of the importance of festival sponsors in providing what John Giddings calls "a safety net", as against demanding an involvement in what the sponsors' own branding departments call "experiential

The political economy of music festivals 93

marketing" (see Forde 2015: 13). Vince Power boasts of making sponsorship a key part of festival economics:[37]

> Well I was the one who started all the sponsorship, I mean heavy sponsorship. I did the biggest deal with Carlsberg first, then I got rid of Carlsberg and did a bigger deal with Carling for Reading and Leeds. So Carlsberg paid us a lot of money, then Carling paid us something like £6 million. But in the end, it's "you can drink anything so long as you drink Carling!"

But Power also goes on to note the problems of sponsor involvement:

> It had to do with hospitality tickets, ways to enhance the ticket, they give you a marquee, a sausage roll and a glass of champagne and make you a VIP. And it gives the feeling to the customer who's actually just bought the ticket, a feeling of like, "We're never good enough. We're the ones wandering around the festival and we can't go into that Vodaphone or Budweiser tent because we haven't upgraded, and there's that big area back there you can't get in with all the superstars."[38]

For Fiona Stewart, managing director of the independent Green Man Festival, *resistance* to sponsorship is a necessary part of her festival's appeal:

> We had Wall's ice cream approach us to be a sponsor last year [2009]. They would have given us lots of money as well, which would have been nice, but then we'd have had to sell their products. Anyway, we've already got handmade ice cream from Wales which our audience is used to and, to be honest, I much prefer it as well.

For another independent festival promoter, Graeme Merifield of the Wychwood Festival (held on Cheltenham racecourse), any sponsorship has to be carefully chosen:

> I think people come to Wychwood because of the music and the experience and if you put things there that went against what we have suggested we stood for, then our audience, quite rightly, would not be happy.[39]

Even the most profit-oriented promoters realise that it is more important for a festival's survival that ticket buyers have the experience they expect than that sponsor demands are met, whatever the cash on offer. As Fiona Stewart puts it, "we have a loyal fanbase and don't want to do anything that would destroy what we have", while Fergus Linehan recalls that when the Edinburgh International Festival faced the "complete collapse" of corporate sponsorship following the 2008 recession, personal giving from individual festival regulars "shot up".[40] Festival sponsors, it seems, can be replaced more easily than festival audiences, and it is to festival audience expectations that we turn next.

94 *The political economy of music festivals*

Notes

1 Quoted in *The Guardian*, July 10, 2015: 12.
2 From an interview with Emma Webster, February 17, 2010.
3 In 1981, John Drummond withdrew the Edinburgh Festival from EMFA as he didn't believe that EMFA activities had anything to offer him. In 1997, by which time EIF had returned to the fold, the European Music Festival Association became the European Festivals Association. In 2010 it claimed 100 members from some 40 countries (Autissier 2009b: 129–30).
4 There are various figures given for the number of annual commercial music festivals in this period, none of which are definitive, not least because there is no agreed definition of what makes a musical event a festival in the first place. Chris Anderton identified over 600 music festivals catering to numerous genres in 2005, of which over 40 per cent could be classed as outdoor events (Anderton 2018: 38). In 2007, *The Guardian* (March 26, 2007: 9) and other media suggested that there were now 450 rock and pop festivals in Britain each year, while market research in 2004 suggested that there were 350 folk festivals alone (Morris Hargreaves McIntyre 2004). All commentators are agreed that festival provision continued to grow until 2011. Anderton's (2018: 38) figures suggest that the outdoor music festival sector doubled in size between 2005 and 2011, from 261 events to 521 events.
5 Quoted from www.huffingtonpost.co.uk/geoff-ellis/t-in-the-park-festivals-have-changed-in-the-last-twenty-years/10/06/2013.
6 The Cambridge Festival was sponsored by Newcastle Brown from 1982–84; the Abbot Ales sponsorship lasted till 1993 when Charles Wells Brewery of Bedford took it on (Laing and Newman 1994: 19).
7 Tour schedule details taken from a Domino Records press release.
8 This can be resented by local artists. British jazz musicians, for example, suggested to us that the "decent" fees paid to visiting jazz stars by some British jazz festivals meant that local acts were expected to play at their usual small venue gig rates. We discuss jazz festivals further in the next chapter.
9 The Association of Independent Festivals was established in 2008.
10 Quotes from "What Does a Music Festival Say About You?", *BBC News*, May 26, 2010, http://news.bbc.co.uk/1/hi/magazine/8692313.stm.
11 For a more academic (and less tongue-in-cheek) attempt to classify festivals, see Stone 2008: 220. Stone also labels festivals primarily by reference to their unique selling points and consumer characteristics rather than by the music on offer.
12 Figures taken from the 2010 UK Festivals Awards report, written by Matt Brennan and Emma Webster and included in the programme for that year's Award ceremony. It can be accessed at http://livemusicexchange.org/resources/the-uk-festival-market-report-2010-matt-brennan-and-emma-webster.
13 Quotes taken from the *Supper* website: www.suppermagazine.co.uk. In 2018, Mondiale sold Festival Awards to CGA, a "food and drink consultancy".
14 For influential early studies here see Hesse (1992) and Rolfe (1992). For the approach applied to local festivals, see Maughan and Bianchini (2004), an impact study of 11 cultural festivals in the East Midlands funded by ACE and the East Midlands Development Agency. For arts festivals, see the BAFA report, *Festivals Mean Business* (2000) and its 2002 *Update*, covering 83 festivals and paying particular attention to their "community contribution".

The political economy of music festivals 95

15 For discussion of the methodology of economic impact studies see Maughan (2009: 58–60). For an interesting critique of the concept of "economic impact" in the cultural sector, see Vrettos (2009).
16 In the 2010s, more urgent questions began to be asked about the environmental impact of festivals, following the 2007 launch of Julie's Bicycle, a charity formed with the aim of reducing the music industry's carbon footprint.
17 See www.musicweek.com/story.asp?sectioncode=1&storycode=1041413&c=1.
18 See http://thescotsman.scotsman.com/funding-woes-force-festivals-to-pull-the-plug.
19 For more on Melvin Benn and Festival Republic, see Chapter 3. During his career, Benn has promoted almost every major British rock festival, from Reading and Glastonbury to Latitude and Creamfields. For his career biography, see https://dlrcoco.citizenspace.com/planning/oel0217/supporting_documents/Appendix%201%20%2024.pdf.
20 Quoted in Forde (2015: 12). Festival No 6 was a "family friendly" festival featuring literature and comedy as well as a wide range of rock and dance acts, held at Portmeirion in North Wales from 2012–18 (it drew a significant part of its audience from Manchester). The festival had flood problems in 2016.
21 The worst festival disaster was at Berlin's 2010 Love Parade when 21 people were killed and 500 injured following a stampede in a tunnel leading to one of the festival sites. The event was never held again.
22 Information taken from a confidential expert witness report on the long-term sustainability of UK festivals.
23 See www.getreading.co.uk/whats-on/music/heaven-sent-4248496.
24 WOMAD was initiated (and owned) by Peter Gabriel and by 2010 had put on festivals in more than 25 countries.
25 Brooman's successor as WOMAD global director, Chris Smith, had previously been Reading Borough Council's Head of Culture.
26 The BBC's extensive coverage of the Glastonbury Festival began in 1997. Serious Staging is the UK's leading provider of festival staging. Quote taken from a company profile, "Supporting Stars", *Festival*, December 2012: 20.
27 See www.ft.com/s/)/f474096c-11e1-8397-00144feab49a.html. PRS figures taken from Page and Carey (2010) and Brookes (2012).
28 The rate was reduced to 2.7% in 2018. See https://pplprs.co.uk/wp-content/uploads/Tariff-Popular-Music-Concerts-modified-2018.pdf. It should be noted that Wenham is only representing the promoters' interests here. For songwriters (represented by PRS), the 3% was great. The promoter might be paying you a pittance festival fee; you'll play at a loss most likely for the "great exposure" (ugh), but if you're the songwriter the festival percentage makes financial sense! (MB)
29 See the celebratory tribute to John Giddings included in *Music Week*, November 2007.
30 For musicians' calculations here, see Paleo and Wijnberg (2006: 12).
31 In 2012, the Isle of Wight Festival suffered major travel chaos—cars stuck in mud and unable to get on or off the site—caused by torrential rain.
32 Figures taken from an interview with Geoff Ellis by John Williamson on August 29, 2002. One of the more significant service providers in this context was the manufacturer of wrist bands. Vince Power recalls using babies' hospital ID-tags before specialist companies (and technologies) emerged.

96 *The political economy of music festivals*

33 The claim to be Britain's best site can be found in various witness statements in the legal argument between the site's owner and BP over the terms of compensation for the site's closure. Following the cancellation of the 2017 festival in the face of a number of problems with the new site, T in the Park came to an end.

34 See Cloonan (1996). In the 2010s, the problems became particularly fraught for promoters using public parks for city festivals. Local councils were easily persuaded that the fees paid were welcome in austere times; local citizens were less happy at being excluded from public spaces by commercial interests.

35 The Deer Shed Festival, launched in 2010 as a one-day event with a capacity of 1000, is still going strong as a "celebration of family friendly music, arts and science" at the time of writing.

36 Information and quote taken from an interview with Geoff Ellis by John Williamson on August 29, 2002.

37 In fact, in most music worlds sponsors had long been part of the festival finance mix, as we'll discuss in the next chapter.

38 Quotes taken from an interview with Matt Brennan, June 5, 2009.

39 Quotes from a BBC business report on May 19, 2010. The acceptable sponsor for Wychwood was Waitrose, which also offered "marketing clout, from mailing lists to magazines". See http://news.bbc.co.uk/1/hi/business/10120490.stm.

40 Private communication—Linehan has been festival director since 2014.

6 Festival worlds

The title of this amazing week [The Sidmouth Folk Festival] doesn't begin to do it justice: it has a completely universal appeal. The title fails to conjure up the colour, excitement, spectacle, verve and vitality that abound. It's as if a benign deity has sprinkled magic dust over the whole town, and I wish I knew how to sprinkle it over the rest of the world.

(Pamela Gold)[1]

When I went to Roskilde [Festival] in like 1980-something, you know, they had a launderette there, they had a wine bar there, it was civilised, people were sitting down and the British festivals seemed to be like "get in there, drink as much horrible beer as you can, if you don't like the band, you piss in a bottle and chuck it at them".

(Vince Power)[2]

Introduction

In their illuminating research report, *From Glyndebourne to Glastonbury*, Emma Webster and George McKay (2017: 4) suggest that contemporary music festivals can broadly be characterised in three ways: greenfield events that predominantly programme music, often involving camping, open-air consumption and amplification; venue-based series of live music events linked by theme or genre, usually urban; and street-based urban carnival. We will cover all these types of festivals in this chapter, but we begin with a historical point: people went routinely to outdoor festivals in Britain long before Glastonbury became an annual musical event.

We don't need to rehearse this history here (see Frith et al. 2013: 177–9), but should draw attention to two kinds of established gathering: *carnivals* (public celebrations in which music-making has a central but secondary place) and *competitions* (at which a large number of performers gather to make music for judges—the first *eisteddfod* was apparently held in Cardigan Castle in Wales in 1176). In Britain, the line of carnival generally runs through pre-industrial religious and harvest festivals to today's village and agricultural

98   *Festival worlds*

shows and from partying traditions in the Caribbean and South Asia to urban UK celebrations of ethnicity such as the Notting Hill Carnival (see Frith et al. 2019: 133–4) and the annual Mela in cities such as Edinburgh (starting in 1985) and Bradford (starting in 1988).

Many such festival programmes include competitions (for the fittest sheep or the biggest leek, for the best cake, the best costume or the best steel band, for tossing a hay bale or singing in Scottish Gaelic) but festivals focused on music competition are more bureaucratic. The British Dance Council, for example (originally set up in 1929 as the Official Board of Ballroom Dancing)

> is the governing body for all matters pertaining to all forms of ballroom, Latin American, and disco freestyle dancing throughout England, Scotland, Wales, Northern Ireland and Channel Islands. One of the main functions of the Council is to formulate and administer the rules for competition dancing.[3]

The National Brass Band Championship of Great Britain has been organised in its present sectional form since 1945; the British Association of Barbershop Singers has staged an annual convention featuring its National Quartet and Chorus contests since 1974; and the World Piping Championship has been held annually in much the same format since 1930, although since 2003 it has been preceded by Glasgow's Piping Live! Festival. The Cardiff Singer of the Year was launched by BBC Wales in 1983 for the opening of St David's Hall in Cardiff; Leeds International Piano Competition was launched in 1963 (and became a member of the World Federation of International Music Competitions in 1965).[4]

Both carnivals and competitions continue to be embedded in the cultural routine of many British communities, whether "community" is defined by locality or shared musical practices or, indeed, by both. Even if school music education has declined over the last 30 years, the Association of Competitions for Music, Dance and Speech (founded in 1904) continues to provide those children who do still have music lessons the opportunity to celebrate their skills by playing for prizes at annual festival competitions. It is important to remember, in short, that the development of music festivals as leisure commodities that we described in the last chapter—organised around selling tickets to the public, and marketed accordingly—has not displaced other kinds of festival activity.

In his pocket history of post-war British festivals, Nod Knowles (2015: 208) remarks:

> Whether sipping champagne and picnicking on the lawn at the Glyndebourne Opera Festival or spliffing up and dancing wildly at Glastonbury or downing a pint and joining in the choruses at Cropredy Folk Festival, audiences, as ever, gravitated towards events that best suited their social attitudes and aspirations.

Knowles suggests that the first post-war arts festivals—Cheltenham, Edinburgh, Bath and Aldeburgh—were nationally conceived, each one "backed and endorsed by the Great and the Good, perfect examples of the patrician spirit of arts provision, especially in the early post-war period".[5] In the 1960s and 1970s, new festivals such as Chester, Harrogate, Chichester and Brighton ("the largest and most established annual curated multi-arts festival in England", founded in 1967) were more likely to be local council and regional arts council initiatives, with an increasing emphasis on local community involvement and educational activities (Knowles 2015: 205). For example, the Spitalfields Festival, which began in 1976 (and has been staged as both a summer and a winter event since 1996), is both determinedly local and a setting for new art music. The most ambitious of such local council initiatives, the biennial Manchester International Festival (launched in 2007), provides an interesting contrast to the Edinburgh International Festival (launched 60 years earlier) in both its blend of high and low culture and its clear sense of celebrating the city that funds it.

The classical music festival

In the classical music world, the remarkable rise of festivals in the last 40 years has been driven primarily by musical concerns, most obviously by organisers' commitment to certain *kinds* of music (hence the York Early Music Festival, started in 1977, and the Huddersfield Contemporary Music Festival, started in 1978),[6] but also often by the interests of particular musicians. The St Magnus International Festival in Orkney, for example, was initiated in 1977 by the composer Peter Maxwell Davies, while the pianist Martin Roscoe is artistic director of both the Ribble Valley International Piano Week (started in 1987) and the Beverley Chamber Music Festival (started in 1993). The Gould Piano Trio with clarinettist Robert Plane have staged the Corbridge Chamber Music Festival in Northumberland every year since 1999 and numerous such small, musician-led festivals are held around Britain every summer, providing "a bedrock for classical music programming in Britain outside of London and a very few other major cities" (see Knowles 2015: 211).

Other provincial classical music festivals were put in place by particular venues—the Buxton Festival, for example, was established to mark the opening of the refurbished Buxton Opera House in 1979—and festival programming is essential economically for London venues too. The Southbank Centre's Meltdown Festival, for instance, curated every year since it started in 1993 by a different musical figure (from George Benjamin to M.I.A., from Yoko Ono to Ornette Coleman), is key to the Southbank's audience development policy.

This is one of the more imaginative examples, but there is in fact a long history of arts centres, concert halls and orchestras highlighting some parts of their year-round programming as a "festival". Following the success of Claudio Abbado's 1985 "Mahler, Vienna and the Twentieth Century"

100 *Festival worlds*

concerts and its Leonard Bernstein Festival in 1986, the LSO promoted "a regular stream of starry performers ... a dazzling series of mega-projects, each built round the personal enthusiasms of a 'star' conductor or soloist who would work with the orchestra for a substantial period of time" (Morrison 2004: 206–7, 210). The Scottish National Orchestra's Musica Nova event, announced in 1971 as "a public forum devoted to the rehearsal, discussion and first performance of five newly-commissioned works", was staged annually until 1990 (Noltingk 2017: 129). This was, in effect, a festival for "professional" listeners, for University of Glasgow music students and young Scottish composers. One such composer, Malcolm Hayes, remembers "an atmosphere which ... was very unLondon ... it had more of a holiday feel to it ... and it had that sort of feeling of a congenial gathering" (quoted in Noltingk 2017: 142).

London Sinfonietta developed a variety of festival programmes in the same period. It staged events pairing a well-known composer with a lesser-known one from 1973, musical surveys from 1980 and Stravinsky Festivals in 1979 and 1981. These events were marketed as concerts *plus*—with heavyweight accompanying programme books, for example; by the 1990s, the group was staging weekend events (*Response*; *Explorations*; *State of the Nation*) that "mixed performances with workshops, discussion and a social environment seeking to develop a shared-interest community". Such concerts offered audiences value for money by combining Sinfonietta performances with other activities—an amateur choir singing Eisler songs for an Eisler event, films, experiments in staging choreography (see Wright 2005: 131–2).

The Barbican Centre, meanwhile, staged a Stockhausen Festival in 1984–85 and then, in collaboration with Radio 3, weekend programmes devoted to a particular contemporary composer (Drummond 2000: 338). Glasgow Concert Hall started promoting Celtic Connections in 1994 to fill the scheduling gap in the Hall's post-Christmas bookings calendar; Sage launched the Gateshead International Jazz festival (promoted with Serious Music) in 2005—again, in part, to fill the summer concert gap; the Southbank Centre ran its 2012 The Rest is Noise programme across its 2012 season. Svend Brown, founding artistic director of the East Neuk Festival and Director of Music for Glasgow Life, explained why he launched Minimal, a festival of minimalist music, in the city in 2010:[7]

> Risk is reduced by festival formats. I've always found, regardless of the type of music, that a festival format sells more tickets and gives a better experience than a one-off concert or even series of concerts. This may be because it suggests intensity, unique experiences, one-off collaborations, out-of-the-ordinary excellence all round. Even the most high-profile ensembles have been known to relax a little and offer something they never would normally. That's worth a lot artistically and it rewards the audience too.
>
> (Quoted in Evans 2012: 49)

Festival worlds 101

Chris Sharp, programmer of the Barbican's contemporary seasons, suggests that "the advantage is that it draws attention to something in a way that an isolated event doesn't". For Jude Kelly, then artistic director of the South Bank, "festivals encourage people to have opinions and ideas ... to have conversations with strangers who have shared the journey". For Lorna Clarke, who directed the BBC's Electric Proms, promoted in the Roundhouse from 2006–10 to support new music collaborations in the Radio 6 (rather than Radio 3) world, in a festival "you're taking an artist out of their comfort zone and you're saying 'Try something else that might not work'" (quoted in *Music Week*, October 6, 2007: 10; Sharp and Kelly in Evans 2012: 49).[8]

The BBC's Promenade Concerts at the Albert Hall are the longest and best-known example of festival programming. BBC coverage is significant for the marketing and income models of many festivals, not just Glastonbury. Each year, Radio 3 broadcasts numerous "live recordings from the festival circuit", which includes not only classical music from, say, Edinburgh's Queens Hall or East Neuk, but also performers from WOMAD, Celtic Connections, the London Jazz Festival and many others.

It is clear that, over the last 40 years, festivals (and festival programmes) have become essential to the vitality of classical music for both audiences and performers. Bruno Frey has provided a useful analysis of the economic factors at play here. On the one hand, festival spending can be understood as a form of *holiday* expenditure (as against payment for routine leisure events).[9] Festival goers are therefore willing to pay more than usual for tickets and to take greater risks regarding what they will go to see in what sort of venue. At the same time, festivals offer greater opportunities (and flexibility) for sponsors while additional marketing support may well be provided by tourist boards. Festival directors also have unusual freedom in their concert programming, in terms of both repertoire and the range and combination of musicians employed—musical possibilities are not restricted by orchestral contracts or the working practices of a specific concert hall. Frey suggests that classical music festivals have lower marginal costs than classical music concert halls, and festival directors may also persuade musicians to lower their fees in return for the career opportunities and the publicity offered by festivals. As a special occasion, a festival is likely to generate far more media attention than a concert hall programme. In Frey's (1994, 2000) words, festivals offer an "*extraordinary* cultural experience" (his emphasis) in their unusual settings, limited duration and unique annual line-ups.

The ideology of classical music, the reason people give for making and listening to music live, is its ability to "transcend" the everyday.[10] This is also true for other kinds of audience, of course, but over the 150-year calcification of classical music concerts into the repetition of known works, silent audiences and, by their own admission, jaded orchestral musicians (see Chapter 9), the classical world does sometimes seem to have become synonymous with a suspicion of the new, the difficult or the startling. Classical music festivals, by contrast, are a way of celebrating music (and the people who play and listen

102   *Festival worlds*

to it) in a way that encourages both adventure and argument. Festivals matter here not just economically, but also ideologically.

The folk festival

In the late 1990s, the English Folk Dance and Song Society (EFDSS) estimated that three million people attended folk festivals every summer.[11] As Michael Brocken wrote in 2003:

> The folk music festival has become an extremely important feature of folk music activity in this country. It has matured into possibly the best medium for presenting the eclectic and idiosyncratic in folk music, whilst at the same time drawing attention to the folk scene as an important feeder network. The festival is seen as part of a pyramid organisation the culmination of which is the explosion of performances at places as diverse as Sidmouth, Cambridge, Fylde, Edinburgh, Cleethorpes, Fort William and Pontardawe.
>
> (Brocken 2003: 125)

The folk festival was not just significant for the folk world. It also embodied an argument about musical community that shaped what was meant by the "festival experience" much more broadly. In 1993, after nearly 30 years of running the Cambridge Folk Festival, Ken Woollard tried to pin down its ethos:

> Some people have likened it to a giant folk club, others to a massive village garden fete and others say it's one big party. I lean towards the latter, but it's a party to which everyone is invited.
>
> (Quoted in Laing and Newman 1994: 22)

In other words, folk festivals established the music festival ideal while their organisers were the pioneers in managing the resulting tension with festival reality—the tension, that is, between communal celebration and financial survival. Three overlapping communities were involved here: the people who lived in the locality in which a festival was held; the musicians, performers and festival crew; and the audience.

In Brocken's (2003: 27) view, "there is considerable evidence to suggest that folk festivals serve primarily as entertainments and annual meetings for an audience of mellow, suburban, middle class people who have literally grown up with festivals" but, as Alan Bearman (in Schofield 2004 202), notes, such people were necessary for folk festival economics.[12] They acted as volunteer stewards; they were "the spirit of Sidmouth": "*everyone* sees themselves as an active participant in the event." The Sidmouth Festival, in Colin Irwin's (Schofield 2004: 214) words, "absorbed the entire town for a whole week … there is an irrefutable spirit of belonging". For Janet Dowling (in Schofield 2004: 213), who by 2003 had been attending the Sidmouth Festival

Festival worlds 103

for 27 years, "it's a community that is spread out across the country, it grows and develops."

The Sidmouth festival had initially been set up by the EFDSS in 1955 as a week-long setting for the teaching of traditional English dance. The event was billed as a Folk Dance Festival, and participants were expected to learn the steps well enough to end the week with a public display. In its magazine, *English Dance and Song*, EFDSS described Sidmouth as "an Ideal Place for a Seaside Holiday with Dancing". The event had local council support and used a variety of local performance spaces; it contributed to the town's portfolio of summer entertainment. The festival week has always included the August Bank Holiday (Schofield 2004: 13).

Sidmouth soon became a regular destination for folk fans and by the end of the 1950s the Festival featured song as well as dance and had begun to shift focus from audience participation to professional performance. In 1962 it became the Sidmouth Folk Festival and over the next 20 years took on familiar festival trappings: stalls for the sales of records, song books and musical instruments, tents for local crafts and produce, a variety of outlets for food and drink (Schofield 2004: 177). The BBC started broadcasting festival performances and the musical fare became increasingly varied, including now not just popular singer/songwriters (Ralph McTell's 1984 booking was taken to mark a significant move away from traditional music), but also an increasing number of performers from the UK's multicultural folk traditions, and indeed from outside the English-speaking world. By 1984, the annual gathering was billing itself as the International Festival of Folk Arts while remaining true to its origins as an educational event. It continued to provide workshops and performance spaces for children and young folk artists, and to showcase performers from educational projects such as Folkworks (first established in the north-east of England in 1988).

At the start of the 1980s, there had been a sense of crisis in the folk world, marked by the closure of longstanding folk clubs, the demise of the established magazines *Folk Review* and *Folk News/Acoustic Music* and the folding of the Jean Davenport folk agency. In a new folk title, *Southern Rag*, editor Ian Anderson noted that the decline of folk clubs coincided with the rising numbers of folk festivals and wondered whether "people now preferred to go to a couple of festivals a year rather than a weekly folk club". His co-editor, Lawrence Heath, "observed that folk enthusiasts were not always able to get to a weekly folk club because of family responsibilities, but that they could take the children to a folk festival" (Schofield 2004: 123).

The rising number of folk festivals was a challenge for Sidmouth's organisers. To be competitive, it had to improve its marketing and further broaden its appeal to both disparate folkies and to the wider array of Sidmouth residents and holiday-makers.[13] On the other hand, it was Sidmouth that had established the festival model its competitors were adapting. The Whitby Folk Week, for example, was launched in 1965 as a local authority-supported seaside English dance festival before evolving into a multifaceted

104 *Festival worlds*

charitable event, successfully promoting "song and dance and storytelling" to a holidaying family audience.

Among the many folk and folk-inflected festivals taking place across the UK every summer by the early 2000s, the only one that could seriously claim to occupy Sidmouth's one-time position at the pinnacle of the folk world pyramid was the Cambridge Folk Festival.[14] As Dave Laing explains, "the decision to hold a folk festival in Cambridge was taken in 1964 by a sub-committee of the City Council" (Laing and Newman 1994: 1). But the festival's driving intelligence over the next 30 years was its organiser, Ken Woollard, who died in 1993. He was a local trade union activist and a stalwart of the Cambridge Folk Club (set up in 1964). His vision of what a folk festival should be was informed by two things. The first was his local club experience: the Cambridge Folk Club featured bluegrass as well as traditional English folk musicians. In Woollard's words, "it was a very popular club because it put on everybody". The second was *Jazz on a Summer's Day*, the film of the 1958 Newport Jazz festival (Laing and Newman 1994: 5–6).

It is easy enough to see Cambridge as a celebration of the second folk revival, of the folk clubs of the 1960s, in contrast to Sidmouth, the festival of the EFDSS and the first English folk revival. But while Woollard had to choose headline acts "to attract the widest possible audience, people new to Cambridge as well as the regular festival-goers", his "unique skill in building up the Cambridge bill was in booking those in the middle and lower ranges". In his words, putting together a festival programme "is like furnishing and decorating a room". He looked for "a musical range and for entertainment value", and explained:

> There are NO superstars at Cambridge. If some musical eccentric tickled his fancy during the year they would invariably wind up at Cherry Hinton Hall during the last weekend in July.
>
> (Laing and Newman 1994: 20–1)

By the mid-1980s, and despite their different starting points, the Sidmouth and Cambridge festivals were equally eclectic: Sidmouth routinely billed singer/songwriters and world music stars; Cambridge featured Morris dancers as well as American country acts.[15] Both festivals attracted not just folk club members but also folk club organisers (and BBC folk music producers) looking for acts to book in future months; both festivals gave clubs the opportunity to promote their own evenings or stage. The Cambridge Festival had a club tent. As Lorna Sargeant explained in 1994:

> Each folk club is allotted so many hours each over the weekend. Some of the audience come into the club tent and stay there the whole weekend. It's a place where new talent wants to try its wings in public and sometimes they don't so much fly as plummet!
>
> (Quoted in Laing and Newman 1994: 140)

Festival worlds 105

Cambridge was as proud of its family atmosphere as Sidmouth, and equally dependent logistically on its "family", which provided its volunteer workforce. Derek Batchelor said:

> From being a paying punter [at the Cambridge Festival] I became one of the site crew for many years—a motley bunch who descended on Cherry Hinton Hall the weekend before the Festival and grafted to put the site together. Marquees were erected by professionals but virtually everything else was built by a dedicated band—some working for their food plus a couple of free tickets. Being paid in cash was a dream of the future.
>
> (Quoted in Laing and Newman 1994: 141)

Both festivals were designed to celebrate the craft and the profession of acoustic music-making. Ralph McTell said:

> Folk festivals are a celebration for people who share a love of all types of acoustic music, so you have to retain a certain humility and work just a little bit harder—after all, you are just part of the whole! ... Apart from meeting your fellow professionals and semis, I sometimes get the feeling that half the audience are writers, strummers and pickers too.
>
> (Quoted in Laing and Newman 1994: 147)

If the Sidmouth and Cambridge folk festivals stood out for their comprehensive mapping of the folk world, their influence can be traced across a variety of smaller or more specialist gatherings. Sidmouth's commitment to instruction in traditional music-making is echoed in, for example, the Fèis movement in Scotland. This was launched in Barra in 1981 and over the next decades built up an annual summer series of Gaelic arts and music tuition workshops across Scotland (Martin 2006). The numerous rural folk festivals featured in EFDSS statistics, from Fairport Convention's Cropredy Festival in Oxfordshire (launched in 1976) to Maddy Prior's Stepping Stones Festival in Kirklinton in Cumbria (launched in 2012), were at once celebrations of local crafts, local communities and local produce as well as showcases for the professional and semi-professional music-making networks that Ralph McTell describes. Celtic Connections is not just a series of public concerts but also, like Sidmouth and Cambridge, a meeting place for talent-spotters—for international agents, bookers and promoters.

By the end of the 1990s, "the folk festival" was also the model for a new generation of "boutique" rock festivals, which put an emphasis on audience participation (Robinson 2015). The Green Man Festival, for example, was started by Danny Hagan and Jo Bartlett in 2003 because they wanted "to get a few friends to do a gig in the Brecon Beacons".[16] Their "template" was, in Will Hodgkinson's (2009: 285) words, "an alternative rock and folk festival with an organic, egalitarian appeal".[17] His description of his Green Man

106 *Festival worlds*

experience echoes those of the Sidmouth regulars quoted by Derek Schofield (2004: 285–6, 287):

> The atmosphere was inspiring. The Green Man had a democratic ethos. There was no major separation between artist and festival-goer and no big back stage area to make ticket-payers feel like they were missing out on the action. My dislike of the big festivals is that they turn rock music into a spectator sport in which the audience dumbly consumes as the on-stage acts earn. At The Green Man you felt that being there meant being involved: that this was a community.[18]

But we will end this section with a different kind of musical community, country and western. From 1969–91, Mervyn Conn promoted the annual International Weekend Festival of Country and Western Music at the Wembley Arena. This featured performances from the leading US country stars, but also gave stage space to British country acts and, more entertainingly, floor space to audience members of local C&W clubs who were as interested as dressing up in Western/cowboy outfits as they were in listening to country superstars.

In the 1980s, the Peterborough Country Music Festival was a similar if smaller scale event, launched by Peterborough Council and promoted from 1986–88 by Jeffrey and Howard Kruger. It was held on the August Bank Holiday and billed as "a great day out for all the family".[19] In the 1990s, Billy Kelly, who had been music programmer for Glasgow's Mayfest, launched the Big Big Country Festival in the city. Initially (in 1993) a weekend event, by 1995 it was an 11-day celebration of country music. More eclectic (and hipper) than Wembley in the range of country music covered, and organised more like an arts than a folk festival (using the Royal Concert Hall, the Old Fruitmarket and the Ramshorn Theatre as its venues), the programme featured visiting US stars and "newcomers and local talent", but not shoot-outs. It was well regarded critically but, as Kelly explained, "we can't put this on commercially because, with international travel and concert fees on top of production and promotion costs, it just doesn't add up financially, even allowing for the good ticket sales". It initially had support from the Glasgow City Council but could not attract backing from other funding bodies and did not survive.[20]

Conn revived his Wembley event in 2012, although since 2013 its place has been taken by AEG's Country to Country (C2C) Festival staged at London's O2 and Glasgow's SSE Hydro Arena—which is, in effect, just a way of labelling a routine commercial promotion of contemporary country music recording stars; the survival of UK country music festivals as such lies elsewhere, in the Tavern Country Music Club's annual event at Brean Leisure Park and Sands Holiday Resort in Somerset. This was first staged in the late 1990s and annually "transforms" Brean Sands as "the whole village goes back

Festival worlds 107

in time with Westerners, Mountain Men, Indians [sic] and American Soldiers, many in Authentic regalia". As the Festival advertisements proclaim:

> If you like Country Music and western/line dance then we direct you to the original home of Country Music in Brean, where you can enjoy many of the top Country entertainers from all around Britain.
>
> The park likes to embrace the lifestyle too, and hosts one of the UK's biggest Country and Western market places at our September Festival, where you will be able to buy anything from clothing to footwear and gifts to jewellery.
>
> Everything you could want is here and there is also a variety of activities for everyone to get involved with including line dancing tuition, re-enactments, shoot outs and every night is topped off with a trilogy![21]

There are echoes here of the way the earliest Sidmouth festivals were marketed: a seaside holiday with participatory dancing lessons and display, a chance to dress up in traditional costume, with the involvement of the specialist music clubs, an emphasis on UK acts, and a bill of pro and semi-pro performers. And the whole event—despite its ersatz US Civil War nostalgia— as characteristically English as, say, Morris dancing.

The jazz festival

In their history of the London Jazz Festival, Emma Webster and George McKay (2017: 24) note the

> marked increase in the number of annual jazz festivals in the UK overall: from ten in 1980 to around forty in 1992, including Ealing, Brecon, Birmingham and the Glasgow International Jazz Festival ... [This reflected] the popularity of festivals as tools for local authorities to enhance local identity and for 'destination marketing' ... as cultural regeneration [policies] gained momentum throughout this period.

In *The List*'s 2011 Guide to Scottish Festivals (produced in association with Creative Scotland), 15 jazz events are included, with jazz festivals being held in Aberdeen, Ayr, Callander, Dundee, Edinburgh, Fife, Glasgow, Islay, Kirkcudbright, Lockerbie, Nairn, the "Northern Edge" (various venues in Aberdeenshire), Orkney, Peebles and Skye. There is no doubt that, among other things, these festivals were indeed "tools for local authorities to enhance local identity". As Martin Gayford had commented in the *Spectator* twenty years earlier:

> On and on from June to September [jazz festivals] roll in unbroken sequence, with quite often the same repertory company of musicians appearing at

108 *Festival worlds*

each in turn. Not for the first time I found myself wondering: are the festivals really a blessing or a curse? … It seems against the spirit of the music for it to be provided by every local authority in the land like social workers and floral clocks.

(Quoted in Eales 2017: 85–6)

The British jazz festival thus became, to a surprising extent, an instrument of state cultural promotion. Less surprisingly, this involved contradictory impulses. On the one hand, jazz was understood as art music, and the jazz festival could be understood as a kind of arts festival (the influential Bath European Jazz Weekend, which ran from 1996–2006, was a strand of the Bath International Arts Festival). On the other hand, jazz was still popular music, and a jazz festival was expected to provide a kind of "traditional" good time, whether in pub sessions or as the background sound of "hospitality venues" or public squares. Jazz in these settings is usually music made by amateurs or "semis" rather than by visiting professionals. Such traditional jazz can be as familiar a sound of seaside entertainment as traditional folk music. According to *The List* guide, the Ayr Jazz Festival offered the "jumpin' scenes of the '20s and '30s"; Callander offered jazz cruises around Loch Katrine; Kirkcudbright offered "music to please traditional tastes"; and Peebles offered Dixieland. Since 1988, Bude, the seaside resort in Cornwall, has had an annual festival of "jazz by the sea" and street parades during the August Bank Holiday weekend, while the Isle of Bute has run a traditional jazz festival in the Rothesay Pavilion during the May Day weekend for holiday trippers from Glasgow.[22]

Such a backward-looking view of jazz can't entirely be ignored by the jazz-as-art promoters. Alison Eales quotes from Sue Steward's 1995 *Daily Telegraph* review of the Glasgow International Jazz Festival, in which she criticises the programming:

Sadly, in this country, "summer jazz" is all too often synonymous with that more feeble dilution of the original Dixie sound, "Trad", and treated as an accessory to eating and drinking … Jazz is a new commodity, treasured for its ability to attract tourists: at worst, it is used to boost trade in bars and cafes with Dixieland menus and decor, and a band in the corner of the room.

(Eales 2017: 165–6)

To explore the issues raised here, we will focus on three jazz festivals, Brecon, Glasgow and London, which in some respects exemplify three types of festival promoter—enthusiast, state and commercial—while also illustrating the ways in which these distinctions are blurred in practice.

The Brecon Jazz Festival was first held in 1984 on the initiative of Jed Williams, a stalwart of the Welsh Jazz Society who ran the Four Boats Inn in Cardiff as a jazz pub (with live music seven nights a week) and in 1991 launched the magazine *Jazz UK*. Brecon was a festival promoted by and intended for jazz buffs, with a programme of British musicians and visiting European as well as American jazz acts. It had the support of the Arts Council of Wales but also established what would become the jazz festival norm: an accompanying fringe festival, a series of free gigs featuring local musicians staged around the town in pubs, restaurants and outdoor public places. By the 1990s, Brecon was established as the most significant annual gathering of serious jazz fans in the UK, but in 2008 torrential rain and significant ticket cancellations following the sudden death of headliner Esbjörn Svensson resulted in a major financial loss.[23] The Arts Council of Wales withdrew direct funding support, though it contracted Orchard, a Cardiff-based commercial events promoter, to organise the festival from 2012. (The Hay Festival had stepped in to run it from 2009–11.) In 2015, Orchard decided the contract was financially unviable and since 2016 the festival has been kept going by a combination of the Brecon Jazz Club, Friends of Brecon Jazz, Brecon Cathedral and Thetr Brycheiniog.[24]

For many of its regular visitors, the Brecon Jazz Festival remains a model of what a jazz festival should be. Created by an enterprising enthusiast (Jed Williams died in 2003), it was a festival that celebrated both dedicated British jazz musicians and dedicated British jazz fans; it was concerned to nurture innovative music as well as to honour jazz history, and for a time it was remarkably successful in balancing the expectations of the Arts Council of Wales and the cultural and financial interests of the town in which it was held. As shown by the commitment of the people who have kept it going for the last decade, Brecon exemplifies what is meant by "a much loved festival".

The Glasgow International Jazz Festival (GIJF) was launched in 1987, but its origins couldn't be more different. Its starting point was a meeting of senior executives from the Scottish Development Agency and the Glasgow Tourist Board who believed, in Alison Eales' words, that "Glasgow needed a new identity—one that would bring new economic opportunities" and that "culture had a key role to play, particularly in terms of improving the city's image" (Eales 2017: 10). A jazz festival seems to have been chosen to meet this policy aim, partly because the chair of the SDA liked jazz and partly because a jazz festival was thought to be a way in which a would-be European city could establish its cultural prestige (Edinburgh already had one). A Jazz Festival Committee was formed:

> At the initial meeting, the name, timing and length of the Festival were determined, along with four main aims: to establish Glasgow as 'a major European jazz centre'; to grow the local audience (particularly the youth audience) for jazz; to attract tourism to Glasgow; and to provide employment opportunities for local professional jazz musicians. Additionally, the Festival's artistic policy was determined: the word 'jazz' was to be interpreted widely, with an international programme representing all styles of jazz.
>
> (Eales 2017: 79–80)

110　*Festival worlds*

The Glasgow Jazz Festival was to be, in the words of Glasgow tourism boss Eddie Friel, "as inclusive as possible" with no "audience sector who felt that they were being left out" and "it was agreed that the new Festival's activities should take place all over the city, encompassing pubs as well as concert halls" (Eales 2017: 79–80). On the other hand, as Bill Sweeney (the Musicians' Union representative on the Jazz Festival Board) remembers:

> Right from the start, it was clear that this was not just enthusiasts wanting to have a jazz festival. … People who were not present were people who ran what Andy Park used to refer to as the traditional Saturday afternoon out-of-tune big band … Certainly in the first four or five years, there was a fair bit of disgruntlement amongst some of the local jazzers, who found that it did create a bit of work around it, the main Festival itself, but it was off the main stages …
>
> (Quoted in (Eales 2017: 102–3)

In Eales' (2017) definitive history of GIJF's first 30 years, two problems stand out. The first is how to establish festival *space*. The folk festival, as we have seen, is a celebration of a real or imaginary rural setting. As Chris Anderton (2018: 117) remarks, while the Cambridge Folk Festival takes place in a suburb of a university city:

> The festival's official website and photo galleries represent it as a leafy, green, outdoor event, with many photographs showing the woods, the nature reserve, the campsites, and festival-goers involved in yoga and tai chi in the grounds. The suburban location is downplayed in favour of a natural, countryside image, further enhanced by photographs of traditionally-dressed Morris dancers, amateur musicians playing acoustic instruments in the park, and children playing with simple toys or paddling in the stream … The focus on the physical environment of the festival is also given preference in television coverage of the event, where interviews with performers are conducted in part of the nature reserve at the rear of the site. This alludes to an imagined history of folk music as simple, rural, close to nature, non-commercial and authentic, even though the genre has been reliant on commercial exploitation and mediation for its success since the 1950s.

The large jazz festival, by contrast, celebrates the city and jazz as a metropolitan music; rather than being focused on one dedicated site, jazz festival performances tend to be spread through a variety of venues.[25] The problem here, as Eales (2017: 238, author's emphasis) argues, is how to *occupy* a complex urban geography: "this can mean the difference between a bona fide *festival* and something which might be better described as a concert series: it is crucial to try to 'control the space between gigs'". While it can point to

Festival worlds 111

the successful development of the Old Fruitmarket as a core festival venue, overall GIJF failed to establish a clear or stable spatial presence in the city.

The second question is how to resolve the contradictory festival aims of attracting high spending tourists and supporting local music-making. This became the central programming issue. In Eales' (2017: 107) words, "at the core of the programme was a small number of high-profile concerts by internationally-famous jazz acts", while local musicians often found themselves playing in pubs or bars in which people had no interest in the etiquette or economics of a jazz performance.

GIJF organisers were having to deal here with the incompatible demands of their funders, the Scottish Arts Council and various local authorities, on the one hand, and those of their corporate sponsors on the other.[26] These issues came to a head during the Royal Bank of Scotland's title sponsorship, from 2002 to 2005. Olive May Millen resigned from her position as artistic director in 2004 saying, according to *The Scotsman*, that "the event is becoming too populist" (quoted in Eales (2017: 199). The problem, as her successor Jill Rodger explains, was that RBS demanded "complete control over everything" and it was "hard when they're waving a huge cheque in front of you; it's really hard. And the Board was obviously saying, 'Well, it's your call but …'." Rodger found herself stuck with a deficit from a concert RBS had demanded:

> They wanted a specific artist on a certain night in the Armadillo as their Branch Managers' event and the only way to get that artist was to *pay*, and it didn't sell. Well it sold, but not well enough, so there's a deficit I'm dragging around with me every year from that one concert. And that was sponsor led (Rodger's italics).[27]

A further problem with this sponsorship was that:

> [The RBS] wanted to see popular programming and bums on seats and that's what we did. We had great audience figures but these possibly were not the type of people that the Arts Council feels it wants to support.
> (quoted in Eales 2017: 201)

The Scottish Arts Council was concerned not only about the quality of the festival's concerts but also about the connection of its events to its local communities. While the Festival had included education and outreach activities from the start—the establishment of the Strathclyde Youth Jazz Orchestra was one of its lasting successes—Eales shows that the extent of these activities became a point of contention in the 2000s when some board members felt, like the sponsors, that more of the festival's resources should be being invested in the big stars who supposedly attracted visitors (Eales 2017: 204).

The London Jazz Festival (LJF) faced similar problems, but resolved them with rather more panache. Its starting point was also a feeling that London

112 *Festival worlds*

ought to have a jazz festival as an expression of its international cultural status; however, the impetus here was provided not by state bureaucrats but, as at Brecon, by remarkably energetic jazz promoters, John Cumming and David Jones, whose "aim was to create a London Jazz Festival that both reflected and contributed to London's status as a world city, as well as functioning as a kind of cultural melting pot" (Webster and McKay 2017: 4).

Cumming, also inspired by the film *Jazz on a Summer's Day*, had extensive experience as a theatre and music tour producer, and during a stint as theatre director at the South Hill Park's Art Centre in Berkshire had developed the Bracknell Jazz Festival, which ran from 1975–87.[28] He also worked as a concert programmer for the Jazz Centre Society and in 1978 was employed on a freelance basis to produce the Camden Jazz Week (which ran from 1974–92). In 1986, Cumming set up Serious Productions as a tour production company. Jones also had a theatre as well as a music background. From 1984–87, he had programmed the Bloomsbury Theatre's Bloomsbury Festival and in 1987 he started the Crossing the Border festival of World Music in Camden. While working for the Bloomsbury Theatre, he had set up Speakout as a production company.

In 1989, Serious and Speakout joined forces in a successful bid to Greater London Arts Authority's Major Concert Promotion Fund for support in running the Moving Forward series of concerts of international jazz and contemporary art music. When Cumming and Jones began planning a London Jazz Festival, they already had extensive experience of working with and for the state cultural sector at both the national and local levels.

There were other important contextual difference between the London and Glasgow jazz festivals. To begin with, London already had a promoter (George Wein) bringing in big US jazz names for the Capital/JVC Jazz Festivals that ran from 1979–97.[29] The LJF had to establish itself as a different kind of jazz festival. And while it is, like GIJF, "an umbrella festival", staging a variety of events in a variety of venues, the vitality of the London jazz scene means, as Webster and McKay suggest, that the festival can act as an "amplifier", bringing attention and new audiences to existing jazz spaces (Webster and McKay 2017: 77).

In other words, the London Jazz Festival had to address the same issues as the GIJF but was in a much better position to do so. One of the initial funding conditions of the London Arts Board, for example, was that as well bringing high-level international jazz into London, the festival would also draw on the grassroots of the scene and highlight London's significance as a year-round music city. This provided the impetus for the festival to involve the diverse communities of London, not least by commissioning new music and encouraging new collaborations. This was an approach Cumming and Jones had brought into their previous music promotions from their theatre experience.

LJF also found it much easier to establish a reasonably stable sponsorship base. The BBC was engaged with the festival from the start and Radio 3 had a direct sponsorship role from 2001–12. Oris, the Swiss watch firm that was title sponsor from 1995–98, was influential in attracting other such international corporate sponsors (EFG, a private Swiss bank, was title sponsor from 2013–16); by the time the Oris deal came to an end, the income from commercial sponsors matched that from state funders. The relative stability of its core funding enabled Serious to employ staff to develop its outreach and educational ideas. Claire Whitaker joined Cumming and Jones as a festival co-director in 1996, and took charge of fundraising strategies, the festival's learning programme and other special projects. Debbie Dickinson, who ran the development agency Jazz Moves, was taken on as a freelance festival coordinator to look after the grassroots programme.

In their celebratory history of Serious and the London Jazz Festival, Webster and McKay (2017: 91, their italics) suggest that, "rather than being *caught* between the art and commercial worlds, Serious have instead managed to create a model that is able to glide *between* worlds with confidence". By balancing box office income, state funding and commercial sponsorship, Serious didn't have to "over-rely on one income stream" (2017: 42). It is, then, an enthusiast *and* a commercial promoter, which is what enables it to act so effectively as a state promoter too. One example of this can be seen in LJF's commitment to bringing in European jazz acts: this is obviously an aspect of the festival's music policy, but it also opens up another line of sponsorship from European cultural agencies. A similar approach, combining artistic and financial considerations, is followed by the Edinburgh International Festival.

In the end, the continuing success of LJF *as a festival* is an effect of Serious's self-conscious role as a live music *producer* (Cumming and Jones prefer this label to "promoter").[30] It is their active curation of the shows they stage that leads to performances that otherwise wouldn't happen, that are not "just another concert". But one reason Serious can do this is because it is, so to speak, the Live Nation of the jazz world. Cumming also programmes the Gateshead International Jazz Festival at the Sage and the Love Supreme Festival at Glynde on the South Downs; Serious runs the Barbican's jazz series and its own year-round national touring programme.[31] As Serious states on its website:

> Serious is a unique force in the field of live music.
>
> The company makes a major contribution to the arts world through a national programme that is internationally recognised, working with a network of partners to ensure the greatest reach for our work; on average each year we produce **over 630 events**, work with **over 2,600 artists**, reach live audiences of **over 250,000** in **over 300 venues**, and have a broadcast reach of **over 44 million**.
>
> (See https://serious.org.uk/what-we-do; their use of bold)

Serious produces events from international festivals to small club gigs; it engages in learning and participation activities through workshops and training programmes; its professional development programme includes artist

114 *Festival worlds*

management and publishing. The success of the London Jazz Festival is one effect of Serious's domination of Britain's live jazz business.[32]

Conclusion

By 2015, music festivals were centrally important both culturally and economically to all British music worlds. In everyday conversation, however (and in the pages of *Music Week*), the term "music festival" was still usually taken to mean a rock festival and the best-known rock festivals were still Glastonbury (which originated in the folk world) and Reading (which had begun by staging jazz and blues).

The period of this book is the period when Glastonbury shook loose from its free-festival trappings and became more professional:

> Looking back on it now you can't quite believe it, but throughout the 1980s CND was selling all the tickets for the festival ... We were responsible for counting all the ticket money. We used to be in these horrible little caravans stuck at various points behind the gates, with all the windows sealed. It was really the most disgusting working conditions, really hot and then people would walk in with thousands of pounds. You'd have a table with it all spread out and we'd be counting all through the night. And then these guys would turn up with tool boxes, like they were mechanics working on the site, and we'd put the money in them ... Then they'd go up to the farmhouse where there was this elderly accountant sitting in Michael's living room who was bagging and banking all the cash.
> (CND's Janet Convery, quoted in Aubrey and Shearlaw 2005: 94)

When Melvin Benn (then working for the Workers Beer Company) first started his Glastonbury visits:

> It was a very strange place to come down to ... You basically entered a bartering culture ... and your first impression was that the franchises and security were a nightmare, the organisation was chaotic. It was totally different from the normal structure at a big event.
> (Quoted in Aubrey and Shearlaw 2005: 123)[33]

By 2002, as we noted in Chapter 5, Benn (now working for Mean Fiddler) had acquired 40% of the Glastonbury Festival and taken charge of its organisation. Chaos was no longer the best way of dealing with the licensing process following years of onsite drug dealing, violence and gatecrashing, culminating in the fence-breaking crush of 2000, and over the next decade Glastonbury became more significant as an annual date for the music business and the BBC than for political activists or the disaffected. As executive Jeff Smith explained to *Music Week* (July 4, 2009), the BBC saw Glastonbury coverage

Festival worlds 115

as an opportunity to raise its profile: "what Glastonbury will do is grow awareness of 6 Music".[34] In Caitlin Moran's words:

> Within the music business itself it's seen as everybody's holiday, like a weekend in the country, the only fresh air that anybody in Soho sees all year. It's a chance to see the bands they'd never get to watch otherwise
>
> (Quoted in Aubrey and Shearlaw 2005: 266)

By the start of the new century, Mean Fiddler also ran the Reading Festival (which in 1999 had become the Reading and Leeds Festival, repeating its programme across two sites). Unlike Glastonbury, though, the Reading Festival hardly seemed to change at all. What the *Daily Telegraph*'s Patrick Smith wrote of the 2014 event could have been applied to the 1994 or even 1984 event:

> Think of the Reading festival these days and one tends to picture large swarms of lager-throwing teenagers running amok in a field, celebrating their exam results to loud and primal alternative music.[35]

In 1993, the writer Andrew Collins admitted that:

> Over that bank holiday I came to realise why, sometimes, Reading is better than Glastonbury. Sure it lacks ley-lines and healing fields and men on stilts, but that merely concentrates the mind. It's all about the music. It has to be. It has nothing else to offer.
>
> (Quote from Carroll 2007: 102)

Ten year later, after playing Reading with his indie rock band The Ordinary Boys, Preston remarked:

> I think the thing about Reading is it is probably the most unpretentious festival there is. The kids go there because there are bands on the list they want to see. The people that organise it know that so they book the bands that people want to see and stay one step ahead of the "trends" or they bypass the trends completely.
>
> (Quote from Carroll 2007: 155)

Glastonbury and Reading were both rock festivals and many bands have appeared on both their bills, but they offered different sorts of rock festival experiences. Andrew Collins thus celebrates Reading's ease of access:

> You can turn up by train and walk to the site. Equally, as I did when the storm clouds formed overhead the year previously, you can walk off the site without a moment's forward planning and get the hell out of there.
>
> (Quote from Carroll 2007: 102)

116 *Festival worlds*

Billy Bragg, however, praises Glastonbury's sense of separation:

> What makes Glastonbury unique among the major rock festivals is that the site is miles away from anywhere. It's not tacked on to a dormitory town or in a purpose-built arena. There's no cosy link with civilisation. The challenge of how to get here is the same for stars and punters alike ... and once you're there you're there. There's no point in trying to come and go as you please.
>
> (Quoted in Aubrey and Shearlaw 2005: 166)

In Chapter 5 we showed how music festivals came to be understood as commodities in the leisure market; in the 2000s, rock and pop festivals thus began to sell themselves by reference to unique selling propositions (USPs), which couldn't just be the musical offering as that was much the same from one festival to another. And so Rockness claimed to be "arguably the most beautiful festival in the world", Guilfest was "a festival held in a park not a field" and Latitude was "not only a festival but a holiday destination" (quotes from *Music Week*, September 26, 2009: 14).

These quotes are taken from a *Music Week* feature on festival PR. "The plethora of festivals means that promoters and the PR professionals representing them have to fight increasingly hard to make themselves heard." Stuart Galbraith told the paper that:

> Festivals have become a rite of passage—you finish your exams, leave school and go to festivals. And now what you've got is the industry starting to capture customers from as early as the age of 10, with festivals like Underage and Camp Bestival, all the way through to 40-, 50-, 60-year-olds.
>
> (Quotes from *Music Week*, September 26, 2009: 17)

In his excellent analysis of the V Festival (promoted by SJM/Metropolis), Chris Anderton (2018: 122) explains the promoters' thinking:

> the target market for the event was 16–34-year-olds: a mix of those attending their first music festival, and older professionals who may have grown up with rock music, but now sought a festival with a varied musical bill and a higher level of service provision than was available in the past.

SJM's Andy Redhead explained:

> We place ourselves in the middle ground as far as festivals go. We are not a "hippy" or "rock" festival, rather a festival for people who want to have a great weekend and see and hear good music in a safe environment.
>
> (Anderton (2018: 122)

Festival worlds 117

In this chapter we have shown that festivals are shaped by the musical cultures from which they spring. The variety of immersive rock festival experiences on offer thus reflect promoters' readings of the varied and sometimes contradictory expectations of their audiences. An illuminating academic study of drug and alcohol use at a 2008 Scottish music festival—presumably T in the Park—suggests that the festival experience here could be described as "controlled hedonism within a situation traditionally associated with unrestrained excess" (Martinus et al. 2010). And director Sofia Olins describes her film *Lost in Vagueness*, shot over 12 years on the Lost Vagueness site at Glastonbury, as a journey from "anti-society DIY debauchery" to "prescribed corporate anarchy", a shift that she suggests is indicative of Britain's modern [rock] festival culture.[36]

The changes described here are in part demographic: one sector of the rock festival audience is made up of established attenders growing older, more staid and more affluent; another sector is young people attending a festival for the first time. Festivals like Reading and Glastonbury can therefore be differentiated by reference to their demographic focus. But we will end this chapter with a different point. In 1993, the Reading Festival featured a Subterranean Dance Stage for the first time. Glastonbury opened its dance tent in 1995 (it became a Dance Village in 2005 and was renamed Silver Hayes in 2013). In 1998, the first Creamfields festival was held on August Bank Holiday in Winchester. What began as a one-day dance event attracting 25,000 people moved the next year to the old Liverpool Airport before becoming an annual four-day event (with camping) on the Daresbury estate in Cheshire. In the next chapter, we turn to dance culture and the dance business.

Notes

1 Quoted in Schofield (2004: 213).

2 From an interview with Matt Brennan, June 5, 2009.

3 For details of the BDC see www.bdconline.org/about_bdc

4 For the significance of international music competitions in the classical world, see McCormick (2015). The Cardiff Singer of the Year was renamed BBC Singer of the World in 2003.

5 Actually, as Richard Witts (2015: 9) argues, Cheltenham—which not only "initiated the post-war arts festival movement" (in 1945) but also, in its dedication to *new* British music, was "the first European town to construct its postwar identity using modernist music"—was a local rather than national initiative, although the Borough Council was less concerned to "raise revenue out of a slim body of [visiting] enthusiasts" than "to retain their town's brand as an elitist enclave".

6 Other notable festivals of "brave new music" are Arika in Glasgow (since 2001), Reverb in London (since 2010), and Ilan Volkov's Tectonics, originating in Iceland and staged annually in various countries, including Scotland, from 2013.

7 Glasgow Life is the charity that delivers "cultural, sporting and learning activities on behalf of Glasgow City Council". The East Neuk Chamber Music Festival started in 2004.

118   *Festival worlds*

8 The event was dropped following BBC budget cutbacks. In 2019, Lorna Clarke was appointed the BBC's Director of Pop.
9 All Tomorrow's Parties, which promoted festivals between 2001 and 2012, when it was put into liquidation, staged its events at Pontins and Butlin's holiday camps.
10 This was one finding from our audience studies at Edinburgh's Queen's Hall—see Behr, Brennan and Cloonan (2016).
11 The EFDSS claim is mentioned in Brocken (2003: 129), but neither the source nor its date is given. In 1982 the EFDSS's *Folk Directory* listed 60 festivals, though there were undoubtedly many more (Schofield 2003: 123). The 2003 MHM report on the impact of folk festivals on cultural tourism suggested that there were now 350 annual folk festivals, "a key sector in the UK's creative economy", but with a total attendance of only 350,000 (Morris Hargreaves McIntyre 2004: 3–4).
12 Alan Bearman programmed the Sidmouth Festival from 1987–2004, when he formed his own agency, going on to represent many of the UK's leading folk artists.
13 Derek Schofield (2004: 145) describes what this meant in terms of management, programming, ticketing and the use of venues—1987 was the key year of change.
14 The Sidmouth Festival folded in 2004 when East Devon District Council withdrew funding support. Festival losses following the appalling weather conditions during the 1997 event had left the organisers with no reserves. In 2005, a Sidmouth Folk Week was organised by a variety of local folk musicians and clubs and by 2018 this was successful enough to take on the name of the Sidmouth Folk Festival again.
15 For an account of the Cambridge Folk Festival in the 2000s see Anderton 2019: 114–9.
16 The Hagans sold their shares in the festival in 2011; it has since been run by Fiona Stewart.
17 The Green Man template was "copied and commercialized elsewhere", by various other festivals that appeared and disappeared during the 2000s (Hodgkinson 2015: 285).
18 Compare the Fence Collective's even more egalitarian (and intimate) Homegame and Away Game Festivals, staged in Anstruther and the Isle of Eigg since 2004 (see Lynch and Larsen 2014).
19 Quote taken from http://jeffreykruger.com/peterborough_country_music_festival.html
20 Quotes from John Williamson's report in the *Glasgow Herald*, May 28, 1997.
21 Quotes taken from the Brean Sands and Brean websites, www.breansandscaravans.com/brean-sands/country-music-festival.asp;   www.brean.com/country-festivals. A "trilogy" in this context is a ritual participatory performance of "Dixie", "Battle Hymn of the Republic" and "All My Trials", in which the dead of the US Civil War are honoured and mourned.
22 Even a musically wide-ranging jazz festival such as Scarborough (launched in 2002) has a strong component of jazz nostalgia—this was certainly an aspect of my experience of attending the Scarborough Jazz Festival in 2014 (SF).
23 Swedish pianist Svensson died in a scuba diving accident.
24 Information taken from a Radnor Express 2017 story: www.brecon-radnor.co.uk/article.cfm?id=104860&headline=Brecon%20Jazz%20no%20longer%20viable,%20says%20study&sectionIs=news&searchyear=2017.

Festival worlds 119

25 Rock and pop festival promoters have also been using this model in recent years—for example, Brighton's Great Escape, Liverpool's Sound City, Sheffield's Tramlines and Cardiff's Sŵn Festival.
26 GIJF's problems with sponsors were exacerbated by BBC Scotland's lack of support.
27 Quotes taken from an interview with Emma Webster, October 30, 2009. The artist was Dionne Warwick. The Royal Bank of Scotland was at this time in full macho-expansionist mode. Its financial collapse began a couple of years later.
28 Information about Cumming, Jones and the LJF taken primarily from Webster and McKay (2017).
29 Live Nation started promoting a similar London Jazz and Blues Festival in 2011.
30 It should also be noted here that Cumming and Jones started out with an eclectic, open-minded and remarkably generous understanding of "jazz".
31 There are other examples of jazz promoter ubiquity, if on a smaller scale. Jim Smith, who was director of GIJF from 1990–92, established the Cheltenham Jazz Festival in 1996; Roger Spence, who established the Scottish jazz promotion companies Platform in the 1970s and Assembly in the 1980s, programmed the first Glasgow Jazz Festival as well as later running the Edinburgh Jazz Festival.
32 John Cumming "stepped back" as a director of Serious in 2019: https:// efglondonjazzfestival.org.uk/news/2019/john-cumming. He died in 2020.
33 The Workers Beer Company was set up as a trading arm of the Battersea and Wandsworth Trade Union Council to provide supplies to bars at music festivals.
34 Jeff Smith has been head of music at BBC Radio 2 and 6 Music since 2007.
35 Quote taken from a festival retrospective in the *Telegraph* magazine: www.telegraph.co.uk/music/jazz/reading-festival-history-and-timeline.
36 See www.theguardian.com/music/2018/apr/28/leaving-lost-in-vagueness-glastonbury-pioneers-hedonism-documentary.

A snapshot of live music in Glasgow in October–November 2007

"Enthusiastic, vociferous and utterly magnificent" was how the *Rough Guide to the World* described Glasgow's gig scene in 2007. Stretching "from gritty pubs to arty student haunts, marvellous church halls to cavernous arenas", Glasgow was hailed as "Europe's rock music capital", with the Barrowland Ballroom in the city's East End singled out as the venue that "really defines the city" (Horne 2007). By the late 2000s, Glasgow was one of the major touring cities in the UK, forming the top of a touring "backbone" that snaked up the centre of the UK (Laing 2008). The largest venue in the city was the Scottish Exhibition and Conference Centre (SECC)[1] and some of the artists appearing in October and November included Arcade Fire (Friday October 26, £23), 50 Cent (Thursday November 8, £30) and The Sex Pistols (Sunday November 18, £35). The Barrowland welcomed Super Furry Animals (Thursday October 18, £17.50), Calvin Harris (Saturday November 10), and saw two sold-out shows by Amy Winehouse (Friday 16/Saturday 17 November, £20), her first gigs after being booed off stage in Birmingham earlier in the week ("Winehouse in Glasgow for concert" 2007). Another "must-do" venue according to the *Rough Guide* (Horne 2007) was King Tut's, which opened in 1990 and was famously the venue where Oasis were spotted and signed by Creation Records' Alan McGee. In 2007, King Tut's was putting on music virtually every night, ranging from indie, rock and dance to singer/songwriters and folk rock from both local and out-of-town artists, including Oceansize (Sunday October 7), Acoustic Ladyland (Tuesday October 9, £8) and Icelandic post-folk experimentalists Amina and Josh Geffin (Thursday November 1, £10).

Less iconic perhaps, but now an important part of the touring network, was the Carling (now O2) Academy, part of Academy Music Group. Some of the highlights in late 2007 were Manu Chao (Wednesday October 10, £15), Underworld (Saturday October 13, sold out), The Verve's first gig in nine years (Friday November 2, £29.50), and The Proclaimers (Thursday November 15, £22.50). The universities of Glasgow and Strathclyde and their respective unions were also still occasional live music venues, with Glasgow's Queen Margaret Union (QMU) putting on The Maccabees (Wednesday October 3, £10) and the university's Gilmorehill Theatre putting on Adele (Tuesday

October 9, £5).[2] Strathclyde's Ramshorn Theatre hosted classical lunchtime concerts, and its Crawfurd Café was one of a number of venues putting on Oxjam charity events in October 2007. At the ABC on Sauchiehall Street,[3] out-of-town visitors included Americans Ani Difranco and Hamell On Trial (Sunday October 7, £17.50), Liverpool's The Coral (Saturday October 20, £16) and London's Dizzee Rascal (Wednesday October 31, £13.50).

Sauchiehall Street's independent venue-nightclub-café-bar Nice'N'Sleazy welcomed both Glasgow-based Zoey Van Goey (Saturday October 13) and Sheffield-based solo artists Stoney and Neil McSweeney (Saturday October 27), and also ran a regular (free) acoustic jam session every Monday evening. Other venues putting on rock and pop at the time included Bloc, Brel, Blackfriars, the Cathouse, The Ferry, the Garage, Barfly and Òran Mór, a converted church in Glasgow's West End, now a theatre-venue-club-bar.

Many of these "live" music venues also held club nights following the gigs to supplement income—which may be why local music magazine *The Skinny* described Glasgow's club calendar at this time as "congested" (McNamara 2007). One of the major nightclubs was The Arches, a bar, arts venue, theatre, live music venue and nightclub built into railway arches underneath Glasgow Central Station.[4] Illustrating the diversity of programming, highlights included minimal techno-ist Murcof (Sunday October 7, £8.50), hard house DJ Judge Jules (Saturday October 13, £19), P-funk legend George Clinton (Sunday November 4, £17.50) and modern composer Max Richter (Thursday November 22, £14.50). One of the longest-running clubs in the city was Pressure, the monthly Detroit techno and electro night, which celebrated its ninth birthday at the Arches with Laurent Garnier and Billy Nasty (Friday November 30, £20). Other clubs included Merchant City's Byblos, which by the late 2000s had become one of the main hang-outs for the city's young African Caribbean population (Campbell 2010).

After several "tumultuous" years following a long period of financial trouble (Westphal 2007), Scottish Opera appointed new music director Francesco Corti in August 2007; its Autumn/Winter 2007 season at Glasgow's Theatre Royal included Rossini's *Barber of Seville* and Mozart's *Seraglio* (both £58–£9). The King's Theatre was the main venue for musical theatre with *Blood Brothers* (October 1–13, £29–£10.50), a Glasgow Light Opera Club performance of *Fiddler on the Roof* (October 23/27, £18–£10) and Andrew Lloyd-Webber's *Aspects of Love* (October 30/November 3, £30–£13).

Glasgow's Royal Concert Hall (est. 1990) was the home of the Royal Scottish National Orchestra (RSNO) and the predominant venue for classical music in Glasgow in 2007. The venue also hosted rock, pop, jazz and folk, and is still one of the main venues for January's Celtic Connections festival (est. 1994) and June's Glasgow Jazz Festival (est. 1987). The nearby City Halls complex in Merchant City was and still is the home of the BBC Scottish Symphony Orchestra, and also the site of the Old Fruitmarket, another venue for rock, pop and jazz; the complex reopened in January 2006 after undergoing a period of extensive renovation.

122 *Snapshot: Glasgow October–November 2007*

Glasgow's traditional/folk scene was going strong in 2007, with much of the action taking place in pubs including Babbity Bowster, Jinty McGinty's and the Three Judges, but also in the National Piping Centre and St Andrew's in The Square, Glasgow's centre of Scottish culture. To celebrate 2007's St Andrew's Day (Friday November 30), St Andrew's in The Square held a "five-day feast" of traditional music, song and dance, alongside a massive free *ceilidh* in the city centre's George Square and country dancing at Sloans (Davidson 2007). The Grand Ole Opry, Glasgow's largest country and western club, was still a feature of the city's live music scene.

Notes

1 This riverside complex was augmented in 2013 with a purpose-built 13,000-capacity music venue, the SSE Hydro.
2 See www.thesun.co.uk/archives/music/90624/mind-that-time-adele-played-a-gig-in-her-jeans.
3 The ABC was taken over by Academy Music Group in 2009 and renamed O2 ABC; it was extensively damaged by fire in 2018.
4 The Arches had its licence removed in 2015 and it closed permanently later the same year (Gardner 2015) following police complaints about drug usage.

Bibliography

The majority of listings data was taken from the October and November 2007 editions of *The Skinny*.

Campbell, Graham (2010) Personal interview with Emma Webster, 22 February.

Davidson, Vicky (2007) "10 things to do for St Andrew's Day", Evening Times, November 28: 27.

Gardner, Lyn (2015) "The closure of the Arches in Glasgow will be felt around the world", The Guardian, June 10, www.theguardian.com/stage/theatreblog/2015/jun/10/arches-glasgow-theatre-closure. Accessed April 2, 2019.

"Glasgow" (2019) UNESCO Cities of Music website, https://citiesofmusic.net/city/glasgow. Accessed March 27, 2019.

Horne, Marc (2007) "Glasgow will rock you like no other city, says Rough Guide", *Scotland on Sunday*, November 4: 12.

Laing, Dave (2008) "Gigographies", paper presented to IASPM UK and Ireland Conference, Glasgow, September 12–14.

McNamara, Sean (2007) "The art of parties", *The Skinny*, October: 47.

Westphal, Matthew (2007) "Scottish Opera, on the mend, appoints new music director", *Playbill*, August 8, www.playbill.com/news/article/6901.html. Accessed March 27, 2019.

"Winehouse in Glasgow for concert" (2007) The Herald, November 17: 8.

7   DJ business

Today in the London listings magazines, there are four very full pages devoted to charting the turbulent sea of the night: five years ago there were none. Not only have the number of clubs and clubbers continued to grow at a remarkable rate, but there has also been a general realisation that the culture of young London—and in many ways the culture of young Britain—is now a nightclub culture.

(Robert Elms, *The Face*, 37, 1988)[1]

Remember I fought against disco all my life, and this battle against disco had gone on and on, but the real moment for me was staring down from the DJ box one night when Mike Pickering was DJ-ing and suddenly going "Oh, fuck, now I get it": the democracy of the art experience, it's everybody—it's the people who made the record, it's the DJ, it's everybody dancing!

(Tony Wilson, quoted in Haslam 2002: 297)

Choose disc. Place on turntable. Put the needle to the record. Become deified and immensely rich ... Why?

(Kevin Le Gendre, *The Observer* June 11, 2000)[2]

Introduction

In *Generation Ecstasy*, a celebration of club music in the 1990s, Simon Reynolds (1998: 7) remarks that, "for the newcomer to electronic dance music, the profusion of scenes and sub-genres can seem at best bewildering, at worst wilful obfuscation". In this chapter, we will not attempt to tell the story of 1990s dance music genre by genre. Our focus is on broader issues.

The general development of electronic dance music was, to begin with, clearly driven by technology. Bennett (2000: 77) writes that it was the emergence of digital recording in the early 1980s that laid the "crucial foundations" for the urban dance scene, not just because of the new kinds of sound manipulation it made possible but also because, following the introduction of MIDI equipment, studio-quality recording could take place pretty well anywhere. Drum'n'bass, for example,

124 *DJ business*

Came about partly due to the Akai S1000 sampler. Launched in 1989, it gave breakbeat pioneers access to techniques that were previously only available in the most hi-tech expensive recording studios, enabling them to manipulate their sampled beats as never before.

(Garratt 1998: 276)

Dance thus became a setting for DIY music-making. For Norman Cook (aka DJ Fatboy Slim), this "DIY attitude" was a continuity of the punk ethos:

An irreverence to the rules, like you can make a record that's really repetitive and isn't very musical and was made at home in your bedroom and doesn't have any chords, drummers, singers, or anyone who can read a musical note.

(Quoted in Brewster and Broughton 2010: 414)

And this is fellow DJ Terry Farley, reflecting in 2009 on the cultural effects of acid house:

It helped push music technology forward. Everyone said it had a great social effect, I don't really think it did. The biggest effect it had was the push and development of music hardware, firstly, and then software. Kids were going out and hearing those records and wanting to make them themselves. I would imagine those that went to those early clubs ended up, a good proportion of them, being involved in music technology. That lit the blue paper for where we are now where we can sit here and make tracks on our laptops. That's what acid house is. It had a few momentary social consequences, like the poll tax riots and the club laws, but it was only made political by the press.

(Quoted in Brewster and Broughton 2010: 379)

Farley might be right that the social consequences of acid house were "momentary", but in that moment the dancers' use of ecstasy was as significant as dance music producers' use of technology. In 1988's "Second Summer of Love", rave events seemed to offer dancers a glimpse of utopia, transforming, "Mundane Britain, with its dreary metropolitan thoroughfares and placid country lanes, into a cartography of adventure and forbidden pleasures" (Reynolds 1998: 9).

Ecstasy was the "happy drug". It turned hooligans into "love thugs" and brought working-class hedonists and sexual bohemians into dance-floor harmony. Suddenly, as Peter Hook (Hook 2009: 191) puts it, "indie kids were dancing too" and the Haçienda DJ Mike Pickering was playing to "an amiable mix of estate kids, students and trendies" (Garratt 1998: 206). For Dave Haslam:

The vibe was so intense, the club so packed, the music just so pure, fresh and mindblowing; DJ-ing at the Haçienda in 1988, 1989 and 1990 was fantastic. It was an unmediated experience. It didn't feel second-hand,

DJ business 125

it wasn't forced, it had no models, it wasn't faked, it wasn't ritualistic; it was immediate ... Nobody was excluded: shop assistants, secretaries, dole-ites, plasterers, thieves, students. I felt at the centre of the pop world, that's one thing, but better still was that I felt in the middle of a huge explosion of energy. Everybody danced: on the stairs, on the stage, on the balcony, and at the bar. They danced in the cloakroom queue. For all I know, they were dancing in the street outside.

(Haslam 1997: 175)

Such euphoria couldn't last. During the 1990s, acid house nights were ritualised. If, in Mike Pickering's words, "the first two summers of ecstasy, of love, was the most special time you'll ever have", after that "it was just boring" (quoted in Hook 2009: 190).

From another perspective, however, it was the successful commercialisation of the acid house scene that marked a significant change in British youth culture. For Brewster and Broughton (2009: 391–2):

Starting in 1988 (for many commentators dance music's year zero) the DJ and his music embarked on an unprecedented project of social change. A new kind of music met a new kind of drug and thousands, eventually millions, of young people discovered a new way of enjoying themselves. House music, having upturned the ways in which music is conceived and created, set about transforming the way it is consumed.

For Dave Haslam (1997: 168—our italics), "since the late 1980s the dance-floor has consolidated its position as *the* focus of British youth culture", as was apparent on the urban club scene.[3] In 1994 Newcastle, for example, the indie rock club the Waterfront started devoting its Saturdays to a dance night, Pigbag. In its manager's words:

Our traditional market is indie music and live indie bands ... but the music scene's changing ... I mean there's the dance culture now, people of 18 have grown up with dance culture ... they haven't grown up with live music culture ... So we're looking more at club nights now ...because that's what your people want. Our house night on Saturday is a good quality dance music night.

(Quoted in Bennett 2000: 88)

In fact, as discussed in our previous volumes, young people in Britain have always grown up with dance, and there are clear continuities from the pre- to the post-acid house dance floor. Richard Norris, Paul Oakenfold's official biographer, provides a succinct summary of the acid house origin myth. In the summer of 1987:

Four friends from South London take a two-week trip to a sun-kissed island off the coast of Spain, hear a DJ called Alfredo play a genre-spinning

126 *DJ business*

selection of good-time tunes at Amnesia while out of their gourds on ecstasy, become fervent disciples of the Ibiza sound, triumphantly return to London armed with the new sound ... *et voilà*, modern dance music as we know it is miraculously born.

(Norris 2008: 85–6)[4]

What this doesn't make clear was that two of these friends, Nicky Holloway and Trevor Fung, were already "stalwarts of the Southern Soul scene", while Oakenfold was an established player in the transatlantic dance record business—he worked for Def Jam's promo company and wrote a hip hop column for *Blues and Soul* (Norris 2008: 57–84). He was also a dedicated Chelsea football fan, and being carried away on the terraces by day and on the dance floor by night was not new to acid house. *Boys Own*, the first fanzine of the new scene, was initially inspired by the Liverpool football fanzine *The End*.[5] In its first issue (published in late 1987) *Boys Own* explained:

We are aiming at the boy (or girl) who one day stands on the terraces, the next day stands in a sweaty club, and the day after stays in reading Brendan Behan whilst listening to Run-DMC.

(Quoted in Garratt 1998: 108)

For many participants in the early days of acid house, who were already accustomed to dancing every weekend to a variety of sounds in a variety of local clubs, pubs and discos, what was most exhilarating about the warehouse parties was not the social mix on the dance floor or the compelling urgency of the music played or even the intensely physical ecstasy buzz, but the sheer *number* of dancers involved. Helen Mead recalls the experience of dancing with ten thousand other people on ecstasy:

[It was] completely fucking mind-blowing, compared with doing it in Shoom [Danny and Jenni Rampling's pioneering acid house club in London] with two hundred people ... And I never remember any sense of worry at those big events. You'd maybe go with five people, and you'd be in these absolutely massive places, and you'd always be wandering off—whether it was 'cos you had your eyes closed and then found you'd danced half a mile away, or going to the toilet, navigating your way through these huge places. But I never remember feeling lost or stranded anywhere.

(Quoted in Reynolds 1998: 76)

From a historical perspective, then, the most striking feature of the acid house explosion was its *scale*, not just as a new kind of communal experience but also as a new kind of musical commerce. We will begin this chapter by examining the development of acid house as a business.

DJ *business*   127

The economy of rave

In his memoir of "the glory days of Acid House", Wayne Anthony (2018: xiv) tells the story of Genesis, a warehouse party business set up in 1988 by "three lads from Hackney". Anthony explains that he got the idea of going into the dance business from KP, a friend he'd made at Spectrum[6]:

> KP had limited experience from arranging a few small gigs in the past. He said it was just a matter of finding a deserted warehouse, printing 500 flyers and distributing them to clubbers we met whilst out painting the town red. He had all his own equipment, including a sound system, some lights and a box of wicked tunes. Costs could be kept to a minimum and amount to no more than a grand: drinks would be on a sale or return basis, flyers costs £80, the doorman would be my stepdad, the bar manager his sister Nikki, DJ Tony Wilson took £100 and KP or myself would be on the door taking the money. We were one big, happy, productive, family affair about to put the G into hard graft.
>
> (Anthony 2018: 19)

In practice, the dance business turned out to involve not just hard graft but also the ingenuity needed to find and occupy suitable spaces:

> There we were, the three of us, bolt-croppers in our hands, breaking open doors, embracing the future. If the police turned up when the party was on—and they usually did—I'd pretend to be George Michael's manager, or from EMI or Channel 4 [running a private event]. It was too exciting to worry or feel frightened.
>
> The fear came later. Our efforts got noticed by the kind of organised criminal gangs who usually rob Post Offices or banks at gunpoint. They read in the media that we could earn half a million quid in one night— but, in truth, we were just kids, off our heads on love drugs, holding hands and cuddling each other.
>
> (Anthony 2018: xiv–xv)

Anthony's memoir combines an uplifting tale of promoter-as-enthusiast with a harder headed assessment of dance promotion as a business. Enthusiasm was necessary for commercial success if Genesis were to overcome the challenges posed to an essentially illicit enterprise: on the one hand by police activity; on the other by criminal activity. Initially, Anthony followed the marketing textbook:

> A title is very important when marketing new ideas, and has to be thought over very carefully before a final decision can be made. We didn't want to change our chosen banner at a later stage for any reason, so the name had

128 *DJ business*

> to be right from the start ... the favoured choice for me was Genesis, a beautiful word that I thought summarised the *Zeitgeist*.
>
> (Anthony 2018: 19–20)

And while the next task for rave promoters like Genesis was to get crowds into venues without the police finding out in advance, Anthony is clear that such shenanigans were only necessary because of the restrictions of licensing laws, which rave promoters learnt to read with a fine attention to detail: "A loophole in the 1982 Public Entertainment Act, for example, meant that rave promoters could avoid the need for an Entertainments licence by claiming to be a private, members-only party on private land" (Garratt 1998: 166). Anthony developed the skills of forging leases and playing the role of an arrogant music biz party organiser. The problem, as he explains, was that

> nobody wanted to rent warehouses to promoters, which meant venues were hard to come by. The clubs didn't have the facilities to accommodate our huge crowds, and the few that were big enough to hold thousands of people closed too early. This left an enormous gap, which had to be filled. We knew that if we didn't grab the opportunity to stage even better parties than before, somebody else would do it.
>
> (Anthony 2018: 55–6)

In effect, "the authorities had *forced* us underground" (his italics):

> When promoters were forced underground, it meant having to deal with unsavoury characters for the protection of your money and your well-being. By 1990, it was getting out of control and we had somehow to legalise events before someone was seriously hurt, or worse.
>
> (Anthony 2018: 117, 199)

Criminal violence on the acid house scene was over-determined. On the one hand, raves were off-the-book cash events, which meant promoters needed (and had to pay for) "protection"; on the other hand, they were—like acid house club nights—sites for systematic drug dealing. Organised criminal involvement was therefore inevitable and the resulting tensions are threaded through both Anthony's account of the demise of Genesis and Peter Hook's account of the demise of the Haçienda. Simon Reynolds describes a typical incident at a party organised in April 1989 by East London rave promoter Labyrinth: "a gang of thugs rushed [into] the dance wielding machetes" after promoter Joe Wieczorek turned down their offer to provide "security". "The incident convinced Wieczorek that the illegal party game was too much of a hassle" (Reynolds 1998: 73–4).

Wayne Anthony notes that within the illegal promotion community itself, there were also rogue operators who tipped off the police about competitors' plans and/or ripped off punters by taking money for events they didn't

DJ business 129

actually stage. This was the context for a meeting in January 1990 at which "the linchpins" of the four biggest dance party organisations—Tony Colston-Hayter (Sunrise, Back to the Future), Anton Le Pirate (Energy/World Dance), Jarvis Sandy (Biology) and Jeremy Taylor (Energy)—formed the Association of Dance Party Promoters in order "to distinguish themselves from the gangsters and cowboys and to present a respectable front to apply for licences" (Anthony 2018: 201; Garratt 1998: 189).[7]

If the rave scene initially seemed to be a reaction to economic bad times (why else would there be so many abandoned warehouses?), increasingly it seemed to signal the potential for economic good times.[8] By 1989, Wayne Anthony was investing at least £25,000 into each Genesis event and the standard ticket price for a major rave had reached £25 (Anthony 2018: 164, 215). In an article for *Q* in the autumn of that year:

> Lloyd Bradley outlined the costs of a typical event: sound system £10,000; lights £5000; marquees and staging £3000; security £5000; DJs £2000; flyers/radio ads £3000; power supply £500; toilets £500; coaches from pick-up points £1000; hire of the land anything up to £10,000.
>
> (Garratt 1998: 172)

The increasing risk that an event would be stopped by the police (see Chapter 4) was one obvious inflationary pressure: promoters had to have alternative sites and reserve sound and lighting systems available,[9] and equipment companies pushed up their prices to ensure a decent advance fee (usually half) in case of cancellation. As crowds got bigger, the cost of spaces rose accordingly, and so did DJ fees:

> DJs who had been happy to play for £100 were suddenly demanding £1000 for a two-hour set. In the space of two parties, Lynn Cosgrave remembers Energy's DJ bill jumping from £1500–2000 all night to £7000–8000.
>
> (Garratt 1998: 172)[10]

Increasing investment also reflected increasingly elaborate staging—bigger and better sound and lights, and sets designed to disguise the scumminess of a warehouse or to transform a dank field. A rave was, after all, *a party* and its promoters were essentially party organisers.[11] As ticket prices rose, so rave audiences

> wanted more than a mirror ball and a few flashing lights. They wanted all the new technologies of pleasure, and they wanted them now. They wanted 15K, 20K, 30K, 40K, 100K of turbo sound, water-cooled lasers in different colours, big screen projections and fairground rides. They wanted bouncy castles, jugglers, magicians, stilt-walkers, fire-eaters and mime artists. They wanted candyfloss, fruit stalls, ice cream and burgers.
>
> (Garratt 1998:158)

130 *DJ business*

In May 1989, Energy held an event in a Shepherd's Bush film studio that offered around 5000 dancers a choice of five laser-filled rooms: a Blade Runner room, Stonehenge, a Greek temple, an Egyptian room and a sushi bar (Brewster and Broughton 2000: 401).

The financial returns from such big events (from 5000 to 25,000 dancers) were potentially huge—Garratt (1998: 172) suggests that the biggest events of the summer of 1989 netted their promoters "somewhere between £50,000 and £100,000". This matches Saunders' calculation that a Sunrise event attended by, say, 20,000 dancers had a turnover of around £250,000 and a profit of around £50,000 (Saunders 1995: 21). The steady rise in costs/profits also increased the financial risk of the illegality of the events: the larger and more profitable a potential rave, the greater the interest of both the police force and criminal gangs. Wayne Anthony (2018: 250) gives voice to the promoters' subsequent frustrations: "We felt pretty pissed off with the government. After all, it was the Thatcherite era that had created the environment that was meant to encourage initiative and entrepreneurs like us."

In Chapter 4 we described the passage in 1990 of Graham Bright's Acid House Bill, the Entertainments (Increased Penalties) Act and the increasingly aggressive and effective policing of illegal parties.[12] As it became more difficult to organise such events, so pressure increased on licensing authorities to enable them to take place legally. The Freedom to Party campaign was less significant here than market forces. Sheryl Garratt (1998: 262) explains:

> In 1990, a new generation of promoters came through to run legal, licensed open-air events and big parties in indoor sports halls and concert arenas, exhibition centres and leisure complexes: Raindance, Amnesia House, Storm, Rezerection, Fantazia, Living Dream, Perception and the Pure Organisation's Dance '90 and Dance '91 events all attracted young, predominantly working-class ravers in their thousands.

Between 1990 and 1992, a rave "overground" emerged, "a circuit of commercial megaraves" bringing between 10,000 and 25,000 dancers "inside giant hangers or under circus-sized tents" and providing them with the expected spectacle, sideshows and vast volume of sound. These promoters got local authority licences by claiming that they forbade "illegal substances", a claim that involved introducing new rituals into raving: "the two hour line, the humiliating body frisk, and the surly bouncer all became part and parcel of the rave experience" (Reynolds 1998: 130).

Initially, late licences for club-based dance events were only provided if alcohol was not for sale; however, breweries were determined not to be excluded from the new dance economy, and campaigned successfully, as we have seen, for relaxation in licensing laws while introducing (and glamorising) youth-aimed drinks such as alcopops. As dancers came indoors, a new generation of club promoters emerged, personified by Geoff Oakes. His club,

DJ business 131

Renaissance in Mansfield, "was going to be a big, all-night club playing acid house music. But it wasn't going to be a rave." Oakes wanted "something beautiful, something refined ... He wanted to transform a working men's club into a sixteenth-century Italian palace", into "a northern, working-class clubbing utopia that would spark a whole new era in British nightlife" (Phillips 2009: 14–5). Oakes persuaded Mansfield officials to give Renaissance a 7.00am licence and booked a big name as resident DJ, an old friend, Sasha.

In contrast to the anything-goes democracy of the original warehouse parties, clubs like Renaissance deliberately offered glamour and exclusivity (exercised through their door policy). If the flyer for Shoom, one of the original acid house clubs, had exhorted "Sensation seekers, let the music take you to the top!" the flyer for one of the new clubs, Miss Moneypenny's in Birmingham, promised "Style, comfort and exclusivity" (Phillips 2009: 85). Suddenly, as Brewster and Broughton 2000: 426) put it, "Things had come full circle. Everyone was dancing in the clubs that acid house and rave were meant to have finished off".

Steven McLaughlin remembers his first experience of Illusions, Blackpool's hottest club in the early 1990s, which was "decked out in shiny black marble" while "a green-beamed laser light system ... pulsed in time to the music":

> Clubland was beginning to change and Illusions was at the cutting edge of this revolution. Disco music and a slow lingering dance at the end of the night were most definitely out; hardcore dance music, piano house and Madchester melodies were definitely in ... The compulsive beats had markedly differing effects on different individuals: for some, it would be a night-long trance; for others, a rush of high-energy whistling bliss. What I didn't fully realise at the time was that how you ended up, either aggressively drunk or deliriously happy, often depended on the drugs you had or hadn't ingested ... pints made people fight but pills made people dance.
> (McLaughlin 2013: 45–6)

McLaughlin went on to work as a doorman, beginning at the local ex-disco "superclub", the Palace (capacity 3000–4000) and ending at the Varsity, and his book shows that while the commercialisation of acid house certainly affected the ecology of the local pub and club scene, this did not mean that all clubs switched en masse to new ways of doing things. The Palace, for example, responded to the demand from local dancers for "a more intimate and uplifting experience in a purer space" by "morphing into something else entirely":

> The locals were jettisoned, the trendy crowd was snubbed and the Palace embraced a revival as a gaudy Las Vegas-style "holidaymakers only" nightspot, revelling in a seedy reputation for cheap beer and easy sex.
> (McLaughlin 2013: 75)

132   *DJ business*

The Varsity, long established in an amusement arcade, was refitted and rebranded as "a bang up-to-date, state-of-the-art fun pub". It now had a £2 entry charge and barred customers wearing jeans, though this did not seem to have much effect on its reputation as a dance-floor setting for as much trouble as fun (McLaughlin 2013: 164, 167). In short, the 1990s development of fun pubs and super-clubs might illustrate how electronic dance music and its DJs changed the dance-floor experience itself—its shape and volume, its sound and look, its kinetic sensibility; but the essence of a good night out for many young people remained much as it had been for decades—getting drunk and having sex—and the mass youth acceptance of electronic dance music could be seen, as Sheryl Garratt (1998: 302) puts it, as "disco's revenge", although Steven Evans (1989: 6–7) suggests a different take:

> On the basis of my observational and interview work, I would argue that there are effectively two distinct nightclub cultures in Sheffield: the commercial discotheque scene ("glitzy palaces") and the alternative nightclub scene ("scruffy dives").

In the 1990s, this "two culture" model became the norm for the club scene across the country.

Dance club as brand

In 1989, old Etonians James Palumbo and Humphrey Waterhouse began planning a London equivalent of New York's Paradise Garage with their clubbing friend Justin Berkmann (whose father ran a wine-importing business). Their initial task was to find a suitable site in a non-residential area, which they did: a disused warehouse on disused land around the Elephant and Castle roundabout. Thanks to Palumbo's City earnings, the trio had the capital needed to transform the building into a club with the capacity for 1500 dancers organised around three spaces: a bar area, a VIP room and a dance floor with "the best sound system in the UK".[13] The immediate task, though, was to get an all-night licence. The strategy here was to work out in advance the licensing board's likely objections and to prepare their solutions:

> They would have metal detectors on the door to search for weapons, an elaborate membership system, entry for over twenty-ones only, no alcohol after 3 a.m. They would get clubbers to testify that there was a demand for all-night clubbing, and to explain that the places they danced in now were unsafe, unregulated and illegal.
>
> (Garratt 1998: 286)

In 1991 they were granted a licence and the Ministry of Sound opened for dancers on September 21; however, for some time thereafter it still had to deal with the issues that had plagued unlicensed promoters: organised

DJ business 133

in-club drug dealing and the incentive to criminal gangs to control club security in order to protect their trade. The eventual solution involved major investment in a highly paid professional door team and, more controversially for clubbers, an agreed code of practice with the local police force: if someone was found with a small amount of an illegal substance for personal use, it would be confiscated and delivered to the police; anyone with a larger amount—for dealing or sharing—would be handed over to the police too (Garratt (1998: 288–90; Phillips (2009: 227–8). This policy was by and large successful. Drug dealing certainly continued but the club was no longer a criminal target. Indeed, by 1998 it was a significant leisure business. Ministry of Sound ran a record label, an internationally franchised radio show, a magazine, an internet site, a shop, a DJ agency, a tour team (which organised 150 events around the world that year), a clothing merchandising company and a sponsorship team (putting together brands and clubs). In 1996–97, the company's turnover was £20 million—£3.5 million from the club, £12.5 million from the label, and £4 million from tours, media, merchandising and sponsorship. By the end of the decade, Ministry of Sound Danceclub Ltd was reporting an annual pre-tax profit of £4.1 million (Garratt 1998: 291–2; Phillips 2009: 229).

The team that launched Cream had a rather different background from the Ministry of Sound's establishment entrepreneurs.[14] James Barton grew up as the son of a market trader on a Liverpool housing estate and started out in the live music business as a ticket tout before promoting Liverpool's first dance music night, Daisy, in September 1988 and DJ-ing at the Underground club. By early 1992 Barton and fellow Underground DJ Andy Carroll had set up an office from which they promoted dance events at the Royal Court and managed Wrexham-based electronic dance group K-Klass (whose "Rhythm is a Mystery" was a major UK hit in 1991). In 1992, clubber Darren Hughes talked Barton and Carroll into starting a new club night, Cream, at the Nation.

The first Cream event was held in October 1992 for around 400 people. By the end of the year, Barton had persuaded the venue's leaseholders to give him more space and Cream began to draw crowds of 1000-plus: "I brought all the football terrace element in and Darren's connections brought in all these camp fashion students" (quoted in Phillips 2009: 231). In May 1993, the club got a licence to stay open until 6.00am and that summer Barton and Hughes formed a new company with Nation boss Stuart Davenport.[15] The club was redecorated and £50,000 invested in developing all three of its spaces: the main room (1400 capacity), the annexe (650 capacity) and the courtyard (850 capacity). Suddenly, in Garratt's (1998: 298) words, "Cream was one of the biggest clubs in the country", its nights attracting more than 3000 people a week, many travelling considerable distances from around the UK. Its success as a club enabled Cream to expand its business into merchandise production and, most profitably, mix CDs. *Cream Classics*, released in 1995, sold over 250,000 copies, "a then unheard-of amount for a dance mix album" (Norris 2008: 269).[16]

134 *DJ business*

As with Ministry of Sound, Cream's success initially exacerbated its drugs problem. By 1995, in Darren Hughes' words, it was becoming "more and more of a drug dealer's paradise" and more and more of a policing and a media target (Phillips 2009: 234). Cream recruited Jayne Casey to the management team as head of PR: she had experience working with both Liverpool City Council and the police in the organisation of performance spaces and events (among other things, she had run the Bluecoat Arts Centre and Liverpool's Chinese New Year festival). She immediately advised Cream to join the local Chamber of Commerce and to document in detail the club's impact on the local economy, using the measures of added value (hotel bed occupancy, for example) that were now shaping urban cultural policies.[17] At the same time, she worked to ensure that the club was proactive in supporting anti-drug dealing measures, telling the local press:

> Cream has over the last three years developed into a thriving business, which plays its part in the economic regeneration of the city. In particular, Cream has acted as a catalyst to the regeneration of the Bold Street area. The position of the company is unequivocally anti-drugs. Obviously we recognise and take very seriously the threat that this widespread practice poses to our business. We are therefore totally in support of Merseyside Police and the action that they have taken to curb the sale of illegal drugs in and around our premises.
>
> (Quoted in Phillips 2009: 236)

As Mark Devlin (2007: 177) notes, clubs like Cream and Ministry of Sound were well aware that "E-consumption was inextricably linked to dance music clubbing—and therefore their profits". It was thus important that they show themselves to be "taking a responsible stand on the issue", providing free drinking water and full-time paramedics, regulating the temperature on the dance floor, and providing "chill-out zones".

Like Ministry of Sound, once Cream got through its early licensing problems it rapidly developed as an international business. It organised its first outdoor event in Britain in 1998, launching Creamfield onto the UK festival market (as noted in Chapter 6), and over the next decade sold Creamfield events globally. There were Creamfield festivals in Spain, the Czech Republic, Romania, Poland, Russia, Chile, Brazil, Australia and Argentina. In 2012 the brand was bought by Live Nation.

For many of the more ideological (or nostalgic) participants in the original illegal scene, the emergence of international commercial operators like Ministry of Sound and Cream marked a betrayal of rave's spirit. "The nation's biggest venues", as Brewster and Broughton (2000: 427) put it, had fallen "for the lure of money and the power that their 'brand' had accumulated". But rave was always an events business and branding was always crucial to it. At the beginning of this section, we noted Wayne Antony's determination to choose a good name for his parties and he would have understood the

DJ business   135

entrepreneurial logic of both Ministry of Sound's mission statement, "We are building a global entertainment business, based on a strong aspirational brand, respected for its creativity and quality" (quoted in Garratt 1998: 292) and James Barton's brief to designer Mark Farrow for a Cream logo:

> The only reference we gave him was the Nike swoosh. We didn't want to look anything like Ministry of Sound, which for us was very London, very authoritarian, a government-type logo. We wanted a clean, modern/industrial look ...
>
> (Quoted in Norris 2008: 268–9)[18]

As branded dance nights developed in clubs all across the UK, so did the demand for star names to play the records: "DJs started racing up and down the motorways to play all of them. It was a gold rush" (Phillips 2009: 90).

DJs and superstar DJs

When DJ Paul Oakenfold agreed to take up a year-long Saturday night residency at Cream in 1998, his contract—negotiated by his agent, David Levy of ITB—ran to 20 pages.[19] It covered not just his fee but also how Oakenfold's name would appear on flyers. He had the right to choose the opening DJ and the contract included detailed technical specifications of the sound equipment he would require. Cream had to supply a sound engineer for each show and pay for Oakenfold's roadie. The DJ expected an input into dancefloor design— "I brought a friend in every week who decorated the room with psychedelic artwork"—and his booth had to be kept clear of other people. Oakenfold was allowed four weeks off a year but couldn't accept another gig within a hundred miles of Liverpool. Most notoriously:

> The contract stipulated that he had to be met by a chauffeur-driven car at Stamford Bridge every time there was a Chelsea match on; if Cream couldn't get him to Liverpool by car, he'd get there by plane. If there were no flights available, they'd have to hire a plane.
>
> (Norris 2008: 273–7)[20]

This can be seen as the moment when the DJ effectively became a rock star. As Oakenfold remembers:

> I got a lot of stick from the media when the rumour went round that I had this massive rider but I'd learnt from touring with U2 that there's a proper way of doing business.
>
> (Quoted in Norris 2008: 276)

From Cream's point of view, Oakenfold's drawing power was worth the expense. In his second year at the club, when he moved from the Annexe

136 DJ business

to the larger Courtyard, "it was full-on Oakenfold mania at Cream", his appearances drawing dancers from far and wide. David Levy, interviewed by *Mixmag*, suggested that just as there were models and supermodels so there were "DJs and super DJs" and so the notion of the superstar DJ was born (quoted in Norris 2008: 283).

If dance clubs needed name DJs to attract a crowd, DJs needed clubs' use of guest DJs to build a name in the first place. In their history of the disc jockey, Brewster and Broughton (2000: 419) suggest that:

> Perhaps the greatest single factor in making the DJ a star was the practice of hiring guest DJs. Promoters found that a big-name, out of town jock could give a considerable boost to a club night's fortunes. To keep up with the demand for their services, the best DJs started playing two, sometimes three gigs a night, eating up thousands of miles of motorway a week, and flying off to Germany, Italy and Japan, where DJ fever was also raging. It was soon standard for a top DJ to roll into a club, play for just two hours, collect his inflated fee and rush off to another engagement.

To maintain their position at the top of the guest DJ list, superstar DJs had to do more than just spin records. DJ Mark Devlin (2007: 20) said:

> Rightly or wrongly, it's not enough to just be a hot DJ that can rock a crowd. It's a marketing-driven game, and you have to have some kind of brand or organisation that you're associated with in order to make it big.

In the long run, most of Britain's best-known DJs had radio shows, initially on pirate stations such as Kiss FM, Invicta and JFM, and later on the BBC. More immediately, it was a short step from playing records to remixing them and from remixing tracks to creating and releasing them, particularly given the technology now involved:

> When a good DJ performs, he [sic] will be layering parts of records over each other, introducing snatches of one into a second, weaving and splicing different elements to make an original suite of music. Similarly, making or remixing a dance record is usually a case of playing around with relatively large chunks of sound (i.e. samples and predetermined rhythms), and combining them to make something new.
>
> (Brewster and Broughton 2000: 379–80)

At the same time, as Norman Cook points out,

> when you're DJ-ing, you spend untold hours just standing watching people dance. And you begin to realize which bits of a record people react to and which bits get them going. You just learn what makes people dance.
>
> (Quoted in Brewster and Broughton 2000: 380)

The most successful DJs thus combined technical mixing expertise with an understanding of the dance floor and did so with a distinctive sound sensibility and flow, which could then be captured on record—Oakenfold's impact, for example, came from his ability to build tension and anthemic release, hence his appeal to U2. Remix albums featuring name DJs became crucial to the finances of the major dance clubs, following the release of Renaissance's *The Mix Collection* (mixes by Sasha and John Digweed) in November 1994.[21]

In his remark about DJs and super DJs David Levy implied that the career of a DJ (like the career of a rock star) was pyramid shaped—a mass of would-be stars at the bottom, with only a few making it to the top. But, just as most professional musicians were not interested in climbing the rock ladder, so most DJs didn't aspire to be superstar DJs. A more useful way of thinking about DJ-ing as a profession is by reference to different kinds of DJ. Mark Devlin (2007: 23–34) suggests that there are in essence three types of working DJ. First there's the "common-or-garden general-purpose DJ", the mobile DJ who provides the music for weddings, corporate events and other public functions, playing whatever is required. Such DJs' continuing income depends on building a local reputation, but what they play is audience led. Their livelihood was enhanced by the 1990s clubbing boom not because they became club DJs themselves, but rather because local pubs took note of new customer expectations. As Haçienda DJ Graeme Park put it, "nowadays every bar has a more-or-less competent DJ whacking out the tunes everyone knows" (quoted in Haslam 2002: 292).

The general-purpose DJ may be looked down on by a club DJ, but like a session musician has the steadier income over time and is rewarded for having skills that a club DJ lacks. Dave Haslam remembers being offered a tempting fee by a fan of his Haçienda sets to play the annual Asda staff night. It turned out to be his "most humiliating" DJ experience. "I DJ-ed for three hours that night, playing something like 45 records, and people only danced to two of them" (Haslam 2002: 304). The problem of playing such events is that "there are so many different people to please" and Bill Brewster makes the point that:

> The mobile DJ may well play the most predictable and tawdry array of pop staples, but the mobile DJ knows how to take an evening from an empty room to peak hour and back again. He knows how to work a crowd. Even if he does this by playing Bachman Turner Overdrive records.
>
> (Quoted in Haslam 2002: 305)

The Secret DJ puts it this way:

> It's a piece of piss to make fans dance. It's a walk in the park making people in Ibiza or Las Vegas dance. It's what they came for. It's being out of your comfort zone that makes a pro.
>
> (Anonymous 2018: 119)

138 *DJ business*

Devlin's second kind of DJ is "the specialist", the DJ who plays only a particular kind of music. In the 1990s, the majority of specialist DJs played nights labelled "by the catch-all terms 'black' or 'urban' music", which covered hip-hop, R&B, soul and reggae. This was the DJ tradition that began in Mod clubs in the 1960s and continued through the Northern and Southern Soul scenes of the 1970s. Most of the pioneering names in Devlin's third category, the "house/dance music DJ", started as specialist DJs before differentiating themselves from their roots in the eclecticism of their playlists and their active involvement in manipulating the sounds they played.

Devlin notes the resulting differences in working conditions. Specialist DJs, for example, had to carry a particularly heavy load of records. Devlin calculates that a specialist DJ needed to take at least 200 discs to a gig to cover a three-hour slot; the house/dance music DJ could organise their three hours around just 30 tunes, each one stretched to ten minutes or more (Devlin 2007: 30–2).

A statistic often cited in DJ histories (without a source being provided) is that by the mid-1990s Technics turntables were outselling electric guitars (Devlin 2007: 66). The implication is that young people were now more ambitious to be DJs than they were to be rock musicians. This may or may not be true but it is certainly the case that there were by now well-organised DJ career-support mechanisms.

The Disco Mix Club (DMC) was launched by ex-Radio Luxembourg disc jockey Tony Prince in 1983. Its immediate purpose was to enable "working DJs to get hold of exclusive mixes of current tunes" but subscribers also got *Mixmag,* a monthly newsletter (Devlin 2007: 67). With the emergence of house music, *Mixmag* was redesigned as a consumer magazine, covering dance culture generally (providing club night listings, for example). When it was sold to EMAP a decade later, its circulation had reached 70,000 and one of its achievements had been to turn DJs into pin-ups.

Tony Prince had started DMC because he was "convinced that mixing was going to be the new skill for DJs rather than chat, and that a rise in the status of DJs was imminent". DMC was, as Haslam suggests, at once a record pool, a trade union, an information point and a business. In 1986 Prince launched an annual mixing contest (modelled on the DJ competitions staged by the New Music Convention in New York) and by 2000 the final of the DMC Technics World Championship was being staged in the Millennium Dome:

> There are five TV crews on stage, fifty-two photographers and 130 journalists. The costs for staging the event, including local heats around the world, the various National Finals, advertising, travel, flights and hotel costs for the World Finalists, the parties and the prizes, is probably something like five million dollars.
>
> (Haslam 2002: 248)

The DMC competitions involve turntablism—the live record mixing skill that emerged in the early days of hip hop. Competitors are judged for their

DJ business 139

technical abilities and performance style rather than for their control of a dance floor, but the events became valuable launch pads for DJs starting out on their careers and fulfilled one of Tony Prince's original objectives: "to take a new art form, expand its possibilities and place it on a platform for the world to see" (Haslam 2002: 248).

Another example of emerging support for a DJ's career in this period was the development of DJ agencies. The key figure here is Lynn Cosgrave, who started out in the dance business as part of Energy and worked with Nicky Holloway at Sin before starting a DJ agency, FXTC, in 1988 (Garratt 1998: 179). Cosgrave explains why she moved from being a DJ to managing DJs:

> One night I was playing at the Lyford Film Studios in Wandsworth and the DJ after me was late and it meant that I would be late for my next gig. When I asked him where he had been, he said he had got lost ... I just thought, these guys need organising and that is how it all started for me.

Cosgrave went on to work for Ministry of Sound (establishing its record label) and Sony (as vice-president of dance), but continued to be an agent as well as running Cosmack Management and Safehouse Production. At Cosmack, she says, "I developed paths for my boys into remixing, production, fashion shows, artist releases, sponsorship, etc. It was the first company to do anything like this, up until then, the DJ had just been a DJ and that was that." At Safehouse, "We produce a lot of our own shows now across the world and deal with a lot of sponsors, merchandise, records."[22]

In his "sensational exposé of what really goes on behind the beat", The Secret DJ suggests that what makes a club name a superstar DJ is not simply the huge adulation and fees that they command but also the vast number of people involved in ensuring their success: a manager plus managerial team; an agent plus agency team of travel bookers and logistics planners; a variety of interns, runners, IT people and tour managers; a driver; drug dealers and some sort of sexual partner; a stylist and a hairdresser; a PR rep and a press agent; and, one could add, a publisher, accountant and lawyer (see Anonymous 2018: 72).

From one perspective, this just shows that to be a successful club DJ is to be part of a successful club DJ business; from another, it suggests that by the end of the 1990s the best-known DJs had taken on all the trappings of pop and rock stardom. Their audiences now, as Dom Phillips (2009: 183) puts it, were no longer "clued up clubbers" or "early adopters" or "opinion formers", but "big, Saturday night pop crowds, facing the front, cheering their DJ gods. They wanted showmen, not introspective DJ trainspotters". One such showman was Norman Cook, the DJ Fatboy Slim. His 1998 album *You've Come a Long Way Baby* sold 1.173 million copies in the UK alone; by then his live shows could no longer be constrained by club settings. His ideal events now were beach parties (65,000 people in Brighton!) or street festivals (360,000 people in Rio!) (Phillips 2009: 206).

140 *DJ business*

Another such showman, Paul Oakenfold, agrees that:

> The DJ is a modern entertainer. There's no difference between a band and a DJ. People spend £15 to come and see me and they want the best night of their life. So that's why I have to get into character ... When I perform they're directly watching the DJ, so they're all watching every move. They expect you to deliver.
>
> (Quoted in Brewster and Broughton 2000: 415)

Dance promoter Crae Caldwell explains the cultural effects of the move by DJs move from club to stadium.

> When a dance act makes it big as a live [act] then they move to a live agent specifically and start doing the live music tour properly ... What'll happen is that the agent will say, "Well, we can make you X amount by touring this *this* way". So it moves from one scene to another ... It becomes a live gig; it's not a club night any more, it's not part of a club night, it's an actual stand-alone headline show, so that falls under the kind of, you know, "the doors open at seven, the show comes down at eleven", kind of vibe. So they become a band, in the traditional sense of being a band ... whereas a live act in a club is part of a night, it's not the headline act. But when they become Daft Punk or Basement Jaxx or Leftfield or Orbital or anyone, then they become a live act in their own right and people will pay to go and see them on their own, rather than as part of an overall package.[23]

Not everyone in Britain's turn-of-the-century dance world liked the idea of DJ as rock star. Brewster and Broughton (2000: 437) sum up one view:

> The greatest success of dance culture is supposed to be that it now has acts that are at home playing American stadiums?!? But it's not a triumph for dance music to disguise itself as something that's existed for 35 years or more.

DJ Jeremy Healey put it more pithily: "DJs went from being the most wankery people to being the coolest persons to being the most wankery people" (quoted in Phillips 2009: 362).

On the other hand, as Devlin (2007: 24) notes, by the end of the 1990s female DJs were rather more common in the house/dance music scene than they were in either the mobile or specialist scenes. Brewster and Broughton (2000: 405) see this as "one cultural side effect of acid house": "In the rushing years at the end of the eighties, anything seemed possible, even the idea that a woman could enter this most male of professions and not be laughed out from behind the desks."

DJ business   141

Nancy Noise and Lisa Loud, for example, were part of Paul Oakenfold's first DJ team at his Future nights at Heaven (see Norris 2008: 108–9) and Lisa Loud went on to became a big-name DJ, featuring in advertising copy for Nivea:

> According to Lisa, DJ-ing is physically demanding and dehydrating. Yet looking good is crucial. Lisa's sun-kissed Balearic look is maintained with simple yet disciplined skincare.
>
> (Quoted in Haslam 2002: 300)[24]

It was the entry of corporate sponsors like Nivea into club business that inspired something of a backlash against superstar DJs in the 2000s. The arguments here in part echoed rock fans' 1970s critique of rock stars for being too commercial. In the dance world, too, distinctions were drawn between "authentic" and "inauthentic" clubs and clubbers.[25] What DJs and dance promoters once did for love or adventure, they were now doing, it seemed, for money and fame—although, as Dom Phillips pointed out after years of reporting on British club culture for *Mixmag*:

> Throughout dance music's history it has always been ruthlessly opportunistic, entrepreneurial and capitalist. It's always been about making money.
>
> (Quoted in Brewster and Broughton 2000: 412)

Conclusion

The contempt of dance fans for DJs who sold out by becoming rock stars drew, ironically, on rock's own narrative of betrayal: from underground adventurer to corporate entertainer, from DIY utopianism to packaged consumption. Such arguments also reflected a generational shift, as electronic dance music began to be sold as EDM to a new generation of dancers at festivals such as Tomorrowland, launched in Belgium in 2005.[26] But other arguments about superstar DJs were more concerned with the particular nature of the disc jockey's musical craft: making a career by playing records made by other people. One common distinction made in the dance literature is therefore between DJs who play records because they want dancers to appreciate the music and DJs who play records because they want dancers to appreciate the DJ.[27] In denouncing the "plastic DJs" who became the big names of the 2010s, The Secret DJ, for example, argues that "spectacle has replaced music as the most important thing in a DJ's performance" (Anonymous 2018: 193). On the other hand, as we have already noted, many of the most successful DJs in the 2000s did not just play other people's music. They were increasingly involved in creating, producing and mixing their own sounds, both in the studio and on stage. In this respect, DJs weren't just becoming rock stars;

142 *DJ business*

they were becoming a new kind of rock musician. We will return to this in Chapter 9.

We will end this chapter with a different take on the arguments here. In an article in *The Observer* in 2000, Kevin Le Gendre starts with the familiar observation:

> The problem now is that DJs think they are gods and the people around them are too mesmerised or obsequious to let them know the truth—that all they do is spin records made by other, more talented people.

Le Gendre accepts that

> DJs have played an important part in the dissemination of black and popular music for years. They were crucial to the birth of rock'n'roll and hip hop. They furthered the cause of disco, where 'the mix'—the continuous flow of beats—moved the energy from the stage to the dancefloor.

But, he argues,

> sometime in the Nineties the DJ became deified. Hitherto invisible, he was moved into the spotlight [and] the issue of creative rights in dance music became blurred in the process: compiling and mixing a CD takes skill but it shouldn't be portrayed as a form of composition.

And, "even more important than the division between the DJs and musicians, is the schism between the superstar DJs and the underground selectors. This echoes the growing divide between dance music and black music".[28]

By "underground selectors", Le Gendre means not the white DJ specialists in black music described by Mark Devlin, but the dancehall MCs who first appeared in Jamaica in the 1950s then became an essential part of British Caribbean dance culture. It was these DJs' sound systems that gave impetus to a different kind of dance business and to a different kind of dance culture, in which live and recorded music are inseparable. This is the topic of our next chapter.

Notes

1 Quoted in Evans (1989: 1).
2 See www.theguardian.com/theobserver/2000/jun/11/featuresreview.review2.
3 In his study of its late 1980s club scene, Steven Evans (1989: 33) found that "virtually three-quarters of young people in Sheffield had been nightclubbing well before their 18th birthdays".
4 If nothing else, this event established the link between dance culture and the package holiday. Ten years later, Ayia Napa in Cyprus was established as *the* site for "a garage holiday"—see Laughey (2006: 160–1).

DJ *business*   143

5 The *Boys Own* team included Terry Farley and Andrew Weatherall, who explains how they met: "Well I lived in Windsor and they lived in Slough and it was that classic suburban thing: people meeting at the one decent clothes shop" (quoted in Brewster and Broughton 2010: 387). *The End* actually began in 1981 as a music fanzine, written by Peter Hooton, who went on to form Liverpool band The Farm.

6 Spectrum was an acid house club night, promoted from April 11, 1988 by Ian St Paul and Paul Oakenfold on Monday nights at Heaven in Charing Cross.

7 Tony Colston-Hayter was already promoting legal parties in equestrian centres around the country (see Anthony 2018: 92; Brewster and Broughton 2000: 399).

8 For an excellent ongoing oral history of this moment in a northern working-class town, when "a small and determined group of young people reclaimed the empty warehouses and mills in Blackburn so they could throw 'Parties for the People – by the people'", see www.acidhouseflashback.co.uk.

9 Some of the free party promoters I knew in Sheffield called them "kamikaze rigs" because they knew that they would almost certainly get confiscated [EW].

10 Police raids on raves also began to involve the confiscation of DJs' records. Paul Oakenfold decided he "didn't want to be put in a situation where I could lose my records" and stopped playing illegal events altogether (Brewster and Broughton 2010: 408).

11 Jeremy Taylor of Energy started out organising Gatecrasher Balls, "grand parties for fourteen- to twenty-year-old Hooray Henries and Henriettas" (Garratt 1998: 151).

12 This followed the creation of a dedicated anti-rave police team, the Pay Party Unit, run from Gravesend but with a nationwide remit (Garratt 1998: 182–3).

13 It was designed by associates of Richard Long, "the audio wizard behind the booming mecca that was the Paradise Garage in lower Manhattan", where he arranged and maintained "the most iconic soundsystem of the modern era". For his career (he died of AIDS in 1986), see https://daily.redbullmusicacademy.com/2016/05/richard-long-feature.

14 This account of Cream draws primarily from Garratt (1998: 296–302) and Phillips (2009: 221–5, 229–32, 234–7).

15 This was the point at which Carroll was eased out of the management team.

16 The album was released by Deconstruction, for whom Barton worked as an A&R man.

17 Casey was responsible for the much repeated claim that 80% of the students who came to Liverpool's universities did so because of Cream. The research had in fact referred to Liverpool's nightlife generally, rather than to Cream in particular (Phillips 2009: 236).

18 Ministry of Sound's portcullis logo, designed by Lynn Davis, remains in Phillips' (2009: 227) words, "one of the most recognisable images in dance music".

19 For ITB and its co-owner Barry Dickins, see Chapter 2. Oakenfold ended up playing at Cream for two years.

20 This apparently never happened.

21 *Mixmag* had started selling mix cassettes to readers in 1992, by which time there was also a black market in remix tapes. The Fat Lads, for example— a pair of Geordies who went clubbing with their DAT machines—did a brisk bootleg business until they went legit, forming Global Underground, a record label that put together licensed remix tracks for the international market (Phillips 2009: 123–4).

144 *DJ business*

22 Quotes taken from an interview on the DMC website: www.dmcworld.net/interviews/movers-groovers-behind-the-music-miss-lynn-cosgrave.
23 Quoted from an interview with Emma Webster, September 30, 2009.
24 For a detailed account of the 1990s career of another prominent female disc jockey, DJ Lottie (Charlotte Horn), see Haslam (2002: 274–83).
25 For a sophisticated analysis of the dance club concept of authenticity, see Thornton (1995).
26 We come back to Tomorrowland in Chapter 10.
27 This was an issue that particularly exercised specialist DJs. See, for example, the blog extracts reprinted at the end of Devlin (2007).
28 Quotes taken from www.theguardian.com/theobserver/2000/jun/11/featuresreview.review2.

8 Moving to a different beat: jungle, bhangra, garage and grime

So I said, "Right I'm going to check out Spectrum next week." The next Monday night we went down there. Me and a couple of lads from Brixton walked in and they were like, "What the hell is going on here?" We saw everyone with smiley t-shirts, with big eyes, chewing their teeth and just walking around in another world. My mates fucked off and left me in there. They were like, "You know what? It's like we've walked into hell. We're going back to Brixton."
(DJ Fabio on his first experience of an acid house night)[1]

Jungle had done something to inner-city youths all over the country that no genre had up until this point. It had given us all an identity. It was UK. It was raw. It was organic. People could relate, and we finally had MCs speaking in their local accent instead of mimicking American slang and lyrics, as well as music that was completely original yet fused cultures we had all grown up on.
(DJ Target 2018: 24–5)

Britpop bleaches away all traces of black influences in music in a mythical imagined past of olde England as it never was, whereas … Bhangra and Jungle are rooted in the urban reality of today's Britain. It's village green versus concrete jungle and we know where we'd rather be.
(Rupa Huq 1996: 79)[2]

Introduction

In Jeremy Deller's 2019 documentary on rave culture, *Everybody in The Place: An Incomplete History of Britain 1984–1992*, archive footage is shown to a school class of teenagers. Their reaction is mostly amazement and laughter, but their most telling response is to Deller's direct questions. Following scenes of rural mayhem, Deller asks the pupils how many of them have ever visited the British countryside: no hands go up. He then asks whether they consider themselves to be British. It seems that no one does. As one young Muslim woman explains, they identify themselves as *Londoners*.

Deller's film suggests that while rave may indeed have re-established the dance floor as the focus of white British youth culture, the history of clubs

146   *Moving to a different beat*

and clubbing since the 1980s can be written from a different perspective. In Volume 2 we noted that the origins of rave promotions lay in the London warehouse gatherings that emerged from the long tradition cf Caribbean house parties and featured sound systems of obvious Caribbean lineage—it was in this scene, for example, that Jazzie B's Jah Rico system became the successful pop act Soul II Soul.[3] By the mid-1980s, such sound systems were, in Lloyd Bradley's words, "easing óut" of the warehouse scene. For Jazzie B, the problem was that "the druggier end of acid house was taking over" and in 1986 he started a new Soul II Soul night at the Africa Centre in Covent Garden.[4] These nights attracted a different kind of crowd from the acid house hedonists:

> Here was a multi-culti, multi-racial, wide-age-ranged assortment of ravers, dreads, b-boys, soul boys, suburbanites, sticksmen, students, tourists and the merely curious ... the sense of community between hosts and crowds was on a par with the first sound-system lawn dances in 1950s Jamaica.
>
> (Bradley 2013: 328–9)

For MCs PJ and Smiley from the Shut Up and Dance sound system, the usual way of telling the acid house story, by reference to Shroom, Spectrum, etc., is therefore misleading:

> The West End didn't do shit, man. The West End didn't even let black people in their clubs anyway. You can't really talk about the West End in terms of bringing up a music ... It's just journalists who don't know fuck all. Trust me I was there. From the beginning. Hopefully I'm there to the end. Trust me it's from Hackney. That's where it all started: places like Dungeons [easily the biggest rave club in England], Roller Express, that place in Tottenham ...
>
> (Smiley, quoted in Brewster and Broughton 2010: 451–2)

For these musicians, jungle—the electronic music style that began to be played in clubs in the early 1990s—was an organic development of rave, but for many ravers jungle's sub-bass frequencies and use of samples from gangsta rap and ragga brought something "dark" to the music. In 1994, Gwen Lawford argued in the fanmag *Rave Scene* that "jungle had killed the spirit of the rave movement with its aggression. It had expunged the gocd vibes from the music" (quoted in Zuberi 2001: 170). Kodwo Eshun later reflected in *The Wire* that:

> All too often, the dislike of Jungle translates into a fear of the Alien Ruffneck, of the Rudeboy from the council estate who's supposedly spoilt the peace-and-love vibe and the dream of trans-tribal unity. Jungle, so

Moving to a different beat 147

this racist myth goes, is what killed Smiley [the icon not the MC] and turned every raver's little Woodstock into an Altamont with bass bins.
(Quoted in Zuberi 2001: 170–1)

Sheryl Garratt (1998: 271) describes how the tensions here affected the club night Rage, launched as an acid house event at Heaven in late 1988. The pioneering Jungle DJs Fabio and Grooverider began playing the club's upstairs bar before moving into the main room in late 1991 and making the night "a laboratory for the new breakbeat science". The club closed in March 1993 and, as Garratt (1998: 275), writes, "there were all kinds of conspiracy theories as to why":

> The word was that the gay clubbers didn't like it in their venue. Or that it was too black. Or that the house scene was running scared. Fabio says the truth is much more pedestrian: the future shock of the sound was too much for many of the regulars. "We totally alienated the Rage faithful. It got so ghettoised. A lot of people stopped coming down, and it got a reputation as a druggy, ragga place where the craziest music was being played."

The nascent jungle scene moved to AWOL (A Way of Life) at Paradise in Islington, launched as a Saturday all-nighter in March 1992:

> Nearly everything played at the club was on dub plate, with special mixes being created by producers exclusively for specific DJs. As with the reggae sound systems, if the crowd approved of a track they would shout for it to be played again and again, the MCs on the mic taking up their chants of "rewind, rewind" until the DJ cued it up once more.
> (Garratt 1998: 277)

The music played, "the overlap of reggae bass, breakbeat and ragga chants", "drew black clubbers to the rave scene in significant numbers for the first time" (Garratt 1998: 278). As early 1990s rave DJ Jumping Jack Frost recalls:

> Living in Brixton, where there's a heavy black, West Indian vibe, I'd get a lot of people saying I was playing gay music. "What are you doin', man?" It was only OK when the drum'n'bass, jungle came in. Up to that point it was never OK, never.
> (Quoted in Garratt 1998: 278)[5]

In the summer of 1993, the Jungle Splash night was established at the Roller Express in Edmonton, featuring "sound clash-style contests, competing for the crowd's loud approval from a boxing-ring in the middle of the arena" (Garratt 1998: 278), while in autumn 1994 DJs LTJ Bukem and Fabio established the

148   *Moving to a different beat*

Speed night at Mars in London's West End for the "mellower underground vibe" of drum'n'bass:

> This was the first new dance sound ever to emerge from Britain, the first that our club culture can truly claim to have invented. It closes the circle between Jamaica, America and Britain, bringing together all the different strands of black music that have shaped our club culture over the past twenty years and remaking them into something new. In retrospect, the frantic scene-hopping of eighties clubland, the jumping from jazz to rap to ska and funk, can all be seen to be leading up to this: the creation of identities that are British, that reflect our experiences growing up in multi-cultural cities.
>
> (Garratt 1998: 281)

In the rest of this chapter, we follow this route through dance-floor history: from jungle and drum'n'bass through garage and dubstep to grime. Our concern is less the stylistic or sonic differences between these various ways of making music than the continuities: the influence of Jamaican dance floor conventions; the importance of the black DIY music business; and the exploration of local cultural, ethnic and class identities.

Sound system culture

To grow up in London's Caribbean communities in the 1980s and 1990s was still to grow up with blues parties. For DJ Fabio (in Brixton), there was

> a massive blues party scene going on. Round the corner from me there was a place called Elland Park. On a Saturday night you could have five, six parties going on, with sound systems. I could hear it from my house. They were in people's houses or they used to rig up a sound system in old squats. There were a lot of squats in those days. We used to go to a lot of the local blues parties when I was 13 or 14. I had a whale of a time, man. That got me going into going out and being in this place with loud music playing. It was great because the blues scene was the original club scene: using huge sound systems, having MCs, not mixing but the whole emphasis on loud sounds ... we used to go to regular clubs and the sound systems were so crap, and you'd get DJs talking shit all night ... it wasn't like that at all. You'd have the host, the MC and the guy who used to play music, it was like this *narration*.
>
> (Quoted in Brewster and Broughton 2010: 439, italics in original)

DJ Smiley from Shut Up and Dance similarly remembers his 1980s Stoke Newington starting point in the organisation of blues parties: "We had to do our own things. Break into empty houses. My brother's a sparks, so he'd get the lighting going. Hype [the crew's DJ] would drive around seeing where

Moving to a different beat   149

there's an empty house" (quoted in Brewster and Broughton 2010: 451). And grime star Wiley explained to a reporter from *The Guardian* (January 24, 2017) that the root of all this grime business [in the 1990s] was house parties, "proper house parties, with a proper system, all across Bow and Newham when we were teenagers. We'd go and jump on the mic, and clash each other". Sometimes they'd bring the decks along too. "In our area, anyone who was having a house party, we would be the guys who came and DJ-ed", recalled Wiley's childhood friend Darren "Target" Joseph.

Unlike soul clubs or raves these events were *essentially* local. As Fabio puts it: "If you went to a blues dance in Battersea, then it would be like, 'you guys aren't from around here.' You could seriously get yourself into trouble" (quoted in Brewster and Broughton 2010: 441). Neither were they youth cultural or fashionable. They were rooted in the historical experience of Caribbean migrants. In his autobiography, Wiley (2017: 39) emphasises the debt grime artists owed to the people who provided the musical experiences of their childhood:

> Not only our parents, but all the seventies, eighties reggae people, Tippa Irie, Smiley Culture, whoever, bro. These guys. We grew up listening to a lot of dub tracks. Dub kind of made us who we are.

For Wiley's teenage friend and future collaborator Flowdan:

> My house was the arena for watching sound system clashes. My parents had a load of videos and we used to watch them again and again. And then we heard the jungle MCs picking up elements of it: the charisma, the style of delivery, the lyricism. Jungle as a UK twist on that world. Up to that point there had been a lot of US-influenced music, but jungle opened our eyes. It made us realise that our accents were allowed. Suddenly we could be ourselves.
>
> (Wiley (2017: 52–3)

The Jamaican sound system had been at the heart of the black music scene in London since the 1950s (the Count Suckle and Duke Vin systems were established in 1956) and it now became the driving force in the development of jungle, garage and grime. Jungle producer Wookie once claimed that "everybody that's in this music scene, their dad was in a sound system or around one and they were influenced by that", and for Bradley (2013: 354, 374) grime "was practically a carbon copy of the original immigrant sound-system way of doing things".

Sound systems were organised as crews (rather than bands). DJ Target describes the formation of the Silver Storm crew: "We were all fans of sound system culture from Jamaica, so we wanted a name that reflected that. Silver Storm sounded like a name you'd hear on a world sound-clash tape" (DJ Target 2013: 31).

150　*Moving to a different beat*

Although the SS Crew (as it was soon known) had "only six of us [including Wiley] doing the shows and the tapes, the rest of the guys we hung with every day in the estate were also part of it" (DJ Target 2013: 32).

One feature of a crew's musical organisation was to split the DJ's conventional role (presenting and playing records) into two, with the DJs focusing on their turntablism skills while the MCs spoke to the dancers. Wiley's father remembers that:

> At early house and garage raves you'd have people grabbing the mic to gee people up, encouraging them to feel good. That was their job, you know. But then, all of a sudden, there was a change. People started grabbing the mic to tell stories. Grabbing the mic and having battles.
>
> (Quoted in Wiley 2017: 55)

DJ Target suggests that it was at the turn of century that:

> UK garage started to show signs of a shift, with an almost subgenre emerging amongst the heavier more instrumental tracks that were making way for MCs to really start spitting bars as opposed to the classic hosting style.
>
> (Quoted in Wiley 2017: 72)

But this move from crews as "a DJ thing" to crews in which the MCs "held the power in their hand" was, he also notes, actually a return to "more of a jungle feel ... in terms of the dynamic between the DJ and the MC". Jungle producer General Levy, who had put together his first crew in 1986 at the age of 15, points out that in the early 1980s:

> There was a lot of Jamaican sound system cassettes coming over here.
> ... This was when the MCs was beginning to become predominant in a lot of reggae music, and it brought a lot of togetherness to black music because it brought back the street slang.
>
> (Quoted in Bradley 2013: 346)

In London, this was immediately reflected in the dance hall shows of the sound system Saxon, which had started performing at parties in Lewisham in 1976 and from the early 1980s began to feature MCs such as Papa Levi. As Bradley (2013: 348) writes, "the dance hall-style MC-ing, with the sort of London twang pioneered by Saxon, became the defining feature of jungle as a stylistic development".[6]

The performing emphasis on the MCs was reflected in the popularity of clashes. DJ Target (2013: 94–5) explains:

> The competitive side of [early grime] culture was magnified in these surroundings, with MCs wanting to prove they were better than the next. Garage lyrics had always been about the club, enjoying yourself and the pretty ladies by the bar, but the younger new waves of MCs were

Moving to a different beat   151

talking about the real-life situations they were going through, the struggle of inner-city life and their immediate surroundings. They also had bars [verses] to fend off other MCs. It wasn't long before MCs were offending each other with their lyrics, and with this came clashing. A staple part of sound system culture, and visible in hip hop with rap battles. The UK was crafting its own arena for MCs to battle for supremacy.[7]

A key influence here was the annual Jamaican event Sting, first staged in 1984 (and readily available on video), "which influenced a whole bunch of grime MCs, and gave us its sound-clashing culture" (DJ Target 2013: 77).[8] This is Wiley's description of the "grime rave" nights he started promoting at the Area in Watford in 2002.

> Eskimo Dance used to be mad. It used to be properly underground. It all came from Sting, you know. The greatest one-night reggae and dancehall show on earth. Badman ting. When man just rush out and spray bars. Just mad.
>
> Eskimo dance had that kind of sound, it had that vibe, and it was a roadblock every time.
>
> MCs would go down to battle each other; to have a clash. But it wasn't all aggro—spitting over a beat is how MCs express themselves. It's a form of poetry.
>
> (Wiley 2017: 132)

Sound system business

Wiley (2017: 79) writes that "when it started grime was a young black man's punk rock. MC-ing is basically the same as singing in punk—shouting on a beat to get a reaction", and in his autobiography he quotes Jamie Collinson, from the underground hip hop label Big Dada:

> A lot of grime wasn't very good on a technical level. I always thought it was a bit like a punk movement, where it was so DIY. 5% of it was absolutely amazing and thrilling and 95% of it was not, but it was exciting because everyone was trying new things, and everyone was allowed to have a go.
>
> (Wiley 2017: 168)[9]

DJ Logan Sama suggests that grime was "so DIY" out of necessity. By the end of the 1990s, the garage scene

> had disassociated itself from the underground, the crew and the MC-ing. There were UK garage committees that were purposefully trying to blacklist artists. They wanted to separate themselves from a council estate scene they considered uneducated, aggy, rough.
>
> (Quoted in Wiley 2017: 94)[10]

152 *Moving to a different beat*

But grime's do-it-yourself way of doing business was not really punk; rather, it drew on what Lloyd Bradley (2013: 336) calls the "savvy outlaw mentality" that had driven the black music business in London since at least the mid-1950s. This business, organised around the sound system, involved a very particular relationship between recorded and live music-making. Sound system events meant playing (and playing with) records; sound system records celebrated a live music-making process. The economic model here did not just feature club DJs promoting the latest dance records (as in disco) or tracks being played to promote a club or DJ brand (as in acid house); rather, in sound system business, no distinction was made between live and recorded music.

This can be seen in DJ Target's description of Dizzee Rascal making his first mark on the grime scene in 2002, when Wiley brought him onto Slimzee's Sunday afternoon show on Rinse FM:

> His college demos had become a bunch of finished tracks, and he had started to find his sound. It was still very raw and industrial, but more polished and organised. His MC style was very different than anything that was out there. Brash, hard hitting and precise, his lyrics relaying life in Bow and growing up in the struggle of east London ... Dizzee and Wiley's set tapes [became] hot property, and were getting shared all over the country, even sold for profit at Sunday markets. Wiley started bringing Dizzee to some of the Pay As U Go sets, and Roll Deep were getting booked more and more too.
>
> (DJ Target 2018: 111)[11]

Here we see tracks being recorded and played on radio with live MC-ing, and these live performances being taped and sold as sets, which then loosely informed what people expected to hear when they went to see the sound systems live. All these steps reflected the fact that sound systems worked both economically and culturally as *collectives* and as *work in progress*.

Bradley (2013: 332) describes how this way of working was developed by Jazzie B's Soul II Soul Sound System in the late 1980s. The first Soul II Soul record release (in 1988)

> was the result of continuing experiment by Jazzie and the collective. In true soundman style, he'd cut specials for his dances on dubplate and see how they went down, honing the music with each attempt, and then give the well-received cuts a push on radio.
>
> It made perfect sense for Jazzie to make records: he had a day job working as a sound engineer, in the studios owned and operated by the first British teen idol Tommy Steele, no less. Having recorded several jazz/funk acts ... he understood the process, and had access to a studio and dub-cutting facilities. He'd been doing some unofficial remixes and

Moving to a different beat 153

mixtape-style acetates for the sound system for a long time and had pressed up some of his own specials for sale in the Soul II to Soul shops.[12]

Even when Soul II Soul signed a recording deal with Virgin, it continued to act as the distributor of its own records:

> We said, 'Right, our record's got to be on a white label and we've got to sell them ... we were selling our records like imports, to all the little record shops, and it was really like a little hole in the market and we filled it. It taught us how to promote and distribute our own music.
>
> (Bradley 2013: 333)

As Jazzie B also notes, although Soul II Soul became hugely successful in commercial terms, neither UK nor US record companies started knocking out Soul II Soul clones:

> They couldn't. Because it wasn't a manufactured thing they couldn't just put a few together ... [they] never got the idea that we were a collective, not a group in the accepted sense.
>
> (Quoted in Bradley 2013: 335)

The reggae influence was equally apparent in jungle, as "the soundman's dubplate [became] the be-all and end-all of his sessions". The consequent demand for these one-off special cuts (the dubplates gave DJs their individual sound in live clashes) led to "a revolution in London's smaller disc-cutting operations". In Wookie's words:

> When jungle and drum'n'bass came in they started cutting dubplates because they'd taken on the whole reggae persona—record a tune on a Thursday night, mix it on Friday, and you're cutting the dubplate on Saturday for the rave that night.
>
> (Quoted in Bradley 2013: 355)

It was thus a natural progression for jungle producers to press multiple copies of their tunes as 12" singles, available not just live in clubs but on their own white labels. Using street-level distributors an MC could shift 15,000, even 20,000, copies of a single popular track (Bradley 2013: 356). DJ Target describes how grime artists followed the same business model. Tunes started as dubplates exclusively for the use of a particular DJ. They were then produced in 250 test-pressings of "exclusive vinyls", followed by 500 pre-release copies, aimed at the next layer of DJs (and only available in specialist shops) before eventually becoming "official releases" (DJ Target 2018: 132).

Of course, this kind of music making was, as Zuberi (Zuberi 2001: 168–9) puts it, "grounded in digital technology". If "house music had needed the

154 *Moving to a different beat*

sound-engineering capabilities of the sequencer", then jungle was "the product of the digital sampler's possibilities", while for grime all that was needed was a laptop. Wiley (2017: 72–3) recalls:

> I went quite quickly from making tracks on my dad's computer to doing it on my own … I was using the same programmes my dad had on his computers—Logic, Fruity Loops. I liked playing instruments, but I saw people getting jobs done quicker on programmes. By the time Logic and all those things came out, everyone was producing on computer. Fruity Loops was the one I made a lot of the early tracks on. It came with a standard 140 bpm setting. You had to look for it to change it, you know, and I was just putting things together on there.

DJ Target remembers being asked to produce a track for Wiley's debut album:

> Up until then, 95% of the beats we made were on our laptops. Logic Pro with a bunch of MIDI plugins was all we needed to get the sounds we wanted.
>
> (DJ Target 2018: 117)

Pirate radio

The most important factor in the development of the London sound system business in the 1980s and 1990s was the activity of pirate radio stations. Asked "How did the house thing come about?" Fabio replied:

> The pivotal point was a pirate station called Faze 1. This was the turning point for everything that's happened to me since. A guy called Mendoza set up a station. This was '84. He said, "I want all of you local guys to come in and do a show." It was a Brixton thing, right next to a pub, and he had a shebeen, an after-hours place, downstairs. But this shebeen, no one ever used to go to. It was our local but he never had more than six people there on a Saturday night. We used to go there, get pissed, go upstairs and play some music. A great set-up.
>
> (Quoted in Brewster and Broughton 2010: 442)

In October 1985, DJs Gordon "Mac" McNamee and George Power launched Kiss FM, broadcasting first to South London then across the whole city; in 1986, rapper Derek Boland set up WBLS. Both stations were black owned, but if Kiss FM represented the new club scene (Kiss promoted nights at the Wag Club, for example, and claimed to have put on the "first ever UK acid house party"), WBLS "shifted the approach away from a kind of border-line cheesy 'radio presenter' mode to a sound-system-centric vibe" (Bradley 2013: 326). Its models were DBC (Dread Broadcasting Company), which had

Moving to a different beat 155

been on air from 1981–84, and LWR, London Wide Radio (the first pirate station to feature regular live mixing on air) on which Derek Boland had been a DJ.[13]

In commercial terms, Kiss FM was by far the most successful of the 1980s pirate stations. Even though the Department of Trade and Industry (DTI), in charge of enforcing broadcast licensing regulations, kept it off air half the time, it could still claim an audience of 500,000 listeners, while in the face of its constant DTI raids WBLS lasted only a few months.[14] Yet the next explosion of illegal broadcasting, focused on the jungle scene, was primarily on the WBLS model:

> It's impossible to overstate the importance of pirate radio for jungle's survival ... At any point between 1992 and 1994 you could scan the FM spectrum and find at least a dozen 'ardcore jungle stations disrupting the decorum of the airwaves with their vulgar fervour and rude-boy attitude—stations like Touchdown, Defection, Rush, Format, Pulse, Eruption, Impact, Function and Kool, to name only the most famous.
>
> (Reynolds 1998: 264)[15]

These stations, transmitted from the top of tower blocks using microwave transmitters that were difficult for the DTI to trace, were so easy to set up that Reynolds (1998: 265) suggests there were more than 60 just in the London area and 600 nationwide in this period. For DJ Target, tuning into these pirates as a young teenager:

> Not only was the music more suited to us and what we were into [than the music on Radio 1 or Kiss], the radio sets were often hosted by an MC, who would drop in with his own lyrics and chats over particular parts of the tracks where there wasn't already a vocal sample. It sounded like London. It sounded like us. We were hooked ... They [the MCs] referenced places we knew, things we were growing up around, even mentioning people's names we were familiar with, even if it was just a shout-out on radio.
>
> (DJ Target 2018: 19)

For MC Novelist, a young teenager in the early 2010s:

> People love to say that our culture came from hip-hop but it actually comes more from the Caribbean ragga scene if anything. You know, actual proper MC-ing, and the only way you can really practise to be like that is on a pirate radio station, because legal radio wants to censor everything so you can't really wild out and just go crazy and do your own thing properly. That's why grime is what it is now. Pirate radio and practising is what made all the MCs how they are ...
>
> (Quoted in Collins and Rose 2016: 300)

156 *Moving to a different beat*

The broadcasting conventions here, in other words, did not mean "playing records" but their live *performance*. For grime artists, pirate radio stations were at the core of crews' creative and collective practice. DJ Target describes how his teenage friends Geeneus and Slimfast (DJ Slimzee) started Rinse FM in 1994:

> Gee and Slim had done the research, learnt about radio waves, transmitters, link boxes and everything else that was needed to launch a station successfully ... They had subletted someone's council flat which was going to be the studio, and all the aerials and transmitters were in place on the various tower blocks in Bow.
>
> (DJ Target 2018: 45)[16]

Setting up crews and radio stations was part of the same process. So Solid Crew came together in sets for Supreme FM and Delight FM (broadcast from the Winstanley Estate in Bermondsey); Pay As U Go came together in sets on Rinse. As DJ Target (2018: 164) explains, 99% of their tracks were first played on radio, a perfect testing ground: "if it didn't work on radio, it probably wouldn't work anywhere else".

For Wiley, the station was essential to the creative process:

> Sometimes he had a new bunch of lyrics he wanted to practise, or a new tune to play, or just fancied doing a set. Although DJs and MCs were only supposed to be in the studio during their own sets, Wiley had definitely earned his green card to turn up and jump in a set if he wanted to. Sometimes it would be during the day and sometimes at 3 a.m. Sometimes he'd want a load of MCs with him, and others he'd want to go and do a solo set so he could really practise. He just loved it. Wiley's pirate radio work ethic is what had pushed him head and shoulders above other MCs from our generation. Nobody had used the tool of pirate radio like he had. He'd make a track, go straight to the radio to play it, then do a killer set which hyped him to make another tune, and so on.
>
> (Wiley 2017: 166–7)

As part of the funding model of most pirate stations:

> DJs and MCs were charged subs, meaning you'd have to pay usually £5 each week before your set—money was needed to buy the equipment that was regularly seized in DTI raids.
>
> (Wiley 2017: 159)

Legitimation?

This era of radio began to change in the 2000s following the launch in 2002 of a new BBC digital radio station, 1Xtra.[17] Ruby Mulraine, one of the key BBC figures in its launch, understood that:

Moving to a different beat 157

IXtra would be dealing with a genre of music that interfaced with its audience in a very unique way, rather than relying on conventional, record company-centred methodology. This was an instant, DIY culture, so the new station's staff had to be immersed in that world ... The trouble ... when we first started, was that some of the artists came to the station and treated it as if they were coming to a pirate station. You'd get artists coming late—*often*—or not turning up whereas something like that on Radio 1 just wouldn't happen.

(Quoted in Bradley 2013: 393–4)

The emergence of 1xtra was certainly significant for grime's move into the mainstream of British popular music. As Bradley (2013: 394) puts it:

No longer did you have to be living on the Stepney estate from which Roll Deep was broadcasting to hear some authentic grime: suddenly kids as far removed as the Hebrides or Penzance could feel part of things.

But in the new digital world, such national radio support meant less than it might once have done. According to grime DJ Logan Sama:

We started out with white labels and tapes, moved on to CDs and MP3s, and now streaming is the biggest thing for us. It [grime] was the first genre in this country to be born with the Internet, to be spread virally. We had the tape packs, the raves and the club nights, but it really exploded when we started file sharing. We were swapping stuff on MSN Messenger all the time, and young producers were using whatever technology they had around them.

(Quoted in Wiley 2017: 94)

Lloyd Bradley (2013: 386–7) explains:

The first generation to grow up with the web, these guys were exploiting it mercilessly for showcasing, podcasting and streaming. When they got a grip on Facebook and You Tube, hilarious rough'n'ready promo videos popped up, filmed on inexpensive digital cameras or sophisticated phones ... and as artists appeared in the clothing they'd been wearing all day, they reinforced the notion of there being little difference between performer and public.

The DIY videos with the most impact were Jammer's *Lords of the Mic* and MC clashes he filmed in the Dungeon (a studio in the cellar in his parents' house). In 2003, Darren Platt launched Channel U, a digital satellite channel, broadcasting videos 24 hours a day and "running on a jukebox type system— viewers called in and gave the three digit code of the video they wanted, and that video would be added to the rotation". By 2004, "more and more artists were shooting videos, knowing they had an accessible platform to aim for"

158   *Moving to a different beat*

(DJ Target 2018: 202–3) and it was not long before Channel U had been joined by online platforms such as SBTV (launched in 2006) and Link Up TV (launched in 2008).

Unlike previous DIY music movements, grime had developed a marketing and promotional model that enabled even its biggest stars, like Wiley, Skepta and Kano (who all had periods signed to major labels) to remain effectively independent. But there are two final points to make about this.

First, this was not a form of amateurism. Grime's commercial success reflected its ability to deal with the nuts and bolts of the music business— managers, agents, bookers, promoters, publishers and so on—and what is noteworthy here is the number of women playing key roles in the infrastructure of this black music business. Sandra Lockhart, for example, was central to the development of dubstep as the path from garage to grime. In 2001 she set up Club FWD (first at the Velvet Rooms in Charing Cross then at Plastic People in Shoreditch); she ran the record label Tempa, Essential Distribution and Ammunition Promotions; she managed Geenius, among others, and took charge of Rinse FM; for a while she was head of A&R at EMI Publishing. Cat Park was station manager of Channel U from 2006–12, when she left to form Ten Letter PR. Chantelle Fiddy and Hattie Collins started out working for *Touch* (a monthly black-oriented lifestyle magazine, published from 1991– 2001) and became the leading press champions of grime in both specialist publications such as *RWD* (first published in 2001)[18] and the mainstream national and music press. Fay Hoyte was project manager for black acts at Virgin[19] and Sarah McKinley and Rebecca Prochnik were agents, the former with Xtreme Talent, the biggest garage agency (founded 1999), the latter with the DJ Agency Elastic Artists (founded 2002)—she represented Wiley.

For these women (as for Ruby Mulraine at 1Xtra), the task was to align the casual DIY conventions of their clients with the professional expectations of the music and media businesses with which they were now working. Rebecca Prochnik explains how booking grime artists differed from booking artists from other genres:

> Although a few have notorious and longstanding teams, the majority of grime artists traditionally have been unmanaged or had very loose management. Also artists often hadn't travelled too much, especially out of the UK. Initially, getting things to run smoothly was a challenge and still can be with younger artists who are used to rolling with a lot of people. This can create a conflict for promoters and the smooth running of shows sometimes. At times it adds to the mood and vibe, but it can be hit and miss and sometimes obscure the talent.[20]

In a 2018 interview with Chantelle Fiddy, Cat Park describes the situation when she arrived at Channel U. The station had already been fined significantly by Ofcom for licence breaches:

Moving to a different beat   159

It was a nightmare; we were watched like a hawk ... There'd been dodgy dealings with payola, people paying under hand to get their videos on the channel, and I just wanted to bring more professionalism to it, really.

[CF] There was also a lot of controversy around artists having to sign a waiver to get their videos on the channel too, right?

Yes. With PPL/VPL, you have to have a licence. Now if we look at a channel like MTV Base, they're dealing with massive artists with publishers, labels, managers—everyone's making money from it, collecting royalties. At the other end of the scale, if we're paying out this massive amount of money for licences but none of the artists are registered to PPL, what's the point? You can't collect if you're not registered. But then it became "Channel U are taking our money".[21]

Our second point is that the sound system business was not just "underground", but had involved specifically *illegal* activities (such as pirate radio). With reference to jungle, Bradley (2013: 359) points out that, "while the lack of regulation may have been creatively stimulating, this free-for-all entailed inevitable copyright problems", especially once the records started having commercial success. Wookie suggests that the musical move from jungle to drum'n'bass primarily involved making jungle tracks without the ragga samples:

The reggae artists and producers have all got connections in London—through the sound systems—and they had started catching on. Whereas things might have been let slide, now they were looking at it thinking "This music's getting big, they're sampling my voice and they ain't paying me no royalties!"

(Quoted in Bradley 2013: 360)

The biggest impact of law enforcement on the development of this music, however, came not from copyright or radio licensing issues but from fear of crimes that hadn't yet happened but might. As we discussed in Chapter 4, the Metropolitan Police introduced risk form 696 in 2006 and DJ Target describes its effect on grime artists:

Form 696 had an almost immediate impact, with the number of events decreasing monthly. Some clubs took grime and hip hop nights off their books completely for fear of being cancelled by the police. Artists began to feel the bite of losing shows and having hardly anywhere to perform in the capital ... grime was being pushed further underground.

(DJ Target 2018: 210–11)

For grime journalist John McDonnell, "Form 696 basically killed off grime for about half a decade. It stopped grime in its original form taking off by

160   *Moving to a different beat*

killing the live music" (quoted in Collins and Rose 2016: 251). For grime MC Razor:

> I would say that Form 696 has actively shut down events that I've wanted to go to or perform at and has discouraged people from working in the industry or the scene that I was in. They've moved to work in deep house, in pop, in rock & roll, because those genres aren't being discriminated against; they can make more money there.
> (Quoted in Collins and Rose 2016: 251)

Even after the form was scrapped (in 2017), problems remained:

> There's [still] a lot of legislation and red tape to be able to put on any sort of music that is based around that culture. It would be easier to say that you're putting on a garage night and get a licence for that, but as soon as you put the word "grime" or "bashment" or any of those genres on your event descriptions, the venues wouldn't want to take the event forward because they would predict that they'd have trouble. The headline is that they are going to scrap Form 696 but in my experience it's very, very rare that authority takes away a restriction like that and doesn't have anything to replace it.[22]

The problem for what MC Razor calls 'authority' was the perceived *culture* of grime. Who and what did this music stand for?

Whose music?

Simon Reynolds (1998: 259) writes that:

> Jungle is often hailed as the first and most significant and truly indigenous black British music ... But even if one concedes jungle's musical "blackness" as self-evident, this only makes it all the more striking that from day one more than half of the leading DJs and producers have been white.

Reynolds (1998: 259) goes on to argue that, in contrast to "the mostly white audience for trance and 'intelligent' techno", jungle had always been multi-racial, defined "not by colour but by class": "Junglist youth constitute a kind of internal colony within the United Kingdom: a ghetto of surplus labour and potential criminals under surveillance by the police." Les Back's ethnographic study of this "colony" in South London in the early 1990s found young people sharing loyalties, origins and identities (in the formation of posses and crews, for example), but also concluded that such "interpretative communities" were not exclusively black or white. On the dance floors and in the clubs, young whites had access to the "sensibilities and programmes" of black London.

Moving to a different beat   161

"Blackness" or "whiteness" were not the only issues here. Back (1996: 219) argues that "there are direct parallels between the development of sound system culture and the emergence of new South Asian musical cultures in Britain during the 1980s":

> Within the context of Britain, music [which originated in the Punjab] has been re-invented. Bands such as Alaap in West London's Southall district incorporated sound sampling, drum machines and synthesizers to produce the new form called *bhangra beat* ... In the Midlands other influences from hip hop and house have been incorporated producing *northern rock bhangra* and *house bhangra*.

The appeal of bhangra was seen by media commentators at the time as cutting across differences of nation, religion, caste and class among British Asian youth while adapting to the cultural conservatism of their parents, most obviously in the emergence of bhangra "daytimers", disco events taking place during or after school hours:[23]

> Daytimers reinforce our culture and values, girls dress in *sulwaars,* boys can come in turbans and get no hassle. The music is our music, and it's their show, not a "*goray*" [white] gig or a "*kale*" [black] show. Do parents want for kids to go out to *goray* shows? Would they rather have Asian kids disowning and abandoning their culture, to become Sharons and Garys tomorrow?
> (Mac, singer with Dhamaka, quoted in Back 1996: 220)

Komal, from the East London bhangra band Cobra, explained bhangra's significance in this way:

> I can remember going to college discos a long time ago, when all you heard was Reggae, Reggae, Reggae. Asians were lost, they weren't accepted by whites, so they drifted into the black culture, dressing like blacks, talking like them, and listening to reggae. But now Bhangra has given them "their" music and made them feel they do have an identity. No matter if they are Gujaratis, Punjabis or whatever—Bhangra is Asian music for Asians.
> (Quoted in Back 1996: 220)[24]

This is not bhangra as traditional Punjabi music, but bhangra beat. Dr Das of Asian Dub Foundation explains:

> We see our music as a natural outcome of having been brought up in this country ... It's not part of a fusion, it's just normal. It's taking in everything that I hear. When I lived with my parents I'd listen to Indian classical music, watch Hindi musicals and listen to Sunrise radio; at the

162   *Moving to a different beat*

same time I was listening to dub, Hendrix and techno. There is no contradiction in putting all these sounds together. It's normal and natural. Our music is the sound of urban London today. It's like a soundtrack. It's real Britpop—not revivalist or nostalgic.

(Quoted in Zuberi 2001: 182)[25]

This music was functional as well as ideological: it was meant for dancing. DJ Bally Sagoo suggests that the problem with the traditional bhangra bands was that:

Every single song was always on a similar line, and based on this typical boy-meets-girl song. They always got to have loads of '*hois*' in there, and so on. Like most of Western youth, Asian kids brought up here also wanted the punchy, racy bass lines, the great drum beat and the powerful female vocals coming across. I wanted to hear, probably, more melodies than lyrics. I just wanted a good beat and a good vibe, a good song on the dancefloor. Because, obviously, that's what makes everybody get up and dance.

(Quoted in Housee and Dar 1996: 90)[26]

One way to trace the history of bhangra in Britain is through its performance spaces. Britain's first bhangra groups, Alaap (put together by Channi Singh in 1975) and Heera (put together by Bhupinder Bhindi in 1979), played in West London temples before taking their sets to weddings and other social functions. Asian dance promoters began to hire bhangra musicians to play alongside local DJs and the increasing demand for their music encouraged the bhangra acts to make their own 12" singles (the Asian recording market in Britain had previously been dominated by cassettes) and the DJs to start mixing bhangra with reggae, soul, funk and hip hop in their club sets.

Young Asian dancers thus began to establish their own dance floor spaces, although how this was done depended on local conditions. In Birmingham, for example, bhangra was shaped by (and in response to) local Anglo-Caribbean culture. The biggest local star, Steve Kapur aka Apache Indian, performed in "a creole language" that "combine[d] Punjabi, Hindi and Patois". After leaving school, he had

worked as a roadie for several reggae sound systems before getting a chance on the microphone to voice his own Handsworth songs. He privately financed the pressing of "Move Over India", a single [released in 1990] that combined Jamaican patois and Punjabi rhymes. After receiving some radio airplay, the single was a local success and then a national hit on the reggae charts.

(Zuberi 2001: 201–2)

Moving to a different beat 163

In London, Asian Dub Foundation was originally set up in 1993 as a sound system at a music workshop in Farringdon organised by free jazz drummer John Stevens.[27] The group's rapper/MC, Master D [Deedar Zaman], had previously been in one of the first Asian sound systems in London, Joi Bangla, formed in the mid-1980s. This group described itself as "Asian punk junglists", and its music (as described by Zuberi),

> incorporates the snicketty chikketty drum break-beats of jungle, but the sound foundations are dub bass lines with Master D's breakneck rapping in both Jamaican patois and London English accents, samples of Bollywood strings, harmonium drones, Indian classical flute and violin, folk drums, and electronic sequencers. Chandrasonic [guitarist Steve Chandra Savale] tunes his guitar like a sitar. Dr Das [bass player Aniruddha Das] says that the group "uses some principles of Indian music that have come down through thousands of years but we're applying technology to it".
>
> (Zuberi 2001: 218–19)

DJ Ritu recalls the bhangra/jungle connection, marked by a new clubbing scene in London:

> Bombay Jungle at the Wag Club was put together by three different sound system promoters in September 1993. A weekly generous helping of bhangra and black music, catering for Asians that enjoy bhangra and for those that don't, yet still want to be the majority rather than the minority race at a club night. Bombay Jungle is an exception in that it's the first night for Asians run by Asians.
>
> (Quoted in Awan 1995: 109)[28]

For MC Radical Sista, who performed with KKKings, "a mixture of Hindi vocals, Punjabi and mellow chill out rap" was "representative of the times we're living in—integrating all cultures is the way forward" (quoted in Awan 1995: 110).

Another setting for Asian dancers in London in the 1990s was Anokha, a club night at Blue Note in Hoxton launched by Talvin Singh and Sweety Kapoor in 1995 and designed to promote the Asian underground music scene.[29] The effect of this electronic dance club night was to make the "lived experiences of this group of British Asians visible in white-dominated British popular culture" (Murthy 2009: 332); the majority of those in the audience were not Asian. Only the Asian dancers, though, could feel part of the ethnic culture that dominated the soundscape:

> Suddenly you felt like not only did you enjoy the bassline and the beats that were going around it ... but there was this sudden Indian sample that you could kind of relate to and when you heard it in the clubs you thought,

164 *Moving to a different beat*

"I know this better than most people, I know these sounds, I know what this is." And people coming up you and asking you ... 'What's that sound, what is that instrument?' ... And suddenly you felt like you are bigger part of that scene ... it kind of made it ours in some sense. You kind of knew the DJs who were producing the music, you knew the club DJs. Friends, older brothers and relatives involved in it ...

(Hanif, quoted in Murthy 2009: 342)

For Asian teenagers in Newcastle, the situation was quite different. In his study of the city's youth in the late 1990s, Andy Bennett found that "very little evening leisure provision is currently made for young ethnic minority groups in Newcastle". There were no club nights, no bhangra scene, no bhangra bands and only two bhangra DJs. If, in Birmingham and London, bhangra beat was the music of a "proactive youth culture", no longer willing to be "trapped" in parental culture, in Newcastle a bhangra event was still "cause for a family outing". Such "traditional" events were important because they enabled an expression of ethnic identity that was otherwise not possible: to appear in ethnic costume in everyday life would be "out of place" (Bennett 2000: 106–7, 110).

Bhangra here was not the new sound of a new kind of Asian-British identity, but the traditional sound of a familial Asian identity. Bennett quotes a young man on a return visit to Newcastle having moved to Birmingham:

Down there you get schools where it's all Asians and Afro-Caribbeans and they've grown up together and that's the way they've been brought up to feel. The Asians listen to reggae and rap and stuff, and they'll have black people singing on their tracks ... the Afro-Caribbeans down there, they listen to bhangra music as well. It's a close-knit sort of thing, they kind of alienate themselves from the English music.

(Quoted in Bennett 2000: 114)

Compare the way the term "English music" is used in a discussion Bennett had in a Newcastle comprehensive school:

SUNIL: None of us likes bhangra really.
AB: What sort of music do you like?
SUNIL: English music
AB: Such as?
SUNIL: Rap
ABDUL KHAN: I like rap and reggae
BOBBY: I like rap as well;
AB: So what is it about bhangra you don't like?
BOBBY: It's too old-fashioned.

(Quoted in Bennett 2000: 114–5)

Conclusion

In his ethnographic report on clubbing in London in the mid-1990s, Ben Malbon quotes an anonymous clubber:

> I've always grown up thinking life is pretty grim, and you've got to fucking work your bollocks off 'cos otherwise you're not going to get anywhere— I've still got a very strong work ethic inherited from my Asian background ... but what I really like about clubbing is just the trash Western, hedonistic nonsense of it all ... and this is happening now and it's my culture, this is the only thing I have that I can call home. I'm not English in the normal sense of the word, and I'm not Indian by any means ... I've just been dumped into this urban nightmare scenario with a blank sheet of paper and I just, I just love it—it's my culture.
>
> (Quoted in Malbon 1998: 281)

A decade later, in May 2005, a flyer appeared in Hackney advertising "Mahatma's Revenge":

> A night that embraces all, from the past, present and future. Translating anarchy-confusion, double identity, hybridity and cultural mutation into soundscapes of eastern influenced beats and breaks, deep broken house, breakbeat and drum & bass. Presented by the now infamous Shiva Soundsystem crew, with live guests [including DJs from San Francisco's Dhamaal crew] and resident DJs.
>
> (Quoted from the flyer, reprinted in Murthy 2009: 340)[30]

This night, like the same decade's Independence Day Mutiny events, when British Asians of Bangladeshi, East-African, Indian, Pakistani and Trinidadian ancestries came together to celebrate India and Pakistan's independence days with both local and visiting DJs, shows how important music had become to second- and third-generation immigrants' explorations of what it meant to be British and Asian, a Londoner and a Bangladeshi, a Muslim, Sikh or Hindu and a Brummie or a Geordie.

Considering these issues with reference to young Anglo-Caribbeans, Les Back (1996: 227) argues that "the culture that is produced here relies not on entities of selfhood" (with music expressing a given identity) but "on the process of becoming more than one". Music such as jungle or bhangra expresses a "collective supplementarity—ragga *plus* bhangra *plus* England *plus* Indian *plus* Kingston *plus* Birmingham" (Back 1996: 227). The black, white and Asian junglists to whom he talked all claimed that their music uniquely belonged to Britain or, more specifically, that jungle was "a London somet'ing". For these citizens, this was music "to feel at home in", "profoundly heterotopic and simultaneously local, national and transnational" (Back 1996: 234). For

166   *Moving to a different beat*

Lloyd Bradley (2013: 385, our italics), focusing on London's black music history, the music had become so pan-racial as to make it impossible to tell what a performer's roots might be: "As an MC-ed art form, grime ... had been designed, however subconsciously, from the *composite* cadence of the capital's youth."

This is the background to young people's identity as *Londoners* in Jeremy Deller's rave film discussed at the start of this chapter. We end it with a different point. Live music is a setting for cultural conflict as well as cultural harmony, and this has been particularly true of the dance floor.

In late 2012/early 2013, a dispute arose in London clubs over the shuffle, "a crouchy, jerky dance style" mostly performed by young black dancers. Kieran Yates reported that:

> Complaints are typically to do with shufflers taking up too much dance-floor space, and dressing in a way which is incongruous with the socially accepted styles favoured by the non-shuffling crowd.
>
> (*The Guardian*, January 31, 2013)[31]

There were echoes in this dance floor spat of similar arguments in the house scene in the north of England in the mid-1980s.[32] At the beginning of the decade, club nights focused on the latest black American dance tracks became leisure sites for local black youth otherwise excluded from the mainstream city centre discos by quotas and dress codes. Nights like The Jive Turkey in Sheffield nurtured the early house scene, while "dayers" – inter-city events on Sundays and Bank Holidays – were also promoted, attracting predominantly black audiences to dance from midday to midnight. The emphasis at such events was on virtuosic and competitive dancing, individually or in troupes, as we described in Volume 2 (Frith et al. 2019: 152–3).

This dance floor culture changed when house nights were invaded by the "love community". As Mangera-Lakew (2014: 33–4) writes, "the rise of un-stylised, unrehearsed dancing to Acid House" could be said to have "democratised the club environment, as there was no precedent for the right or best way to dance". But these changes could also be described in another way:

> The drug crowd was incompatible with the black scene's system of creating status through dance ... [and] ... house went from being a genre predominantly popular amongst unemployed black people in the North, to a nationally consumed genre with a majority, white, wage-earning audience.
>
> (Mangera-Lakew (2014: 33–4)

In London, this was the moment when, as we have already described, the original black house sound systems "eased out" of the acid house scene and set in place the music-making dynamic that led from jungle to grime. Our point here is twofold. First, the arguments and disputes about music and identity

Moving to a different beat 167

that inform this chapter refer not just to who was performing and what was being performed, but also to audience expectations, to dance floor behaviour, to the social *etiquette* of listening to live music. Second, live music history is a history of places, venues and spaces, and more importantly a history of the ecological relationship *between* performance spaces. Audiences and the live music ecology are the topics of Chapters 10 and 11. In Chapter 9 we consider the changing fortunes of performers in music worlds with professional conventions that seemed to be well established by 1985. So how did rock, classical, jazz and folk musicians adapt to digital technology and new cultural and commercial ideologies?

Notes

1 Quoted in Brewster and Broughton (2010: 442).
2 In 2015, Rupa Huq became Labour MP for Ealing Central and Acton.
3 One impetus for the move from houses to warehouses was the 1981 New Cross fire, in which 13 teenagers were killed when flames swept through a birthday celebration. This led, among other things, to increased police action to prevent such gatherings.
4 Manchester-based DJ Greg Wilson notes that "as Ecstasy swept in, House [ironically] went overground". Black participants in the original northern House scene were also "eased out" and had "to reinvent the wheel, coming away from the scenes they had established to create fresh underground scenes … and to forge their own musical direction" (quoted in Mangera-Lakew 2014: 36).
5 For an excellent account of the cultural complications of DJ-ing in 1990s London see Frost (2017).
6 For the Saxon story, see https://thevinylfactory.com/features/the-story-of-saxon-sound-system. For Papa Levi, see http://uncarved.org/dub/papalevi.html.
7 For examples of clashing as "the essence of grime", see DJ Target (2018: 215–28).
8 Sound clashes had long given Jamaican DJs an opportunity to test their sonic skills against other sound systems, but stage shows put MCs in front of bigger audiences—Sting was set up to give dancehall fans a night of head-to-head clashes between their favourite performers.
9 Big Dada, which released some of Wiley's work, was a subsidiary of Ninja Tunes, the trip hop label founded by Coldcut in 1990.
10 For more on these garage committees (apparently formed in 1999 by "deejays, producers and promoters [at] the top of the scene") and their attempts to control venues' booking policies, see Bradley (2013: 368).
11 Pay as U Go and Roll Deep were sound systems of which both DJ Target and Wiley were members. For the economic significance of mixtapes for grime, see DJ Target (2018: 141–3).
12 After designing a logo for its party flyers, Soul II Soul developed its own look (clothing and hair styling) and started selling tee shirts and other fashion-based merchandise, initially in market stalls and then in its own shops (Bradley 2013: 315–25).
13 LWR had started (as London Weekend Radio) at the beginning of 1983. Originally a pop station, it was relaunched as a soul/reggae/hip hop outlet in September 1984. For a detailed history of London pirate radio, see Hebditch (2015).

14 Kiss FM went off air at the end of 1987 in order to prepare an application for a licence, which it was granted in December 1989.

15 Kool FM was the longest lasting of these, broadcasting from Hackney from 1991 before switching to the Internet in 2000. In late 1992, Kool also started to promote events, launching its *Jungle Fever* night in August 1993.

16 Since 2010, Rinse FM has been a licensed community radio station for "young people living and/or working within the central, east and south London areas".

17 Although this certainly didn't put a stop to pirate broadcasting. An Ofcom report in 2007 found that 16% of adults in Greater London still said they listened to illegal broadcasters. See www.ofcom.org.uk/research-and-data/tv-radio-and-on-demand/radio-research/illegal-broadcasting.

18 *RWD* developed an interesting financial model. It was freely distributed and therefore had a big enough circulation (around 100,000) to attract advertisers while acts paid to have their tracks, videos and profiles included.

19 In 2018 Hoyte was appointed marketing director of EMI.

20 Quote taken from www.musicweek.com/live/read/grime-week-skepta-embodied-the-shift-earth-agency-s-rebecca-prochnik-reflects-on-scene-s-growth/069561.

21 Quoted from *Trench,* https://trenchtrenchtrench.com/features/the-tipping-point-01-cat-park-channel-u-and-the-future-of-grime.

22 Quoted from an interview with Emma Webster, November 15, 2017.

23 For an entertaining survey of British press coverage of bhangra in the late 1980s, mostly "focused on the repressed-Asian-youth angle", see Huq (1996: 65–7).

24 Back takes these quotes from Baumann (1990: 87, 91).

25 Sunrise Radio, the UK's first commercial Asian radio station, was launched in Bradford on November 5, 1989. For the history of British Asian radio, see Khamkar (2016).

26 For Sagoo's career, see Zuberi (2001: 205–10).

27 Stevens had been a leading figure on the British free jazz scene since forming the Spontaneous Music Ensemble (SME) in 1966. From 1983 he worked with Community Music to bring improvised music making to youth clubs, community centres and mental hospitals. He died in 1994. Asian Dub Foundation played the 1997 London Jazz Festival with Nitin Sawhney.

28 Bombay Jungle was succeeded by the Hot'n'Spicy night at the Limelight, which ran from 1994–99.

29 In Birmingham, similar club nights were Chak De Phattey at The Church from 1996 and Shaanti at the Que Club from 1999. The Blue Note in Hoxton was also the home of Goldie's Metalheadz night.

30 Murthy notes that the flyer's writer was clearly well versed in cultural studies!

31 See www.theguardian.com/music/musicblog/2013/jan/31/foot-shuffling-ban-house-club.

32 The argument here draws primarily from Mangera-Lakew (2014), which in turn draws primarily from an interview with DJ Greg Wilson.

9 Making a musical living

When everything's free, who's going to pay a musician to be professional?
When I started, in the 60s, you bought a record and, at the end of a long chain,
a band got a few bob … now you can download [a CD] with a click, and if you
pay anything at all it's only small change … the future now is for amateurs.
(Jon Hiseman, 66, jazz drummer, interviewed by Dave Gelly
in the April 2011 issue of *Jazz Journal*)[1]

As a musician you've got be an accountant, you've got to be a salesman,
you've got to have a marketing qualification, you've got to be able to do
funding applications, you've got to be articulate, you've got to have a good
phone voice … having to constantly sell yourself is exhausting … All I do is
sit on my computer all day replying to emails, sending emails, catching up on
some accounts from last year, hoping that the phone's going to ring and some
gigs will come in.
(Eric, 28, jazz saxophonist, interviewed by
Umney and Kretsos 2013: 582)

Introduction

In 2009, *IQ*, the live music trade paper, ran a special feature on "the super
managers", the managers who now handled those elements of a rock
musician's career that had once been the responsibility of a record company.
Brian Message from Courtyard Management (who handled Radiohead's
affairs) explained to *IQ* that the manager's task now was to develop "multiple
revenue streams" in "the creation and sustaining of *an artist business*" (*IQ* 24
[Q2] 2009: 14, our italics).

A key part of artist business was developing a direct relationship between
musician and fan. Malcolm McKenzie from SuperVision Management
(a specialist in hard rock and metal acts) said:, "[This] requires you to do
more work but the upside is that a direct-to-fan business is profitable at a
much lower sales base and therefore much earlier in the process" (*IQ* 24 [Q2]
2009: 14–5).

170 *Making a musical living*

In this model:

> Recorded music is a marketing cost, not a revenue stream. In reality, these days, the packaging has more fiscal value than the music does. You make records to market your band and create an emotional connection with the audience and you make your money from touring and selling T-shirts. I often joke that I'm not in the music business but the clothing business.
>
> (*IQ* 24 [Q2] 2009:17)

In 2010, *Music Week* reported that that year's MIDEM, the annual international music industry jamboree, was focused on "the monetisation" of live music, with panellists highlighting ways in which artists could increase their live income, whether by selling ads for video screening between stage performances or by using data-capture to help them connect with fans for download sales (*Music Week,* February 6, 2010: 16). In *IQ*, Malcolm McKenzie had explained the audience development strategy here: to turn prospects into friends, friends into customers, customers into fans and fans into superfans—the top 5% of a band's followers who spend far more on music and merchandise than anyone else, but who also need careful nurturing. It was this process for which data access and control were essential, as we discussed in Chapter 3 (*IQ* 24 (Q2) 2009: 18).

Such discussions of bands as brands could be read as evidence that digital technology had seen off the self-conscious distancing from raw commerce typical of rock musicians. But a recurring theme of this history has been that the continuities in musical culture are just as significant as the changes. This is particularly true for musicians, whose lives and careers are not easily divisible by decades, and for audiences, whose understanding of live music is shaped by experience. As Angus Batey wrote in *The Guardian* on February 20, 2009:

> [In the rock world] the mechanics may be changing—My Space pages replacing demo tapes, music sold independently on line—but the Transit van trawl around the toilet circuit remains a cornerstone rite of passage for aspirant rock stars, and [rock] audiences are taught to mistrust anyone who hasn't paid these dues.[2]

In this chapter, we will examine what it means to be a performing musician in the digital age while recognising that "the digital revolution" in music was shaped by existing assumptions about creativity and professionalism as well as by historical consciousness. We will trace the issues here across different music worlds—rock and pop, classical, jazz and folk—while understanding that making a living from music involves similar problems and opportunities for all musicians, and that in this period they all had to deal with not only technological innovations but also the effects of globalisation, economic austerity and the changes in state policies we described in Chapter 4.

Rock's last rites

In the preface to his history of the music scene in Northampton between 1988 and 1996, Derrick Thompson (2008) notes that throughout this time the town had "top rate bands" playing New Orleans jazz, soul, Beatles covers, reggae, folk and Irish folk-rock, "as well as dozens of bands playing variations of Indie music, Dance music, Rock and Pop".[3] Thompson's book, which is primarily about Northampton's rock musicians, is one of a number of oral histories documenting rock music-making in particular localities in the 1980s and 1990s—histories that complement Sara Cohen's (1991) anthropological study of two rock bands in mid-1980s Liverpool.[4]

Cohen (1991: 38) suggests that for rock musicians in this period, "being in a band was a way of life":

> The sense of camaraderie and enjoyment involved was exhibited in the way in which musicians tended to fondly discuss and reminisce about past exploits with their band or with previous bands. Tales were told about wild goings-on travelling to and from gigs and what "a laff" they had, or about how close the band had come to getting "a deal" and what they should have done but did not. It was also revealed in the way in which band members charted the history of their band, describing in detail the movement of members from one band to another as if relating the genealogy of their own family.

In Volume 2 of this history, we described the development of a new kind of musical career in the 1970s—becoming a rock star— and by the mid-1980s this career model was as familiar to young musicians around the country as the rules of a favourite board game: form a band with friends, play local gigs, find a manager, get an agent, trail round the toilet circuit, make a demo, sign to a record company and publisher, release a single, get radio play, release an album, buy on to a tour as a support act, employ a press agent, sell merchandise, make videos, supposedly earn and spend millions, fall out with manager, agent, record company and fellow band members (in that order). Go back to square one.[5]

The rules of the rock band game could be remarkably detailed. Remembering his first tour with Inspiral Carpets, Tom Hingley (2012: 32) writes that, "as with all groups, a massive over-importance is attached to the order in which band members are dropped off at home at the end of the tour". By then rock's behavioural conventions were as familiar to audiences as to musicians, which is why young rock fans assumed so readily that they too could become rock stars.[6]

In his entertaining heavy metal memoir, for example, Seb Hunter (2004: 201) describes his move from being a metal fan to forming a metal band as a natural progression, in which learning how to make the music was tied up with learning how to dress and behave as the audience. By the end of the 1980s,

172 *Making a musical living*

small town metal fans and bands had their own music magazine, *Kerrang!*, their own outdoor festival, Masters of Rock, and their own gathering points in London: "landmarks, tourist spots, pubs, clubs, gig venues and shopping", where metal conventions could be learnt.[7]

Throughout the 1980s, it seems rock musicians were still trying to hang onto to the 1960s sense of counterculture by which rock was originally defined. By the end of the decade, however, so-called "indie-rock" was not really "rebellious and anti-establishment" at all. The "credibility" of rock musicians now, suggests Louise Wener, was determined not by individuality but by conformity with a strict code of practice:

> Even though your record company is shelling out many thousands of pounds on your behalf—videos, photo shoots, recordings, producers, PR gurus, tour budgets, marketing and drugs—you can, and must, remain unsullied by the stench of filthy corporate lucre that surrounds you by virtue of having once fashioned your own record cover out of brown paper.
>
> (Wener 2010: 161–2)[8]

Among the best-established codes of rock practice were the gender rules. Seb Hunter (2004: 239) describes metal as "so overwhelmingly masculine that there was literally no space within it for women"[9] and Sara Cohen (1991: 204) writes that, "although women are, in general, notably absent from rock music, that absence was particularly notable in Liverpool": the compilation album of local bands funded by Liverpool City Council was unashamedly entitled *Jobs for the Boys*.[10] In Volume 2 we cited Mavis Bayton's findings that the combination of punk rock and second-wave feminism resulted in "the single largest surge of women into rock music-making in the UK". But if for a moment in the late 1970s and early 1980s it seemed as if "we were on the edge of a breakthrough", by the end of the decade "the whole rock-and-roll world remained overwhelmingly male" (Bayton 1998: 22, 63).

Like Cohen, Bayton argues that the masculine ideology of rock music-making meant both that male bands saw women as "a threat" and that women musicians were wary of rock's institutional norms—the endless touring, for example—as part of what Louise Wener (2010: 223) calls "a musical bloke-fest". But while the overwhelming laddism of 1990s rock is obvious, it did not altogether exclude women. In 1994, for example, Maggie Mouzakitis was appointed tour manager for the ultra-laddish band Oasis:

> When she first arrived, we thought it a mad decision to employ her as our tour manager. She looked about 12 with her American accent, baseball cap and ponytail. But [manager] Marcus [Russell] had been right. A sisterly touch would be just the thing to keep control of five young men.
>
> (McCarroll 2011: 148)[11]

For successful female musicians, rock's retro ideology was perhaps less of a challenge than the broader cultural changes of the Thatcher era, particularly

Making a musical living 173

its competitive individualism and valorisation of conspicuous wealth. Tracey Thorn (2014: 234–5) remembers the 1980s becoming a "very much more conservative decade":

> The female icon you were supposed to revere above all others was, of course, Madonna, and no one could have seemed more alien to me. A shiny, brash, Teflon-coated embodiment of AMBITION, she was absolutely a version of feminism but not the one I felt I'd signed up to ... Manipulating men, using your feminine wiles "to your own advantage", above all exploiting a simplified version of your own sexuality was suddenly the name of the game again.

For Louise Wener (2010: 287–8), by 1995 "the coterie of frank, gutsy women fronting guitar bands had been watered down with giggly 'girl power'":

> You wake up one morning in the midst of the beer-swilling, coke-fuelled, self-important macho parody that is Britpop's death rattle and say, haven't we been here before? Justine [from Elastica] aping Christine Keeler on the cover of *Select*, Sonya Echobelly falling out of her shirt in *iD*, Cerys Catatonia pouting half naked on the cover of a lad's mag, and how the hell did I end up being photographed in a wet-look PVC catsuit carrying a gun? I look ridiculous. Like sexy liquorice.
> This wasn't part of the plan ... This is neutered and neat. Conformist and traditional. Same as it ever was. Indie Playboy. Don't be stupid. Look what we've won. The right ... to rave all night and take our kit off in *Loaded* and call ourselves ladettes. The right to have celebrity fashion photographers ask us to undo extra buttons on our shirts every time they take our picture.[12]

Within a decade, young men's quest for rock's Holy Grail, a record deal—the talisman of fame and fortune—was becoming more problematic anyway. Amanda MacKinnon, who moved from playing in a successful band, Bis, to managing an unsuccessful band, Multiplies, describes the effects of the decline in record company investment—"you don't earn a lot from being in a band any more"; and music press influence—"you don't really hear about new music anymore, you have to find it [for yourself] on the internet" (quoted in Harvey 2005: 101–2).[13] In the words of Colin Hardie (who for a while managed Mogwai), a record company might still

> sign a band [but] that band would be lucky to get enough money to get wages out of it, it's very much a development deal ... not enough to actually make it practical for a band to be fulltime, or if they are they've got a quality of life pretty similar to being on the dole.
> (Quoted in Harvey 2005: 132)

Hardie therefore worked for his bands with Simbiotic, a Glasgow-based internet company formed in June 2002 by Natasha Noramly (from another

174　*Making a musical living*

Glasgow band, Fuck-Off Machete) and computer scientist Graham Collins to support bands' e-commerce and digital distribution. Simbiotic provided them with bespoke websites and publicity platforms. By 2003, the company was managing 22 online shops and a distribution network for a number of small record companies and artists from the indie sector; by 2005 it had around a hundred such clients.[14] This was a technologically necessary (rather than ideologically driven) form of DIY business. In the digital age, all musicians and their managers had to do these things for themselves.

Volume 2 documented how the dominance of record companies in the development of the rock business in the 1970s had the paradoxical effect of making live performance the essence of the rock experience—hence the growing importance in the 21st century music business of heritage acts and tribute bands, to which we will return. In the post-rock digital world, by contrast, the decline of record company power went alongside the increasing significance of the recording studio in establishing a musician's "brand". And the digital recording studio was not only an ever more flexible space but could now easily be set up in musicians' bedrooms. Already in 1995, as Louise Wener remembers:

> [The studio] is where the glamour really sits. The TV shows, the autographs, the parties, the videos, all the stuff you grow up thinking will be glossy and exhilarating, really aren't. The after gig parties meld into one another after a while, differentiated only by how wasted everyone is. But making a recording is utterly different every time you attempt it. It changes from moment to moment, even in the seconds it takes to rewind the tape and try another take. You can spend hours, days, trying to recreate a simple four-track demo that you've made in your bedroom and sometimes you can never quite find it. Music is slippery and elusive, and chasing it, taming it, making it fit together is where the good stuff is.
>
> (Wener 2010: 245)

The effects of these various changes on careers in popular music can be illustrated by comparing the working lives of guitarist Adrian Utley and drummer Gordy Marshall.

Utley started out in a Northampton rock band, The Army, then found work with various dance and cabaret bands in holiday camps in Devon. In 1986 he moved to Bristol and joined the Glee Club, which specialised in playing sparky but easy-listening supper-club jazz at society weddings. The band was booked for an appearance at the Glastonbury Festival, where Utley was recruited by Tommy Chase to join his jazz quartet, while continuing to play as a side man for visiting American blues acts, with The Bog Town Playboys (a 50s R&B band) and on Jeff Beck's Blue Caps project.[15] In 1993, Utley joined forces with producer/engineer Geoff Barrow and singer Beth Gibbons to record Portishead's *Dummy*, one of the most influential records of the 1990s.[16]

Making a musical living   175

Barrow and Gibbons had met at an Enterprise Training Scheme in Bristol in 1991, and Portishead's music was a significant strand of what became known as trip-hop, the Bristol Sound that emerged from local sound systems' experiments with breakbeats, hip hop and dub. The most prominent of these crews, Wild Bunch, had evolved into the era-defining Massive Attack.[17] Geoff Barrow had also started out in rock bands (as a drummer) before becoming a tape operator at the local Coach House Studios, where he had worked on Massive Attack's debut album, *Blue Lines*.

If the first part of Utley's career would have been familiar to any working rock musician since the 1960s, Portishead represented a new approach to music-making. Dom Phillips (2009: 116) writes that "the 1990s is too often seen as the decade of Britpop ... but Britpop, despite its vitality, was essentially a derivative sound, one that took classic 1960s guitar pop and updated it. Dance music, meanwhile, was hurtling forward". Adrian Utley's professional career was now tied into this forward movement.

Tracey Thorn, from the band Everything But The Girl, describes a similar trajectory. Increasingly disillusioned with 1980s indie-rock, she accepted an invitation to play with Fairport Convention at the 1993 Cropredy Festival and discovered a way of making music "without constant compromise and meddling by record companies" (Thorn 2014: 372).

> One day I am onstage in a country field in front of a crowd of bearded real-ale folkies, euphorically singing a Sandy Denny anthem as the late afternoon sun dips behind the trees and hedgerows. And then, almost the next day, or so it seems, there is a phone call from Massive Attack asking me to collaborate and sing on their second album.
>
> Thorn (2014: 272)

Everything But the Girl's music developed thereafter as what Thorn calls a "bizarre hybrid" of indie rock and dance floor. The key factor for Thorn was not so much the exhaustion of traditional rock tropes as the evolving expectations of electronic music with beats. "It could be melodic and heartfelt, as well as experimental. Slow and moody. Atmospheric" (Thorn (2014: 310).

The origins of the indie rock/dance floor hybrid lay in the late 1980s club boom in acid house music, which we discussed in Chapter 7. Brewster and Broughton (2000: 373) describe the effects of this on music-making in Manchester:

> Even after acid house had swept the UK, Manchester's take on the music remained distinctive. It was here, as the eighties closed, that 'indie dance' was born, when local bands like the Happy Mondays combined guitar-based rock with the new dancefloor aesthetic.

Brewster and Broughton describe Paul Oakenfold's mix of Happy Mondays' "Step On" (a top ten hit in 1990) as "a clever reconstruction of rock to make

176 *Making a musical living*

it palatable to a market that had learned how to dance", and the band's manager Nathan McGough explains why a couple of years earlier the Mondays'
second album, *Bummed*, had been launched at the London acid house club
Spectrum:

> It was our way of positioning this music within the cultural framework
> of acid house. From the beginning of '88, through to the album launch
> in November, the whole scene had exploded. It had this fucking vertical
> take-off from the spring through to the autumn. There was a feeling
> at the time that was very tangible. We were experiencing a paradigm
> shift.
>
> (Norris: 2008 167–8)

It was a shift also marked by the second great indie dance hit of 1990, Primal
Scream's "Loaded", mixed by Andrew Weatherall:

> Andrew Innes [rhythm guitarist of Primal Scream] was in Spectrum one
> night and he said "We've got this track and you can do whatever the fuck
> you like with it". That was "Loaded". I made one attempt where I reined
> back a bit because I didn't want to upset them. I played it to them and
> Innes said, "No man, fuckin' destroy it!"
>
> (Quoted in Brewster and Broughton 2000: 390)[18]

These new approaches to rock music-making were not just driven by club
culture but were also an effect of the transformation of the recording process
generally by digital technology. For Bobby Gillespie, working with Weatherall
meant learning about "rhythm and space ... The sampler gave us a whole
new of palette of colours ... a whole new world of psychedelic possibilities".
While the recorded results were an exhilarating confusion of 1960s acid rock
and 1990s acid house, the live tour that promoted *Screamadelica* was essentially an old-fashioned in-your-face rock 'n' roll show (Reynolds 1998: 107).
Primal Scream was not one of the bands that used the new technology to take
a new approach to live performance.[19]

By contrast, Pet Shop Boys explicitly defined their live music strategy
against rock.[20] When the duo launched their first tour in 1989, they had already
released four albums and 12 hit singles, two video collections and a feature
film, but had only performed live four times, and two of those appearances
were on TV (Heath 1991: 1–2). This was not a rock way of doing things and
band members Neil Tennant and Chris Lowe were at pains to explain that
their tour would be quite different from "a traditional rock'n'roll show".
They described "the special lighting" and the technology that would allow
them "to transmit all the programmed music at the push of a button from a
small computer set-up on one side of the stage". This way, "the music being
generated from a computer bank", the stage would be left free to showcase
the most important aspect of their concerts, "the role of Derek Jarman both

Making a musical living 177

in shooting the films to be projected behind the performance and in directing the whole show" (Heath 1991: 5–7).

Much of what is being described here doesn't sound radically different from a prog rock spectacle or the dramatic staging of a Madonna show.[21] And, anyway, it was soon clear that dance musicians were very willing to meet rock audience expectations. As we have seen, the UK's rock festivals became increasingly dance-friendly during the 1990s and dance-based groups like The Prodigy, Leftfield and the Chemical Brothers became major festival draws (Brewster and Broughton 2000: 429). Such bands might, in Phillips' (2009: 116–7) words, replace "choruses with screaming roars of synthesisers, guitar solos with cascades of beats, charismatic singers with visuals and flashing lights", but they were also delighted to exhibit the conventional stadium values of spectacle and excess.

One reason Neil Tennant had given for distinguishing a Pet Shop Boys show from a rock gig was that:

> It's directed, in the same way you direct a play or a musical, whereas a rock'n'roll show is supposed to be "spontaneous, maan" even though it's exactly the same every night.
>
> (Heath 1991: 5)

By this time, it was not at all clear that a rock 'n' roll show *was* supposed to be spontaneous, which is where Gordy Marshall's career comes in. By the end of the 1980s, Marshall had a well-established reputation as a freelance drummer. He played on cruise ships, in the pit and on tour with West End musicals and as a musician-for-hire by rock revival package shows. In 1992, Marshall successfully auditioned to join the Moody Blues for an upcoming international tour. For the next two decades, he played all the band's live shows; this became his most regular freelance gig.[22]

Marshall thus now had the classic rock tour experience we outlined in Volume 2: the resignation of all personal responsibility to the tour schedule; the subordination of musical decisions to the Moody Blues' stage technology and travelling technicians. On the other hand, the Moody Blues no longer had record company tour support; they were no longer on the road to sell a new release. Rather, what was on offer was "the Moody Blues experience"— exactly the same experience for sale night after night.

There were also new rules for a rock tour featuring mature rather than young musicians. The most important tour imperative was "Do not get sick!" or, more explicitly, "Do not give a cold to the singer!" Without the singer, the show couldn't go on.[23] And the Moody Blues now preferred concert hall venues to arenas. It was more comfortable to play several nights in a small venue than one night in a large one once the objective was no longer to reach as many potential record buyers as possible. For years, the Moody Blues played fortnight-long residences twice a year in Las Vegas; later they were booked annually for nightly performances on a cruise ship.

178 *Making a musical living*

By 2010, touring heritage acts like the Moody Blues were a significant part of Britain's live music business alongside the ever-growing number of jukebox musicals and tribute bands.[24] The most successful of the former were the Abba musical *Mamma Mia,* which opened in the West End on April 6, 1999 and is still running there at the time of writing, and the Queen musical *We Will Rock You,* which was panned by reviewers when it opened at the Dominion in 2002 but ran there without a break until 2014.[25] The pioneering jukebox show, however, was *Buddy—The Buddy Holly Story,* which ran in London for 12 years after its opening in 1989 before moving to Broadway; it continues to thrive as a touring show.

Buddy was co-produced by Manchester promoter Stuart Littlewood, who had started his own career at the tail end of the rock'n'roll era in 1962. Another well-established promoter, Tony Denton (who started out in 1982), pioneered a different kind of nostalgia show: the historical package tour, beginning in the 1990s with *The Best Disco in Town* (1970s disco acts) and moving on in the 2000s to *Here & Now* (1980s pop acts) and *Once in a Life Time,* initially featuring ageing heart-throbs David Cassidy, the Osmonds, David Essex and Les McKeown's "legendary" Bay City Rollers. Denton quickly discovered that nostalgia package shows had a particular appeal to the corporate sector ("the 30-plus market", in his words):

> We have 30-odd artists that do *Here & Now* shows [and} for the corporate work we don't exactly call it *Here & Now,* but we say people can create their own *Here & Now* show, where you get three artists for the price of one, basically. If Belinda Carlisle walks out and does four big hits, and then Kim Wilde comes out it is a bit of a talking point for an event ... Marc Almond and Chic always go down really well for corporates.
>
> (Quoted in *Music Week,* July 28, 2007: 24)

According to Georgina Gregory, the first tribute band was White, a US group that in 1991 recreated a Led Zeppelin concert. This was to go further than the already familiar cover bands. A tribute band doesn't just meet a demand for classic live rock, but offers the experience of a particular show (Gregory 2012: 42–3). Much has been written about tribute bands in terms of performance theory and/or postmodernism, but our interest here is how they fit into the twenty-first century popular music business.[26] Tribute bands by their nature rely exclusively on live rather than recording income, tribute band musicians have to be highly professional and technically skilled (often rather more so than the musicians in the original bands). They have to sound and play right for a focused and knowledgeable audience and they *always* have to deliver what they promise. At the same time, tribute bands tend to be self-managing and self-promoting, musicians for hire, not unlike wedding or ceilidh bands (Gregory 2012: 81–3).[27]

In opting for the tribute path, though, musicians choose an odd life in rock terms. They will do a lot of playing in which what matters is not their own

Making a musical living   179

musical creativity but their technical precision and physical condition. And a tribute band performance does not involve the usual fan/star boundaries: band and audience are expressing a collective fandom. Gregory comments on the friendliness of tribute shows, on their popularity in small venues in which the original bands would never have agreed to play.

The recurring term in the marketing material for nostalgia shows is "classic". Audiences are promised classic acts, classic songs, classic sounds and classic shows. In other musical worlds, paying homage to musical traditions has long both shaped and been challenged by performing conventions. We examine the changing lives of musicians in these worlds in the next two sections.

Working in classical music and jazz

The classical musician

In 1995, journalist Danny Danziger (1995) published a book of interviews with 51 members of the London Philharmonic Orchestra. This was not a happy band. Nearly all the musicians he talked to complained about the workload and the stress, the women described the sexism and, in general, players rued the fact that the years of investing time in their skills and money in their instruments had resulted in such paltry financial rewards and prospects: "there's very little career structure in the orchestra for a rank-and-file player: you just sit there and that's it for life, and you remain on the same money. It's a fairly thankless task" (Danziger 1995: 110). Dermot Crehan, principal of the second violins, summed up the general feeling of disaffection:

> It's just the sheer amount of work we have to do; we all work very hard and long hours, and we don't get that much time off. Also, the repetition gets to you after a while, you're just doing the same thing day in, day out. You can imagine, we're working together seven days a week, with the same people, on the same platform, it gets very monotonous. After a while, it gets harder and harder to get your enthusiasm going.
> (Danziger 1995: 48)[28]

Over the next 20 years, orchestral culture did change. New players were increasingly recruited directly from conservatories; they had greater technical and professional skills. Already in 1995, LPO violinist Colin Harrison noted that "overall standards in the music world have gone up markedly in the last few years, you can almost guarantee anybody joining now is going to play better than the chaps who have been there for the last thirty years" (Danziger 1995: 95), although a fellow player complained that "quite a few of the London bands are turning into glorified youth orchestras, with very self-centred youngsters not respecting the age and experience of the older players" (Danziger 1995: 52).

180 *Making a musical living*

One aspect of such changes was the rising number of women orchestral players. A survey of the major UK orchestras in March 2010 found the percentage of female membership now ranged from 28.42% in the LSO to 50% in the BBC Scottish Symphony Orchestra; the average for all UK orchestras was around 40%.[29] What hadn't changed was the derisory pay. In 1990, *Cultural Trends* reported that the average annual salary for an orchestral musician was around £25,000 (rather less for the players in opera companies). In real terms, salaries had, if anything, gone down since 1975 (Feist and Hutchison 1990: 23–34). In 2004, the MU headlined a press release "Musicians' Union Fear Crisis for Future of Classical Performance". This followed a survey of MU members under contract to UK orchestras, which found that musicians who had, on average, been employed in the profession for 22 years were "still only earning £22,500 gross per annum" and were still complaining about "anti-social working hours and a feeling that their work was financially undervalued". With average annual costs of £3200 for clothing, instrument maintenance and insurance, orchestral players were taking on an increasing amount of additional non-orchestral work to survive (MU press release, September 9, 2004).[30]

In his 2004 study, *Professional Music-Making in London*, Stephen Cottrell (2004: 191–2) uncovered "a general level of dissatisfaction among many of my erstwhile colleagues". The cutbacks in funding by both state cultural agencies and the record industry reinforced classical musicians' sense that they now lacked even the cultural status they had once enjoyed. Audiences were declining; orchestral employment itself increasingly meant outreach and community work. Add to this much of the film music industry moving from London to Eastern Europe, the decreasing investment of recording companies in studio sessions and the decline of music teaching work for local educational authorities, and it is not surprising that classical musicians (more than three-quarters of whom were self-employed) felt beleaguered (Cottrell 2004: 192–3).[31]

Cottrell (2004: 66) describes the characteristics of a freelance musical labour market in which supply outstrips demand: the power of the fixer, the complex social relations of the depping [deputising] system and musicians' consequent dependence on "a web of socio-musical connections". These are long-established work processes in the classical world, of course, reflecting the "vicissitudes of an insecure profession" (Cottrell (2004: 78). What changed in the new century was the discursive context. As Susan Coulson (2012: 254). documents in her study of musicians around Newcastle, to be a freelance musician hustling for work was now to be engaged in "cultural entrepreneurialism". A 2006 report on musical careers commissioned by the MU and BASCA thus focused on the need to "encourage musicians and composers *to find, create and exploit new and emerging routes to the market*" (Massingham 2006: 42–3, our italics).[32]

The new entrepreneurialism applied to musical organisations as well as to individual performers. According to LSO flautist Gareth Davies (2013: 125):

> In 21st-century classical music, it's no longer enough simply to do a concert: an overture, a concerto, a symphony plus interval drinks. Now we all have to have marketing to keep up with other, more fashionable art forms.

The key to orchestral policy became branding. Ananay Aguilar quotes Chaz Jenkins, head of LSO's record label, LSO Live: "By running our own label we've increased the value of the LSO brand."[33] LSO Live was not set up to be a particularly significant source of income (although it turned out to be so, as we described in Chapter 4) but "to reify and consolidate the group's sound identity, to demonstrate the musicians' abilities, and thus to grow and *promote* the brand" (Aguilar 2017: 113–14, our italics). Edward Dusinberre (2016) describes the recording of the Takács Quartet's Beethoven cycle in the early 2000s as the classical recording industry was collapsing.[34] Decca had recorded the group's first two Beethoven CDs but the Quartet itself was now expected to cover the costs of "hotel rooms, hall rental and fees for a sound engineer and producer", costs of around $100,000. The group raised the money through a combination of crowdfunding, donations and benefactors, and was thereby able to determine the recording venue and the recording team as well as to budget more time for rehearsals. The question now was "were we ready to make the bold interpretative choices that would give our recording an individual stamp, distinguishing it from those recordings already available". Although this is decidedly not Dusinberre's language, the point of the recording was less to bring in income than to enhance the Takács Quartet's "brand" on the international live music circuit (Dusinberre 2016: 130–7).

For many musicians, entrepreneurialism became necessary simply in order to sustain a livelihood in which they could be creative. This is Rosa, one of Susan Coulson's interviewees:

> You asked me earlier on, did I ever see myself as a business. Absolutely not – I probably reacted sort of like this [makes a mock gesture of horror], because I've never seen that I've had anything to do with business at all. For me, that's another world, to think in terms of profit or money ...
>
> (Quoted in Coulson 2012: 254)

This sums up the classical musician's dilemma: their high cultural status (on which their living depends) is tied up with their low economic status (the public belief that they don't care about money). RSNO players Lance Green and Katy MacKintosh put it this way:

> I think we are just so far behind in the music business, because people seem to think that it is not a business and that it is music ... And so the [brass] section carries on [underpaid and overworked] because it is somehow acceptable because it is not a normal business.
>
> (Green et al. 2014: 369)

182 *Making a musical living*

But these musicians didn't want to think that what they did was a business either; they were, to use a label that became familiar in the 2000s, "reluctant entrepreneurs".[35] There is a tension here, as Cottrell (2002) puts it, between classical performers' economic and musical capital. In a study of female classical players, Christina Scharff (2015: 106) discovered that, "reflecting the entrepreneurial ethos of the cultural industries, many musicians described themselves as products that had to be sold. At the same time, they disliked the practice of selling themselves." Women musicians were particularly reluctant to engage in self-promotion:

> First, self-promotion is associated with pushy behaviour that conflicts with normative expectations that women are nice and modest, and gives rise to dilemmas in the performance of femininity. Second, self-promotion is regarded as a commercial activity and positioned as un-artistic. Taking into account that women have been constructed as the artist's "other", engagement in self-promotion may threaten their already tenuous status as artists. Lastly, the notion of selling yourself may evoke the spectre of prostitution due to the sexualisation of female musicians and the fact that it is mainly women who sell their bodies.
>
> (Scharff 2015: 106)

One solution to these dilemmas was to give up on the problems of making money from music altogether. In Denziger's LPO book, the viola player Julian Shaw is quoted as saying:

> Essentially, I love music more than I love the orchestra. Ninety per cent of concerts are what I call craftsmanship concerts, you do them as well as you can, and it is unlikely that the earth is going to move. The time the earth moves for me is when I am playing violin duets at seven o'clock in the morning with my eight-year-old daughter, or when I am playing in a concerto with a not very good semi-professional orchestra who are in love with music.
>
> (Danziger 1995: 181)[36]

We can add two general points to this personal testimony. First, in understanding the world of the contemporary professional classical musician, it is important to recognise the sheer number of amateur classical music makers in the UK. In 2019, Barbara Eifler, chief executive of Making Music, concluded from a survey of her members (mostly adult leisure-time music groups) that there were at least 800,000 people participating in amateur local music making in the UK and that these musicians were essential to British everyday life.[37] Without them, there would be "no brass band to play carols at Christmas, no choir to accompany the civic occasion, the funeral, the wedding, the school or village fête".[38]

Making a musical living   183

The second point is well made by violinist and music writer Ariane Todes: the amateur scene is essential for the survival of a classical music profession. Todes plays with the Corinthian Chamber Orchestra, "one of the many amateur orchestras in London":[39]

> Generally we play well and our concerts are usually exhilarating, but essentially we do it for the sheer love of it and no one is going to confuse us with the London Symphony Orchestra. My colleagues are doctors, lawyers, classical music industry people, teachers, administrators, nurses and IT specialists, among many other professions. Many studied at music college and could have become professional musicians (I studied at postgraduate level at the Royal Academy of Music, for example). Instead, we all have day jobs, but put on six concerts a year, each with an intense series of rehearsals. Many of us play chamber music and work with other groups.[40]

As Todes argues, amateur musicians are essential for the sustenance of the classical music business.[41] They provide professional musicians at all levels with audiences and performing opportunities; they are vital for the income of venues (whether halls or rehearsal spaces); they hire music and buy scores and equipment; they employ piano tuners and instrument repairers; they pay for music lessons and to attend workshops and summer schools; they are subscribing members of choirs, brass bands and recorder societies; above all, they celebrate the pleasure of music-making and music-listening as vital social and communal activities.

The jazz musician

In 2009, the veteran horn player Terry Johns (a long time member of the LSO) wrote a letter to BBC Radio Scotland producer Bill Lloyd on the occasion of the broadcast of a concert by Glasgow's Cooperation Band, that year's winner (for the 29th time!) of the Scottish Brass Band Championships:

> They are amazing aren't they? There is a completely natural beauty and energy in brass band music that beguiled me when I was a young man, and gave me a desire for the musical life. As a boy I somehow by-passed the Rock and Roll revolution. I was too busy, I think, playing the cornet in the colliery band, while secretly trying to sound like Chet Baker. But the moment finally came when I decided against jazz as a means of making a living, which is why I'm now able to take regular meals and have warm clothes for the winter.
>
> (Johns 2011: 155)

Johns' throwaway remark here is interesting in two respects. On the one hand, he is pointing to the similarities between the lives of jazz and classical

184 *Making a musical living*

musicians. The findings of Cottrell's study of London's classical musicians are thus echoed in Umney and Kretsos' study of London's jazz musicians: the same over-supply of musicians driving "the downward pressure on fees", the same dependence on depping and "the economy of favours", the same need to maintain good relations with fixers, the same networking importance of "the elite London music colleges" and the same tension between organising a living from music and sustaining creative autonomy (Umney and Kretsos 2013).[42]

On the other hand, Johns is also taking for granted that rates of pay are even worse in the jazz than in the classical world. In 2012, trumpeter Jack Davies carried out his own survey of British jazz musicians. It revealed that 89% of his respondents got less than 50% of their income from live performance, 77.1% of them got less than 30% and 39.1% of them got less than 10%. In Davies' words, such figures "back up the assertions that the British jazz scene is predominantly 'amateur'—musicians are unable to earn a living from their art, and have to find income elsewhere".[43]

A couple of decades earlier, Harry Christianson focused an academic study of jazz musicians in the Midlands on a specific career stage: performers who'd started playing in the 1950s and 1960s as young men and were returning to the stage after their children entered their teens or their marriages broke up. These players all had jobs and used their non-music income to subsidise their music work, often accepting gigs that played well below MU rates. For them, jazz was a hobby but involved accepting paid gigs of all kinds— weddings, parties, festivals and pub jazz-club nights. Such "paid amateurs" (still the bedrock of many local jazz scenes and festivals) were in it not for the money but for the enjoyment of self-expression, improvisation and making music with other players, who they often only ever met on stage. As in the classical world, such musicians shared a strong ideology of *not* being commercial, of playing out of a love of jazz (Christianson 1987).

By the 2000s, though, young would-be jazz professionals were also increasingly encouraged to think of their music as their *product*. In his guide to how to make it as a jazz musician, Chris Hodgkins offers indicative pieces of advice, such as:

> Think about who your audience is. Ensure your image matches your sound ... The font, images and words you use are often an audience's first introduction to your music.
>
> (Amy Pearce, promoter and programmer for Serious Music)

> Before presenting your group or collective you need to have all components together ... website, 2–3 video links (and not just YouTube, ideally a professional video) of not more than 4 minutes each, high resolution photos that can be copied from the website, a short bio and a more elaborate bio, tour history (if that exists) showing cities and venues, links to audio files, press (if available) and contact info. And don't forget to

Making a musical living   185

regularly update the site. There is nothing more irritating than looking at "old news" … Additionally one needs links to a Facebook page and other social media.

> (Ina Dittke, promoter with the European Jazz Network; quotes from Hodgkins 2017: 71–2).[44]

It could be argued that jazz musicians are more responsive to this sort of advice than classical musicians because of jazz's greater emphasis on individuality. On the other hand, issues of self-expression in jazz are complicated by the importance in the jazz world of players' *social* identity, in terms of gender and race for example.

In 1995, an Arts Council England review found that 85% of the UK's professional jazz musicians were male. Among musicians generally, the figure was 75% (McKay 2005: 245)[45] and, as in the rock world, any challenge to the status quo had come from a combination of feminism and DIY, through the impact of the Feminist Improvisation Group, for example (it was formed in 1977). In the jazz world, the issue was not just women's exclusion from male music-making networks, but also the feminist challenge to male music-making practices. All-woman big bands like Sisterhood of Spit and Lydia D'Ustebyn's Swing Orchestra not only established new female musician networks but also gave their members opportunities to explore and express their own musical ideas, opportunities not so readily available to, say, an all-woman chamber group in the classical world (for the arguments here, see McKay 2005: 292–6).

In the early 1980s, young black musicians also found themselves excluded from the existing jazz networks. Cleveland Watkiss remembers:

> We'd go to Ronnie Scott's and they'd be looking at us suspiciously, like what are these black kids hanging around this club for and following us around the club thinking we were there pick-pocketing.

Juliet Kelly explains that these musicians

> felt ostracised and that's why they built up the community groups and that's why they were forced to make their own special nurturing places because they weren't invited or welcomed on the [existing London jazz scene].
>
> (Quotes from Doffman 2014: 120–1)

Hence the importance of the Abibi Jazz Art Music Collective, set up by Courtney Pine and Jeune Guishard in 1984,[46] and the Jazz Warriors, whose first appearance in the Fridge in Brixton in January 1986 became "a catalyst for many Black British players":

> Jazz Warriors was a time, an era, when something happened. [The] reason … was because … myself and Courtney [Pine] were fed up of hearing,

186 *Making a musical living*

from the white jazz musicians, "Oh, yeah they're great players, but they can't read". And we just said, I'm fed up with this. Sick of this ... So we just said, "Oh, we've had it, let's do our own thing".

("A black saxophonist", quoted in Dueck 2014: 265)

In Gary Crosby's words, "we wanted to express ourselves ... in a jazz-like fashion, and there were no opportunities, so ... people were setting up their own clubs" (quoted in Dueck 2014: 265). Crosby went on to be artistic director of Tomorrow's Warriors, a music education/professional development organisation he founded in 1991 with Janine Irons. In 1996 they also established Dune Music, a jazz promotion business that included artist management, a record label and music publishing.

The importance of such black-led music-making projects was not just as a way of dealing with the musicians' exclusion from the white jazz establishment. As with feminist musicians, it also involved an argument about jazz process and jazz community and, in this case, jazz tradition. As Gary Crosby comments:

So we call ourselves "artistes" but actually the roots of this thing is nothing to do with artistes, it's entertainment. Or it's an artist who is an entertainer, who's entertaining, or it's an entertainer who can be an artist. But the real basis of this music is functionality, functionality to its community, *that's* the real basis ... For me, the Eurocentric thing has become "artist" ... I classify them as failed classical musicians, really. They have very little respect for the tradition ...

(Quoted in Dueck 2014: 209)

Whatever the stylistic and aesthetic differences between the players to whom Byron Dueck talked, black British musicians all

seemed to prioritize forms of musical interaction distinct from those privileged in the conservatoire. It was not so much the difference between aural learning and note reading, but rather the difference between a musical outlook that prioritized technical excellence and one that emphasized participation.

(Quoted in Dueck 2014: 209–10)

The questions here about what it meant to be a jazz musician, about tradition, participation and community, were also being asked in the folk world.

A folk resurgence?

In 2007 FolkArts England ran two "Folk Industry Focus Days" as part of a conference describing itself as "the biggest gathering of folk activists, promoters and media folk since, well, who knows?!" Simon Keegan-Phipps and Trish Winter (2014: 489–90) argue that the use of the term "folk industry" here was indicative of the folk world's growing professional engagement with commerce and evidence of what they call an English "folk resurgence".

> Folk festivals have become increasingly popular; the demography of folk audiences is getting younger—folk is enjoying considerable and growing popularity with people in their teens, twenties, and thirties; and folk has moved beyond the boundaries of the folk scene and toward popular cultural contexts like Mercury Music Awards nominations and mainstream music festivals. The media profile of folk has shifted, with greater media visibility for folk music in both arts and popular entertainment television programming, for example.

This resurgence coincided with the increased use of the internet for the distribution of musical and promotional material:

> The social and music networking site MySpace was particularly instrumental at the turn of the twenty-first century in enabling amateur and semiprofessional musicians to be heard by an active/selective audience ... However, the increased opportunities for self-distribution and self-promotion might also be read as moving folk music into line with a larger hegemonic economy in which musicians are able—and encouraged—to become professional (or rather professionalized) by working on a self-funded basis to begin the process of profile and popularity building. That is, artists are encouraged to invest their own time and money in order to obtain the first indicators by which the industry may assess their economic potential.
>
> (Keegan-Phipps and Winter (2014: 500–2)

Underlying the argument here is the assumption that the folk world was no longer ideologically based in folk clubs but organised around new institutions: folk festivals (which we discussed in Chapter 6), folk radio and academic folk courses. The result was that folk musicians no longer shared "a discourse opposed to mainstream cultural developments". This is perhaps most evident in the emerging importance for folk music careers of the Radio 2 Folk Awards (which started in 2000).[47] Karine Polwart is clear that her award "was the difference between having a career and not having a career". Her album sales increased tenfold, taking her "into another level of game ... immediately your name is on the radar of bookers and, you know, getting gigs" (as well as press coverage, better distribution, managerial representation and "above all" radio play). This was also the moment for her to step up in new media terms, creating her own digital sites and establishing a permanent fan network.[48]

188 *Making a musical living*

The veteran fiddler Dave Swarbrick had a more jaundiced view of this development, relating it to the *lack* of paying gigs for young musicians:

> And unless they get some recognition, such as sales on a CD, they're not going to get anywhere. [And] the only way they're going to get sales nowadays is if they're nominated for an award from the BBC.
>
> (Quoted in Bean 2014: 357)

There were equally disparate views about the impact of the new folk degrees we described in Chapter 4. Writing in 2018, Josh Dickson suggested that the Royal Conservatoire of Scotland's traditional music degree (which he ran) was both the cause and an effect of traditional performers finding a place in the "mainstream" of Scottish music. RCS graduates, he found, were more outward facing than previous traditional musicians and more eclectic stylistically. There was "a growing alignment" between the ways in which aspiring traditional, classical and jazz musicians thought about their work (Dickson 2018: 87–8).

Eclecticism and "outward facing" have, however, always been a dynamic factor in the folk world. As Simon McKerrell points out, Scottish traditional music-makers have a long history of seizing any opportunity to make a living from their music. One of his examples is Capercaillie, a group formed in 1984 in Oban High School that was fully professional by 1985. Capercaille developed "a very successful recording, touring and promotion business", drawing on popular music influences such as "lush keyboard harmonies and lively percussion" and crossing genres as they built a large fan base, increasing their use of syncopation, chromaticism and jazz influences (McKerrell 2011: 7–8). In 2007, the band's accordion player, Donald Shaw, became artistic director of Celtic Connections, which as we have seen was a music festival and promotional showcase shaped by the development of the global market for world music (and the Glasgow Tourist Board) rather than by folk awards or degree courses.

The suggestion that folk clubs were losing their significance for the folk world is also problematic. This was certainly an aspect of John Leonard's thinking when his independent production company, Smooth Operations, took on responsibility for Radio 2's folk show. He deliberately shifted the show's emphasis away from clubs, arguing that the more influential acts were not to be found on the club scene any more (see Bean 2014: 365), but to dismiss folk clubs for their "conservatism" is to forget their importance as the setting in which even the most adventurous performers in "new folk" started out. For John McCusker, folk clubs are "where you learn your craft, where you learn to speak to an audience, how to entertain" (quoted in Bean 2014: 357); for Karine Polwart, her early experience of "the whole session scene" was crucial for her understanding of music-making as the work of a "collaborative community".

Making a musical living 189

A sense of community remains significant for folk musicians' attitudes to market ideology. Martin Carthy makes the point that for musicians, folk clubs are places where they can make "terrible mistakes" and still be "supported and looked after". Clubs give performers a valuable creative freedom: "people will allow you to do what you like—and you belong to them" (quoted in Bean 2014: 380).

In his reshaping of *Folk on 2*, John Leonard argued that folk clubs had been run by the same people for forty years and that therefore "the clubs had stayed much the same and they were impossible to go to as a newcomer". The clubs "could not grasp the [new] culture. And so new people are not going to them". For Dave Swarbrick, by contrast, "clubs are better now than they ever were". Their continuing members were "more involved"; casual attenders had dropped away. The clubs now provided "the nicest possible atmosphere on the whole scene to play to, because you're playing to people who appreciate what you're doing" (quoted in Bean 2014: 385–6). Realising this, folk musicians continued to start new clubs. Sam Lee, for example, opened the Magpie's Nest in 2006 because "we wanted a [place for] the new folk and the old folk and the no folk", offering open mic sessions for both self-proclaimed folk singers of various sorts and singer-songwriters who were only "touching upon" the tradition. The Magpie's Nest was "the instigation for a lot of other [new] folk clubs in London" (Bean 2014: 356).

In an investigation into "the health of the UK folk club" carried out in 2015, Stephen Henderson discovered three types of provision: the familiar "singaround" club, the open mic night and the concert club. The singaround club was in good shape and its weekly sessions remained crucial for new artists learning the ropes; open mic nights were an increasingly significant feature of pub folk nights, often promoted by the musicians themselves; concert clubs, featuring admission prices and star names, were in decline, not least because of competition from arts centres.[49]

Eliza Carthy's move from singing in back rooms in pubs to headlining in concert halls and festivals exemplifies the "resurgent" folk career described by Keegan-Phipps and Winter (2014), but Carthy herself suggests that her music became popular because it gave audiences access to a kind of non-commercial culture, to the folk community still nurtured in the folk club. In her words, mainstream audiences are opening up to the idea of acoustic roots music because "people aren't always happy with what's shoved in front of them any more" (quoted in Phipps et al. 2005: 32).

Conclusion

This chapter has been focused on musicians working in worlds in which there seemed to be, by the mid-1980s, well-established career conventions. Our interest was in the ways in which these conventions had to change over the next 30 years. There are themes here that turned out to cut across all these

190 *Making a musical living*

music worlds: the decline of record company power and investment; the rising importance of social media; the increasing demands for individual entrepreneurialism; the shifting boundaries between the amateur and professional performer, between live and recorded performance and, indeed, between the different musical worlds themselves. For all players struggling to make a living from music, the challenge is to maintain an acceptable balance between integrity and opportunism, between replaying the past and shaping the present. Their success here is dependent on the other key figures in live music culture: the people who provide musicians with performances spaces and opportunities, and the people who pay to see them play. We return to performance spaces in Chapter 11. In the next chapter, we consider audiences and their expectations.

Notes

1 See www.jazzjournal.co.uk/magazine.php?id=214. Hiseman died in 2018.
2 www.guardian.co.uk/music/2009/feb/20/zarif-soul-music-kindred-spirit.
3 In terms of change and continuity, it is interesting to compare this description with Dave Allen's account of the range of live music regularly available in Portsmouth in 1956 (see Frith et al. 2013: 63).
4 For other accounts of local music scenes in this period, see Martin Roach (1990) on rock in Stourbridge; Ed Jones (1999) on being "a failed rock star" in Wigan; Seb Hunter (2004) on being a "heavy metal addict" in Winchester; and Will Carruthers (2016) on the counter-cultural community that spawned Spacemen 3 and Spiritualized in Rugby.
5 Nearly all rock memoirs of this period follow this narrative (e.g. see Hingley 2012), but the best account is that of Jones (1999), perhaps because his journey ended in failure without really passing through success. Unusually, Jones also provides contract and income/expenditure details (e.g. see 1999: 81–2 and 179–80).
6 For an excellent academic account of the rock band as a social institution, see Behr (2010).
7 *Kerrang!* was launched in 1981 as a special supplement in *Sounds*; by 1987, it was a weekly glossy.
8 Louise Wener was singer, songwriter and guitarist in the successful 1990s indie band Sleeper.
9 This is an ideological rather than an empirical assertion. For a rather more subtle account of gender, metal and female fan engagement, see Hill (2016).
10 In Derrick Thompson's Northampton history, there are very few women pictured among the many men. The only female group featured is Strung Out Sisters, a string trio who had met in Leicestershire school orchestras and worked with veteran local singer/songwriter Tom Hall. The trio still work as a wedding and ceilidh band (Thompson 2018: 189–91).
11 Mouzakitis went on to have a distinguished career as a live event band manager. Cara Anderson, dressing room/production assistant on Stereophonics' 2010 tour (and one of only two women in the 77-person crew) remarked in an interview with Emma Webster (March 2, 2010) that some bands "specifically ask for female tour managers" as they want a "caring manager", not a testosterone-filled one.

12 For a good account of the gender politics of the indie scene during this period, see Davies (1995).

13 By the 2010s, "finding it for yourself" meant being guided by commercially driven algorithms.

14 Figures taken from Williamson et al. (2003: 120) and Harvey (2005: 84–5).

15 The Blue Caps, featuring guitarist Cliff Gallup, were Gene Vincent's backing band and a major influence on Britain's 1960s beat groups.

16 Details here taken from Thompson (2018: 167–71).

17 We discuss the origins of this scene in Volume 2 (Frith et al. 2019: 45, 129, 158).

18 "Loaded" and other Weatherall mixes featured on *Screamadelica,* Primal Scream's 1991 album, the first winner of the Mercury Music Prize.

19 For a discussion of the technology involved here, see Prior (2018: 60–95). Primal Scream eventually took *Screamadelica* on the road as an album show in 2010.

20 Massive Attack provides another example of digital musicians who initially sought to provide on stage "a complete audiovisual experience that goes beyond the basics of the sound system yet avoids the clichés of the rock concert" (Zuberi 2001: 159–61).

21 Chris Heath (1991: 112) quotes Janet Street-Porter raving "I *love* the lights! I could *tell* it was done by somebody who'd never done a rock show." In fact, as Heath notes, Patrick Woodroffe, the lighting designer, "does little else but rock shows and is soon off to do the Rolling Stones".

22 Details of Marshall's career taken from Marshall (2012).

23 As we write this, it has been announced that the latest Rolling Stones tour has been called off because Mick Jagger has a health problem. For the growing difficulty of providing tour insurance for ageing bands, see Eamonn Forde, "Sex and drugs and rock'n'roll insurance", *The Guardian*, October 30, 2015, www.theguardian.com/music/2015/oct/30/band-tour-live-music-insurance-blur-morrissey-robbie-williams.

24 We could also mention here the increasing number of bands performing their "classic" albums in their entirety—something they certainly didn't do when the albums were originally released.

25 *Mamma Mia* also spawned two hit films, while the Queen musical clearly inspired the equally successful movie *Bohemian Rhapsody.*

26 For a useful overview/collection of academic writing on tribute bands, see Homan (2006).

27 This is clear at "The World's Biggest and Best Tribute Festival", Glastonbudget, an annual three-day event that has been held in Wymeswold, Leicestershire since 2005. Bands have to audition for a place on the bill.

28 Constant touring, which the orchestra needed to do for its financial survival, exacerbated these problems.

29 Figures from a survey published on William Osborne and Abbie Conant's website: www.osborne-conant.org/orch-uk.htm.

30 The survey also drew attention to the continuing lack of career development. An orchestral position was both very difficult to get and very difficult to move on from.

31 Surveys of conservatoire graduates by Janet Mills and colleagues at the Royal College of Music suggested that typical post-1991 graduating students spent at least two-thirds of their working time teaching and less than a third performing. If

192 *Making a musical living*

their graduating ambition had been to be an orchestral player or, failing that, to be a full-time freelance performer, they soon found that the work was not available. (The statistics here are taken from the trombone study: Burt et al. 2006: 38–9; see also Mills 2006.)

32 The British Academy for Songwriters, Composers and Authors (BASCA) was founded by Ivor Novello in 1947. It changed its name to the Ivors Academy in 2009.

33 Jenkins had "come from a background of popular concert production to work in the marketing department of the LSO" (Aguilar 2017: 101).

34 In September 1997, Decca's full-time classical music production staff of sound producers, engineers and drivers was made redundant.

35 Something they had in common with many rock musicians, who didn't want to think of themselves in business terms either (Hayes and Marshall 2018).

36 For an instructive discussion of amateur musicians as the real music lovers in France, see Hennion et al. (2000).

37 Making Music is "the UK's number one organisation for leisure-time music, with a membership of over 3700 groups representing around 200,000 music makers across the UK". See www.makingmusic.org.uk/about-us.

38 Quoted from a letter to *The Guardian* (February 15, 2019). A 2005 Music Industries Association report, *Attitudes to Music in the UK*, reported that 37% of UK households included at least one person who played a musical instrument. The most popular instruments were the guitar (37% of the instruments named) and keyboards/piano (35%) (MIA 2005: 2–3).

39 To get a sense of the remarkable number of such orchestras (and choirs) in the UK, and their employment of professional singers, players and conductors, listen to BBC Radio Radio 3's Friday and Saturday morning call-outs of the weekend's amateur concerts.

40 See www.elbowmusic.org/single-post/2018/03/22/17-reasons-to-love-amateur-musicians.

41 A similar argument can be found in the Policy Studies Institute report *Amateur Arts in the UK*, published almost 30 years earlier. Its authors note that in 1989/90 members of the National Federation of Music Societies (founded in 1935 to bring together amateur choral societies, orchestras and music clubs) "spent an estimated £5.7 million on professional engagements" (Hutchison and Feist 1991: 109).

42 By 2010, jazz performance was taught at all the UK's conservatories. Between 2012 and 2015, the total number of students completing undergraduate and postgraduate courses annually rose from 55 to 180 (Hodgkins 2017: 121).

43 Davies surveyed 92 musicians, the majority of whom were between the ages of 21 and 50. See http://jdodavies.blogspot.co.uk/2012/04/british-jazz-survey.

44 In fact, by then most performer videos on You Tube were probably professionally made.

45 A 2016 evaluation of PRS for Music's "Women Make Music" project notes that in 2011 87% of PRS's composer/songwriter membership were male—see Tom Fleming Consultancy 2016: 1.

46 Jeune Guishard-Pine later left jazz management to become a distinguished and influential child psychologist.

47 Note that the *BBC Young Musician* competition, launched in 1978, is equally important for careers in classical music.
48 Polwart quotes taken from an interview with Sean McLaughlin (2012), which includes a useful study of the effects of awards on the Scottish folk music business.
49 Thanks to Stephen Henderson for access to his unpublished study.

A snapshot of live music in Sheffield in October–November 2007

October 2007 started with Sheffield band Arctic Monkeys voted "best act in the world today" at the Q Awards in London ("Winners in full ..." 2007). The band's win came two years after the *NME* coined the term "New Yorkshire" as an umbrella for up-and-coming bands from the region such as Sheffield's Bromheads Jacket, the Long Blondes and Reverend and the Makers, and Leeds' Kaiser Chiefs. Indeed, for an intense year or so it felt to some in Sheffield that London's music media had decamped up north, similar to the early days of Cabaret Voltaire and The Human League in the late 1970s (cf Roberts 2004).[1] The Boardwalk (formerly the Black Swan) had particular cachet as it had recently counted Arctic Monkeys' frontman Alex Turner as one of its barmen and was a regular musicians' haunt at the time. In October 2007, it hosted artists including King Creosote (Wednesday October 3), John Cooper Clarke (Thursday October 25) and Wilko Johnson (Sunday October 28), as well as tribute acts including the Bon Jovi Experience (Friday October 5) and Letz Zep (Friday October 19).

November 2007 saw the acquisition of the leasehold by Academy Music Group of the former Roxy nightclub, a vast sticky-floored institution that had opened in the 1970s as the Top Rank but closed as a nightclub in the late 1990s. It reopened in April 2008 as the 2100-capacity Carling (now O2) Academy Sheffield ("Venue information ..." 2019). Prior to this, Sheffield's three most significant medium-scale rock/pop touring venues had been the Leadmill, Plug and the University of Sheffield's Student Union. The Leadmill began in 1980 as a cooperative arts and performance space in what later became Sheffield's "Cultural Industries Quarter" (cf Brown et al. 2000), but has since focused almost exclusively on live music, and in the period of our interest, Idlewild (Saturday October 13), The National (Saturday November 3) and Calvin Harris (Friday November 9) played in this converted Victorian flour mill.

In the 1500-capacity Octagon venue at Sheffield Union, Happy Mondays (Monday October 1), Runrig (Thursday October 4), Editors (Monday October 22), Ash (Thursday October 25) and Biffy Clyro (Thursday November 15) performed, while the Union's smaller Fusion and Foundry venues were entertained by The Cribs (Saturday October 6, sold out), weekly drum'n'bass

Snapshot: Sheffield October–November 2007   195

night The Tuesday Club and weekly indie rock night Fuzz Club. Other smaller venues included the rock and metal-focused Corporation, Plug and The Casbah, while pubs like The Grapes, The Shakespeare, The Washington, The Harley and West Street Live were also busy putting on local and out-of-town bands.

At the largest end of the touring circuit, the out-of-town Hallam FM Arena (opened 1991, cap. 13,600), hosted artists including Rush (Saturday October 6, £45), Stereophonics (Friday November 9, £28.50) and Michael Bublé (Saturday November 27, £37.50).

Sheffield's club scene in the late 1990s had enjoyed international attention via superclub Gatecrasher One (fka The Republic). The club had played a dominant role in the city's clubbing scene for a number of years—both for student events and for big name DJ-led trance/house nights—although by early 2007 the eponymous Gatecrasher night was limited to special one-offs, reflecting a general nationwide decline in club-going as the 2000s went on. A devastating fire in June 2007 led to the venue's demolition ("Nightclub collapses ..." 2007). Other Sheffield club venues at the time included multi-roomed venue Plug, Uniq and DQ Bar, with Embrace and Kingdom catering for more mainstream chart-orientated events, and smaller music pubs/bars like Dulo, The Harley and The Shakespeare also hosting occasional DJ-led events. Club nights at Plug included the venue's second birthday co-presented with MTV Dance (Friday October 5, £8), drum'n'bass heavyweights Goldie and Shy FX (Friday October 19, £8) and the fifth birthday of breaks night Urban Gorilla (Friday November 23 and Friday November 30). Penelope's, a club that had been closed for years, reopened in 2007 and hosted garage and dancehall night Kabal, with resident Toddla T (Ottewill 2007).

The municipal council venue and traditional home of symphonic music in the city through its concert series was Sheffield City Hall. As part of the Sheffield International Concert Season, violinist Nicole Benedetti and the Royal Liverpool Philharmonic Orchestra performed an evening of popular classics, presented by the Classic FM Hall of Fame (Thursday October 11, £25–£7.50), while in the same series Manchester's Halle Orchestra performed Berlioz, Shostakovich and Rimsky-Korsakov, conducted by Yan Pascal Tortelier (Saturday October 20, £25–£7.50). The City Hall also hosted a mixture of jazz and rock/pop acts, including Tony Christie (Monday October 8, £25), Rufus Wainwright (Friday October 19) and Beverley Knight (Saturday October 27). More regular jazz gigs took place at Millennium Hall at the Polish Catholic Centre, many promoted by Sheffield Jazz (est. 1992), while jazz also happened at the Abbeydale Picture House and the Showroom Cinema's café bar, plus smaller venues such as Ruskin's Wine Bar and Cubana.

Other venues for classical music included Sheffield Cathedral and the Crucible Theatre Studio. Kicking off their new autumn season in October 2007 were the Sheffield Bach Choir, which sang Handel, Monteverdi and Scarlatti at the cathedral (Saturday October 6, £13–£10). Also starting a new season that weekend were chamber music specialists Music in the Round, whose autumn season began with six-piece Ensemble 360's performance

196 *Snapshot: Sheffield October–November 2007*

of Mendelssohn, Hindemith and Brahms at the Crucible Studio (Friday October 5, £14–£9.50). Music in the Round's series wasn't solely about classical chamber music, however, as folk singer Roy Bailey and acoustic guitarist Martin Simpson performed at the Crucible Studio on Saturday October 6. In general, folk music in Sheffield was mostly pub-based and in 2007 regular sessions took place at the Hillsborough Hotel, Kelham Island Tavern and Fagan's. A more unusual venue for folk music was the regular "folk train", which took musicians between Sheffield and Manchester with music provided for part of the journey and a pub stop in the Peak District before heading back to town.

Note

1 Singer Little Lost David described the Sheffield scene in 2007 as, "Diverse and the strongest it's been for many years; lots of unique nights and little venues giving live music a chance". Speaking a year later, however, Boardwalk promoter Chris Wilson spoke of the post-Arctic Monkeys hangover experienced by some Sheffield musicians: "When the spotlight slowly started moving away from Sheffield, I think a lot of bands thought, 'That's it, we may as well give up'. And [the scene] seemed to go *completely* flat" ("Little Lost David" 2008).

Bibliography

Listings taken from *Sandman Magazine* (October and November 2007) and the *Sheffield Telegraph* (October 2007).

Brown, A., O'Connor, J. and Cohen, S. (2000) 'Local music policies within a global music industry: Cultural quarters in Manchester and Sheffield', *Geoforum*, 31:4, pp. 437–51.

"Little Lost David" (2007) *Sandman Magazine*, October, p. 12.

"Nightclub collapses in city fire" (2007) BBC News, June 18, http://news.bbc.co.uk/1/hi/england/south_yorkshire/6765331.stm. Accessed March 20, 2019.

Ottewill, J. (2007) 'Late licence', Sandman Magazine, November.

Roberts, E. (2004) 'Sheffield in a league of its own', Yorkshire Post, June 3, www.yorkshirepost.co.uk/news/analysis/sheffield-in-a-league-of-its-own-1-2544187. Accessed March 20, 2019.

"Venue information: O2 Academy Sheffield" (2019) Academy Music Group website, https://academymusicgroup.com/companyo2academysheffield. Accessed March 20, 2019.

Wilson, C. (2008) Personal interview with Emma Webster, Sheffield, August 21.

"Winners in full: Q Awards 2007" (2007) BBC News, 8 October, http://news.bbc.co.uk/1/hi/entertainment/7033815.stm. Accessed March 20, 2019.

10 Live music experience in the digital age

> What kind of rational cost–benefit calculation might lead people to go to a concert? The answer, clearly, has to do with the things that are not delivered by even the highest quality headphones.
>
> (Nicholas Cook 2013: 395)

> I am sick and tired of people going on about "accessibility" without considering those who want to enjoy the music in peace, and how *inaccessible* so many concerts have become for us as a result of such a "laissez-faire" attitude. The nadir has to be the time when one person had the nerve to accuse me of being "rude" because I had pushed her camera (without in any way touching her) downwards (without causing her to lose hold of it and without causing any damage) to prevent her taking a photograph during the music. Upon pointing out to her that photography is prohibited (as had been announced prior to the concert), she suggested that I could have "talked" to her to explain that, in response to which I pointed that that this would have been impossible *during* the music.
>
> (Quoted from a discussion of ticketing policy on Norman Lebrecht's *Slipped Disc* web site)[1]

> I'm such a dork, I just screamed out loud. Good thing I'm the only one home! WE'RE LIVE IN CAPE TOWN AND IT'S FRIDAY NIGHT!!!!!!!!!!!!!!!! You should see me—I think I'm going to faint soon … Honestly, I've got tears almost coming from my eyes right this moment! OMG!!!! I'm hearing Bono live!!!!! I'm crying!!!!
>
> (Extract from a U2 fan thread accompanying the band's appearance in Cape Town, February 18, 2011)[2]

Introduction

As we documented in Chapter 1, by 2010 consumers were spending more on live than on recorded music, and multinational entertainment corporations dominated Britain's live music commerce. In this world of live music as big business, market researchers were increasingly commissioned to clarify exactly

198　*Live music experience in the digital age*

what it was that audiences wanted, to define the *audience experience* and to determine what was expected from a *festival event*.[3] Yet, as a concept, "the audience" remained somewhat ill-defined.

In the public sector, the concern has been "audience building". Arts councils, for example, now expect the musical organisations they support not just to increase their box office income but also to develop more social diversity in their customer base, whether through educational programmes or presentational devices.[4] In this context, "audience building" has often become, in effect, a policy for popularising the kinds of musical events whose cultural value lies in them not being popular; the problem is that the exclusivity of such concerts is an important part of their appeal to their existing audiences.

During his musical journey around Britain, Nige Tassell (2013: 238) thus found that, all over the country, "loose bands of volunteers have surrendered their time in the service of [live] folk music"—and, one could add, in the service of live jazz in the local jazz club and live classical music in the extensive network of local music societies. In the classical world, orchestras and chamber groups are also dependent financially on subscribing "friends", who by their nature are both the most conservative and, it seems to newcomers, most cliquey members of the audience. "*They're* the people who aren't so willing to change," says Tracy Johnston, concert manager of Music in the Round in Sheffield. In developing a devoted audience, "you almost create your own monster, but at the same time you *need* them, and at times of change it's also nice to have some steadiness" (her emphasis).[5]

There is an issue here for commercial promoters too. Rock fans, for example, are sensitive about the exclusive value of their favoured acts and quick to spot "selling out", to accuse artists of sacrificing their distinctive sounds to the tastes of a broader audience, just as they are quick to distinguish between an act's "real" fans and the "socialites" who are at a gig for the atmosphere or the prestige.[6] In Daniel Cavicchi's words (about Bruce Springsteen's fans):

> Fans see ordinary audience members as passively responding to the more obvious and superficial elements of rock performance, interested only in having fun, partying, and being entertained. But by strongly weaving their performance experiences into their daily lives, fans see their own participation in rock performance as far more active, serious, and interpretive, as shaped by something larger than the performance itself.
>
> (Quoted in Pitts 2005: 267)

One problem with the audience-building model is that "the audience" cannot be understood simply as a gathering of individual consumers being persuaded to make the same cultural market choices; rather, it is a fluid entity made up of people with different kinds of musical knowledge and commitment. If, as customer services manager Gordon Hodge notes, "a lot of [audience] complaints come from the difference between people's expectations and what

Live music experience in the digital age   199

they actually get", it is equally clear that different audience members have different expectations.[7]

The recurring market research question "What do audiences want?" can often be rephrased as "What do audiences want _besides the music?_" For example, in 2017 _IQ_ reported on a questionnaire survey of "young concertgoers", commissioned by the ticketing platform Eventbrite; it found that, for Millennials, gigs were not "about the music" at all. Rather, these audience members treated live events "as a form of self-expression [and] self-improvement", with 69% saying that attending a show was "the best way to show other people what they stand for" (quoted in _IQ_, June 21, 2017).

What is at issue here, however, is what is meant by "a concert experience", and in this chapter we consider the history of live music audiences from a different perspective: ethnography. Our questions are these. What are the social, cultural and musical conditions that produce different kinds of audience? How have audiences changed since 1985? How have they adapted to digital technology? In what ways, to paraphrase Martin Barker (2013: 71), have audiences communally produced _new_ ways of "doing liveness"?

What makes live music special?

The value of a concert as a commodity is usually taken to lie in its _uniqueness_. Tracy Johnston, like other promoters, suggests that her audiences value the live music experience _because_ it is unique:

> Because no two concerts are ever the same. Let's face it, we're all watching for the point someone's wig falls off or whatever happens, aren't we? [laughs]. And I think musically, no two performances of any chamber work—any work—are ever _exactly_ the same.
>
> (Johnston's emphasis)

The musical experience provided by a particular concatenation of performer and audience in a particular place and time is, by its very nature, unrepeatable. The audience members present can thus claim to "possess" something that anyone not there can never have: the experience—and the memory—of _being there_ (Cohen 2014).

The uniqueness of a concert performance is routinely used as a sales pitch by promoters, but its uniqueness needs unpicking. An essential part of the concert experience, for example, is that it is shared with other people. This is a clubber on the pleasures of his nights out: "Yeah, it's the music that does it—totally. You cannot beat loud music of whatever sort mixed with a load of like-minded people" (quoted in Malbon 1998: 281). And this is Alex Reedjik, general director of Scottish Opera since 2006, on the appeal of opera:

> It's a very rich and complex art form and I think that it's best enjoyed in an auditorium in a shared experience with other human beings. And

200 *Live music experience in the digital age*

I think that's what we all crave in a funny way—whether it's opera or not—human beings collectively crave the shared experience.[3]

This points to another component of a live performance's uniqueness: a shared witness. Audiences go to concerts to *see* music being made. Jazz fans thus value the

> visual immediacy of seeing performers interacting, with the exchange of gestures and movements helping to draw listeners' attention to the structure of the music, and the close proximity of players and listeners giving a sense of shared participation in a musical event.
>
> (Burland and Pitts 2014: 28)

Seeing the performers is equally important for audience members at classical music concerts "in creating a sense of musicians' engagement in the event". Classical audiences too look for "evidence that players were enjoying the performance and appreciating one another's playing" (Burland and Pitts 2014: 28).

This is witness as a socially constructed experience. The pleasure of live music is not just watching music being made; it is watching music being made as part of an audience. In her jazz ethnography, Elina Hytönen-Ng (2017: 82) concludes further that "the experience of a live performance is jointly created by the audience, the venue and the musicians". This is what makes a gig "unique and virtually unrepeatable each time": a situation in which "the musicians' and audience's relationship takes on an interactive form". As a classical fan in Sheffield put it:

> Recordings are all excellent, and broadcasts are wonderful, but it's a combination of the excitement of the performers transferring this to the ears of the audience, which a radio or a CD can't possibly compete with. There's an empathy between, a hidden string between the player and the audience ... with a recording or a broadcast, there's something in the middle which blocks that intimacy.
>
> (Quoted in Burland and Pitts 2014:130)[9]

Visual evidence of such communication is central to the ideology of musical authenticity:

> In a number of musical genres, particularly folk, jazz and rock, live music remains the test of quality and authenticity, as well as an important developmental experience for musicians ... live music can be seen by fans as something that enables them to witness the extraordinariness and uniqueness of musical talent and hard work.
>
> (Burland and Pitts 2014: 11)

In the rock world, this can be seen, paradoxically, in the popularity of tribute bands. Nige Tassell describes going to see The Smiths Indeed and asking one fan (who was clearly too young to have seen The Smiths themselves) whether "it's a problem that tonight's entertainment is a tribute act"? The reply: "I just want to hear the songs live. Where else am I going to hear them?" (Tassell 2013: 98). It was as if hearing The Smiths' songs live authenticated them even though it was not actually The Smiths onstage. As Tassell 2013: 99) argues, what mattered here was that the songs were heard as a *collective* performance:

> Even a sing like "Jeanne"—a B-side from very early in The Smiths' career—is met with word-perfect accompaniment ... The evening becomes a communal celebration ... made jointly by band and crowd alike.

For tribute band audiences in general, as Georgina Gregory (2012: 138) writes, "the traditional division between performers and audiences is [not] clear cut, since both could be defined as fans", but even in musical worlds where there are clear differences between performers and audiences, the experience of collective participation can be essential to people's pleasure. One recurring theme in ethnographic audience research is the importance of a perceived *intimacy* between musicians and their listeners. In a discussion of a particular classical performer, one of Stephanie Pitts' informants explained why she was a devotee of Sheffield's Music in the Round festival:

> It's the venue, and the atmosphere, the approach, because at the cathedral she was just very much, you know, [a] wonderful performer, on a stage, strutting her stuff sort of thing; whereas in Music in the Round, you know, she talked; there's this sort of feeling between the audience and the performer, which is just, just makes the whole thing so different and so exciting
> (Quoted in Pitts 2005: 260)

What makes a performance in an intimate venue "so different" is that audience members feel at home there—it's their space. "Intimacy" describes a kind of social relaxation, a shared informality marked by performers talking to the audience, often jokily and always with a clear sense of the locality.

In many music worlds, however, such performed togetherness is also a way of dealing with an ongoing tension: who is actually in charge here— the performers or the audience? Even in the notably intimate setting of a pub back room or small social club, performers may be torn between being "musicians", in charge of their own performance, and "entertainers", ceding control to the audience (Frith et al 2019: 38).[10] A jazz musician interviewed by Hytönen-Ng (2017: 77) expressed a common complaint:

> People visit venues in order to spend time with their friends and socialise. In these situations attention is not on the music or what is happening on stage, and music becomes a mere background affair.

If performer–audience relations may involve different expectations and ongoing negotiation, so may relations between audience members. While

202 *Live music experience in the digital age*

members of audiences in all music worlds describe their enjoyment of gigs with reference to "like-minded" people this necessarily involves dealing with (or excluding) people who are not like-minded. In her ethnography of popular music scenes in Sheffield, Josie Robson writes:

> At smaller gigs, I have consistently found the audience composition reflects that of the group onstage, who are ... almost always male ... many women, and to my great surprise as a cultural researcher, I numbered amongst them, are rendered "out of place".
>
> (Robson 2006: 127)

At the very least, acceptable and unacceptable gig behaviour is a matter of etiquette, which newcomers have to learn. Tassell spent time observing the Red Lion Folk Club in Kings Heath Birmingham, run by Della and Chris Hooke. Della explained:

> "We're a pretty serious and silent venue. We're like a little theatre." Were anyone intent on offering a single whispered observation to the person next to them, I imagine Della would make a pretty formidable peacekeeper, ssshhhing people from the sidelines with all the fervour of a militant librarian. Not that she needs to.
>
> (Tassell 2013: 235)

A regular at the Music in the Round Festival in Sheffield told Stephanie Pitts:

> We brought a cousin of my partner and his wife (our guests for the weekend). They had been to the festival before—but find the intimacy, energy, emotion and enthusiasm of the audience and the performers hard to take. We realised afresh how privileged we are, how special the festivals are—and how sad and purist lots of folks are! They will not be invited again—we have too many other friends who *do* want to come.
>
> (Quoted in Pitts 2005: 261)

And a jazz musician in Hytönen-Ng's study reflected that:

> It's a terrible thing to say this, but you see people who've been dragged along, who didn't really want to come. And it's usually wives and girlfriends who don't want to be there a lot of the time, you know. And I say, "Look, it's only two hours of this. We're going to get through it you know. We're gonna get two hours of jazz, but we're gonna get through this. Okay?" And you can see them sort of [relax] ... because you've hit on exactly on what they're thinking, they start laughing.
>
> (Quoted in Hytönen-Ng 2017: 72)

The question here is what it means to listen to music "as a jazz fan"—that is, with a particular kind of identity that is brought by audience members to a jazz

Live music experience in the digital age 203

club, but also learned in—and shaped by—their jazz club experiences. Burland and Pitts (2012) suggest that appropriate listening at a jazz club involves a combination of commitment (fans need to indicate their commitment to jazz as a musical form by their continuous response to what they hear); the right level of comfort (provided by the promoter) with good sound and sightlines, sociable seating and easy access to and from the bar; and connection, a sense of a tangible relationship with both performers and other audience members. What seems to matter most to the jazz audience is that a gig has the right "atmosphere", something that is determined by how the venue is organised and managed, by the behaviour of other audience members and by the quality of performance in terms of its direct engagement with the audience as well as its skill. Jazz audiences are distinct in expecting a degree of improvisation in how they listen; they have to decide when to be silent, when to be noisy, when to be still, when to be exuberant, and there is not necessarily audience agreement about this. Indeed, there is noticeably more audience dissatisfaction at jazz than at folk gigs, more irritation with people in the next seats, more grumbling about organisers' carelessness, more criticism of musicians for misjudging the occasion whether by being too introverted or too extroverted (Burland and Pitts 2012).

Julie Haferkorn (2018: 158) describes the similar problems that had to be addressed by promoters trying to attract new audiences by putting on classical music in "nightclubs and other non-traditional venues". Again there was a tension between treating a concert as a setting for "listening or socialising". The Little Orchestra (founded in 2014) advertises its events in this way:

> We've designed a night out that is social, relaxed, intimate and fun … Arrive and enjoy some drinks with friends and maybe make some new ones.
>
> (Haferkorn 2018: 158)

In selling classical music as entertainment, just like any other leisure activity, the new classical promoters have had to address a number of questions:

> Is the music, which is seemingly the prime focus in a traditional concert hall, just a by-product of the non-traditional event? And does it matter what the audience's motivation is to attend, be it to relax, socialise, or be intellectually simulated or educated?
>
> (Haferkorn 2018: 158)

Robert Ames, from the London Contemporary Orchestra (founded in 2008), argues that audiences attend for both social *and* musical reasons: "if people come for the social experience I hope they are inspired by the music. If they come simply for the music I hope they have a good social experience" (Haferkorn 2018: 159). This might seem like a formula for audience dissatisfaction—the "serious listeners" distracted by the "socialisers" at the bar, but Ames suggests that his audiences become, in effect, self-regulating.[11]

204 *Live music experience in the digital age*

Maggie Faultless from The Night Shift (a concert series staged in pubs, warehouses and rock clubs by the Orchestra of the Age of Enlightenment since 2006) told Haferkorn:

> You might think that the informality of these venues would create a casual relationship with the music—I'm often asked if pub venues mean it's noisy, but not a bit of it (the clink of a few glasses from the bar aside). In fact we've found that there seems to be an enhanced degree of listening as people are much more directly involved in the music making, and this intense listening creates the atmosphere of the performance.
>
> (Haferkorn 2018: 159)

It is, concludes Haferkorn (2018: 159), the informality that makes such performances "unique and particularly welcoming to new attenders". By "redefining the 'listening situation', the spectrum of what is acceptable in terms of etiquette and behaviours at classical music concerts is changing". It should be added, though, that promoters need to have a performance "set-up *designed* to create a focused listening environment", in the use of lighting, programming and amplification for example, thus creating what Ames calls "a really *big* listening experience" within the informal setting (quoted in Haferkorn 2018: 159, his emphasis). Gabriel Prokofiev, who launched his Nonclassical club nights in 2014, adds that all levels of engagement are fine, "people are listening when they are standing by the bar ... [That's] still a valid experience" (quoted in Haferkorn 2018: 160).

A similar set of promoter/musician/audience negotiations is described in Adam Behr's (2012) ethnography of the seemingly very different world of pub-based open mic nights in Edinburgh. Were people there to listen while they drank or to drink while they listened? What effect did the way performers were staged have on their performances? At open mic nights, the host has a particular significance. They are the figure through whom the audience is mediated (and to whom the performer, in effect, plays) *and* through whom the performers are mediated (and to whom the audience, in effect, responds). What seems to be the simplest of all forms of public entertainment—"just get up and play what you like!"—in fact involves a complex set of gestural rules (Behr 2012).

As these various examples show, appropriate audience behaviour has to be learned, may be contested and varies greatly both across and within different musical worlds. The only general conclusions to be drawn are, first, that there is no such thing as a passive audience; there are, rather in Martin Barker's (2013: 70) words, "different modes of participation" and, second, that changes in audience expectations and behaviour involve demographic processes, as new audiences grow up and existing audiences age. As rock promoter John Giddings explained to Adam Sweeting in 2007:

> Music fans in their forties, fifties or sixties are no longer prepared to put up with the squalor of sweaty clubs and instead demand the kind of

Live music experience in the digital age 205

comfort enjoyed by opera fans. And they're prepared to pay extra for the privilege. The audience gets older, earns more income and wants to enjoy what they know. It's like going to a classical concert to hear music you loved from the past. You've got 50,000 people sharing the experience. It's not like going to a football match where if you cheer you're liable to get beaten up by the guy sitting next to you. We seat the audience, because they want their own three feet of space. They stand up, but they don't want to have to push against other people. Twenty years ago they would have done.[12]

The audience sense of togetherness, in other words, can take different physical forms, including jostling for position or sitting in one's own space. Either way, live music is experienced as *communal*, as membership of some kind of club. Jon Savage once suggested that:

Yes, basically dance music is community, togetherness, and a lot of rock music, listening to it is very atomized. The archetypal kind of rock thing is The Smiths and people listening in their bedrooms. Coming together to see concerts but not really linking up to the extent that the dance community does. The gay community became visible and was able to some extent to find itself through dancing because of the nature of the music. Its whole rhetoric, the way it works, is about community.

(Quoted in Smith 1995: 198)

But this is to value one kind of "togetherness" over another. While gay dancers in the 1990s may have had a particular intense sense of community on the dance floor (a safe space in contrast to everyday life), for Smiths fans the audience experience had a different narrative. For many people, in fact, participation in a live event precedes and follows the event itself. It involves planning and anticipation beforehand, and discussion and reliving the highlights afterwards. In their study of audiences at the Queen's Hall in Edinburgh, Adam Behr and his colleagues (Behr et al. 2016) show how going to a gig involves not just buying a ticket but choosing who to go with, planning where to meet them, how best to *prepare* for a show. And the Queen's Hall bar turned out to be a crucial social space after the gig too, a place where people could go for a debriefing ("everyone in agreement that it had been a splendid show—good venue, good sound, good visuals, great band. Much to discuss" (quoted in Behr et al 2016: 15).

Similarly, in his study of Sheffield clubbing, Steven Evans (1989) writes that "many people could clearly specify a typical, often rigid routine" that they would follow on a night out: getting ready with friends, meeting others at pre-arranged pubs and bars. On arrival at the club, the women would always go straight to the toilets ("That's what they do, you know. Just to look at themselves, put some makeup on, wind's blown their hair out of place"), order a drink, walk around the club to "see who was in" and then stand around or

206 *Live music experience in the digital age*

find a seat ("often in exactly the same place as on previous visits"). Evans is describing a going-out ritual that has changed little since the 1950s dance halls, and that remains as important for meeting potential romantic partners as it does for celebrating friendship groups.[13]

In Chapter 1 we described how developments in ticketing technology put an end to the need to queue all night for tickets to the major shows—another long lasting pre-show ritual—but in some music worlds the queue has continued to be important:

> Through winter 2016 and early spring 2017 I've been waking up at 2 or 3am and taking the nightbus across London from my Peckham flat to a music venue. I don't know who I'm going to find but since there's a pop or rock gig on the following night, the fans will be there, wanting to be the first in. It doesn't feel particularly exclusive to any type of music, as long as the fan base includes a lot of them. When I say "them" I mean almost exclusively teen girls, since that is who I find every time.
>
> (Ewens 2019: 31)

These girls lived across southern England and knew each other through meeting in such queues. They always queued for shows and went to as many as they could afford, queuing for music "as disparate as hardcore punk and bubblegum mainstream pop". They were avid users of mobile phones and the internet, and were committed queuers because "the waiting connects the public and private parts of fandom" (Ewens 2019: 35):

> The time these girls wait in the queue is the time during which they get to possess the experience of the gig—the music, the crush of bodies, the thrill, the proximity to their idols. They're looking forward with all their hearts to something that might seem miserably brief ... but by queuing, they're making the wait that might irritate or be ignored by you or me into a mini break from reality.
>
> (Ewens 2019: 41)

This was in some ways the most enjoyable part of these fans' live music experience: sharing the anticipation and the tension, being with friends who had the same expectations. There are echoes here of people's fond memories of the daily queue outside the Royal Albert Hall for cheap standing tickets for the BBC proms. Even after the 2017 changes brought in by on-the-day online sales and the security needed to control a crowd hanging around a public building, the *BBC Music Magazine* website was still providing tips for potential queuers:

> If you are planning to stand in the Arena (at just £6!) and you want to get near the front, get there very early! Like Wimbledon, some Prommers show an extraordinary devotion to the cause—for a major work such as

a Mahler symphony, you can expect the queue to start forming from as early as 8am.

Bring a book to help pass the day or, if you are feeling really sociable, you could even talk to your fellow concert-goers. Presuming they want to talk to you, that is ... [but] ... if you are joining the Proms stalwarts in the queue you may need to rely on them when times get tough. When the heavens open and you are left with no umbrella; when you lose track of time and run back to the Albert Hall after your allotted 30-minute break is over and need someone to cover for you; when it's 30 degrees and you are without sun cream or simply when you're sitting in sheer boredom wanting someone to talk to, your fellow Prommers will come in handy. Picnic eggs and/or sausage rolls are recommended for getting the conversation started.[14]

Another kind of queue culture developed in the 1980s, outside clubs. By the mid-1990s, as Ben Malbon (1998: 276) writes, "the rituals of the queue and the door [had] become situations in which the clubbers act out certain roles in order to gain entry to the club—they behave as they are expected to behave". Like the people queuing in other music worlds, clubbers thus enjoyed collective rituals of anticipation, although here with an edginess, a sense of danger not obvious in other queues—commercial dance clubs were places to meet strangers as well as friends, to negotiate leisure in the big city.

Queues and other pre-gig rituals could be said to encapsulate, in their own ways, the paradoxical appeal of live music: its blending of the extraordinary and the everyday. Folk singer Jim Moray speaks for people in all music worlds:

> I want to be taken to another place when I go to see somebody. All that "I'm just like you" presentation undermines the songs that might be magical and mysterious and extraordinary. Presenting them in an ordinary way feels like a travesty.
>
> (Quoted in Tassell 2013: 241)

Or, as a Sheffield musician told Josie Robson in answer to the question: "What's the biggest buzz you get out of music?"

> It's still the live thing, going to see bands live, being overtaken and *overwhelmed* by whoever it is that's on stage, that's the best feeling ever. *Doesn't happen that often* now but it can be just the most amazing experience even without the use of drugs [laughter].
>
> (Quoted in Robson 2006: 127, our emphasis)

For Richard Smith (developing Jon Savage's point above), being *overwhelmed* by music at gay clubs in the mid-1990s was the essence of clubbing as a collective experience.

208 *Live music experience in the digital age*

The DJ teases us by mixing Deborah singing "deeper love, a deeper love, got a deeper love, a deeper love" into the record he's playing. Real quiet at first, then louder and louder and louder 'til we all know what's coming next. Then there's that "Whoomph!" like a needle dragged right across the record and we're there. Here we go again … "Well I got love in my heart, it gives me the strength to make it through the day, pride is love PRIDE is respect for yourself and that's why I'm not looking for …" BAM! The thing explodes. We all explode … All us boys together clinging. Somehow managing to have a good time in these terrible times. We know the world outside is shit and that all there really is is us. Drugs are just part of the glue that joins us together. What we're really rushing off is each other.

(Richard Smith in *Gay Times*, September 1994)[15]

For the fan girls in Hannah Ewens' study, the key term was *excitement*. Ewens describes a scene in the authorised One Direction documentary that was shown in cinemas in 2013:

"These girls are crazy about One Direction and I have no idea why," [Simon] Cowell says, like a hopeless dad, rather than a shrewd businessman who has helped build a lucrative product. Cut to neuroscientist Dr Stefan Koelsch dressed in a starched white lab coat … surrounded by computers and holding a model brain in his hands. "As soon as Directioners listen to music and find the music pleasurable," he says, splitting the brain with his hands and pointing to all its cavities and pathways, "what happens in the brain is that a neurochemical called dopamine is released and provides feelings of joy and happiness, shivers, goosebumps, strong pleasure." "The girls are not crazy," he says, "The girls are just excited."

"I were in the cinema in Glasgow with my friends," remembers Hayley, "And when that scene came on the whole cinema of girls just burst into applause, screaming and cheering. Finally an accurate representation of us; we were happy that someone had hit the nail on the head. My friend joked afterwards, 'Well, at least we know why we cry when they walk on stage. Science'."

(Ewens 2019: 25)

Earlier in this chapter, we quoted Daniel Cavicchi's description of Bruce Springsteen's self-identified "real fans"—real fans because their experiences of Springsteen's concerts were woven into their daily lives. But one doesn't have to be a fan in this way—whether of Bruce Springsteen or One Direction—to find live music entangled in one's emotional life, an entanglement as obvious at a karaoke bar as at an indie gig by a new rock band, a gig at which most of the audience are parents, siblings and school and family friends, at once proud, fearful and, indeed, excited.[16] In 2012, the artist Grayson Perry visited a social club in Sunderland for his research for *The Vanity of Small Differences*. In the television documentary about this project, as described by Lynsey Hanley:

Live music experience in the digital age 209

We see Perry watching a tearful woman in late middle age holding on—tenaciously but tenderly—to the arm of a young club singer while he performs a ballad she has requested. It turned out that the singer's mother had died not so long ago, and the woman holding on to his arm had been one of her best friends.

(Hanley 2017: 215)

The pleasure of live music involves a sense of both distance and closeness between performers and audience members. On the one hand, by the 1990s spectacle was the driver of the appeal of stadium rock and rave, and over the next two decades bands and DJs had to become ever more spectacular:

They're playing big rooms, like 10,000 each night, like here, they've got to make it more than just a band turns up and just plays the songs. People want to be entertained for their money they spend on the ticket, and that's part and parcel of what they get now. They expect to see, like, playback video screens, lasers, cannons, confetti drops, the whole shooting match.

(Graeme Roberts, Production Manager for the Stereophonics 2010 show at Glasgow's SEC)[17]

On the other hand, the 2010s also saw the development of the "house gig".[18] Emma and Jan Webster, for example, launched Music Inn in 2009, initially in their home in Glasgow, then in their home in Oxford. By 2013, the BBC was reporting that:

Simon and Snesha Holderness like nothing better of an evening than to settle down at home, put their feet up and listen to some of their favourite music.

In fact, they like it so much that they invite a select group of people to join them in their conservatory for a bite to eat and to share their experience.

Oh, and the performers come too.

The Sussex couple are among a small but growing band of people in the UK who host house concerts—live performances by professional musicians in cosy front rooms, home extensions or out on the patio among the shrubs and flower beds.

(*BBC News* report, April 26, 2013)[19]

The promoters of such contrasting events have equally contrasting anxieties: a stadium promoter has to ensure that audience members are individually engaged by what's happening on a stage they can hardly see; house concert promoters have to preserve something of the "mystery" of a visiting performer. What these promoters share with all promoters is the understanding that the experience of live music is an experience of *time and space*. In the

210 *Live music experience in the digital age*

second half of this chapter, we examine how digital technology has changed both the spatial and the temporal parameters of live music events.

The digital audience

> On the last weekend of 2006, the New York Metropolitan Opera launched a new initiative. Captured by up to a dozen high-definition digital cameras in front of more than 3000 attendees, a live performance of Mozart's *The Magic Flute* was beamed to 100 digitally equipped cinemas in the USA, the UK, Canada, Norway—and, with a delay, Japan.
>
> (Barker 2013: 2)

The Met had always been a pioneer in the use of new technology (in the live radio broadcasts of its performances, for example) and its use of livecasts in cinemas was quickly copied by other opera companies.[20] In 2007, Glyndebourne struck a deal with Odeon cinemas in Britain and by 2015 the Royal Opera House was offering live screenings in more than 400 cinemas in the UK and 60 in territories elsewhere. By then ROH had its own DVD label and through its BP sponsored "Big Screens" project offered free live outdoor summer screenings in public parks and squares. In the words of the company's managing director of enterprises, Alastair Roberts, "we regard all these digital technologies as ways of extending our audience reach", from the 2256 available seats in Covent Garden (almost always filled) to "the tens of thousands watching ... the Big Screens or the hundreds of thousands who see our work at local cinemas."

> We were in the business of live theatre with occasional television and radio broadcasts. Now we're in the business of live theatre plus ... Almost every time a new technology comes along, we use it.
>
> (quoted in Stewart 2015: 14)

While no one now doubts the importance of livecasting for opera companies' finances, research suggests that, rather than introducing cinema audiences to opera, livecasts brought opera lovers to the cinema. English Touring Opera found, for example, that the average age of the cinema audience for live opera was 68—considerably higher than the average age of people attending ETO's live shows (Stewart 2015: 14). ETO also found that if one of its live stage performances in a particular town clashed with a live ROH cinema performance, the ETO's audience was significantly reduced. "Liveness" was clearly valued by opera fans ("encore" screenings, showing live recordings on a later day, fare far less well in box office terms than "authentic" live showings), but the issue for opera fans was not live versus not live, but rather one kind of liveness against another.[21]

Reflecting on these issues, Andrew Stewart quotes "digital music consultant" Andy Doe (ex-head of classical music at iTunes and ex-COO of the record label, Naxos). Doe's view was that however people consumed opera, the quality of the audience experience was what mattered:

> There is a hunger out there for authentic experience. There's a danger that the excitement of any art form like opera can be diminished by the trend to present everything in this highly-polished, highly packaged digital world. What people want, in my opinion, is an experience that is honest and compelling, whichever way they access it.
>
> (quoted in Stewart 2015: 15)

The question is what is meant by an "authentic" and "honest" audience experience. This issue has been addressed most systematically by Martin Barker. Here, to begin with, are sample quotes from Barker's audience research:

> It was a fantastic performance in excellent quality at a local cinema in great comfort with friends.
>
> It's comfortable in the cinema and you get a great view of the auditorium too at the beginning. Our local cinema has a good system for ordering drinks for the interval which is great. The only thing you miss out on is the excitement of a live event but actually it was pretty exciting at our cinema—everyone clapped at the end!
>
> We are opera fans and spending half our time far away it is great to be able to access it in a local cinema.
>
> I had a bottle of wine and my wife beside me and a good view of the action ... with superb sound to boot.
>
> (quoted in Barker 2013: 32)

Barker asked his research sample how the experience of live opera in the cinema compared with the experience of live opera in an opera house.

> Obviously not the atmosphere of being at the theatre, but the interviews and behind scenes shots made up for it.
>
> Obviously lacks the every night an *event* feel—but the directed camera actually adds to the emotional impact. I think this is a really valuable addition to the availability of arts.
>
> You actually get a better view of the performance than in the actual theatre. The sound is always excellent. Obviously the atmosphere is not the same although the audiences do often respond with applause.
>
> (quoted in Barker 2013: 63)

A recurring theme for Barker's respondents was their enjoyment of livecast opera as a *local* event—they could now go to grand opera in a familiar place with familiar people:[22]

> Nothing could improve the experience in a good quality cinema like the Picturehouse at all. All the better points were that the Picturehouse is

212 *Live music experience in the digital age*

comfortable (luxurious seating), clean and the staff are welcoming; there isn't the snobbery that there is at the Opera House and you can still feel part of the production by dressing up just as you would at the Theatre.

(quoted in Barker 2013: 63)

For the audience, then, livecasting made opera more accessible, both materially and emotionally. The use of close-ups and back stage shots heightened the sense of participation; the use of cinematic editing conventions enhanced the feeling of being *present* at the event. In the words of Barker's respondents:

Larger than life ... surprisingly intimate, great visibility, and interesting introductions.
  Strangely more absorbing, because camera operator expertise presents a huge variety of shots and engages the concentration more deeply in the performance.
  Better because you're practically there on stage with the singers rather than seeing them from some distance in a live theatre. You ... miss the immediate excitement of a live performance and being in the presence of great artists, but surprisingly this is no big deal.

(quoted in Barker 2013: 63)

This was an experience still being shared with—and shaped by—other people, by the like-minded members of the cinema audience with whom one could discuss the performances over a drink at the bar at interval. It was obviously the case that in the cinema there was no interaction with the performers: "the only slightly weird thing is that everyone feels they want to applaud the best things but it is silly to applaud a cinema screen" (quoted in Barker 2013: 63),[23] but then such interaction was perhaps not really very significant for the opera audience in the theatre either. An opera is such a carefully constructed collaboration between so many different skilled workers that it leaves little room for improvisation, for the ad hoc, for the sense that each performance really is "unique". For most members of the theatre audience an opera performance is special because this is the only time they'll see it and, as a locally created cultural experience, an opera livecast will similarly be recalled as *a special event*.

The opera lovers who didn't like livecasts objected to them for a different reason. For these audience members, liveness is about "retaining control" of their experience; they want to manage their own responses to a performance, and not have them shaped by a film director (Barker 2013: 65):

Those who are most committed to the importance of physical co-presence are the ones who are most likely to say that they do not like being brought too close to the performers. This leads, they argue, to the loss of something they need if they are to have what they desire: a critical relationship. They need a certain distance to be able to sustain what they need: a clear sense of the illusion of the performance.

(Barker 2013: 69)[24]

The opera fans who did like the enhanced effect of being *immersed* in an opera (to use Barker's term) resembled in this respect the cinema audiences for the live streaming of (ex-)boy bands, who also shared the excitement of seeing and hearing their idols in close-up and behind the scenes. For both audiences, cinematic techniques intensified the wow! factor. Take That's 2015 London O2 Arena show, for example, reached cinema goers in "twenty-two territories", selling 10,500 cinema tickets in the UK (figures from *Music Week*, March 29, 2008: 9).

In general, however, rock and pop events have not been live screened in cinemas as systematically as operas, although such showings have been used to launch new albums: Madonna's 2000 album, *Music*, and David Bowie's 2003 album, *Reality*, were both launched with special concerts (a "secret gig" in Bowie's case) streamed to cinemas globally. In 2008, Stefan Demetriou, director of audiovisual at EMI, announced a deal with Odeon cinemas:[25]

The tie-in allows fans "to get closer to the live experience", by providing access to gigs and events which otherwise they might not be able to attend. "The big-screen, surround-sound experience literally ensures that every seat is the best in the house".

(Quoted in *Music Week*, March 29, 2008: 9)

But the EMI/Odeon tie-in didn't develop as a significant money-maker and live streaming of rock music quickly focused on computer rather than cinema screens. Radiohead, for example, staged a gig in 2008 for 200 people in a small London venue that was streamed, in real time, on their website (radioheadtv) with their usual record producer, Nigel Godrich, in control of sound. The idea was to establish a new kind of "intimacy with their fans" (Quoted in *Music Week*, March 29, 2008: 9).

The key players in the development of this kind of live casting were YouTube, Facebook and AEG Digital, who moved from using their services to promote upcoming shows and festivals to providing an expansion of the live music experience itself. Fabian Holt describes how, from 2008, "the marketers of Tomorrowland [Europe's biggest EDM festival, staged in Belgium] pioneered a kind of festival marketing movie that creates a digital extension of the fictional event world". The use of multiple camera angles, the "flow of footage of stages, backstage areas, tents, parties, travelling, and much more" provided "instant participation for audiences not physically present" (Holt 2016: 277–8). At around the same time in Dalston, Blaise Bellville, working with Femi Adeyemi's online radio station NTS and later the US-based video service Ustream, launched Boiler Room, which streamed live DJ

214   *Live music experience in the digital age*

sets online "so that people could watch them from their bedroom". Within a decade, as Sam Wolfson reported in *The Guardian,* "clubbers themselves [were] documenting every part of their night out on Instagram Stories and broadcasting it back to their mates who decided to stay at home".[26]

As Burland and Pitts (2014: 175) concluded:

> The experience of "live music" is not simply, and only, dependent upon an individual actually "being there"; audiences can engage with live performances, in real time, but remotely, relying on others to share their experiences online ... thereby extending the audience "community" in ways previously unimaginable (even as recently as the 1990s).

Even the jazz world, which is ideologically centred on the live, improvised performance, has extended "its audience community" in this way. In their 2010 study of "the cultural importance of the online experience to jazz fans", Tim Wall and Andrew Dubber (2010: 161–2) write that:

> The most prominent technologies and applications where we found fan activity were blogs, discussion boards and fora, dedicated website pages, online radio stations and other forms of streamed and downloaded audio and video services ... What is notable ... is the quantity of fan activity devoted to live jazz performances within the noncommercial spaces on the internet. These are apparent, amongst other materials, in the availability of recordings of live events, fan-produced reviews of live events, information about live performances, encyclopedic listings of musicians' live performances, and discussions about performances.

The history of jazz in Britain has always involved a special relationship between live and recorded music. The original jazz clubs brought people to pub rooms to listen to records together, and studio recordings are packaged as if they were live events, with detailed information about personnel, instruments, the time and place of the recording, the number of takes and so forth. The digital "extension" of the jazz audience and its participation in live music involves new ways of supporting old fan practices, new ways of sharing "data".

The same point could be made about the use of social media in other music worlds. Lynsey Hanley remembers what it was like to be a dedicated pop fan in the 1980s (which was not very different from what it had been like to be a dedicated pop fan in the 1950s, 1960s and 1970s):

> We wrote to each other across whichever agonizing divide we were trying to breach, all from points of isolation. These days a social life unfettered by locality has been made possible by mobile phones and the internet. Back then, when there was one phone in the living room, and the possibility of instant communication with like-minded people was restricted

Live music experience in the digital age 215

to those with ham radio facilities, the exchange of letters—along with newspaper snippets, duplicate stickers, promises of meetings and other affirmations of *there being a point to it all*—was all there was.

(Hanley 2017: 107, her italics)[27]

By contrast, Lucy Bennett 2012: 548) describes how, by 2010:

> even though they are not physically present and are in different time zones, [U2] fans are gathering to share their opinions and knowledge and the excitement surrounding this specific event, in such a way that they not only feel part of the "live" music experience, but also create their own. Some construct and post possible set-lists, sharing their own predictions, while others play the songs being performed as the songs are texted in. After the concert, the interest continues, with fans posting footage and songs from the show on YouTube and sharing their photos ... While some fans use social media to send bulletins to other fans throughout the concert, others take the connection further by using a facility called 1000Mikes—self-described as Radio 2.0—to broadcast the entire show to them as it happens. The volunteer show attenders use their mobile phone to connect to the platform, which then generates a personal live broadcast channel, which other fans can access and listen in to through the website.

What Bennett is describing here is a new kind of audience for live rock and pop that emerged in the 2000s, an audience that is present at the events not bodily but rather via mobile phone access to the internet and on social networking sites. For such listeners physical absence from the show itself is compensated for by a more intense engagement with what is going on, expressed through a running commentary on the music as it is played. As we have already argued, the meaning of a musical event is always been shaped by anticipation and recollection; social media both socialise and formalise this temporal arc, condensing the process and making even the most individual emotional flow a matter for public scrutiny. Because this virtual audience cannot be seen listening, their musical response has to be continuously articulated in words. For an absent audience, silence is not an option; as a result, the virtual audience can, paradoxically, lay claim to an equally intense sense of participation and fellow-feeling, an equally strong feeling of *being there* as the "real" audience.

Conclusion

It has long been argued that the concept of "live music" only became necessary when people began to listen to recorded music, to listen (for the first time) to music that was not live (Auslander 1999), and one historical consequence of this conceptual binary has been to pitch the live and the recorded against each other as competing ways of listening. This was the driving force

216　*Live music experience in the digital age*

of the Musicians' Union's long campaign to "Keep Music Live!", for example. But this is to play down the reality that the "live music experience" has been mediated technologically in other ways too. Long before the live streaming of opera was a regular cinematic event, the live music experience was being shaped for various audiences by live performance on film, whether *Jazz on a Summer's Day* in 1959, S*aturday Night Fever* in 1977 or *Spice Girls the Movie* in 1997. Even more significantly in Britain, the BBC—first on radio, then on television—developed its own conventions of the "live broadcast", whether of dance bands from London hotels in the 1930s, rock groups in studio sessions in the 1960s and 1970s or BBC orchestras from municipal concert halls and the BBC Proms from the Royal Albert Hall all through these years. As we have shown in our previous volumes, the history of live music in Britain necessarily involves the history of broadcasting.

If participating in a live music event, being in the audience cannot always be confined to being in a particular place, nor can what is meant by the live music *experience* be confined to a particular time. In advance, as we have already noted, it involves planning, ticket buying, queuing, anticipation; afterwards it involves reminiscence, saving the tickets, memorialising. Social media haven't changed these processes; rather, they have enable them to happen in new ways technologically (from the polaroid to the selfie), on a bigger scale, in more extended networks and in ways that can be commercially shaped and exploited more easily, as promoters and marketers join in the conversations. From an audience perspective, in short, digital media have not so much transformed the live music event as changed the *environment* in which such events are staged. The ecology of live music is the subject of the next chapter.

Notes

1　See https://slippedisc.com/2017/08/bbc-now-has-two-classes-of-proms-queues.
2　Quoted in Bennett (2012: 550).
3　By the end of the 1990s, "the experience economy" was a familiar term in the marketing literature (e.g. see Pine and Gilmore 1998) and music festivals had become an important topic for the rapidly expanding academic field of event management.
4　This is my experience, for example, as a Trustee of the Queen's Hall in Hexham, which is funded by ACE and Northumberland County Council (SF).
5　Quoted from an interview with Emma Webster, June 30, 2009. Music in the Round is, in its own words,

> the leading national promoter of chamber music. We bring people and music closer together through our unique, informal and informative style of "in the round" performances, touring to numerous venues around the country as well as presenting two concert series and the annual Sheffield Chamber Music Festival.

See www.musicintheround.co.uk.
6　We take the distinction between "fans" and "socialites" from a study of the audience at the 2008 Wireless Festival in Leeds (Henderson and Wood 2009).

Live music experience in the digital age 217

7 Hodge, then working at the Glasgow Royal Concert Hall, quoted from an interview with Emma Webster, December 16, 2009.

8 Quote taken from an interview with Emma Webster, October 20, 2009.

9 There have been examples of people gathering in public places to listen intently (rather than dance) to records, from the early British jazz clubs in the 1930s to contemporary London "audiophile clubs" where, as *The Guardian* reported in 2016, fans get together each week "to listen to a record in its entirety, played from original vinyl over speakers and amps that cost more than most of their homes". See www.theguardian.com/music/2016/jan/07/ spiritland-brilliant-corners-london-audiophile-bars.

10 For detailed analyses of two particular moments of audience–performer negotiation—the encore and the request—see Webster (2012) and Hytönen-Ng (2017).

11 For comparable self-regulation through the use of spatial "zones", see Wendy Fonarow's (2006) pioneering anthropological study of British indie gigs.

12 Quote taken from an airline magazine but I don't know which one (SF)! Giddings is implicitly describing the thinking behind London's O2 here—see Chapter 2.

13 In her study of the culture of femininity in the East End of Glasgow, Adele Patrick (2004) found that it wasn't uncommon for women to enjoy getting ready together so much that they didn't actually make it to the gig.

14 See www.classical-music.com/article/5-top-tips-attending-bbc-proms.

15 Reprinted in Smith (1995: 229–30)

16 For karaoke see Drew (2011). For music, emotion and everyday life, see Clayton (2008).

17 Quoted from an interview with Emma Webster, March 2, 2010.

18 At the end of the 1990s, Pete Doherty and Carl Barât had staged Libertines gigs in their flat, but this was more in the spirit of punk DIY.

19 Quoted from www.bbc.co.uk/news/uk-england-22206434. For the house gig scene, see Emma Webster's report posted on January 31, 2014 to Live Music Exchange: http://livemusicexchange.org/blog/gig-in-your-house-national-house-gig-network-launched-today-emma-webster/. Country house gigs have, of course, a long and continuing history in the classical music world.

20 The business of "livecasting" had, of course, been pioneered by Live Aid.

21 There is also a cost factor here. The average ticket price for a live screened opera outside London is well under £20, which means that audience members can go to several such showings for the cost of just one ticket for the staged event.

22 Opera showings have become most important for small, independent, arthouse or community cinemas (rather than multiplexes), where seats are bookable and the bar feels more like a theatre bar than a branded food and drink outlet.

23 This was a dilemma in the rock world too. The 2009 premiere of Julien Temple's Dr Feelgood documentary *Oil City Confidential* was simulcast across British cinemas; it was followed immediately by a streamed live performance by Wilko Johnson: "it was a bizarre experience. Some people applauded, some didn't" (personal communication from Mark Percival). It could be argued, though, that clapping is anyway not just for the performers but a celebration of being in an audience.

24 How intervals are treated in the cinema can be another problem here. For me, these backstage shots "broke the fourth wall" and took away some of the sense of theatrical mystique. For example, having Renée Fleming being interviewed about

218 *Live music experience in the digital age*

her upcoming roles just before the fourth act of *Aida* began took me out of the performance completely (EW).

25 EMI was then owned by the hedge fund Terra Firma, which also owned the Odeon business.

26 See www.theguardian.com/music/2018/mar/14/the-new-rules-of-clubbing-from-illegal-raves-to-spacehopper-hedonism. Ustream is owned by IBM, Instagram Stories by Facebook.

27 For insight into how contemporary fan communication works see Hannah Ewens' report on Beyoncé's online "beyhive", which organises the global exchange of news and gossip between hundreds of thousands of "bees" divided into sub-groups. Ewens (2019: 133) interviewed Lela, the administrator of one such group, a "small" one of around 47,000 fans.

11   The live music ecology

What I loved was Roger's idea of what you could do with a demographic, he knew what his demographic was. His people were, for better or worse, about thirty; they could be school teachers, social workers whatever, they were the ones who had disposable income, they were the ones nobody catered for.

(C.P. Lee on Roger Eagle, promoter at the International, Manchester, from 1985–1991, quoted in Sykes 2012: 248)[1]

Have you ever found a venue that you think is perfect but that people won't go to? Yep. Absolutely. Several times. And ... Actually a case in point in Rotherham at the minute, with the arts centre, is a really nice space for chamber music, but people won't come through the front doors, because it's seen as a council building—it's part of the library; it's a horrible front; it's a really ugly looking building—and they just think nothing good can be in there, so they don't bother coming through. If they came through they'd see a nice cafe, an intimate space, a performance space with good acoustics, and free parking. I don't see what more you can want! But they won't come through the front doors.

(Tracy Johnston, Concert Manager, Music in the Round, 2009)[2]

To ensure that cultural and economic enrichment continues, we need to make sure we do all we can to protect the music ecosystem of the [Sheffield] City Region. We need to nurture and support the venues, particularly smaller and grassroots venues, that are the bedrock of the local music scene.

(UK Music 2019)

Introduction

We have argued throughout this history that live music has to be approached ecologically. Ecology is the scientific study of the relationship between living organisms and their environment; it is a branch of the natural sciences. Our perspective is not scientific in this way, but we do approach live music history through the lens of cultural ecology. We are interested in the environments in which live music-making practices develop and change, in their fragility

220 The live music ecology

and resilience. One of our questions, for example, is how the materiality of a musical place (its size, shape, acoustic and physical accessibility) affects the construction of musical meanings. The buildings in which music happens today may or may not have started out as musical sites; even if they did, the musical ideology inscribed in their physical and acoustic design may or may not be compatible with the listening expectations of later musical communities. Either way it's obvious that buildings don't just exist in people's minds. Live music is a cultural practice that is embedded in—and depends on—a material setting.[3]

Similarly, a musical event is not just the result of ideological agreement among the people who, in reaching such agreement, form a musical world. A live musical event involves constant negotiation with people who are not part of this world. In her ethnographic study of a successful pub-based jazz club in the south of England, Elina Hytönen-Ng (2017: 70) shows that:

> The promoter is dependent and constrained by technical equipment available, the physical space and the support provided by the pub staff, the available finances, as well as the musicians wanting to work at the club. For the customers to come back their needs and interests should be met. The management needs to receive enough of an exchange value in order to allow the events to take place within its premises. The cooperative links influence the kind of art and music that can be or will be produced within the club.

A live music event is an effect of the interdependence of music worlds, regulatory worlds and commercial worlds. Promoters and venue owners know that state authorities routinely make decisions without any reference to live music at all, which nevertheless have profound consequences for what kind of music can be made where, when and for whom.

The ecological issues we want to consider in this chapter are *sustainability* and *adaptation*. The sustainability of live music became a particularly contentious issue for British policy-makers in the period of this volume, an issue that was both the cause and an effect of an increasing use of ecological arguments in live music discourse. Local authorities were challenged to understand that decisions about public transport or new housing schemes could have significant consequences for the ability of existing venues to survive; large promoters were challenged to understand that the pursuit of competitive policies that put small operators out of business would, in the long term, have a significant impact on their own businesses. An ecological approach means tracing the relationships between different performance spaces in the local environments in which *all* live musical activity occurs. In looking at these ecosystems in terms of survival and adaptation, we will examine first the recurring argument over the last decade that "grassroots venues are in crisis" and second, promoters' own understandings of the local music environment.

The live music ecology 221

Crisis? What crisis?

In recent years, local newspapers have begun to celebrate long-gone music venues as part of their nostalgia marketing. In 2017, for example, the *Birmingham Mail* ran a feature on the "live music venues we have loved and lost"; in 2019, the *Newcastle Chronicle* headlined a story "Newcastle's legendary rock venue, the Mayfair Ballroom, closed its doors on this day 20 years ago".[4]

Venue closure stories have become commonplace in national news pages too. On December 12, 2008, *The Guardian* story was, "Last Orders. Across the UK, rock pubs are closing down. Yes, they're grimy, smelly and loud—but we can't afford to lose them." The reporter, Anita Bhagwandas, mourned the closure of Maltsters in Pontypridd, the Swan and Bottle in Uxbridge, The Old Swan in Wrexham (now "a trendy wine bar") and the Flapper and Firkin in Birmingham (a city once famed for its rock pubs now had only Scruffy Murphy's). In London, the survival of the Devonshire Arms in Camden, the goth pub, was taken to be remarkable.

On November 26, 2010, *The Independent*'s Rob Sharp reported that "the recession has decimated small venues". The trigger for his report was the closure of Lumiere. Its demise followed the closure of other well-known London venues: the long-established 100 Club and the Astoria in Charing Cross (a victim of London's Crossrail development) and the relatively new Flowerpot in Kentish Town; and the demise of Barfly in Cardiff, Glasgow and Liverpool.[5] Sharp blamed the financial difficulties for these venues not only on the recession but also on property developers, rising local rates and rents, and competition from the large corporate-owned venues. Without small venues, he asked, how will new bands "hone their craft"?[6]

By May 26, 2012, the headline story in *The Observer* was "Rock Music under threat as small venues go bust across Britain. Venues where top bands started out are shutting down as rent rises and falling audiences spell crisis for gig promoters."[7] This story mourned the end of the Bongo Club in Edinburgh, Charlotte in Leicester, TJ's in Newport and the Horn in St Albans;[8] the crisis for gig promoters was also affecting venues in Cardiff, Bristol, Belfast, Leeds, Sheffield and Manchester. The paper quoted The Horn's promoter, Hansi Koppe:

> In good times people will go and see a new band just to hear what they're like. Now if it's a band nobody has heard of then people aren't so keen to pay the money to see them. They'd rather go and see a cover band down the pub where it's free. But that's not what we're about. We're a little rock'n'roll sweatbox.

Bongo's manager Ally Hill despaired that, despite Bongo's cultural and financial success, Edinburgh University (which owned the premises) wanted the site back to build offices.

222 *The live music ecology*

Playing places like this is the groundwork bands need, the stepping-stone. And even when they've made it big, live music needs every rung in the ladder it can get … it's not just bands who cut their teeth here but sound and lighting engineers, promoters, even bar staff.[9]

Such stories gave weight to the launch of the Music Venues Trust (MVT) in 2014.[10] The MVT was set up "to protect, secure and improve UK Grassroots Music Venues for the benefit of venues, communities and upcoming artists":

We aim to secure the long-term future of iconic Grassroots Music Venues such as Hull Adelphi, Exeter Cavern, Southampton Joiners, The 100 Club, Band on the Wall, Tunbridge Wells Forum, etc.

These venues have played a crucial role in the development of British music over the last 40 years, nurturing local talent, providing a platform for artists to build their careers and develop their music and their performance skills.

We work to gain recognition of the essential role these venues fulfil, not only for artist development but also for the cultural and music industries, the economy and local communities.[11]

MVT's discursive impact was quickly evident. UK Music's Manifesto for the 2015 General Election included the demand for "consistency in live music regulation across entertainment licensing and the planning system" and for the protection of small venues, so that "music can flourish at local levels" (UK Music 2015: 10). Later that year, London's "grassroots music venues rescue plan" was launched by the Mayor of London's Music Venues Taskforce. In 2019, a DCMS Parliamentary Committee report concluded that the UK had lost 35% of its grassroots venues between 2007 and 2015; it criticised the government, the cultural sector and the music industry for failing to identify the "crisis and to act to stop it".[12] In the words of an accompanying MVT press release:

Five years ago, we launched Music Venues Trust in response to the challenges facing our venues. We did that because we strongly believed that Grassroots Music Venues were not properly being understood by those key stakeholders, and we believed that the collective loss of hundreds of these venues had long term social, cultural and economic impacts that were much more serious and important than the loss of any one single venue, no matter how important or loved that venue was. With your help and support, we've grown this cause into an effective and meaningful campaign that has made a real change in the way venues are perceived, treated and valued.

(MVT March 19, 2019)

In its lobbying activity, MVT had primarily deployed two arguments, one about the organisation of urban space and the other about the structure of

The live music ecology   223

live music commerce. At MVT's first Venues Day event in 2015, for example, Ministry of Sound's Lohan Presencer griped that housing always "trumps music": the noise complaints of incoming residents were always favoured over the interests of established music venues. MVT thus campaigned successfully for the agent of change principle that was incorporated into England's National Planning Policy Framework in July 2018.[13] Paragraph 182 of this planning guidance stated:

> Planning policies and decisions should ensure that new development can be integrated effectively with existing businesses and community facilities (such as places of worship, pubs, music venues and sports clubs). Existing businesses and facilities should not have unreasonable restrictions placed on them as a result of development permitted after they were established. Where the operation of an existing business or community facility could have a significant adverse effect on new development (including changes of use) in its vicinity, the applicant (or "agent of change") should be required to provide suitable mitigation before the development has been completed.

At MVT's 2015 event, another speaker, Steve Lamacq, warned that live music was going the same way as football, with the large big city venues/clubs attracting all the money and small local venues/clubs in a state of decline. Lamacq worried that if 15-year-olds couldn't get to a gig on a bus, they might never go to a gig at all; he suggested that funds needed to flow down from the corporate to the grassroots level to ensure the survival of venues accessible to all. It was in the interests of the major entertainment corporations to protect small venues for the good health of the live music economy as whole.[14]

The argument that performers and audiences should have access to a variety of different-sized venues was by then a commonplace of music policy documents, as can be seen in Paul Carr's (2011) analysis of the live music industry in Wales for the Welsh Music Foundation and EKOS's report on the music sector in Scotland for Creative Scotland. Carr (2011: 39) concluded that Wales needed a better supply of venues to enable acts to perform at all stages of their career, while EKOS (2013: ii) suggested more sanguinely that Scotland is "well-served in general by the range and geographical scope of music promoters—and the venue stock is generally good".

The issues in Wales were explained to us by Guto Brychan from Club Ifor Bach in Cardiff (founded in 1983 as a members' club for Welsh speakers):

> There are lots of nightclubs in Cardiff so we provide an alternative night out to the chain venues in the city centre. There weren't that many options for bands to perform back in the late 1980s and early 1990s. It was hardgoing in terms of providing a live music infrastructure in the city and there weren't really any "grassroots" venues catering for that audience. And there weren't that many other levels of venues here to support artists

224   *The live music ecology*

coming through. One of the issues that's always faced us as a city, I think, is that we've got venues at certain levels but there are gaps in the provision. So when you're starting off with a new band, you might get them at the 200 capacity level, but then there wasn't a 500 cap; there was a 1000 but there wasn't a 2000 or a 5000. So bands would come at the start and they wouldn't come again till much later in their career ... And that's something that's started to change recently. Venues like the Tramshed have opened up which is 700–1000, and the Union can do 1200 to 1500, but after that then you haven't really got anything until you get to the Motorpoint which is 8,000, and then after that there's the Millennium Stadium which is up to 70,000. So there's a lot of gaps over the 1500 capacity size.[15]

Brychan is considering venue provision here from an urban perspective. The Carr and EKOS reports, with their broader geographical brief, were also concerned with rural venues; both reports pointed to the importance of the state-supported touring networks that had, in the past, been developed by Community Music Wales and the Scottish Arts Council.[16] In England, such activity is exemplified by the Highlights rural touring scheme (covering Cumbria, County Durham and Northumberland), which was developed in the 2010s with the financial support of the relevant county councils and Arts Council England, using volunteers from more than 70 village halls and communities.[17]

While there can be no doubt about the limitations of live music provision documented in policy reports and the threat to existing venues publicised by the Music Venues Trust, from a historical point of view, the discourse of a venue "crisis" is problematic. A "grassroots venue" is not just some kind of natural species that needs protection from human interference in its habitat. There is another ecological question to ask here: how do venue ecosystems *adapt* to such interference? In NESTA's 2017 mapping analysis of London's club scene (prepared in response to "widespread concern" about club closures) its authors, Antonio Lima and John Davies, suggest that

one would expect clubs to have a high closure rate as venues come and go out of fashion and people move on. Many of the most famous clubs, held to define a given period, for example Studio 54 in the 70s, the Hacienda in the 80s and 90s, no longer exist. The question is therefore not whether clubs are closing, which will always happen, but whether the pattern of closures is systematically changing London's nightlife.[18]

Club promoters have always been sensitive to the effects of population change and fashion on the dance floor. Mark Ross, Sheffield DJ and club promoter, said:

Part of the reason we gave [Urban Gorilla] up was because I think our tastes were becoming less in line with what the rest of the people were

The live music ecology 225

into, possibly as we got older. And the younger kids started to get into different styles of music and maybe we were starting to lose touch a bit.[19]

For Martino Burgess, co-owner of the Lakota Club in Bristol, its survival has been dependent on spotting new dance floor trends:

> There's always that risk with Lakota: it has to move really fast. I mean, we found ourselves ... the scene that I personally was caught up in was the house/techno scene and that did really well, but when that went mainstream, people stopped going to Lakota and started going to more mainstream clubs doing it .... Whatever scene you're into there comes a point when that comes to an end, and you've *got* to know what the next scene is.[20]

Property development and the enforcement of noise regulations are not the only causes of urban venue closure. There can be many change factors involved: demography and fashion as we've mentioned, the geography and nature of crime, the shifting patterns of drug and alcohol use. In her report on the discussions at the 2015 Venue Day, Emma Webster observed that

> some venues are noticing that their audiences are growing older and that it was becoming increasingly difficult to attract a younger audience; it was suggested by some people that young audiences may be staying in and socialising online instead of going out to local music venues.

Webster speculated that what these venues offer is not what younger people are now looking for:

> For example, live music and alcohol have had a strong relationship for many years, with festivals in particular associated with heavy drinking. However, research in the UK appears to suggest that the proportion of young adults who reported that they do not drink at all increased by more than 40% between 2005 and 2013, and it may be that live music is starting to move away from its traditional links with social drinking. In addition, venues, particularly those literally underground, may have poor or non-existent wi-fi connections, which again may be putting younger audiences off. Could we, then, be heading for a return to 1950s coffee bars but this time with added superfast wi-fi connections?

Competition between venues for new audiences has long been the norm. In his unpublished history of the council-owned Free Trade Hall in Manchester (another "legendary" venue, which became a concert hall in 1951), Richard Lysons shows how it was "squeezed from both sides" from the mid-1980s as indie and world music acts were booked into International One and Two (opened in 1985 and 1987), mainstream pop, rock and country acts into the Apollo (from 1988) and new rock and pop acts into Academy One (from 1990).

226   *The live music ecology*

The Free Trade Hall closed in 1996 (when the Bridgewater Hall opened) and is now a Radisson Hotel, The Edwardian.[21]

Among the online comments on the 2012 *Observer* story we quoted earlier, there were several dismissing the notion of a "venue crisis" as "bollocks!" "For every venue closing, there is another independent absolutely thriving," wrote one reader. "We've more choice than ever before." "Independent promoters will always find great places to put on gigs," wrote another:

> I have promoted gigs in Nottingham for over 10 years and venues come and go, good and bad. If there are no good venues (and by good I mean: a friendly owner, location people are willing to travel to, decent PA/sound guy and good beer) then you make our own! Put gigs on in practice rooms, artists' spaces, community halls. If people want cheap then you put gigs on in these places and do BYOB. Build your own PA!

In 2014, an *NME* writer went inside "Britain's DIY venue revolution":

> Amid the gloom about some of our most treasured venues closing, there is also some good news: Britain's DIY scene is having a resurgence that is leading to a growing community of music fans clubbing together to set up new spaces on their doorsteps.
>
> (*NME*, September 20, 2014: 12–13)

Among the venues described were Unity Works in Wakefield, a space for art and music events set up by 375 local residents who in 2013 formed a co-op and raised £4 million to purchase and restore a derelict Grade 2-listed building; JT Soar in Nottingham, a fruit warehouse turned all-age music/arts venue and rehearsal space with a recording studio; and The Lughole, a volunteer run, not-for-profit space in Sheffield. For all of these venues doing-it-yourself was the inspiring idea. The Lughole, for example,

> grew out of a need for a space where we could do our own thing, free from the constraints of "regular" venues and the rules, atmosphere and attitudes that they perpetuate. With this in mind we formed a collective, went out and (eventually) found a building (a pretty horrible disused factory), pooled our meagre personal finances, recruited other like-minded individuals and set to. After a couple of months' hard work getting set up, the Lughole opened its doors on New Year's Eve 2013. It has since gone from strength to strength, attracting bands from all over the world, countless different genres and people from all walks of life.[22]

For JT Soar:

> The DIY ethics extend to the drinks policy with a bring your own bottle approach avoiding the issue of pricey drinks (so often cited as a bugbear

The subsequent fortunes of these venues were mixed. Unity Works went into administration in 2017; the building was taken over by a commercial entrepreneur and developed as a conference centre. The Lughole faced "continuing threats and pressure from both Sheffield council and private developers", and in 2017 launched an appeal for funds for a new building, which seems to have been unsuccessful. JT Soar continues to be a much-used venue.

DIY venue making is not only inspired by the ideology of punk or indie rock. In his book on Franz Ferdinand, Hamilton Harvey (2005: 107) writes:

> Looking for alternative spaces is … a well-established practice in the art world. Glasgow had long developed a strong tradition of artists finding and converting spaces in which to display their work.

Hence the "legendary" Chateau, the art/performance space established by the band in the early 2000s in a run-down "mostly empty six-storey art-deco workshop and warehouse set a few yards off Bridge Street" (Harvey 2005: 113).

And on February 26, 2009, *The Guardian* ran a story on "one of the country's best-kept musical secrets: an informal network of London soul singer-songwriter open mic nights", publicised by word of mouth among musicians:[24]

> Tonight's example, it turns out, is fairly typical. There's little in the way of promotion, even inside the venue; no written mention of the singer/songwriters who troop up to the microphone for their twenty minute sets. The pub itself, Monkeychews in Chalk Farm, considers itself so far off the beaten track that its website carries the slogan: "Seek and ye shall find". Yet the audience—in the main, performers and their friends—pay polite, careful attention, and the atmosphere is enthusiastic and supportive.[25]

In 2018, Sam Wolfson reported on a quite different kind of DIY activity:

> Illegal raves have been a fixture of British partying for decades, but figures released last week by the Metropolitan police show that in London in the past year their number nearly doubled, from 70 to 133, and events are getting bigger. In the past few months, police have shut down parties ranging from a rave in Liverpool accessible only by an underground tunnel, to parties in a field in Berkshire and an industrial estate in West Sussex. Last year in Hounslow, West London, 1500 people descended on a closed-down Morrisons, set up sound systems and kept going until riot police stormed the venue. These events often end with minor skirmishes. When police tried to close down an event at a disused bank in Deptford, South London, in January 2017, crowd violence caused injury to officers.

228   *The live music ecology*

[DIY] Promoters have seen the eradication of traditional clubs as a challenge. "The more clubs that close, the more the illegal scene grows; people are always going to find somewhere else to do it," says Clair Stirling AKA Eclair Fifi, a renowned club DJ who has had shows on Radio 1 and NTS.

This movement is being led by some extremely young people. Ticket prices and a clampdown on fake IDs means legitimate clubs are completely out of reach for them. Teenage party fixers will scout out empty locations, climb in through an open window and then start spreading the news.[26]

What we see here (as in different ways with the Lughole and the Chateau) is the survival of particular strands of DIY promotional practice (punk, performance art and rave) as musicians, promoters and audiences adapt to new circumstances. Survival and adaptation are equally apparent in musical worlds with different histories. In the jazz world, for example, what is immediately noteworthy is the longevity of key venues: the Concorde Club in Eastleigh, Hampshire, has been open since 1957, Ronnie Scott's in Soho and The Bull's Head in Barnes since 1959, The Old Duke in Bristol since the late 1960s, the Band on the Wall in Manchester since the 1970s and The Four Bars Inn in Cardiff since 1987.[27]

In 2009, in a critical study of the BBC's music policy, Jazz Services described the live jazz scene as "vibrant" less because of the survival of these old clubs than because a new generation of jazz players had found a variety of new spaces in which to play. Acoustic Triangle had put together 120 dates in a year by playing many of them in churches and cathedrals; new urban jazz spaces had opened up around the colleges in Manchester, Newcastle, Cardiff and Birmingham, where jazz was now taught. Barak Schmool from F-ire Collective explained that:

> Some people want to play in rock venues that have a different energy about them, where everyone is standing bunched up close together. Other people need the street; some people need a more relaxed jazz club, so people are creating music for different environments and this has never happened before.
>
> (Quoted in Nicholson et al 2009: 9–10)

Young London jazz musicians began playing in the Total Refreshment Centre, an old West Indian social club in Stoke Newington, the Church of Sound, an old Clapton church, and at club nights like Steam Down at the Buster Mantis bar in Deptford.[28] For these musicians, the variety of venues needed was a matter of audience culture as well as audience size. In the words of saxophonist Nubya Garcia:

> It's more about who's in the audience. I'm honoured to play Ronnie Scott's, but if the audience doesn't want to be there, or they haven't come

to see me, that isn't a gig that's the same as playing in a warehouse where your people are, your musical family, they're with you from the beginning until the end, they're not a passive audience. Each venue has its own vibe.[29]

A quick look at the tour schedules of contemporary folk musicians reveals a similar mix of venues: folk clubs and pub rooms; theatres, arts centres, libraries, schools and universities; city, town and village halls. These examples are taken from Faustus's Cotton Lords Tour in 2018; from other bands' schedules we could add hotels, churches and barns, aged care homes, bowling clubs and trains. Promoters and agents have to be ingenious in putting tours together but what is described here does not suggest a venue crisis. In the words of Biyi Adepegba of promotion company Joyful Noise (which he started with Barbara Pukwana in 1990), "There's African music going on all over Britain all of the time. Everywhere from churches and community halls to bars, clubs and stadiums" (quoted in *The Guardian*, September 10, 2010: 11).

On September 12, 2009, *Music Week* reported that the independent ticketing agency WeGotTickets had signed a deal (which is still in place) to "showcase and sell tickets" for all events promoted by Making Music's 2800 member groups,

> which includes choirs, orchestras, music clubs, samba groups and barbershop choruses and represents more than 200,000 volunteer musicians and music lovers. Making Music's members promote more than 10,000 events per year to an audience of 1.6m people.

There are two final points to be made here. On the one hand, venue closure reports are not in themselves indicative of a decline in the overall provision of live music; venue closures and openings are a normal and continuing occurrence in the history of live music. On the other hand, the health of the live music ecosystem is determined not simply by the number of venues available, but also by their variety and interdependence. The clubs with which MVT campaigners have been most concerned, for example, are significant not because of their "legendary" status, but because such dedicated music venues for amplified music continue to be important for the sustenance of strong local live music scenes. It is to local scenes that we now turn.

Putting promoters in their place

Early on in our research we decided that the best way to understand the importance of locality for live music was through case studies and we picked on three cities: Bristol, Glasgow and Sheffield. We chose them for a mixture of reasons. They were cities with which we were familiar; they had contrasting populations and histories; they were known for their distinctive music cultures.[30]

230   *The live music ecology*

This is most obvious in the case of Glasgow, which has been a UNESCO Music City since 2008: "Glasgow is a vibrant city with a legendary music scene that stretches across the whole spectrum from contemporary and classical, to Celtic and country. Its venues are equally varied and the city hosts an average 130 music events each week".[31] For Karen Taylor, Head of Events at the Glasgow Royal Concert Hall, there is "a *massive* provision of classical music in Glasgow" (her emphasis): the BBC Scottish Symphony Orchestra at the City Hall on a Thursday, the Scottish Chamber Orchestra at the City Hall or Royal Conservatoire of Scotland on a Friday, the Royal Scottish National Orchestra at the Concert Hall on a Saturday and Scottish Opera at the Theatre Royal during its opera seasons.[32] For independent promoter Peter MacCalman, Glasgow is, simply:

> The best city for music in Scotland. We've got more venues, we've got a much broader diversity of music outputs ... and a discerning audience. It's got an audience that are going to see a lot of different *styles* of music, rather than necessarily being a rock audience or a classical audience ... There's a lot on offer in Glasgow so to draw a crowd out you've got to put on something that's interesting.

There are two historical factors involved here. First, by the end of the 1990s Glasgow had developed a solid independent music infrastructure. In their different ways, the Sub Club, "a new club for a new type of music" (launched in 1986) and Craig Tannock's various small cafe/bar venues (the first, 13th Note, opened in 1997) established a distinctly Glaswegian music scene. By 2005, in Hamilton Harvey's words:

> Go to Glasgow on any night of the week, and you'll be able to sample just about any genre of pop music, from guitar pop to post-rock to electronica and on to a host of bands for whom there is no present classification. Meanwhile, classical, jazz, country and folk all thrive as they have done for decades.
>
> (Harvey 2005: 174–7)[33]

Second, Glasgow City Council had a strong promotional presence: in 2006 the Concert Hall (opened in 1990) was joined by the refurbished City Halls and the converted Old Fruitmarket, and this venue portfolio ensured a continuing balance of state, corporate and independent promoters.[34] At the same time, Glasgow is a big enough city to provide potential performance spaces for a wide range of enthusiast promoters.[35] The city's international reputation for music is an effect of the vitality of its live music ecosystem.

Bristol and Sheffield have more chequered musical reputations. Bristol has had important folk and jazz scenes since the 1950s (described in our previous volumes) and, as an important slave-trading port, long established British

African and Caribbean populations.[36] The Bristol Sound of the late 1980s and 1990s (including such acts as Massive Attack and Roni Size, Tricky and Portishead) reflected Bristol's particular multi-ethnic, bohemian culture (see Chapter 9). But by the end of the 1990s, the city's distinct live music/club scene had lost impact as clubs became nightclubs and DJs replaced live bands. There was general agreement among the Bristol promoters we interviewed that the city no longer had the right spread of venues, though there was some disagreement as to what was lacking. For a local commercial promoter, all that was needed was

> a big venue, we need a 10,000 capacity venue, but aside from that we've got every other venue you could dream of, I think ... [perhaps] too many at the kind of 350 capacity, that's the problem.

For Graeme Howell (then director of the Colston Hall), Bristol "suffers from not having an arts centre type venue". The Colston's new 200-capacity space was therefore planned to be "the kind of missing space below the St George's level".[37]

Sheffield's music history cannot be disentangled from the history of the steel industry although, as Owen Hatherley writes in his essay on Pulp (formed in 1979, dissolved in 2002):

> Aside from steel, it is a city best known outside the UK either among fans of modernist architecture ... or for various experimental pop musics. This was the home of The Human League/Heaven 17, Vice Versa/ABC, Cabaret Voltaire, Comsat Angels, and after a fallow period in the mid-80s, its techno-city rep, the sense it was Britain's analogue to Detroit, in the way its electronic musicians held a ruinous, deindustrialised present to account for its failure to create a future ...
>
> (Hatherley 2011: 40–1)

Although the council in Sheffield was one of the pioneers of Labour's cultural industries policies (see Chapter 4) and established a successful venue, the Leadmill, in Sheffield's "cultural industries quarter", it has not been a significant music promoter or as active as Glasgow's city council in intervening in the local cultural economy.[38]

Tom Boulding, landlord of long-established folk pub Fagan's, told us that "they do *like* music in Sheffield; they actually do like music, and they see it", but he also noted the increasing importance of the student market for local promoters following the city's industrial decline. In fact, university students were a significant source of audiences, musicians and club promoters in all our three cities, even though student unions were no longer the important venues they had once been. In answer to the question "Are student unions significant in any way, shape or form?" Isla Angus from Glasgow's Toutpartout Agency put it most bluntly: "No".

232   *The live music ecology*

Sheffield's changing music demographic is also reflected in the history of its working men's clubs. Ken Green, South Yorkshire CIU Branch Secretary, explained:

> They're committee driven, these clubs, so there is a committee that sort of run all the aspects and the secretary just collates it; carries out the committee wishes ... I contact the agent, we tell the agent *when* we want entertainment, roughly, broadly what type of entertainment at certain times in the year; and give them a budget, a budget to work to. (Green's emphasis)

These entertainment agencies have a long history of servicing variety clubs, holiday camps and cruise ships, but Green notes that his own club, which once had entertainment five to six nights a week, now—like almost all such clubs—features a live performance only once a week. The clubs could not compete with home entertainment and were less and less used for music although Alan Deadman, promoter of the Juju Club, used the Crookes WMC for a while.[39]

> There was a big walk-up audience at Crookes Working Men's Club. The housing around Crookes was attractive to a lot of first-time buyers and a lot more students lived in the area, so you had those two elements. And they came! And it was their local—they came and they didn't even know what was on. They just came because they knew they would have a good time. Whereas there wasn't really a walk-up audience [at the Boardwalk, the venue in Sheffield city centre to which the club moved] ... and that is an issue, depending on where they are, in some town venues.[40]

Mark Ross, promoter of Urban Gorilla nights, described another issue with Sheffield's city-centre venues, following changes in the licensing laws.

> A lot of bars have turned into clubs, basically ... Part of me thinks that it's a good thing and part of me thinks that's *not* a good thing, because there's a lot of not very good little venues, which are actually bars but are running as clubs that are just ... Yeah, they don't feel right because they were built to be a bar ...

Finding the right venues

For promoters, the task is not just to find a venue or even to find a good venue, but rather to find the *right* venue—and that is not a simple matter. It needs to be right for the promoter, right for the performers and right for the audience, and the alignments here are not necessarily straightforward. The alternative rock promoters interviewed by Robert Cluley, for example, got "annoyed" when the audience did not recognise "the difference between their events and

The live music ecology   233

those of the horrible local venue". These promoters had a clear idea of how the shows they were putting on should be experienced. Their shows were typically

> defined in opposition to a generic local music venue. In each interview the name of this venue changed but the complaints were uniform, such as "a horrible, horrible venue. It's like a total pissy horrible metal, horrible old punk ... literally, you go there if you kind of like the grime and the dirtiness".

Cluley describes these promoters as would-be "engineers of aesthetic experience", to which end they needed to attract people who respected what they were trying to do, something that was impossible in both "grotty venues" and commercial spaces used "just for the sake of putting the band on" (Cluley 2009: 378–9).

Glasgow indie promoter Fielding Hope (from Cry Parrot) also faced the challenge of finding the right venues for his bands, but was more flexible ideologically:

> So to us that's quite a creative process in the way that it's not just find any venue that's X size; we like to vary it about quite a lot and try and find new, interesting places and not always the same place as well ... We also like doing it in dives, sometimes, and kind of really grimy pubs like the Captain's Rest before it got done up ... We kind of like abstract venues where it's exciting because it's somewhere different, and it's grimy and it's a bit oppositional and it's quite exciting to see the bar staff get pissed off, in a way [laughs].

Eventually, though, Cry Parrot had to move its shows to more established venues "because they have technical set-ups and can make every band happy" (relieving them of the time and effort required to get PA systems into grotty sites) while attracting broader audiences "because they are music places to which people already regularly go".[41]

Any space can be used as a venue, but for an event to work the space used needs to be perceived as *suitable* by everyone involved. Tracy Johnston, the concert manager of Music in the Round, describes a venue she used that had been set up as part of a school:

> But they'd never programmed *anything* but us three times a year. So no one knows it exists; there's no signs, there's no presence on the website; it is *not* a public venue. And then they wonder why audiences won't come.

Contrast Tony Benjamin's description of the Coronation Tap cider house in Clifton in Bristol:

234   *The live music ecology*

Jan, the woman in the couple who run it, absolutely wants it to be a really good music venue. It's a tiny wee pub with absolutely *no* chance of being a good music venue. Fortunately, for *her* really, they've kind of found some of the right people in the Bristol music scene—acoustic music and jazz—made the right connections and they've brought their friends. A lot of the gigs here are called "somebody and friends" and the "and friends" is almost a house band but it's a really, really *good* house band.

The Cori Tap is "hideously overcrowded" and "uncomfortable"; one can't physically get to the bar when it's full, which it is two to three nights a week. This is, one could say, a good music venue for its regulars *because* it is a bad one. Its apparent unsuitability as a music space has become a key part of its appeal.

Promoter Peter MacCalman classifies the venues available to him in Glasgow under three headings: venues operated by the council, corporate venues (such as King Tut's or the ABC) and venues on the underground scene. For him, all are "good venues", all are easy to work with. "Unfair" competition for audiences comes from the pub promoters of free gigs, their policy driven by the need to maximise alcohol sales rather than by a concern for musical careers or listeners.

Another way that promoters can categorise venues is to distinguish between *multipurpose* venues (open for any kind of commercial hire), *arts centre* venues (which stage art/music/performance events and are usually state subsidised) and *music* venues (which only host live music).[42] In practice, multipurpose and arts centre venues operate in much the same way. For Karen Taylor from the Glasgow Royal Concert Hall, "I'd say about two hundred [events each year] will be brought in by promoters and thirty-five will be our own promotions, just for the auditorium itself. Roughly."[43] GRCH gets artists on their way up to selling out the SECC and on their way down from superstardom:

And then maybe we also appeal to artists with an older audience, like Tony Bennett or somebody like that. Someone that's not appropriate for them to perform in the SECC because their audience want a nice comfy seat and they want a good acoustic and all that.

But many of the Concert Hall's bookings are routine, following an annual schedule: the jazz festival in June–July; the RSNO's two concert seasons; Raymond Gubbay's Christmas show; the City of Glasgow Chorus in December and May; the National Youth Orchestra of Scotland in the Easter and Summer holidays; the Fiddle Orchestra in September; Celtic Connections in January. Glasgow's Concert Hall is at the heart of the city's taken-for-granted cultural life.[44]

Suzanne Rolf, Director of St George's Bristol, makes a similar point about its importance as a local resource. A large proportion of the people who hire St George's are "part of the very vibrant local church and orchestral scene".

The live music ecology   235

It's quite unusual to see a programme like St George's where, say, a local school, or local amateur choir, is being cited next to a very well-known international artist … It's always been really important to us that we do that because I think that we're kind of citing that we're part of the *community*. And St George's is here for us to put music on, but actually there's still lots of capacity there for musicians who live nearby to use it.

For Graeme Howell, at Colston Hall, it is equally important to appeal to all sectors of Bristol's audience for music: "We'll have Motorhead followed by the Philharmonia Orchestra followed by Grace Jones," and to ensure that like other council services the Colston Hall is available to all communities. The Hall, for example, hosts the events staged by such specialist music promoters as the Asian Arts Agency, launched as a community-based organisation supporting South Asian arts in Bristol in early 2000.[45]

A good civic venue, then, has the flexibility to be used by a variety of promoters and audiences while preserving a sense of local identity. For promoters using music venues, the requirements are different. Crae Caldwell from Slam Events in Glasgow said:

> The night is what makes the night, not the owner of the venue. The venue's just a shell for the night to take place in … [though] … if you tried to do a Slam night in somewhere like O'Couture or … one of the ABC clubs, it would fail dismally because they're too corporate and they're too shiny … The ownership of like the GI Group and that kind of thing—Stefan King [venues]—it's a different vibe.[46] They wouldn't want [Slam], they want young drinkers in, they don't want a different crowd that is difficult for them to manage … It's a different way of running operations and certain clubs [like Slam] wouldn't work in it and certain clubs do: R&B and, you know, the sort of prevalence of these cheesy pop types … they want nights that sell booze, and lots of it, to fund their clubs.

Sheffield DJ and promoter Ralph Razor explained:

> As a promoter I just like a venue, you know, where they leave you alone, and have decent facilities, i.e. a PA that works, and that sort of thing, and reasonably priced drinks. I think venues are what you make of them, 'cos we always, we're quite into décor, so we can kind of transform spaces to make them look a bit different … [and] … What I've found is, there's actually been some venues we've been at where the security have actually really got into the music and stuff, and because we're quite picky on the door—not in an elitist sense, just because we don't want, kind of, you know, townies in—so they got to know the regulars, and they've got really into the night and been really supportive.

For corporate promoters looking for spaces into which to put bands at the "beginning of their trajectory", a good "feeder" venue is one with a decent

236   *The live music ecology*

sound system and the right sort of attentive audience. In Glasgow, Robin Morton—then co-owner of the bar/venue Brel ("a hundred capacity maximum acoustic venue in the West End"), where he promoted gigs to give "a stepping stone to artists"—was thus contracted to promote such gigs for DF; another major promoter, PCL, used Captain's Rest (and, more recently, Broadcast) for its starter gigs, while Regular used Holly Calder's Eyes Wide Open club for starter gigs at Barfly and the Twisted Wheel.

As we have already noted, for many musicians playing gigs before they reach this stage (and often after it, too) means promoting themselves. In the words of Chris Trout from Sheffield band Smokers Die Younger:

> If you're a musician within the independent sector, sooner or later you end up *having* to put on gigs 'cos no other cunt's going to do it.

In his memoir of the early days of Belle and Sebastian, Stuart David writes:

> There were a few places scattered around the city [Glasgow] where singer-songwriters could turn up and do open mic spots. They all took place on different days of the week. On Monday nights there was the Star Folk Club in the Society of Musicians building on Berkeley Street. Tuesday evenings it was the Glasgow Songwriters, downstairs in Blackfriars in the Merchant City. Open mics at the Halt Bar took place on Wednesday nights and Saturday afternoons and Alistair decided we should make our debut there on a Saturday, because there was usually less drinking and a more discerning crowd through the day.
>
> (David 2015: 20)

There are probably many more open mic nights in Glasgow now. Adam Behr (2012) writes that while there were just a handful of such nights in Edinburgh in the 1990s, there were over 20 regular nights by 2012 and Steve Parkhouse, then concert manager at St George's, confirmed that there were "loads" of them in Bristol in 2009.[47]

Asked if there were enough venues in Bristol for local working musicians in jazz and folk, Tony Benjamin replied:

> I think there probably are. As I say, a lot of the time the musicians make their own venues, you know, and get a venue when they haven't got one. They'll dep for each other, they'll be at each other's ... gigs.[48]

Understanding local audiences

For musicians, as for all promoters, establishing a venue meant understanding local audiences, their leisure patterns and travel habits. Karen Taylor of the Glasgow Concert Hall was aware that "lots of people I know in the Southside [of Glasgow] won't travel west for a show!" while Hayley Pearce of the Bristol venue Thekla remarked that as students are "mostly our target market", there were far fewer Thekla gigs in the summer vacation.[49] But the most pressing problem for promoters in all our cities was to make sense of the geographical focus of the night-time leisure economy: the city centre. Tony Benjamin, speaking in 2009, said:

> I mean, the problem with Bristol City Centre is nobody lives there, so it's a completely un-owned area after dark, once the business stuff has closed. And then it's all kebab shops and bars and fights. Promoters have to bear in mind that this crowd might arrive.

Ben Dubisson, who ran the small indie/underground Bristol club Native from 2005–09, talked of "the *town* crowd", mainstream club goers, young, drunk and violent who took over Bristol city centre on Friday and Saturday nights.

> *Were you trying to keep that element out?*
> You don't have to. With certain music and certain drinks, they just won't come in. If you don't sell alcopops ... People, whatever they say, really want to be with the kind of people *they* are, that's apparent.

For promoters, then, an understanding of their likely audience demographic dictates both the choice and the spatial organisation of the venues they use. As we saw in Chapter 10, being with "like-minded" people is essential to many people's understanding of a good gig, and this does pose problems for venue managers trying to increase the number or variety of their concert-goers or to change their market position. Gordon Hodge, customer services manager at the Glasgow Royal Concert Hall, said:

> I think that there are people who come to shows at the Concert Hall because they come to shows at the Concert Hall, and they have an expectation of what a show's going to be like. There are *other* people, when you get touring productions—like Ray Davies, like the Bootleg Beatles—who come because it's Ray Davies or the Bootleg Beatles, and they would go whether that was at the ABC, the Academy, the Barrowlands; they would go anywhere. And *they* as long as there's a bar and as long as the person they're seeing is on the stage, are generally easily pleased.

Steve Parkhouse, concert manager of St George's in Bristol, speaking in 2009, said:

> St George's is quite a unique venue and we've only ... We're trying to change the audience ... putting on more world music concerts and more, attracting more ethnic people in and younger people in.

One problem here was the hall's historical building status and its protected flooring: it had to be a seated venue and no drinks could be taken in.[50] Another was its existing audience:

238   *The live music ecology*

> We get the same people virtually all the time for a classical audience, especially the lunchtime concert. If it's a folk audience, for example, Tom Paxton's been coming now for twenty, thirty years, you'll get the same people who saw him the *first* time he's come round.

Like many such venues, St George's is also dependent on volunteers (as stewards, for example), whose willingness to work for the hall depends on it not changing its ethos.

Gary Prestwich, the Hall's marketing director, identifies another issue here. Bristol venues like Fiddlers and Thekla have the younger audiences that St George's would like to attract but:

> If you *go* to those venues, the people are going there for a good time that's not necessarily wholly dependent on the music ... I mean they *are* going down to see certain groups—they're not just going down to see everybody—but when you *get* there, you look at some of these people drinking at the bar and you're thinking "You haven't heard a word of what they're singing!" ... And they'll come away and they'll say "Oh we've had great fun watching this band" but if you ask them what they actually played, they probably wouldn't know at all. And that's a bit different to here, where's it's much more driven by actually listening to the music. (his emphases)

The tension between audiences who want "a fun time and a bit of drink with some nice noise in the background" and audiences who want to listen is difficult to resolve in any space.

Another way promoters think about like-minded audiences is as *scenes*, which are particularly important for the success of indie promoters and venues. For Fielding Hope of Glasgow's Cry Parrot, "our audience" is the "art crowd"; half of them are

> normally familiar faces ... people in their late twenties and thirties [who] tend to come along because they're part of ... they know the people in the CCA, hang out at 13th Note, Mono and Stereo, are interested in subculture and modern music, and have been since the 1980s.

In Bristol, Mark Wolf set up Mr Wolf's as a vegetarian venue in 2002:

> *Who's it for?*
> Primarily I would say 22- to 35 year-olds, generally with a background in media or arts or music. And that's about it, really.

The club's manager, Ross McRae, added that Mr Wolf's did sometimes have problems with people coming in "who don't really fit the venue".

Tony Benjamin makes a different point about Bristol's close-knit jazz scene. When the Future Inn Jazz Cafe was launched in the city, it was designed to fill a gap in local jazz venue provision:

> The idea is it's got a proper stage, proper sound equipment and a good piano, and tables and chairs and you can sit and have your food brought to the table, and therefore get that kind of respectability into the music.

As Benjamin notes, this was a new venture in Bristol, promoting jazz in a dedicated space that was neither a pub back room nor a concert hall nor, like the Metropolis club, using jazz as intelligent dance music. What the new promoters had to understand, though, was that it would be "bad manners" for it to stage jazz on a Friday, thus competing with the Be-Bop Club, founded in 1989 and still staged weekly in the function room of The Bear on Fridays.[51] Bad feeling created on the existing jazz scene would not be outweighed by the attraction of a new—and likely more fickle—jazz audience.

Conclusion

The purpose of this chapter was not to provide a historical census of live music in our three cities (we discuss census data in the next chapter), nor to determine which city is "healthier" in ecological terms, nor even to show how cities can be understood through musical activities and memory (for this approach, see Cohen 2007). Rather, we wanted to explore what it means to be a promoter in a particular locality, how different kinds of promoter think about venues and audiences and how they situate their activities within complex taste, commercial and ideological networks. That said, we can make some general points about the history of live music in British cities over the last two to three decades.

First, it was apparent in all our cities that students are centrally important for the promotion of both commercial and "alternative" entertainment. Second, equally apparent is the increasing significance in local music scenes of the city centre arts centre model—venues that are state subsidised, multi-purpose and civically self-conscious. Third, the stadium is not really part of a local live music ecology (though it might have local economic benefits). It is about bringing people into a city (touring rock and pop stars and their fans) and has little significance for local music-makers.[52]

In terms of historical change, there was in all the cities we studied a steady turnover of clubs and club nights on the dance scene, while venues and promotions for specialist audiences in classical music, folk and jazz had a not-ably long life, not least because they intrinsically involve enthusiast promoters, as described in Hytönen-Ng's (2017) study of a jazz club:

> Running the club is a way for the promoter to maintain his own work as a musician. The promoter's reasons for doing the work are purely musical;

240 *The live music ecology*

to provide a small city with good quality music, offer work for fellow musicians, to work with established musicians both off- and on-stage, and to keep up his own musical competence. His aim has not been to make profit, rather to keep the performances going from one year to the next.

(Hytönen-Ng 2017: 70)

Demographically, as ageing youth music, rock fits uneasily somewhere between the fashion-driven dance world and the relatively settled status of folk, jazz and classical music. The problem with grassroots venues, to return to the first part of this chapter, is due at least in part to the difficulties of creating cross-generational "like-minded" audiences. At the local level, a sustainable live music scene has as much to do with people as with property. On the one hand, there has to be the right balance of state, corporate, independent and enthusiast promotions. On the other hand, among promoters, performers and potential audiences, there has to be a good distribution of *musical motivations*—the right mix of reasons why people want to make and listen to music live. The live music economy is not simply about promoters and/or venues competing with each other for audiences and ticket income; it involves other ways of valuing and sustaining music, which is the topic of the next chapter.

Notes

1 Eagle had previously been DJ at the legendary Twisted Wheel in Manchester, promoting all-nighters from 1963–66, and ran the equally legendry Eric's in Liverpool from 1976–80.
2 Interviewed by Emma Webster June 30, 2009.
3 For an excellent example of this approach to local live music history see Helen Southall's study of dance bands in Cheshire (Southall 2015).
4 See www.birminghammail.co.uk/whats-on/music-nightlife-news/birmingham-live-music-venues-loved-13364623 and www.chroniclelive.co.uk/news/history/newcastles-legendary-rock-venue-mayfair-16789178.
5 Although the 100 Club's closure was announced in 2010, it was saved by a sponsorship deal with Converse and remains open. The UK chain of Barfly venues was completely gone by the end of 2011.
6 See www/independent.co.uk/arts-entertainment/music/news/the-toughest-gig-in-town-2144017.html.
7 See www.theguardian.com/music/2012/may/26/rock-music-venues-bust-britain.
8 The Horn was, in fact, being refurbished and soon reopened as a music venue.
9 In 2013, the Bongo opened in new premises, under Edinburgh's central library.
10 See Behr et al. (2014) for a clear academic account of the grassroots venue problem that MVT sought to address.
11 Quoted from the MVT website: http://musicvenuetrust.com.
12 The House of Commons DCMS Committee's *Live Music Inquiry* was published on March 19, 2019.
13 The agent of change principle had originally been developed in Australia.

The live music ecology   241

14 Information about 2015 Venues Day discussions taken from Emma Webster's report for Live Music Exchange: http://livemusicexchange.org/blog/ten-things-learned-at-venues-day-2015-emma-webster.

15 Quoted from an interview with Emma Webster, November 8, 2017.

16 SAC established Tune Up in 2003 "to bring high quality live music to communities the length and breadth of the country".

17 For a more extended policy discussion of venue provision in a rural area, see the *Review of Orchestral Provision in Yorkshire*, written by G. Devlin and J. Ackrill and published by ACE in 2005. A summary can be found at http://livemusicexchange.org/resources/a-review-of-orchestral-provision-for-yorkshire.

18 See www.nesta.org.uk/blog/the-clubbing-map-what-has-happened-to-london-nightlife. NESTA, the National Endowment for Science, Technology and the Arts, was set up (with National Lottery funding) to promote innovation in 1996.

19 Mark Ross interviewed by Emma Webster, May 8, 2009.

20 Martino Burgess interviewed by Emma Webster, April 8, 2010; Burgess's emphasis.

21 Thanks to Richard Lysons for giving us access to his work.

22 Quoted from www.punktastic.com/news/sheffield-diy-venue-the-lughole-needs-your-help, December 11, 2017.

23 Quoted from www.fredperry.com/subculture/article-subculture-uncovered-jtsoar, March 8, 2018.

24 Such nights, according to reporter Angus Batey, "helped nurture the careers of hitmakers including Amy Winehouse, Corinne Bailey Rae and Estelle".

25 See www.guardian.co.uk/music/2009/feb/20/zarif-soul-music-kindred-spirit.

26 See www.theguardian.com/music/2018/mar/14/the-new-rules-of-clubbing-from-illegal-raves-to-spacehopper-hedonism. *NME* ran a similar report the same month: www.nme.com/features/nme-investigates-rave-culture-2275118.

27 In 2017, the jazz club at the Four Bars had to move to the smaller Flute and Tankard when its original premises was closed, refurbished and reopened as Dempseys.

28 For the history of Total Refreshment Centre (which was closed down by Hackney Council for safety reasons in 2018), see Warren (2019).

29 Quoted from an April 2019 interview by Mark Evans in the Emirates inflight magazine: https://openskiesmagazine.com/london-swings.

30 In journalistic terms, Britain's most famous music cities are probably Liverpool (Cohen 2007) and Manchester (Haslam 2000). In this context, London is a collection of localities.

31 Quote taken from the Cities of Music Network website: https://citiesofmusic.net/city/glasgow. For an overview of Glasgow's recent music history, see Anderson (2015) and for a useful anthology of articles on Glasgow's most significant venues, see Molleson (2015).

32 Karen Taylor's words taken from an interview with Emma Webster, February 9, 2010. Unless otherwise stated, all quotes in this section are taken from interviews carried out by Emma Webster between 2008 and 2010. For details, see Webster (2011).

33 Glasgow's famous country venue, Glasgow Grand Ole Opry, opened in 1974.

34 In Chapter 6 we described how the Fruitmarket's potential as a flexible venue was developed by the Glasgow Jazz Festival.

242 *The live music ecology*

35 The city of Glasgow's population is around 600,000; the population of the greater Glasgow conurbation is double that. Bristol's population is around 450,000 with 650,000 in the Bristol metropolitan area. The equivalent figures for Sheffield are 575,000 and 725,000.

36 For the history of Bristol as a music city, see Jones (2018).

37 In 2014, Howell became head of Shetland Arts.

38 Local promoter Stuart Basford recalls that when he first worked at Sheffield City Hall, it was run for the Council "by someone who had been in charge of the libraries ... Her job at the library was made redundant and the manager's job at the City Hall was vacant so they put her in that". She had no previous experience of the live music business.

39 In another Yorkshire city, Leeds, Nathan Clarke turned the Brudenell Social Club into the city's best-loved independent venue. The Brudenell is situated to the immediate north of Leeds' two universities in an area largely populated by "students, musicians, young professionals ... and that kind of more musical type". Not the usual membership of a working men's club! (Clarke interviewed by Emily Roff, January 24, 2009)

40 The Boardwalk was an incarnation of the famous Sheffield rock pub the Black Swan.

41 In 2014, Fielding Hope also became senior producer at London's avant-garde venue Cafe Oto.

42 Terms taken from Scarles (2009: 44–5).

43 Most of the Hall's own promotions are for Celtic Connections. Commercial promoters such as Live Nation, DF and SJM are regular Concert Hall users.

44 It is also hired out for weddings, conferences and meetings ("we do all the catering").

45 See https://asianartsagency.co.uk/about-us.

46 O'Couture was a bar/club on Sauchiehall Street; it closed around 2014. The G1 Group is "Scotland's largest and most diversified hospitality group, with a collection of over 50 venues in Glasgow, Edinburgh, St Andrews, Aberdeen and just about anywhere else you can think of". Stefan King began his venue career with the launch of Club X in 1990. See www.g1group.co.uk.

47 Behr (2012) is the definitive study of open mic nights.

48 An important space here was the Bristol Folk House, an adult education centre hosting "live music events in the café and our large hall as well as festivals such as our Cajun Festival and Harmonica Festival".

49 Thekla is a venue on a boat originally sailed (from Sunderland) to Bristol by Ki Longfellow and her husband, the musician Viv Stanshall. It opened in Bristol in 1984 as a theatre space, closing in 1986 and then reopening in the 1990s and early 2000s as an underground nightclub, becoming part of Bristol's burgeoning drum'n'bass scene. The boat was bought and refurbished in 2006 as a live music venue and club by Nottingham venue owners Daybrook House Promotions (DHP). The DHP Family are now one of the biggest promoters in the country: www.musicweek.com/live/read/dhp-family-talks-small-venues-and-disrupting-the-status-quo/078875.

50 At the Glasgow Royal Concert Hall, black matting is used for touring productions that are going to use a large lighting rig so the stage floor (which is a light, maple wood colour) doesn't get damaged. This also maximises the lighting effects!

51 The Be Bop Club didn't operate in the summer during student vacations and the festival season. The Metropolis jazz funk nights ran from 2008–12; it is now a mosque. The Future Inn still has a weekly jazz night—on Thursdays—in its basement space.

52 See Martin Cloonan's definitive analysis of the development of the Glasgow Hydro (in Behr et al. 2017: 18–21).

The Rolling Stones, Twickenham, August 20 and 22, 2006

The Rolling Stones' two shows at London's Twickenham Stadium, the home of English Rugby Union, in August 2006 illustrate many of the changes in the UK's live music industry which have been illustrated throughout our three volumes. These changes were not simply those associated with the transformed status of a band that had gone from playing local gigs to touring globally as the self-proclaimed "greatest rock and roll band in the world"; they also reflected the ways in which the staging of popular music had developed over the years. However, the Twickenham shows also illustrate a number of continuities, showing that for promoters the *business* of live music continued to revolve around deciding which artists to promote, which venue to put them in and how to attract an audience. Let us begin with the changes.

These gigs were part of the Bigger Bang tour, which was eventually to run from August 10, 2005 to August 26, 2007, covering five continents.[1] One major change was, of course, the sheer scale of the shows. A band that started in pubs and clubs in and around London now needed an aircraft hangar in Toronto in which to rehearse.[2] Whereas in 1976 the Stones played London's biggest indoor venue, Earls Court (capacity around 19,000), they now played one of its largest outdoor stadiums (capacity 82,000).

If the Stones gigs in 1963 were promoted by an enthusiast promoter (albeit one with an eye on the main chance), in 2006 the promoter was listed on the ticket as the tour sponsor, American Express. Whereas in 1963 the band members flyposted its gigs themselves in order to attract audiences, they now staged a press conference in New York to announce the tour. "In keeping with tradition", the Rolling Stones also "performed a surprise club show on August 10, 2005 at the Phoenix Concert Theatre [in Toronto] before an audience of 1000, each only paying $10 (the Phoenix's regular cover charge)".[3] At the other end of the scale, the tour included a free gig on February 18, 2006 at the Copacabana Beach in Rio de Janeiro, Brazil. Broadcast on television, the gig was allegedly the largest rock concert of all time with a reported live audience of two million.[4] The tour also included the band's first dates in China and two benefit performances at the Beacon Theatre on Broadway for the Clinton Foundation, added so the Stones' stage performance could be filmed by Martin Scorsese—*Shine a Light* was released in 2008.

The Rolling Stones Twickenham, August 2006   245

The tour was draped in money. Whereas Brian Jones once moaned that Stones gigs didn't make the band anything, these gigs were part of the most profitable tour undertaken by any artist, earning over US$550,235,000, the largest tour income ever up to that point.[5] The lavish stage set was designed by Mark Fisher, who had previously designed the sets for the Stones' *Steel Wheels/Urban Jungle* (1989), *Voodoo Lounge* (1994) and *Bridges to Babylon* (1997) tours and would go on to design the set for the *50 and Counting* tour (2012–13). Where once they mixed with the audiences at small clubs, now the Stones' images had to be projected on to huge screens as they played. In these tour venues they could not easily be seen by the naked eye of much of their audience.

In some ways, then, everything had changed, but in others it remained the same. A venue still had to be found, ticket prices set, customers attracted and those involved paid. By this point, The Stones would obviously seek to play those places that maximised their returns, but this was not always straightforward. The Twickenham gigs were originally scheduled for Wembley Stadium, for example, but had to be moved following the delay to the tour caused by Richards' accident (see note 1). And although on the tickets American Express was listed as presenting the show, its production was actually undertaken by the Canadian entrepreneur Michael Cohl, who, as we discussed in Chapter 2, had been the Stones' tour promoter (greatly increasing their live income) since 1989.[6] Tickets were priced at £40, £60, £90, £150 and £340, meaning that the highest price for an individual ticket was now rather more than the total fee the band was paid in the mid-1960s, even allowing for inflation.

The shows themselves consisted mainly of "classic" Stones tracks, with a few new numbers—primarily from the album that gave the tour its name—thrown in. That album had been critically well received, marking something of a return to the band's rhythm and blues roots.[7] However, by this point artists like the Rolling Stones were no longer touring to promote an album; rather, the album had become primarily a means of marketing a tour—within two years the value of live music in the UK would exceed that of recorded music (see Chapter 1). So while the album was critically well received and its sales were respectable (according to EMI, by March 2006 the album had sold 2.6 million copies), the revenues the band received from the record were dwarfed by what they made from their shows. In order to have the biggest financial bang, in short, the Stones *had* to be on the road. This was not to be The Last Time, but it was to be The Most Lucrative Time.

Notes

1 In April 2006, Keith Richards suffered concussion after falling from a tree during a tour break; some dates had to be rearranged and the tour run extended.
2 See https://en.wikipedia.org/wiki/A_Bigger_Bang_Tour.
3 Such surprise shows were announced on the day of performance by local radio stations with tickets available in local outlets, though hardcore travelling fans often

246   *The Rolling Stones Twickenham, August 2006*

seemed to know about them in advance: thanks to one such fan, Lee Marshall, for this information.

4 All statistics of tickets and records sold on this tour taken from https://en.wikipedia.org/wiki/A_Bigger_Bang_Tour.

5 This would be exceeded by the returns from U2's 360 degree tour (2009–11).

6 In 2006, Cohl's company, CPI, was taken over by Live Nation but this didn't affect the Stones' tour arrangements.

7 See www.metacritic.com/music/a-bigger-bang/the-rolling-stones.

12 Conclusion: the value of live music

As a cultural industry music is unique—and uniquely important—because so much of its commercial success depends on people making and listening to music for its own sake, without economic concerns at all.

(Williamson et al. 2003: 128)

So I think we need more understanding of the audience's relationship between value, cost, experience, that sort of thing. Because one of the things I think is really interesting is the secondary ticketing market, or the touts or whatever. I mean, it's an interesting thing in that for some reason, people who are willing to pay £300 for a Kasabian ticket are not seen as real fans, even though they're paying perhaps ten times over the odds to go and see the show ...

(Graeme Howell, Director Colston Hall, Bristol 2010)[1]

For the global real estate sector, I believe there's a missed opportunity in using music to increase value, create better communities, engage local residents and generate better outcomes.

(Shain Shapiro, CEO Sound Diplomacy 2018)[2]

Introduction

During much of the 2000s, the world of commercial entertainment was dominated by the public appetite for live television talent shows. *Pop Idol* (developed by ex-Spice Girls manager Simon Fuller) ran from 2001–03; *The X Factor* (developed by ex-*American Idol* judge Simon Cowell) was launched in 2004 and followed by his *Britain's Got Talent*, launched in 2007. The final of its 2009 series was reportedly watched by 17.3 million viewers, almost two-thirds of the British TV viewing public.

The two Simons had started out in the record industry (Fuller at Chrysalis, Cowell at EMI), but were now major players in television commerce, the advertising market and the global format trade. Their programmes contributed significantly to the UK's pop star-making machinery (although neither of the biggest stars thus created were show winners—Susan Boyle came second in the final of *Britain's Got Talent* in 2009; One Direction third in *The X Factor*

248   *Conclusion: the value of live music*

final in 2010). Our interest here, however, is the place of these programmes in the history of live music.

TV talent shows were not new. *Opportunity Knocks* ran on commercial television from 1964–78, *New Faces* from 1973–78 and, as we discussed in Volume 2, the demise of these programmes was a major blow to the variety club circuit (Frith et al. 2019: 33–4).[3] The new century's shows, though, were different in two respects: first in their use of mentors; second in their phone-in voting process. On the one hand, this meant that the "professional" shaping of "amateur" performers became part of the entertainment.[4] On the other hand, in the new world of digital communication and social media, public engagement with these shows was far more extensive, immediate and intense than in the 1970s—it was regularly claimed, for example, that more people voted in TV talent show finals than in political elections.[5] Overall, then, the effect of these shows was to make the value of live music a topic of everyday conversation, whether in arguments about what made a particular performer or performance "good" or "bad", in assessments of winning contestants' enhanced earning power and Simon Cowell's growing fortune, or in assertions that the "talent" in these shows was shaped with such commercial cynicism as to be worthless.

This chapter brings to an end not just this book but our history as a whole. We will therefore use it to draw some conclusions from the story we have told and, in particular, to address the question of value. As this is our concluding chapter, it also seems appropriate to return here to the starting point of our research: a mapping of the music industry in Scotland commissioned by Scottish Enterprise in 2002. Two of us (Cloonan and Frith) were involved in that project, and the finding that most struck us was that live music was in many respects the most important sector of the Scottish music business (Williamson et al. 2003: 26–36). This was striking, given the neglect of this sector in most studies of the music industries at that time and its marginal position in music policy debates.

One problem here, as Dave Laing (2012: 1) later commented, was that in comparison to the record company sector, the live music business had "no comparable comprehensive statistics, no comparable international trade associations and few comparable national ones". If the live music promotion business was centrally important to the music economy, as our Scottish research suggested, surprisingly little seemed to be known about it—hence the research project that led to our three-volume history.

Since then, the situation has changed greatly, not least (as we described in Chapters 1 and 2) because the decline of record sales led to increasing attention being paid to ticket sales. In Laing's (2012: 7) words:

> The involvement of authors' collection societies in this research is significant here. These bodies in the past collected a large proportion of songwriters' royalties from recorded music sales, but now find these

mechanical royalties in free fall. They are therefore paying much greater attention to live performance as (hopefully) a growing alternative.

One issue a collecting society like PRS for Music faced was how the "value" of live music related to its composer and publishing members' licensing fees (we discussed this in relation to festivals in Chapter 5). In 2015, the society carried out a systematic consultation with its members on its popular music concerts tariff:

> A publisher response said that the market had changed significantly, from a model that was predominantly driven by ticketing income consisting of a legitimate primary sector and an illegitimate secondary sector, into a multi stream revenue model in which items like food, drink, merchandising, parking and legitimate secondary ticketing directly or indirectly subsidise live event ticket prices, but revenues from which are only obtained by venues and promoters.
>
> (PRS for Music 2015: 6)

The question was whether PRS fees should continue to be calculated against box-office takings only.

Live music is also now routinely included in the collaboration of music industries and government in their common agenda of promoting British music as an economic good (Cloonan 2007: 67–8). Such collaboration has meant not just the creation of government/live music industry committees (as we described in Chapter 4), but also the increasing importance of the economic statistics of the sector. As UK Music puts it on its website:

> The success of the music industry is largely dependent on the talent it works with. But, like all other industry sectors, it is also affected by many factors outside its control such as the UK's economic performance, the shade and priorities of Government and public opinion. However, backed by strong, hard evidence and robust research the music industry can influence Government thinking and the media agenda. UK Music is, therefore, committed to an extensive programme of research which defines the industry's place within the country's cultural and economic framework and can also inform and influence current debate and decision making.[6]

It is such research that we will first consider.

Music by numbers

In the last decade, there has been an endless flow of reports on the economic value of live music, reports displaying ever more ingenuity in determining the extent of its economic impact. In its 2017 response to the government's

250   *Conclusion: the value of live music*

Green Paper, *Building on our Industrial Strategy*, for example, UK Music noted that:

> The export strength of the live sector has grown by 35% in the past year. This is attributable to a 16% increase in overseas music tourists visiting the UK. In 2015, 767,000 people visited the UK for festivals and concerts. Music tourism as a whole generates £3.7 billion to the economy.

The measurement of the economic value of live music has become equally important for local authorities, hence the routine use of local economic statistics in "impact" reports on music festivals (see Chapter 5) and in the planning documents for new concert halls and arenas (see Chapter 4). Here there is also an emphasis on music tourism, on the importance of live shows for inward investment in selling a city as an attractive place to visit or in which to live and work.

For us, the interest of such reports lies less in the overall economic benefits claimed than in what is being measured and how. In their report. *The Value of Jazz in Britain,* for example, Mykaell Riley and Dave Laing (2006) estimated that there were at least 45,000 jazz performances a year in the UK, but also noted that their economic value could not just be measured by box office figures. Jazz performers also got fees for "free to enter" gigs; jazz promoters' income included public subsidy (primarily from the Arts Councils and the BBC) and commercial sponsorship.

In the jazz economy, secondary ticketing was not a significant factor; elsewhere, it was. In his 2012 overview paper, Laing estimated that the annual value of secondary sales in the UK was £172 million, equivalent to 18% of primary spending on tickets, while in 2009 total sponsorship in the live sector had been £23 million (Laing 2012: 3–4).[7]

Even such a careful and well-informed music researcher as Dave Laing acknowledges that many of the figures in his own reports and in those of other people are based on educated guesswork. It is certainly true that to read these economic studies, one after another, is to enter a kind of fantasy land in which the figures presented with most certainty are, in fact, the most nebulous, while an amazing variety of business sectors, from mobile toilets to real estate, are shown to be generating value from live performance.[8]

The general point here is not in dispute. One theme we have explored in our history has been the expansion of the activities that need to be included in "the live music economy". In Volume 2, for example, we described the increasing professionalism of the concert business by reference to the emergence of new enterprises—specialist security companies, transport companies, sound technology companies and so forth (Frith et al. 2019: 66–75). On October 30, 2010, an article in *The Guardian* celebrated the 25th birthday of the Sheffield-based company Snakatak, "a catering firm that specialises in feeding pop and rock bands—and their entourages—while on tour". The company, which has

Conclusion: the value of live music   251

around 40 employees, is still going strong at the time of writing and it is obviously not the only catering firm in the live music business.

It is certainly true, then, that live music now generates income for a great variety of enterprises; the question is how this is to be measured. And in the period of this volume, the problem of which economic data to include in calculations of the value of live music has become even more complex. For the global entertainment corporations we described in Chapter 2, for example, the "value" of an audience is not just measured by the money immediately realised by venues, promoters and performers from ticket, bar and merchandise sales, but also by the potential return an audience offers advertisers and retailers and the potential income generated by a gig's contribution to the development of a musician's "brand". In the digital world, significant value is also, as we've seen, extracted from the data "harvested" from audiences, and such data can be gathered from virtual as well as real concert-goers (as we discussed in Chapter 10).

The value of live music is equally difficult to measure with numerical accuracy at the other end of the gig business. As we discussed in Chapter 9, the economy of classical music, jazz and folk is dependent on the activities of numerous unpaid people: amateur musicians, enthusiast promoters and volunteers who provide their services for free, whether collecting tickets or providing performers with board and accommodation, decorating the stage or providing sound and lights, running a website or providing audiences with refreshments and programme notes. To complicate matters further, the people doing these things are often also themselves performers, and at a local level folk and jazz clubs, music societies and karaoke nights are crucial for the business model of pubs, printers and community centres. While some of the activities here can be measured by cash flow, the quantification of others depends on often-dubious calculations of the "money equivalent" of people's "time expenditure".

Statistical measures of live music are put together for a purpose: to provide a rational basis for investment decisions, whether by national governments, local authorities or private companies. As we discussed in Chapter 3, however, live music promotion is not an altogether rational business. This is indicated, paradoxically, by the secondary ticketing market, which *is* ruled by the movement of supply and demand. It exists, though, precisely because the primary ticket sellers—the promoters—don't work with this model. For them, the most important feature of the live business is *risk*, which has to be considered in both the short and long term (Cloonan 2012). Promoters aren't only anxious about *this* concert covering its costs, they are also concerned to ensure that audiences will *continue* to come to their events, that musicians will *continue* working with them as their careers develop.

Of course, promoters have an interest in numbers. They have to set ticket prices and estimate profit margins, to count seat sales and calculate how much more to spend on publicity. But they also know that such numbers

252 *Conclusion: the value of live music*

may turn out to be illusory. There are components of a successful promotion that promoters can't control, most obviously the weather (as we discussed in Chapter 5 with reference to the finances of festivals). A further complication here is that promoters necessarily work in two worlds—the music industry and the leisure industry—and in a business that is both systematically regulated and somewhat anarchic. What most promoters value about live music—the reason why they took up the trade—is not something that can be measured empirically. A good gig, as many of our interviewees told us, is not always the same thing as a profitable gig, even if promoters can only continue to put on good gigs if their businesses are profitable.

The benefits of music

We began this volume with an account of a benefit concert, Live Aid. The "benefit" here—the concert's value—was defined in cash terms, as the sum of the money raised for famine relief. Benefit concerts have been staged in Britain since at least the eighteenth century. (Handel organised the first of many benefit concerts for The Foundling Hospital in Bloomsbury in 1749.) As a musical event promoted to make money for charity, Live Aid was unusual only for its audience reach: in this kind of event, the people who attend the concert are not usually the people who benefit from it.

Benefit shows as ambitious as Live Aid are rare, but small-scale charity concerts are routine. They are used to raise money for the church roof, a school swimming pool, cancer research, a beloved venue; they are a form of crowd funding for the support of the family of a roadie who has died in an accident on the road or to help to pay for a musician's visa application They may, like the numerous benefits for striking miners in the 1980s, have political ends, to raise consciousness as well as cash, and in this case their audiences may benefit directly, enjoying the musical sense of solidarity and uplift.

The suggestion that the value of live music lies in its "benefits" has become familiar in the last couple of decades. Benefits may be defined in individual or social terms; concert attendance is shown to be beneficial for, say, individual health and communal cohesion. In 2017, the UK Live Music Census thus found that live music enhances social bonding, is mood-enhancing, provides health and wellbeing benefits, is inspiring and forms part of people's identity. It is usually assumed that such benefits also, eventually, have an economic impact but the discourse of cultural benefit has been primarily developed by arts agencies looking for a more flexible way of accounting for the value of their work than a balance sheet.[9]

This was not the language used by the 1950s Arts Council we described in Volume 1, for which the arts needed no instrumental justification (see Frith et al 2013: 46–50). But the Thatcher government's reshaping of Britain's political ideology (as discussed in Volume 2) meant a more robust argument was now needed about cultural value and what made artistic goods different

Conclusion: the value of live music 253

from other consumer items. This was the context for a major AHRC research initiative, the Cultural Value Project, launched in 2013 to address two questions: Why do the arts matter? And how can we to capture their effects?

> The Project had two main objectives. The first was to identify the various components that make up cultural value. And the second was to consider and develop the methodologies and the evidence that might be used to evaluate these components of cultural value.[10]

From our perspective, the most interesting aspect of the project's final report is its attempt to "reposition" the *individual* experience of arts and culture (our emphasis):

> Far too often the way people experience culture takes second place [in assessments of its value] to its impact on phenomena such as the economy, cities or health. There are two problems about displacing attention in this way. In the first place it leads to a neglect of such issues as reflectiveness, empathy and imagination that have as their starting point individual experience. And, secondly, it ignores the fact that some of the most important contributions of arts and culture to other areas are embedded in that individual experience: perhaps not economic impact but rather the capacity to be economically innovative and creative; perhaps not urban regeneration ... but rather the way small-scale arts assets and activities might help communities and neighbourhoods; and for health not just clinical arts therapies but also the link between arts engagement and supporting recovery from physical and mental illness.
> (Crossick and Kaszynska 2016: 5)

The individual experience of the arts was also the focus of the flow of live music statistics from the audience surveys we discussed in Chapter 10. The economic assumption in these was that the value of a concert for its audience members can be represented by the money they are willing to pay to attend, and while this was not the AHRC Project's starting point, its research questions are much the same. What is it that cultural consumers think they are buying? What does a concert *do* for them? What *is* the experience that defines the "experience economy"?

The live musical experience

At the start of Volume 1, we noted Glenn Gould's confident 1966 comment on the future of live music:

> In an unguarded moment some months ago, I predicted that the public concert as we know it today would no longer exist a century hence, that its function would have been entirely taken over by the electronic media.

254   *Conclusion: the value of live music*

> It had not occurred to me that this statement represented a particularly radical pronouncement. Indeed I regarded it almost as a self-evident truth.
>
> (Quoted in Frith et al 2013: x)

Fifty years later, this truth is no longer self-evident, although we should add, first, that in 1966 most cultural economists agreed with Gould and, second, that we haven't reached 2066 yet. Gould's assertion can certainly be taken to show the folly of predicting the effects of new technology, but there was also a flaw in his argument that had nothing to do with the electronic media: Gould assumed that the concert experience he valued was the concert experience valued by everyone else.

In Chapter 10 we suggested that ethnographic research provides insights into "what audiences want" that are not apparent in market researchers' surveys. Stephanie Pitts makes two useful points about this in her reflection on her own concert fieldwork. First, although the answer to "What are concert-goers doing when they listen?" is not easy to determine, "it is fairly certain not to be what is going on in the head of an academic music researcher". Second, the concert experience is not just listening to music; it is also, necessarily, listening to music *as a member of an audience* (Pitts 2019: 14).

This is particularly obvious for festivals (see Chapter 6) and in dance culture (see Chapter 7), but it also explains, for example, the importance of musical events for the shaping of African, Caribbean and Asian British experiences (see Chapter 8). While any particular audience is made up of people with different musical expertise and expectations, "the audience" is, at the same time, a collective entity, which takes different forms in different music worlds. It is not just that certain sorts of music call forth certain sorts of audience (and audience behaviour); these audiences also express how music is valued (and thus performed and presented). In Chapter 10, we discussed the ways in which audiences are put together in advance of gigs and after they are over, in the *social* rituals of anticipation and recall; in Chapter 11, we suggested that the reiterated description of musical audiences as gatherings of "like-minded" people is to acknowledge that there are different sorts of musical gathering, different kinds of audience, different ways of being like-minded.

Many people in contemporary Britain enjoy the live music experience as members of different audiences; they go to a chamber concert one night, a stadium rock show another; to see an established jazz act one week, a new folk group the next. Nevertheless, what makes any particular audience like-minded is its *exclusion* of people who aren't "real" fans—hence Graeme Howell's comment quoted at the start of this chapter: "authentic" participation in live performance, it seems, is not a matter of spending lots of money on a ticket from Viagogo. Whether as a volunteer helping at a music society or free jazz club or as a fan queuing with other fans to get the best floor view of a new pop act, audience participation is a form of *advocacy*—advocating, that

Conclusion: the value of live music   255

is, both the music *and* its audience (which is one reason for clapping—even at a livecast, as we discussed in Chapter 10).

This takes us back to the question of what a "good gig" is and how it can be measured. In researching "the qualitative judgements" made by audiences for various kinds of concert promoted by the Queen's Hall in Edinburgh, Behr, Brennan and Cloonan (2016: 15) argue that:

> Policy makers need not only to resist political imperatives to assess all art in instrumental terms, but to understand those attributes which make up intrinsic value … Our respondents were clear that they went to music to forget about monetary concerns and to have a transcendent experience. The fact that that experience had to be paid for did not concern them much. Above all, they showed that all talk about the value of artistic activity remains abstract until that art is experienced. When it is, the value ascribed goes well beyond the merely economic … There was a clear sense from our research that engaging with art was part of what it is to be truly human insofar as it gives meaning to a wider range of often more quotidian experiences.

As Ruth Finnegan (1989) suggested 30 years ago, the starting point of understanding the value of live music is the interplay of transcendent and everyday experiences. If nothing else, our history confirms that live music remains a component of the unfolding of human lives: growing up and growing old; sex and courtship; work and leisure; settling and resettling; friendship and identity; ambition and disenchantment; celebration and loss. The value of music is the value of life, which is why a good gig is hard to define but easy to recognise: what audience members describe as "transcendence" is an intense feeling of *presence* and *flow*. It is both an intensely individual experience of being sociable and an inescapably social experience of being oneself. From a historical point of view, what needs stressing here is that such musical experiences provide people with memories: they shape people's sense of themselves. One of the key live music pleasures (as we discussed in Chapter 9) is re-living such experiences, hence the commerce of tribute bands and heritage acts and the rituals of annual music gatherings, whether at Northern Soul All-Weekenders, seaside folk and jazz festivals or the BBC Proms.

Last words

Our history of live music in Britain has been organised around three main drivers of change: technology, demography and ideology. The effects of technology (on recording, amplification, digital storage and communication) have been the most obvious, but the movement of populations (whether through migration or age cohorts, by social mobility or transport systems) and changing social mores and political ideas (best summarised as liberalism and neo-liberalism) have been equally significant. All these factors played a role in

256 *Conclusion: the value of live music*

another underlying theme of this history: the effects of globalisation or, as it is more often described in live music history from rock'n'roll to Live Nation, Americanisation.

In driving change, though, these factors were shaped by the ways in which they were adapted to existing leisure institutions. From this perspective, as we have often noted, continuities are as significant as changes. This is obvious, for example, in the history of social dancing. The 1970s disco (and the DJ) and 1990s electronic dance music club (and the super DJ) were the effects of new technologies, new kinds of hedonism and new urban economies: dance floors become qualitatively louder and bigger. But there are also obvious continuities in the Saturday night out since its dance hall days—in its alcoholic and sexual charge, for example, as is obvious today to anyone who walks around any city centre.

We have also documented the continuing importance in British music history of commercial leisure institutions that long pre-dated the period of our volumes, the pub and the cinema, and the continuing significance of established state cultural institutions, the BBC and higher education (universities, colleges, conservatories and art schools). The impact of the BBC on live music careers and resources is woven through all our volumes; the role of the higher education sector in providing live music spaces, audiences, promoters and performers is equally striking. In the 1950s and 1960s, metropolitan universities and art colleges provided essential settings for folk, jazz and experimental music clubs; in the 1960s and 1970s, colleges all over the country became key sites for the performance of live rock music. Student entertainment officers now competed with commercial promoters, many so successfully that an apprenticeship in a student union became the most common starting point for a career in the live music business. In the 1980s and 1990s, however, the contribution of higher education to this business began to change. Conservative government moves to tighten the regulation of student union funds made it harder for them to offer subsidised beer and ticket prices (Day and Dickinson 2018); Labour governments' moves to relax alcohol licensing laws meant increasing competition from pubs as music venues, as we noted in Chapter 11. In most British towns and cities in the twenty-first century, it is the student audience not the student union that provides a vital component of the market for live musical entertainment.

We finished writing the final draft of this book on the day Britain left the EU. We can't predict what effect this will have on the future of the UK's live music economy, although looking back it doesn't seem that joining the EU made much difference to promoters' lives. A more pressing source of political anxiety is the future of the BBC; on the evidence of our history, its demise as a public service broadcaster would have a devastating effect on live music businesses and on the income and work opportunities of musicians, as well as changing the contours of the country's live music culture.

We finished our final edit of this book, however, during the global coronavirus pandemic, which is undoubtedly the biggest crisis the live music business has ever faced. It is certainly depressing to be completing a history of live music in Britain at a moment where there is no work for performing musicians and no venues open in which they can perform. It seems sometimes as if the history of live music has, indeed, come to an end. What we can safely predict, though, is that live music will continue to be an essential part of everyday life. When promoters and performers do at last get back to business, perhaps what they do will be valued more than ever before.

Notes

1 Quoted from an interview with Emma Webster, March 31, 2010.
2 Sound Diplomacy is a consultancy founded in 2013 "to empower cities and places to achieve their social, cultural and economic goals through music and the night time economy". Quote taken from a blog celebrating MIPIM, "the world's leading real estate market event", https://blog.mipimworld.com/urban-planning/value-music-real-estate-sector.
3 Tony Hatch, the famously blunt judge on *New Faces*, can be seen as a precursor of Simon Cowell.
4 In 2011, the BBC reportedly paid £22 million for *The Voice*, a talent show format developed in the Netherlands, in which chosen contestants were assigned not mentors but "coaches". It ran on the BBC from 2012–17, when the format was acquired by ITV.
5 Of course, the income from public calls to their "special" phone lines contributed significantly to these shows' profits.
6 See www.ukmusic.org/research.
7 O2 was by then paying £4.5 million a year for naming rights to the Academy chain.
8 In this context, the 2017 Live Music Census, funded by the Arts and Humanities Research Council and involving project partners UK Music, Music Venues Trust, the Musicians' Union and Live Music Exchange, is a model of focus, clarity and common sense (see Webster et al. 2018).
9 It should be noted here that the Foreign Office-funded British Council has long used the concept of "soft power" to justify its promotion of international tours by British musicians—the (immeasurable) benefit here is to the UK's global reputation.
10 See https://ahrc.ukri.org/research/fundedthemesandprogrammes/culturalvalue project.

Bibliography

Aguilar, A. (2017) "Pioneering the orchestra-owned label: LSO Live in an industry in crisis", Ramnarine, T.K. ed. *Global Perspectives on Orchestras*, New York: Oxford University Press, 100–118.

Anderson, R. (2015) *Strength in Numbers: a Social History of Glasgow's Popular Music Scene, 1979–2009*, Ph.D. thesis, School of Culture and Creative Arts, Glasgow University.

Anderton, C. (2008) "Commercializing the carnivalesque: the V Festival and image/risk management", *Event Management* 12(1), 39–51.

Anderton, C. (2011) "Music festival sponsorship: between commerce and carnival", *Arts Marketing: An International Journal* 1(2), 145–58.

Anderton, C. (2018) *Music Festivals in the UK: Beyond the Carnivalesque*, London: Routledge.

Anonymous (2018) *The Secret DJ*, London: Faber & Faber.

Anthony, W. (2018) *Class of 88*, London: Virgin Books.

Aubrey, C. and Shearlaw, J. (2005) *Glastonbury: An Oral History of the Music, Mud & Magic*, London: Ebury Press.

Auslander, P. (1999) *Liveness*, London: Routledge.

Autissier, A.-M. (2009a) "A short history of festivals in Europe from the 18th century until today", in Autissier, A-M. ed. *The Europe of Festivals*, Toulouse: éditions de l'attribut, 21–41.

Autissier, A.-M. (2009b) "Festival associations: points of reference or platforms for cultural globalisation?", in Autissier, A-M. ed. *The Europe of Festivals*, Toulouse: éditions de l'attribut, 125–35.

Awan, S. (1995) "Full of Eastern promise: women in South Asian music", in Cooper, S. ed. *Girls! Girls! Girls! Essays on Women and Music*, London: Cassell, 100–112.

Back, L. (1996) *New Ethnicities and Urban Culture*, London: UCL Press.

Barker, M. (2013) *Live to Your Local Cinema. The Remarkable Rise of Livecasting*, Houndmills: Palgrave Macmillan.

Baumann, G. (1990) "The reinvention of Bhangra, social change and aesthetic shifts in Punjabi music in Britain", *Journal of the International Institute for Comparative Music Studies and Documentation Berlin* 32(2), 81–95.

Bayton, M. (1998) *Frock Rock. Women Performing Popular Music*, Oxford: Oxford University Press.

Bean, J.P. (2014) *Singing from the Floor: A History of British Folk Clubs*, London: Faber & Faber.

Behr, A. (2010) *Group Identity: Bands, Rock and Popular Music*, Ph.D. thesis, University of Stirling.

Behr, A. (2012) "The real 'crossroads' of live music—the conventions of performance at open mic nights in Edinburgh", *Social Semiotics* 22(5), 559–73.

Behr, A., Brennan, M. and Cloonan, M. (2014) *The Cultural Value of Live Music from the Pub to the Stadium: Getting Beyond the Numbers*, http://livemusicexchange.org/resources/%EF%BF%BCthe-cultural-value-of-live-music-from-the-pub-to-the-stadium-getting-beyond-the-numbers-adam-behr-matt-brennan-and-martin-cloonan-2014. Accessed November 30, 2020.

Behr, A., Brennan, M. and Cloonan, M. (2016) "Cultural value and cultural policy: some evidence from the world of live music", *International Journal of Cultural Policy* 22(3), 403–18.

Behr, A., Brennan, M., Cloonan, M., Frith, S. and Webster, E. (2016) "Live concert performance: an ecological approach", *Rock Music Studies* 3(1), 5–23.

Behr, A. and Cloonan, M. (2020) "Going spare? Concert tickets, touting and cultural value", *International Journal of Cultural Policy* 26(1), 95–108.

Bennett, A. (2000) *Popular Music and Youth Culture*, London: Macmillan.

Bennett, E. and McKay, G. (2019) *From Brass Bands to Buskers: Street Music in the UK*, Norwich: Arts and Humanities Research Council/University of East Anglia.

Bennett, L. (2012) "Patterns of listening through social media: online fan engagement with the live music experience", *Social Semiotics* 22(5), 545–57.

Bradley, L. (2013) *Sounds Like London: 100 Years of Black Music in the Capital*, London: Serpent's Tail.

Brennan, M. (2011) "Understanding Live Nation and its impact on live music in the UK", *Situating Popular Musics: IASPM 16th International Conference Proceedings*, 69–75.

Brennan, M. and Webster, E. (2010) *2010 UK Festival Awards Report*, London: UK Festivals Awards.

Brennan, M. and Webster, E. (2011) "Why concert promoters matter", *Scottish Music Review*, 2(1), 1–25.

Brewster, B. and Broughton, F. (2000) *Last Night a DJ Saved My Life: The History of the Disc Jockey*, London: Headline.

Brewster, B. and Broughton, F. (2010) *The Record Players. DJ Revolutionaries*, New York: Black Cat.

Brocken, M. (2003) *The British Folk Revival. 1944–2002*, Aldershot: Ashgate.

Brookes, N. (2012) *Adding Up the Music Industry 2011*, London: PRS for Music.

Bruck, C. (2012) "The man who owns L.A.", *The New Yorker*, January 16, 46–56.

Budnick, D. and Baron, J. (2011) *Ticket Masters: The Rise of the Concert Industry and How the Public Got Scalped*, Toronto: ECW Press.

Burland, K. and Pitts, S. E. (2010) "Understanding jazz audiences: listening and learning at the Edinburgh Jazz and Blues Festival", *Journal of New Music Research*, 39(2) 125–34.

Burland, K. and Pitts, S. E. (2012) "Rules and expectations of jazz gigs", *Social Semiotics* 22(5), 523–43.

Burland, K. and Pitts, S.E. (2014) *Coughing and Clapping. Investigating Audience Experience*, Farnham: Ashgate.

Burrows, T. (2009) *From CBGB to the Roundhouse. Music Venues Through the Years*, London: Marion Boyars.

260 *Bibliography*

Burt, R., Oakes, L. and Mills, J. (2006) "Working in music: the trombonist", *Research Perspectives in Music Education* 10, 29–41.

Carr, P. (2011) *Investigating the Live Music Industry Within Wales: A Critical Analysis*, Cardiff: Welsh Music Foundation.

Carroll, I. (2007) *The Reading Festival: Music, Mud and Mayhem—the Official History*, London: Reynolds and Hearn.

Carruthers, W. (2016) *Playing the Bass with Three Left Hands*, London: Faber & Faber.

Charles, P. (1997) *I Love the Sound of Breaking Glass*, London: The Do-Not Press.

Christianson, H. (1987) "Convention and constraint among British semi-professional jazz musicians", in White, A.L. ed. *Lost in Music*, London: Routledge and Kegan Paul, 220–40.

Clayton, I. (2008) *Bringing It All Back Home*, Pontefract: Route.

Cloonan, M. (1996) *Banned! Censorship of Popular Music in Britain 1967–1992*, Aldershot: Arena.

Cloonan, M. (2002) "Hitting the right note? The new deal for musicians", *Journal of Vocational Education and Training* 54(1), 55–66.

Cloonan, M. (2007) *Popular Music and the State in the UK: Culture, Trade or Industry?*, Aldershot: Ashgate.

Cloonan, M. (2012) "Selling the experience: the world views of British promoters", *Creative Industries Journal* 5(1–2), 151–70.

Cloonan, M. (2016) "Negotiating needletime: the Musicians' Union, the BBC and the record companies, c.1920–1990", *Social History* 41(4), 353–74.

Cluley, R. (2009) "Engineering great moments: the production of live music", *Consumption Markets and Culture* 12(4), 373–88.

Cohen, S. (1991) *Rock Culture in Liverpool: Popular Music in the Making*, Oxford: Oxford University Press.

Cohen, S. (2007) *Decline, Renewal and the City in Popular Music Culture: Beyond the Beatles*, Aldershot: Ashgate.

Cohen, S. (2014) "'The gigs I've gone to': Mapping memories and places of live music", in Burland, K. and Pitts, S.E. (eds), *Coughing and Clapping. Investigating Audience Experience*, Farnham: Ashgate, 131–45.

Collins, H. and Rose, O. (2016) *This is Grime*, London: Hodder and Stoughton.

Competition Commission (2010) *Ticketmaster and Live Nation*, London: Competition Commission.

Connolly, M. and Krueger, A.B. (2005) *Rockonomics: The Economics of Popular Music*, Cambridge, MA: National Bureau of Economic Research.

Cook, N. (2013) *Beyond the Score: Music as Performance*, New York: Oxford University Press.

Cottrell, S. (2002) "Music as capital: deputizing among London's freelance musicians", *British Journal of Ethnomusicology* 11(2), 61–80.

Cottrell, S. (2004) *Professional Music-Making in London. Ethnography and Experience*, Aldershot: Ashgate.

Coulson, S. (2010) "Getting 'capital' in the music world: musicians' learning experiences and working lives', *British Journal of Music Education* 29(3), 255–70.

Coulson, S. (2012) "Collaborating in a competitive world: musicians' working lives and understandings of entrepreneurship", *Work, Employment and Society* 26(2), 246–61.

Crawford, R. (1997) *Banquo on Thursdays: The Inside Story of 50 Years of the Edinburgh Festival*, Edinburgh: Goblinshead.

Crossick, G. and Kaszynska, P. (2016) *Understanding the Value of Arts & Culture*, Swindon: AHRC.

Danziger, D. (1995) *The Orchestra: The Lives Behind the Music*, London: HarperCollins.

David, S. (2015) *In the All-Night Café: A Memoir of Belle And Sebastian's Formative Year*, London: Little, Brown.

Davies, G. (2013) *The Show Must Go On: On Tour with the LSO in 1912 and 2012*, London: Elliott and Thompson.

Davies, L.L. (1995) "Velocity girls: indie, new lads, old values", in Cooper, S. ed., *Girls! Girls! Girls!*, London: Cassell, 116–23.

Day, M. and Dickinson, J. (2018) *David versus Goliath: The Past, Present and Future of Student Unions in the UK*, Oxford: Higher Education Policy Institute.

Denselow, R. (1990) *When the Music's Over: The Story of Political Pop*, London: Faber & Faber.

Department of Culture, Media and Sport (2009) *Consultation on Ticketing and Ticket Touting*, London: DCMS.

Devlin, M. (2007) *Tales from the Flipside: Exploding the Myth of the Superstar DJ Lifestyle*, Milton Keynes: AuthorHouse.

Dickson, J. (2018) "The changing nature of conceptualisation and authenticity among Scottish traditional musicians: traditional music, conservatoire education and the case for post-revivalism", in McKerrell, S. and West, G. eds, *Understanding Scotland Musically: Folk, Tradition and Policy*, London: Routledge, 81–92.

DJ Target (2018) *Grime Kids: The Inside Story of the Global Grime Takeover*, London: Trapeze.

Doffman, M. (2014) "'What you doin' here?' The sounds, sensibilities and belonging(s) of Black British jazz musicians", in Toynbee, J., Tackley, C. and Doffman, M. eds, *Black British Jazz*, Farnham: Ashgate, 111–32.

Donald, J. and Greig, G. (2014) "Orchestrating a flash mob: reach and reputation", in Beech, N. and Gilmore, C. eds, *Organising Music: Theory, Practice, Performance*, Cambridge: Cambridge University Press, 262–9.

Drew, R. (2011) *Karaoke Nights: An Ethnographic Rhapsody*, Lanham MD: Altamira Press.

Drummond, J. (2000) *Tainted by Experience: A Life in the Arts*, London: Faber.

Dueck, B (2014) "Standards, advantage, and race in British discourse about jazz", in Toynbee, J., Tackley, C. and Doffman, M. eds, *Black British Jazz*, Farnham: Ashgate, 199–220.

Dusinberre, E. (2016) *Beethoven for a Later Age: The Journey of a String Quartet*, London: Faber & Faber.

Eales, A. C. (2017) *Bunting and Blues: A Critical History of Glasgow International Jazz Festival, 1987–2015*, Ph.D. thesis, Glasgow University.

EKOS (2013) *Music Sector Review*, Edinburgh: Creative Scotland.

Evans, M. (2012) "Curating the creatives", *Muso* 98, 48–49.

Evans, S.T. (1989) "Nightclubbing: an exploration after dark", paper presented at the British Psychological Society (Scottish Branch) Annual Conference, University of Strathclyde.

Ewens, H. (2019) *Fangirls: Scenes from Modern Music Culture*, London: Quadrille.

262 *Bibliography*

Feist, A. and Hutchison, R. eds (1990) *Cultural Trends 1990,* London: Policy Studies Institute.

Finnegan, R. (1989) *The Hidden Musicians: Music-Making in an English Town,* Cambridge: Cambridge University Press.

Fonarow, W. (2006) *Empire of Dirt: The Aesthetic and Rituals of British Indie Music,* Middletown, CT: Wesleyan University Press.

Forde, E. (2015) "Festival economics", *The Guardian,* July 10, 12–13.

Forde, E. (2016) "Metropolitan man", *IQ Magazine,* March, 43–56.

Frey, B.S. (1994) "The economics of music festivals", *Journal of Cultural Economics* 18, 29–39.

Frey, B.S. (2000) *The Rise and Fall of Festivals,* Zurich: Institute for Empirical Research in Economics, University of Zurich, 1–16.

Frith, S. (1999) "Mr Smith draws a map", *Critical Quarterly* 41(1), 3–8.

Frith, S., Brennan, M., Cloonan M. and Webster, E. (2013) *The History of Live Music in Britain, Volume 1: 1950–1967,* Farnham: Ashgate.

Frith, S., Brennan, M., Cloonan M. and Webster, E. (2019) *The History of Live Music in Britain, Volume 2: 1968–1984,* London: Routledge.

Frost, J.J. (2017) *Big Bad and Heavy: Sex and Drugs and Drum and Bass,* London: Music Mondays.

Garratt, S. (1998) *Adventures in Wonderland: A Decade of Club Culture,* London: Headline.

Geldof, B. (1986) *Is That It?,* Harmondsworth: Penguin.

Green, L., Mackintosh, K. and Gilmore, C. (2014) "Playing in the Royal Scottish National Orchestra", in Beech, N. and Gilmore, C. eds, *Organising Music: Theory, Practice, Performance,* Cambridge: Cambridge University Press, 366–71.

Gregory, G. (2012) *Send in the Clones. A Cultural Study of the Tribute Band,* Sheffield: Equinox.

Hadfield, P. (2006) *Bar Wars: Contesting the Night in Contemporary British Cities,* Oxford: Oxford University Press.

Haferkorn, J. (2018) "Dancing to another tune: classical music in nightclubs and other non-traditional venues", in Dromey, C. and Haferkorn, J. eds, *The Classical Music Industry,* London: Routledge, 148–71.

Hall, S. (1988) "Brave New World", *Marxism Today* (October) 24–9.

Hanley, L. (2017) *Respectable,* London: Penguin.

Harvey, H. (2005) *Franz Ferdinand and the Pop Renaissance,* London: Reynolds & Hearn.

Haslam, D. (1997) "DJ Culture" in Redhead, S., Wynne, D. and O'Connor, J. eds, *The Clubcultures Reader,* Oxford: Blackwell, 168–79.

Haslam, D. (2000) *Manchester, England: The Story of the Pop Cult City,* London: Fourth Estate.

Haslam, D. (2002) *Adventures on the Wheels of Steel: The Rise of the Superstar DJs,* London: Fourth Estate.

Hatherley, O. (2011) *Uncommon: An Essay on Pulp,* Winchester: Zero Books.

Hayes, J. and Marshall, L. (2018) "Reluctant entrepreneurs: musicians and entrepreneurship in the 'new' music industry", *British Journal of Sociology* 69(2), 459–82.

Heath, C. (1991) *Pet Shop Boys, Literally,* Harmondsworth: Penguin.

Hebditch, S. (2015) *London's Pirate Pioneers: The Illegal Broadcasters who Changed British Radio,* London: TX Publications.

Bibliography 263

Henderson, S. and Wood, E. (2009) *Dance to the Music: Fans and Socialites in the Festival Audience*, Leeds: UK Centre of Events Management, Leeds Metropolitan University.

Hennion, A., Maisonneuve, S. and Gomart, E. (2000) *Figures de l'Amateur: Formes, Objets, Pratiques de l'Amour de la Musique Aujourd'hui*, Paris: La Documentation Françoise.

Hesse, R. (1992) *Arts Festivals in the UK*, London: Policy Studies Institute.

Hill, R.L. (2016) *Gender, Metal and the Media*, London: Palgrave Macmillan.

Hill, R.L. (2018) "Sexual violence at gigs", http://livemusicexchange.org/blog/sexual-violence-at-gigs-rosemary-lucy-hill. Accessed November 20, 2020.

Hingley, T. (2012) *Carpet Burns: My Life with Inspiral Carpets*, Pontefract: Route.

Hodgkins, C. (2017) *Where Do You Want to Be? A Business Planning Manual for Jazz Musicians*, www.chrishodgkins.co.uk/business-education/where-do-you-want-to-be-a-business-planning-manual-for-jazz-musicians-chris-hodgkins-2017. Accessed November 20, 2020.

Hodgkinson, W. (2009) *The Ballad of Britain*, London: Bloomsbury.

Holt, F. (2016) "New media, new festival worlds" in Baade, C. and Deaville, J. eds, *Music and the Broadcast Experience*, Oxford: Oxford University Press, 275–92.

Homan, S. ed. (2006) *Access All Areas: Tribute Bands and Global Pop Culture*, Maidenhead: Open University Press.

Hook, P. (2009) *The Haçienda. How Not to Run a Club*, London: Simon and Schuster.

Housee, S. and Dar, M. (1996) "Remixing identities: 'off' the turntable", in Sharma, S., Hutnyk, J. and Sharma, A. eds, *Dis-Orienting Rhythms: The Politics of the New Asian Dance Music*, London: Zed Books, 81–104.

Hunter, S. (2004) *Hell Bent for Leather: Confessions of a Heavy Metal Addict*, New York: Fourth Estate in America.

Huq, R. (1996) "Asian kool? Bhangra and beyond", in Sharma, S., Hutnyk, J. and Sharma, A. eds, *Dis-Orienting Rhythms. The Politics of the New Asian Dance Music*, London: Zed Books, 61–80.

Hutchison R. and Feist, A. (1991) *Amateur Arts in the UK*, London: Policy Studies Institute.

Hutnyk, J. (1996) "Repetitive beatings or criminal justice?", in Sharma, S., Hutnyk, J. and Sharma, A. eds, *Dis-Orienting Rhythms. The Politics of the New Asian Dance Music*, London: Zed Books, 156–89.

Hytönen-Ng, E. (2017) "Contemporary British jazz musicians' relationship with the audience: renditions of we-relations and intersubjectivity", in Tsioulakis, I. and Hytönen-Ng, E. eds, *Musicians and their Audiences*, London: Routledge, 69–85.

Johns, T. (2011) *Letters from Lines & Spaces*, Milton Keynes: Lightning Source.

Jones, E. (1999) *This is Pop. The Life and Times of a Failed Rock Star*, Edinburgh: Canongate.

Jones, R. (2018) *Bristol Music: Seven Decades of Sound*, Bristol: Tangent Books.

Keegan-Phipps, S. and Winter, T. (2014) "Contemporary English folk music and the folk industry", in Bithell, C. and Hill, J. eds, *The Oxford Handbook of Music Revival*, New York: Oxford University Press, 489–509.

Khamkar, G. (2016) *The Evolution of British Asian Radio in England 1990–2004*, Ph.D. thesis, Faculty of Media and Communication, University of Bournemouth.

264   Bibliography

Knowles, N. (2015) "Reflections on the festival business", in Beech, N. and Gilmore, C. eds, *Organising Music: Theory, Practice, Performance*, Cambridge: Cambridge University Press, 205–12.

Knowles, T. (2017) "English folk law: a brief introduction to pub licensing", *International Journal of Traditional Arts* 1, 1–4.

Krueger, A.B. (2005) "The economics of real superstars: the market for rock concerts in the material world", *Journal of Labour Economics* 23(1), 1–30.

Laing, D. (2012) "Calculating the value of live music: motives and methods", http://livemusicexchange.org/blog/whats-it-worth-calculating-the-economic-value-of-live-music-dave-laing. Accessed November 20, 2020.

Laing, D. and Newman, R. eds (1994) *Thirty Years of the Cambridge Folk Festival*, Ely: Music Maker Books.

Laughey, D. (2006) *Music and Youth Culture*, Edinburgh: Edinburgh University Press.

Lebrecht, N. (2001) *Covent Garden: The Untold Story*, London: Pocket Books.

Lowenstein, R. (2014) *A Prince Among Stones: That Business with the Rolling Stones and Other Adventures,* London: Bloomsbury.

Lynch, J. and Larsen, G. (2014) 'Organising and playing a boutique festival', in Beech, N. and Gilmore, C. eds, *Organising Music: Theory, Practice, Performance*, Cambridge: Cambridge University Press, 218–25.

Malbon, B. (1998) 'Clubbing: consumption, identity and the spatial practices of every-night life', in Skelton, T. and Valentine, G. eds, *Cool Places: Geographies of Youth Cultures*, London: Routledge, 266–86.

Mangera-Lakew, N. (2014) *The Absent Roots of House Music in the UK: Recovering the History of Northern Black Scenes in the 1980s*, BA dissertation, University of Sheffield.

Marshall, G. (2012) *Postcards from a Rock & Roll Tour*, Droxford: Splendid Books.

Martin, K. ed. (2006) *Fèis: The First Twenty-Five Years of the Fèis Movement*, Portree: Fèisean nan Gàidheal.

Martinus, T., McAlaney, J., McLaughlin, L.J. and Smith, H. (2010) 'Outdoor music festivals: Cacophonous consumption or melodious moderation?', *Drugs: Education, Prevention and Policy* 17(6), 795–807.

Massingham, A. (2006) *Status Quo…? An Exploration of the Status of Composers, Performers and Songwriters in the UK's Creative Economy*, London: Musicians' Union and the British Academy of Composers and Songwriters.

Maughan, C. (2009) "The economic and social impact of cultural festivals in the East Midlands of England", in Autissier, A-M. ed., *The Europe of Festivals*, Toulouse: éditions de l'attribut, 51–60.

Maughan, C. and Bianchini, F. (2004) *The Economic and Social Impact of Cultural Festivals in the East Midlands of England*, London: Arts Council England.

McCarroll, T. (2011) *Oasis the Truth: My Life as Oasis's Drummer*, London: John Blake.

McCormick, L. (2015) *Performing Civility: International Competitions in Classical Music*, Cambridge: Cambridge University Press.

McKay, G. (2005) *Circular Breathing: The Cultural Politics of Jazz in Britain*, London: Duke University Press.

McKerrell, S. (2011) "Modern Scottish bands (1970–1990): cash as authenticity", *Scottish Music Review* 2(1), www.scottishmusicreview.org/index.php/SMR/article/view/22. Accessed November 20, 2020.

McLaughlin, Sean (2012) *Locating Authenticities: a Study of the Ideological Construction of Professionalised Folk Music in Scotland*, Ph.D. thesis, Edinburgh University.

McLaughlin, Steven (2013) *Clubland UK. On the Door in the Rave Era*, Edinburgh: Mainstream.

Mills, J. (2006) "Working in music: the pianist", *Music Education Research*, 8(2), 251–66.

MIA (2005) *Attitudes to Music in the UK*, Great Bookham, Kent: Music Industries Association.

Mintel (1986) "Concerts and concert going", *Leisure Intelligence* 16, 113–42.

Molleson, K. (2015) *Dear Green Sounds: Glasgow's Music Through Time and Buildings*, Glasgow: Waverley Books.

Monopoly and Mergers Commission (1988) *Collective Licensing of Public Performances and Broadcasts in Sound Recordings*, London: HMG.

Morris Hargreaves McIntyre (2004) *The Impact of Folk Festivals*, London: Association of Festival Organisers/Arts Council England.

Morrison, R. (2004) *Orchestra—the LSO: A Century of Triumph and Turbulence*, London: Faber.

Murthy, D. (2009) "Representing South Asian alterity? East London's Asian electronic music scene and the articulation of globally mediated identities", *European Journal of Cultural Studies* 12(5), 329–48.

Myers, J.P. (2015) "Still like that old time rock and roll: tribute bands and historical consciousness in popular music", *Ethnomusicology* 59(1), 61–81.

Nicholson, S., Kendon, E. and Hodgkins, C. (2009) *The BBC: Public Sector Radio, Jazz Policy and Structure in the Digital Age*, London: Jazz Services Ltd.

Noltingk, J. (2017) *The Scottish Orchestras and New Music, 1945–2015*, Ph.D. thesis, Glasgow University.

Norris, R. (2008) *Paul Oakenfold. The Authorised Biography* London: Corgi.

Office of Fair Trading (2005) *Ticket Agents in the UK*, London: OFT.

Osgerby, B. (1998) *Youth in Britain Since 1945*, Oxford: Blackwell.

Page, W. (2009) *Adding Up the Music Industry for 2008*, London: PRS.

Page, W. (2011) "Wallet share", *PRS for Music Economic Insight*, 22, November 18.

Page, W. and Carey, C. (2010) "Adding up the UK music industry for 2009", *PRS for Music Economic Insight* 20, www.prsformusic.com/-/media/files/prs-for-music/research/economic-insight-20-adding-up-the-uk-music-industry-for-2009.ashx. Accessed November 20, 2020.

Paleo, I.O. and Wijnberg, N.M. (2006) 'Popular music festivals and classification: a typology of festivals and an inquiry into their role in the formation of musical genres', *International Journal of Arts Management* 8(2), 50–61.

Parkes, S. (2014) *Live at The Brixton Academy: A Riotous Life in the Music Business*, London: Serpent's Tail.

Patrick, A. (2004) *A Taste for Excess: Disdained and Dissident Forms of Fashioning Femininity*, Ph.D. thesis, University of Stirling.

Pearce, D. (2013) *Dizzie Gillespie was at My Wedding: Jubilance and Woe—a Jazz Musician's Lot*, Richmond: Bill Scott and Iain Hannah.

Phillips, D. (2009) *Superstar DJs Here We Go!*, London: Ebury Press.

Phipps, C., Tobler, J. and Smith, S. (2005) *Northstars*, Newcastle-upon-Tyne: Zymurgy.

Pine, B.J. and Gilmore, J.H. (1998) "Welcome to the experience economy', *Harvard Business Review*, July–August, 97–105.

266 *Bibliography*

Pitts, S.E. (2005) "What makes an audience? Investigating the roles and experiences of listeners at a chamber music festival", *Music and Letters*, 86(2), 257–69.

Pitts, S.E. (2019) 'Understanding audiences: what are concert-goers doing when they listen?', in Barlow, H. and Rowland, D (eds), *The Experience of Listening to Music: Methodologies, Identities, Histories*, Milton Keynes: The Open University, https://ledbooks.org/proceedings2019. Accessed November 20, 2020.

Prior, N. (2018) *Popular Music, Digital Technology and Society*, London: Sage.

PRS for Music (2015) *Popular Music Concerts Tariff 'LP'. Summary of Consultation Responses*, London: PRS for Music.

Reid, G. (2007) "Showcasing Scotland? A case study of the MTV Europe Music Awards Edinburgh03", *Leisure Studies* 26(4), 479–94.

Reynolds, S. (1998) *Generation Ecstasy: Into the World of Techno and Rave Culture*, Boston: Little, Brown and Co.

Reynolds, S. and Owen, F. (1986) "These loafers kill Tories", *Melody Maker* November 8, 20–21.

Rijven, S., Marcus, G. and Straw, W. (1985) *Rock for Ethiopia*, Exeter: IASPM.

Riley, M. and Laing, D. (2006) *The Value of Jazz in Britain,* London: Jazz Services.

Roach, M. (1990) *The Eight Legged Atomic Dustbin Will Eat Itself*, London: Independent Music Press.

Robinson, R. (2015) *Music Festivals and the Politics of Participation*, Farnham: Ashgate.

Robson, J.E. (2006) *Finding the Female Fan: A Feminist Ethnography of Popular Music in Sheffield*, Ph.D. thesis, Sheffield Hallam University.

Rogers, J. (2013) "Total rewind: 10 key moments in the life of the cassette", *The Observer*, September 1, www.theguardian.com/music/2013/aug/30/cassette-store-day-music-tapes. Accessed November 20, 2020.

Rolfe, H. (1992) *Arts Festivals in the UK*, London: Policy Studies Institute.

Salter, C. (2011) "Ticketmaster: Rocking the most hated brand in America', *Fast Company*, June 21, www.fastcompany.com/1761539/ticketmaster-rocking-most-hated-brand-america. Accessed November 20, 2020.

Saunders, N. (1995) *Ecstasy and the Dance Culture*, London: Saunders.

Scarles, M. (2009) *An Investigation of the Popular Live Music Industry in Edinburgh*, MA thesis, University of Edinburgh.

Scharff, C. (2015) 'Blowing your own trumpet: Exploring the gendered dynamics of self-promotion in the classical music profession', *Sociological Review* 63(1), 97–112.

Schofield, D. (2004) *The First Week in August: Fifty Years of the Sidmouth Festival*, Matlock: Sidmouth International Festival Ltd.

Schulze, H. (2015) *Bruce Springsteen Rocking the Wall: The Berlin Concert that Changed the World*, Berlin: Berlinica.

Scottish Government (2013) *Instrumental Music Tuition in Scotland: A Report by the Scottish Government's Instrumental Music Group*, Edinburgh: Scottish Government.

Shapiro, H. (1990) *Waiting for the Man. The Story of Drugs and Popular Music*, London: Mandarin.

Smith, C. (1998) *Creative Britain*, London: Faber & Faber.

Smith, R. (1995) *Seduced and Abandoned: Essays on Gay Men and Popular Music*, London: Cassell.

Southall, H. (2015) *Dance Bands in Chester: An Evolving Professional Network*, Ph.D. thesis, University of Liverpool.

Stewart, A. (2015) "A night at the opera", *The Musician*, Spring, 12–15.

Bibliography   267

Stone, C. (2008) "The British pop music festival phenomenon" in Ali-Knight, J., Robertson, M., Fyall, A. and Ladkin, A. eds, *International Perspectives of Festivals and Events: Paradigms of Analysis*, London: Routledge.

Stopps, D. (2014) *How to Make a Living from Music*, Geneva: WIPO.

Sykes, B. (2012) *Sit Down! Listen to This! The Roger Eagle Story*, Manchester: Empire Publications.

Tassell, N. (2013) *Mr Gig: One Man's Search for the Soul of Live Music*, London: Short Books.

Taylor, M. and Towse, R. (1998) "The value of performers' rights: An economic approach", *Media Culture and Society* 20(4), 631–52.

Thompson, D.A. (2018) *Have Guitars ... Will Travel. Vol. 4*, Northampton: Whyte Tiger.

Thorn, T. (2014) *Bedsit Disco Queen*, London: Virago.

Thornton, S. (1995) *Club Cultures: Music, Media and Subcultural Capital*, Oxford: Polity Press.

Tom Fleming Consultancy (2016) *Women Make Music Evaluation 2011–2016*, London: PRS Foundation.

UK Music (2015) *Manifesto*, London: UK Music.

UK Music (2019) *Sheffield City Region Music Report*, London: UK Music.

Umney, C. and Kretsos, L. (2013) "Creative labour and collective interaction: the working lives of young jazz musicians in London", *Work, Employment and Society*, 28(4), 571–88.

Valéro, V. (2002) "Le Festival de Rock, entre passion et désenchantement", *Volume!* 1(1), 113–123.

Vrettos, A. (2009) "About the economic impact studies of arts festivals", *Economia della Cultura*, 3, 341–50.

Wall, T. and Dubber, A. (2010) 'Experimenting with fandom, live music, and the internet: applying insights from music fan culture to new media production', *Journal of New Music Research* 39(2), 159–69.

Ward, A. (1997) "Dancing around meaning (and the meaning around dance)", in Thomas, H. ed., *Dance in the City*, London: Macmillan, 3–20.

Warren, E. (2019) *Make Some Space*, London: Sweet Machine.

Webster, E. (2010) "King Tut's Wah Wah Hut: initial research into a 'local' live music venue", *iaspm@journal* 1(1), 24–30.

Webster, E. (2011) *Promoting Live Music in the UK: A Behind the Scenes Ethnography*, Ph.D. thesis, University of Glasgow.

Webster, E. (2012) "'One more tune!' The encore ritual in live music events", *Popular Music and Society* 35(1), 93–111.

Webster, E., Brennan, M., Behr, A. and Cloonan, M. (2018) *Valuing Live Music: The UK Live Music Census 2017 Report*, http://uklivemusiccensus.org/wp-content/uploads/2018/03/UK-Live-Music-Census-2017-full-report.pdf.   Accessed 20 November 2020.

Webster, E. and McKay, G. (2016) *From Glyndebourne to Glastonbury: The Impact of British Music Festivals*, Norwich: AHRC/University of East Anglia.

Webster, E. and McKay, G. (2017) *Music from Out There, In Here: 25 Years of the London Jazz Festival*, Norwich: University of East Anglia.

Wener, L. (2010) *Different for Girls: My True-Life in Pop*, London: Ebury Press.

Whyton, T. (2015) 'Brilliant corners: the development of jazz in higher education', in Papageorgi, I. and Welch, G. eds, *Advanced Musical Performance: Investigations in Higher Education Learning*, Farnham: Ashgate, 21–31.

268   *Bibliography*

Wiley (2017) *Eskiboy*, London: Windmill Books.

Williamson, J. and Cloonan, M. (2016) *Players' Work Time: A History of the British Musicians' Union, 1893–2013*, Manchester: Manchester University Press.

Williamson, J., Cloonan, M. and Frith, S. (2003) *Mapping the Music Industry in Scotland*, Glasgow: Scottish Enterprise.

Wilson, N. (2014) *The Art of Re-enchantment. Making Early Music in the Modern Age*, Oxford: Oxford University Press.

Witts, R. (1998) *Artist Unknown: An Alternative History of the Arts Council*, London: Little, Brown and Co.

Witts, R. (2015). "Shopping and Fricker: The origins of the Cheltenham Festival of Modern British Music and the 'Cheltenham Symphony'", *The Musical Times* *156*(1931), 9–21.

Wolf, B. (2017) "The British Symphony Orchestra and the Arts Council of Great Britain: examining the orchestra in its economic and institutional environments", in Ramnarine, T.K. ed., *Global Perspectives on Orchestras*, New York: Oxford University Press, 282–300.

Wright, D.C.H. (2005) 'The London Sinfonietta 1968–2004: A perspective', *Twentieth-Century Music* 2(1), 109–36.

Zuberi, N. (2001) *Sounds English: Transnational Popular Music*, Urbana, IL: University of Illinois Press.

Index

Acoustic Triangle 228
Adepegba, Byi 229
Aguilar, Ananay 181
Alaap 162
Ames, Robert 203
Anderson, Ian 103
Anderton, Chris 87, 110, 116
Angus, Bob 32, 35, 37, 43
Angus, Isla 231
Anschutz, Philip 21–2, 26
Ansel, Barry 16
Anthony, Wayne 127–9, 130
Anton Le Pirate 129
Arctic Monkeys 84
Asian Dub Foundation 161–63
Azania-Jarvis, Alice 85

Back, Les 160–65
Baker, Eric 20, 77
Ballantine, Rob 76
Barker, Martin 199, 204, 211, 213
Barrow, Geoff 174–5
Bartlett, Jo 105
Barton, James 133, 135
Batchelor, Derek 105
Batey, Angus 170
Bayton, Mavis 172
Bearman, Alan 102
Beer, Dave 62
Behr, Adam 89, 204–5, 236
Belle and Sebastian 236
Benjamin, Tony 233, 236–7, 239
Benn, Melvin 25, 88, 89, 114
Bennett, Andy 164
Bennett, Lucy 215
Berkmann, Justin 132
Betesh, Danny 16, 29, 30, 37, 39, 43, 49
Bhagwandas, Anita 221
Bhindi, Bhupinder 162

Birchall, Hamish 65–7
Block, Derek 31
Bog Town Playboys 174
Boland, Derek 154–5
Botten, Matt 23
Boulding, Tom 231
Bowdery, Philip 31
Bowie, David 10, 12, 14, 213
Boyle, Susan 247
Bradley, Lloyd 129, 146, 152, 157, 166
Bragg, Billy 5, 6, 116
Brewster, Bill 137
Bright, Graham 61, 130
Brocken, Michael 102
Brooman, Thomas 89
Brown, Svend 100
Bruck, Connie 22
Brychan, Guto 223
Burgess, Martino 225
Burrows, Tim 20–1

Caldwell, Crae 140, 235
Campbell, David 21
Capercaille 188
Capshaw, Coran 19
Carr, Paul 223
Carroll, Andy 133
Carthy, Eliza 189
Carthy, Martin 189
Casey, Jayne 134
Cavicchi, Daniel 198
Chambers, Tim 40
Chase, Tommy 174
Chemical Brothers 177
Christianson, Harry 184
Citron, Alan 19
Clarke, Lorna 101
Clayman, Barry 31, 39, 49
Clement-Jones, Tim 66

270 *Index*

Clerk, Carol 6
Cloonan, Martin 38, 44, 59
Cluley, Robert 233–4
Cobuzzi, Gene 18
Cohen, Sara 171–72
Cohl, Michael 11, 14, 31, 43–4
Collins, Andrew 115
Collins, Graham 174
Collins, Hattie 159
Collinson, Jamie 151
Colston-Hayter, Tony 61, 63, 129
Conn, Mervyn 106
Convery, Janet 114
Cook, Nicholas 197
Cook, Norman 124, 136, 139
Cooper, Gareth 89
Corfield, Steven 90
Cosgrave, Lynn 129, 139
Cottrell, Stephen 180, 182, 184
Coulson, Susan 181–82
Cowell, Simon 208, 247–48
Crawford, Iain 72
Crehan, Dermot 179
Crosby, Gary 186
Cumming, John 112–13

Dammers, Jerry 8
Danziger, Danny 179
Das, Aniruddha (Dr Das) 161
Davenport, Jean 103
Davenport, Stuart 133
David, Stuart 236
Davies, Gareth 180
Davies, Jack 184
Davies, John 224
Deadman, Alan 232
Deller, Jeremy 145, 166
Delsener, Ron 11
Demetriou, Stefan 213
Denselow, Robin 8
Denton, Tony 178
Desmond, Denis 30, 32, 43
Devlin, Mark 134, 136–9, 142
Dickins, Barry 2, 31, 42, 49
Dickinson, Debbie 113
Dickson, Josh 188
Digweed, John 137
Dittke, Ina 185
Dizzee Rascal 152
Dodds, Conal 34, 37, 44
Doe, Andy 210
Donald, Jane 40, 83
Dowling, Janet 102

Downey, Caroline 30
Downs, Bertis 18
Dubber, Andrew 214
Dubisson, Ben 237
Dueck, Byron 186
Dunn, John 44
Dunstan, Guy 46
Duran Duran 31, 37
Dusinberre, Edward 181

Eagle, Roger 219
Eales, Alison 108–11
Eavis, Michael 87
Eifler, Barbara 182
Ellis, Geoff 30, 34, 64, 83–5
Elms, Robert 123
Eshun, Kodwo 14
Evans, Steven 132, 205
Everything But The Girl 175
Ewens, Hannah 206, 208

Fabio 145, 147–9, 154
Fairport Convention 175
Farley, Terry 61, 123
Farrow, Mark 135
Faultless, Maggie 204
Faustus 229
Ferguson, Brian 88
Ferrel, Mike 11
Fiddy, Chantelle 158
Finnegan, Ruth 255
Flowdan 149
Forde, Eamonn 33, 90
Franz Ferdinand 227
Frey, Bruno 101
Friel, Eddie 110
Frost, Jumping Jack 147
Fuck Off Machete 174
Fuller, Simon 247
Fung, Trevor 126

Galbraith, Stuart 31, 116
Garcia, Nubya 228
Garratt, Sheryl 130, 132–3, 147
Garvey, Guy 3
Gayford, Martin 107
Geeneus 156
Geldof, Bob 1, 7
General Levy 150
Gibbons, Beth 174
Giddings, John 3, 31, 42–3, 91,
  204
Gillespie, Bobby 176

Index 271

Gillinson, Clive 71
Gold, Pamela 97
Goldsmith, Harvey 2, 7, 21, 38, 43
Gould, Glenn 253–4
Gould Piano Trio 99
Graham, Bill 7, 11
Green, Ken 232
Green, Lance 181
Gregg, Paul 30, 32
Gregory, Georgina 178–9, 201
Grooverider 147
Gubbay, Raymond 46, 234
Guishard, Jeune 185

Haferkorn, Julie 203–4
Hagan, Danny 105
Hall, Stuart 1, 6
Hallett, Rob 31, 33
Hanley, Lynsey 208, 214
Hanlon, Jef 3, 29, 37, 44, 45
Hansen, Brent 57
Happy Mondays 175
Hardie, Colin 173
Harrison, Colin 179
Harvey, Hamilton 227, 230
Haslam, Dave 124, 125, 137–9
Hatherley, Owen 231
Hayes, Malcolm 100
Healey, Jeremy 140
Heath, Lawrence 103
Heera 162
Henderson, Stephen 189
Hill, Ally 221–2
Hingley, Tom 171
Hiseman, Jon 169
Hobbs, Liz 46
Hodge, Gordon 198, 237
Hodgkins, Chris 184–5
Hodgkinson, Will 105–6
Holden, Anthony 24
Holloway, Nicky 126, 139
Holt, Fabian 213
Hook, Peter 124, 128
Hope, Fielding 233, 239
Howell, Graeme 231, 235, 247, 254
Hoyte, Fay 158
Hubbard, Nathan 19
Hughes, Darren 133–4
Hunter, Seb 171–2
Huq, Rupa 145
Hytönen-Ng, Elina 200, 220, 239–40

Irwin, Colin 102

Jagger, Mick 14
James, Matt 34
Jammer 157
Jazz Warriors 185–6
Jazzie B 146, 152–3
Jenkins, Chaz 181
Johns, Terry 183
Johnston, Tracy 198–99, 219, 233
Joi Bangla 163
Jones, David 112–3

Kano 158
Kapoor, Sweety 163
Kapur, Steve (Apache Indian)
 162
Keegan-Phipps, Simon 187, 189
Kelly, Billy 106
Kelly, Jude 101
Kelly, Juliet 185
Kemp, Mark 34, 41
Knight, John 24–5
Knowles, Nod 71, 98–9
Knowles, Tim 67
Komal 161
Koppe, Hansi 221
Kretsos, Lefteris 184
Krueger, Alan B. 2–3, 12
Kruger, Jeffrey and Howard 106

Laing, Dave 104, 248, 250
Lamacq, Steve 223
Latham, Paul 10, 29, 30, 35–40,
 43–44, 48, 50
Lawford, Gwen 146
Led Zeppelin 23, 178
Lee, C.P. 219
Lee, Sam 189
Leftfield 177
Le Gendre, Kevin 123, 142
Legg, Barry 62
Leiweke, Tim 22
Leonard, John 188–9
Levy, David 135, 136, 137
Lima, Antonio 224
Linehan, Fergus 93
Littlewood, Stuart 45, 49, 178
Lockhart, Sandra 158
Loud, Lisa 141
Lowe, Chris 176
Lowenstein, Rupert 11–12, 14
LTJ Bukem 147
Lydia D'Ustebyn 185
Lysons, Richard 225

272 Index

Mac 161
MacCalman, Peter 230, 234
MacKinnon, Amanda 173
MacKintosh, Katy 181
Madonna 14–15, 25, 177, 213
Makie, Mark 29, 49
Malbon, Ben 165, 199, 207
Mangera-Lakew, Nyasha 166
Marshall, Barrie 2, 35, 36, 37
Marshall, Gordy 174, 177
Massive Attack 175, 231
Masson, Gordon 38
Maxwell Davies, Peter 99
Mays, Lowry 13
McCusker, John 188
McDonnell, John 159–60
McDowell, Kathryn 74
McGough, Nathan 176
McIntosh, Genista 70
McIntyre, Phil 32
McKay, George 85–6, 97, 107,
    112–3, 185
McKenzie, Malcolm 169, 170
McKerrell, Simon 188
McKinley, Sarah 158
McLaughlin, Steven 131–2
McLeish, Henry 59
McNamee, Gordon 154
McNicol, Richard 74
McRae, Ross 238
McTell, Ralph 103, 105
McVay, Derek 48
Mead, Helen 126
Merifield, Graham 93
Message, Brian 169
Millen, Olive May 111
Mitchell, Michael C. 7
Moody Blues 177–8
Moore, Gillian 74
Moran, Caitlin 115
Moran, Simon 21, 30, 32, 33, 43–4
Moray, Jim 207
Morrison, Richard 71–2, 74–5,
    100
Morton, Robin 236
Mouzakitis, Maggie 172
Mulraine, Ruby 156–7, 158

Noise, Nancy 141
Noltingk, Jacqui 74, 100
Noramly, Natasha 173–4
Norris, Richard 125–6
Northcote, John 26, 32–3

Norton, Anne 57
Novelist 155

Oakenfold, Paul 125–6, 135–7, 140,
    141, 175
Oakes, Geoff 130–1
Oasis 41–2, 172
O'Cathain, Detta 57
Olins, Sophia 117
One Direction 208, 247–8
Osgerby, Bill 5, 60–63

Page, Will 3
Palumbo, James 132
Papa Levi 150
Park, Cat 158–9
Park, Graeme 137
Parkes, Simon 33, 36, 42
Parkhouse, Steve 236, 237
Parsons, Andrew 77
Pearce, Amy 184
Perry, Grayson 208–9
Phillips, Dom 139, 141, 175, 177
Pickering, Mike 123, 124–5
Pitts, Stephanie 201–3, 214, 254
PJ 146
Plane, Robert 99
Platt, Darren 157
Pleasants, John 20
Polwart, Karine 187, 188
Portishead 174–175, 231
Power, George 154
Power, Vince 32–34, 39, 41, 42, 43, 49,
    92, 93, 97
Presencer, Lohan 223
Preston 115
Prestwich, Gary 238
Primal Scream 176
Prince, Tony 138–9
Prior, Maddy 105
Prochnik, Rebecca 158
Prodigy, The 177
Prokofiev, Gabriel 204
Pukwana, Barbara 229

Radical Sista 163
Radiohead 169, 213
Rapino, Michael 13–15
Razor (MC) 160
Razor, Ralph 235
Redhead, Andy 116
Reed, Nick 73
Reedjik, Alex 199

Reynolds, Simon 123, 128, 155, 160
Richards, Keith 14
Riley, Mykaell 250
Ritchie, Ian 74
Ritu (DJ) 163
Roberts, Alastair 210
Roberts, Graeme 209
Robson, Josie 202, 207
Rodger, Jill 111
Rolf, Suzanne 234
Rolling Stones , The 1, 11–12, 14, 20
Roscoe, Martin 99
Rosen, Fred 17–18, 26
Rosie, Fiona 64
Ross, Mark 224–5, 232

Sagoo, Bally 162
Salter, Chuck 19
Sama, Logan 151, 157
Sargeant, Lorna 104
Sasha 131, 137
Savage, Jon 205, 207
Savale, Steve Chandra (Chandrasonic) 163
Saxon 150
Scharff, Christina 182
Schmool, Borak 228
Secret Disc Jockey, The 137, 139, 141
Sharkey, Fergal 66–7
Shapiro, Shain 247
Sharp, Chris 101
Sharp, Rob 221
Shaw, Donald 188
Shaw, Julian 182
Sillerman, Robert F.X. 10–11, 13, 26
Singh, Channi 162
Singh, Talvin 163
Sisterhood of Spit 185
Size, Roni 231
Skepta 158
Slimzee 152, 156
Smiley 146, 148–9
Smith, Chris 59
Smith, Jeff 114–5
Smith, Patrick 115
Smith, Richard 207–8
Smith, Tony 35
Smiths, The 200–1, 205
So Solid Crew 156
Soul II Soul 146, 152–3
Sparrow 62
Springsteen, Bruce 34, 198, 208
Stereophonics 48, 209

Stevens, John 163
Steward, Sue 108
Stewart, Andrew 210–11
Stewart, Fiona 93
Straw, Jack 57
Stud, Andrew 67
Svensson, Esbjörn 109
Swarbrick, Dave 188–89
Sweeney, Bill 110
Sweeting, Adam 204

Takács Quartet 181
Take That 37, 213
Talbot, Martin 21
Tannock, Craig 230
Target, DJ 145, 149–57, 159
Tassell, Nige 198, 200–1, 202
Taylor, Andy 31
Taylor, Jeremy 129
Taylor, Karen 230, 234, 236–7
Tennant, Neil 38, 176–7
Thompson, Derrick 171
Thorn, Tracey 173, 175
Tissera, Rob 62
Todes, Ariana 183
Tricky 231
Trout, Chris 236

Umney, Charles 184
Utley, Adrian 174–5
U2 2, 15, 135, 137, 197, 215

Valéro, Vanessa 87

Wall, Tim 214
Waterhouse, Humphrey 132
Watkiss, Cleveland 185
Weatherall, Andrew 176
Webster, Emma 35, 86–7, 89, 90, 97, 107, 112–13, 209, 225
Webster, Jan 209
Webster-Jones, Kate and Oliver 92
Wener, Louise 172–4
Wenham, Alison 90
Whitaker, Claire 113
White 178
Whyton, Tony 75
Wieczorek, Joe 128
Wild Bunch 175
Wiley 149, 150–2, 154, 156, 158
Williams, Jed 108–9
Williams, Robbie 32

274   *Index*

Wilson, Tony 123
Winter, Trish 187, 189
Winterman, Denise 85
Witts, Richard 71
Wolf, Mark 238
Wolfson, Sam 214, 227–8
Wookie 149, 153, 159

Woollard, Ken 102, 104
Wright, David 69–70, 74

Yates, Kieran 166

Zaman, Deeder (Master D) 163
Zuberi, Nabeel 153–4, 162–3

Printed in the United States
By Bookmasters